RADIO
FOR THE
MILLIONS

RADIO FOR THE MILLIONS

Hindi-Urdu Broadcasting Across Borders

ISABEL HUACUJA ALONSO

Columbia University Press
New York

Columbia University Press
Publishers Since 1893
New York   Chichester, West Sussex
cup.columbia.edu

Library of Congress Cataloging-in-Publication Data
Names: Huacuja Alonso, Isabel, author.
Title: Radio for the millions : Hindi-Urdu broadcasting across borders / Isabel
    Huacuja Alonso.
Description: New York : Columbia University Press, [2023] | Includes
    bibliographical references and index.
Identifiers: LCCN 2022023157 (print) | LCCN 2022023158 (ebook) |
    ISBN 9780231206600 (hardback) | ISBN 9780231206617 (trade paperback) |
    ISBN 9780231556569 (ebook)
Subjects: LCSH: Radio broadcasting—South Asia. | India—History—Partition, 1947– |
    India-Pakistan Conflict, 1947–1949—Radio broadcasting and the conflict.
Classification: LCC HE8699.S714 H83 2022 (print) | LCC HE8699.S714 (ebook) |
    DDC 384.50954—dc23/eng/20220525
LC record available at https://lccn.loc.gov/2022023157
LC ebook record available at https://lccn.loc.gov/2022023158

Cover design: Noah Arlow
Cover art: Shutterstock

For abuela, mamá, and Bibi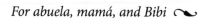

CONTENTS

LIST OF FIGURES

NOTE ON TRANSLITERATION

I use the sound-based transliteration system outlined in the *Essential Urdu Dictionary* (Hachette, UK, 2015), which emphasizes pronunciation over spelling and is appropriate for both Hindi and Urdu. To make the text more readable, I do not transliterate names (of people and places) and Hindi-Urdu words commonly used in English and instead use the most common spelling conventions in roman script.

Urdu

ا	a	آ	ā	ب	b	پ	p	ت	t
ٹ	ṭ	ث	s	ج	j	چ	c	ح	h
خ	x	د	d	ڈ	ḍ	ذ	z	ر	r
ڑ	ṛ	ز	z	ژ	z	س	s	ش	š
ص	s	ض	z	ط	t	ظ	z	ع	a
غ	ǧ	ف	f	ق	q	ک	k	گ	g
ل	l	م	m	ن	n	و	v/ū/o/u	ہ	h
ی	y/ī/i/e	ے	y/e						

Hindi

अ	a	आ	ā	इ	i	ई	ī	उ	u
ऊ	ū	ए	e	ऐ	ae	ओ	o	औ	au
क	k	ख	kh	ग	g	घ	gh	ङ	n
च	c	छ	ch	ज	j	झ	jh	ञ	n
ट	ṭ	ठ	th	ड	ḍ	ढ	ḍh	ण	n
त	t	थ	th	द	d	ध	dh	न	n
प	p	फ	ph	ब	b	भ	bh	म	m
य	y	र	r	ल	l	व	v	श	š
ष	š	स	s	ह	h				

RADIO
FOR THE
MILLIONS

INTRODUCTION

Tuning In to a Radio History

O n the evening of December 30, 1953, Ameen Sayani, the twenty-year-old radio host of the new program *Binaca Geetmala* (Garland of songs), announced the most popular song of the year.[1] The program, which ranked Hindi film songs according to listeners' letters and record sales, aired on Radio Ceylon, a commercial station based in Ceylon (now Sri Lanka) but with target audiences in India and Pakistan. Demonstrating his knack for showmanship, Sayani played a fanfare of trumpets before announcing *Geetmala*'s winning tune from the film *Baiju Bāvrā* (Crazy Baiju, 1952): "Tū Ganga kī mouj, maiṅ Jamuna kā dhārā" (You are the wave of the River Ganga. I am the current of the River Jamuna).[2] While the song's triumph surely excited many listeners, it likely did not surprise them. "Tū Ganga kī mouj" had topped *Geetmala*'s charts for weeks and had been a favorite on Radio Ceylon's other film-song programs. However, in the context of the period's politics of sound, this song's success was quite significant.

Nearly a year earlier, B. V. Keskar, the newly appointed Indian minister of information and broadcasting, had ordered that the national radio network, All India Radio (AIR), stop broadcasting Hindi film songs from all its stations. Keskar, a classical music enthusiast, hoped to usher in a revival of classical music and believed that Hindi film songs' growing popularity threatened Indian classical music's survival. The controversial ban, which lasted half a decade, was part of an ambitious campaign to remake the soundscape of the newly formed Indian nation through the medium of radio and to define national identity in communal terms. Keskar linked classical music to the revival of an imagined ancient Hinduism and favored Hindu musicians over Muslim. He also promoted on the airwaves a Sanskritized version of Hindi—devoid of words of Arabic and Persian (read Muslim) origin—as India's national language, a language that was unlike the more inclusive idiom that Sayani and most Hindi film songs employed.[3]

The reference in "Tū Ganga kī mouj" to the two rivers of North India was also highly symbolic. It alluded to the *Ganga-Jamunī tehzīb*, the notion that this region's culture was a fusion of Hindu and Muslim elements, an idea acutely threatened by the 1947 Partition of India into separate Indian and Pakistani nation-states. In the midst of Keskar's campaign against film songs, the reference to the two rivers also could be heard as a metaphor for the two types of music—*filmi* and classical—eventually merging into a single body of song.[4] After all, the song's composer, Naushad, who had also come up with the original idea for the film and composed all of its songs, led the film industry in defending its music against the government's assault.[5]

Excluded from AIR's playlist, "Tū Ganga kī mouj," and *Baiju Bāvrā*'s other songs found a home on Radio Ceylon, which had just inaugurated a Hindi-language program. One reason that this station—based in Ceylon but aimed at Hindi-Urdu-speaking audiences in India and Pakistan—was able to quickly gain a large following was that listeners in colonial India had been conditioned to tune in to foreign shortwave stations during World War II. During the height of the war, many had tuned in to Axis radio news broadcasts and to the speeches of the anticolonial Axis-sympathizing leader Subhas Chandra Bose (Netaji) as a counter to British reports of the so-called "good war" (see chapters 1 and 2). In the 1950s, listeners dissatisfied with AIR's programs once more fiddled with their receivers and found Radio Ceylon's newly inaugurated Hindi film-song programs, including Ameen Sayani's *Geetmala*. One listener in Bombay spoke for many when he wrote to *Movie Times* in February 1953 to express his satisfaction with Radio Ceylon's new Hindi film-song programs: "The change" in programming, he remarked, "is most welcomed."[6]

Sayani's voice was also "most welcomed" in newly formed Pakistan, where *Geetmala* and Radio Ceylon's other Hindi film-song programs gained popularity and competed with the national network, Radio Pakistan. The impact of the show can be seen in its tremendous legacy. In 2007, more than fifty years after beginning his career at Radio Ceylon, Sayani, now seventy-five years old, visited Pakistan for the first time.[7] He spoke before the packed Arts Council auditorium in Karachi about his lifelong love affair with Hindi film songs and his career with Radio Ceylon. He charmed the audience with his characteristically energetic greeting of *"bahino aur bhāīyo"* (sisters and brothers) and replayed clips from his old radio programs, which likely included Naushad's "Tū Ganga kī mouj" as a tribute to the idea of a *Ganga-Jamunī tehzīb*.

Another of Naushad's famous film compositions, "Āvāz de kahāṅ hai" (Where are you? Call to me) from the 1946 film *Anmol Ghaṛī* (Precious watch/moment), shares a similar story as it also became a powerful anthem for unity at a particularly contentious moment. Shortly after the end of the 1965 Indo-Pakistan War and largely in response to Radio Pakistan's campaign to incite anti-Indian sentiment, Indira Gandhi, then Indian minister of information and broadcasting, inaugurated a new radio service directed at West Pakistan. Although this AIR service technically targeted only "foreign" Urdu-knowing audiences in Pakistan, it quickly gained popularity in North India as well, where Urdu was widely understood. Rather than ignore this unexpected domestic audience, Urdu Service broadcasters sidelined the official aims of a service run by the Indian government and designed programs that consciously and intentionally catered to audiences on both sides of the divide.

One of the AIR Urdu Service's most successful programs was a weekly show called *Āvāz De Kahāṅ Hai*, named after Naushad's memorable song, which featured the singer-actress Nur Jehan's melodious voice calling out to her childhood love, assuring him that despite the passing of years, "*duniyā merī javāṅ hai*" (my world is still young). During the thirty-minute radio program, the host, Abdul Jabbar, played Hindi film songs from pre-Partition days and read excerpts from letters by listeners in India and Pakistan recounting memories of a pre-Partition subcontinent. While somewhat mawkish, *Āvāz De Kahāṅ Hai*, like other Urdu Service programs, enabled cross-border connections at precisely the moment when travel across the western Indo-Pakistan border came to a halt and the border was effectively solidified.[8] Jabbar's program opened and closed with the melodious voice of a young Nur Jehan, addressing listeners on both sides the border, asking: "Where are you? Call to me."

The stories of the circulation of the songs "Tū Ganga kī mouj" and "Āvāz de kahāṅ hai" on the radio airwaves raise many questions about radio and sound's place in the subcontinent's popular cultures and about the medium's entanglement in the nation-making projects that so profoundly marked the twentieth century. What is the significance of film songs' (and films') circulation on the airwaves? What are the aesthetic and commercial implications of this convergence? What was radio's role in the end of British rule in the Indian subcontinent? What do Radio Ceylon and the AIR Urdu Service's robust transnational publics tell us about the cultural and political possibilities of the medium and the contentious politics of language in the region? Above all, the stories of these two songs invite us to ask, what was radio's role in the making and unmaking of the subcontinent's borders? These are questions that animate this book.

Radio for the Millions brings together two fields rarely in conversation: first, twentieth-century South Asian history, particularly works on the end of empire, World War II, independence, and the subsequent Partition of India and, second, the rich and growing literature on sound studies, especially works on radio. A study of radio and the politics of sound uncovers (or makes audible) important crevices in the state-making projects of the twentieth century. Radio listeners and broadcasters used the medium of radio to challenge state powers in their everyday lives and in so doing enabled the survival of the idea of the Indian subcontinent as a homeland undivided by religious nationalism, even after the 1947 Partition. Conversely, by tuning in to the golden age of radio on the Indian subcontinent, *Radio for the Millions* rethinks assumptions of how the medium connects with audiences.

Drawing on a wide-ranging collection of sources, including government documents, recordings, letters to radio stations, diaries, and oral interviews with broadcasters and listeners, this book centers on historical moments of intense cultural and political change when debates about the meaning and purpose of radio broadcasting moved to the forefront.[9] Specifically, it analyzes three key moments, which make up the book's three separate parts: World War II and the peak of the anticolonial movements in South Asia; the difficult first decade of independence; and the 1965 Indo-Pakistan War, the second military conflict between India and Pakistan over the contested state of Kashmir, and its aftermath. During each of these moments, the colonial administration, the Indian government, and the Pakistani government turned to the medium of radio to assert their legitimacy and cultural authority. However, as this book will demonstrate these state broadcasting projects faced substantial challenges and had to contend with persistent rivalries.

During World War II, pro-Axis radio stations from Germany, Japan, and Japanese-occupied Southeast Asia filled India's airwaves, bringing news of the war from an Axis perspective to listeners in India. In the decades following the war and the 1947 Partition, Radio Ceylon's Hindi film-song programs fostered cross-border connections as they invited listeners to welcome film songs and playback singers into their everyday lives. Similarly, broadcasters from the AIR's Urdu Service, founded in 1966 in reaction to the previous year's Indo-Pakistan war, promoted cross-border links at precisely the time when the western Indo-Pakistan border became impassible.[10] Despite repeated and consistent efforts from British, Indian, and Pakistani politicians to usurp the medium for state purposes and mold identities, radio largely escaped the states' grasp.

For each of these key moments, I focus on a particular radio genre—news, music, or drama—that became the subject of debate during the period. News broadcasts were especially important during World War II, and as the war moved east, eventually reaching India's doorstep, listeners' hunger for news about the global conflict only increased. In the decades after independence, radio became the primary medium through which people experienced music, and AIR's controversial radio reforms ensured that the relationship between music—both classical and *filmi*—and national identity became a passionately debated topic, within both the government and the general population. Finally, what I call "dramatic radio," which includes not only radio plays but also broadcasters' enactment of listeners' evocative letters to radio stations, was an important genre during the 1965 Indo-Pakistan War and its aftermath. I turn to the aesthetic and political implications of this genre in the book's third and final section.

By studying these three different genres alongside one another we can account for the medium's influence in the region and trace its changing form and purpose. Indeed, an important contribution of the present study is that it connects seemingly unrelated stories, events, and individuals. After all, few would imagine that Viceroy Linlithgow's speeches during World War II and the impressive musical oeuvre of the playback singer Lata Mangeshkar belong in the same narrative. During World War II, when news dominated the airwaves, the medium had a clear political character, but after independence, radio leaned more toward the aesthetic as music and dramatic performances filled most broadcast hours. Yet as I show in subsequent chapters, music and drama broadcasts were not any less political than news broadcasts. In this sense, it is not that radio was "defanged" per se, but rather that in the postcolonial period the medium moved toward more artistic aural representation of political issues. In my analysis of radio music and dramatic radio performances, I emphasize their political significance while recognizing their aesthetic contributions.

Radio for the Millions is also organized around language. I analyze stations and networks that broadcast in Hindi, Urdu, or both. Some stations promoted a national language (postindependence AIR and Radio Pakistan), and others sought to appeal to a large transnational population (pre-independence British-run AIR; Axis radio stations, including Subhas Chandra Bose's Azad Hind Radio; and Radio Ceylon). By framing my analysis around language groups, I propose a new geography for the study of radio centered on language groups rather than on national borders, imperial borders, or specific radio stations or networks.[11]

Hindi and Urdu are North Indian languages. They share the same grammar and vocabulary in colloquial speech but are written in different scripts— Hindi in Devanagari (a Sanskrit-derived script) and Urdu in Nastaliq (a Persian- and Arabic-derived script)—and have developed distinct literary traditions. Literary Urdu borrows words from Persian and Arabic, and literary Hindi draws from Sanskrit. Scholars of South Asia have argued that Urdu's and Hindi's separate identities were cemented during the communal turmoil that marked the last years of the British Empire in the subcontinent.[12] After independence, Urdu became the national language of Pakistan and Hindi the preferred national language of India. "Partition killed Hindustani," Alok Rai famously noted.[13] Hindustani is the name used to suggest an inclusive language that is neither "Hindu Hindi" nor "Muslim Urdu." *Radio for the Millions* demonstrates that, on the airwaves, Hindustani did not "die." On the contrary, it remained a viable project.

It is also important to point out that Hindi and Urdu are by no means marginal languages on the world stage.[14] Quite the opposite, if we consider nonnative speakers, together Hindi and Urdu can compete with English and Spanish for the second-most-spoken language in the world.[15] Therefore, far from a "local" or "ethnic" study, *Radio for the Millions* is a study of the medium's global dimensions.

Across Borders and Beyond Nations

This book benefits from a rich tradition of scholarly works on radio that explores radio's role in places as distinct as France, Egypt, Israel, and Japan and examines how the medium fashions collective identities and listening publics. Analyzing the medium's many artistic contributions and its links to politics, this scholarship has shown how radio's development was enmeshed in larger discussions about sound and how radio became a "platform of political engagement."[16] New works on radio drama also offer fresh theoretical tools that enable us to "read" radio broadcasts with the same care and detail that we might approach written texts or images.[17] In this book, I draw on many insights of this body of scholarship.

Yet despite the diversity of methods and regions studied, the majority of scholarly works on radio share the common framework of the nation. Some radio histories explicitly link radio to nationalism, arguing that the medium helped build imagined national communities or that radio networks unequivocally supported the state's interests.[18] Other works make the nation-state the point of departure or arrival without presenting an explicitly nationalist argument.[19] More recently, scholars have begun to question this familiar narrative, paying attention to the medium's transnational connections. Michele Hilmes, for example, studies important connections and interchange between broadcasting institutions in Britain and the United States, and Derek Valliant analyzes interchanges between French and American broadcast institutions.[20] These works show that while the national (and imperial) framework cannot be fully jettisoned (the vast majority of stations in this era were funded and run by the state and unabashedly projected imperial or national interests), the unboundedness of the air—and the resistance of airwaves to national and imperial controls—was one of the constituent features of radio broadcasting that fueled the ambitions of its magnates and practitioners. Similarly, works on Black and Latinx radio in the United States have explored how the medium enabled minoritized communities to fashion powerful counterpublics.[21]

I build on the insights of these two distinct streams of scholarship (transnational broadcasting institutions and minoritized radio) while pushing scholars of radio to consider how the medium contests state projects. Although *Radio for the Millions* certainly acknowledges (and examines) the important relationship between radio and nationalism (and British imperialism), it demonstrates that furthering state agendas is hardly where the medium proved most successful in the region. It was in the undoing of borders and in actively challenging cultural, linguistic, and political agendas of imperial and national governments where radio in South Asia ultimately left its deepest grooves.

Soundscapes

Radio for the Millions argues that radio forged a transnational soundscape that defied state borders and identities even as the 1947 Partition had rendered the idea of united India a political impossibility. Studying an earlier period, Manan Ahmed Asif has shown that "European understanding of India as Hindu" effectively replaced "an earlier, native understanding of India as Hindustan, a home for all faiths" and contributed to the internalization and naturalization of the idea of separate Muslim and Hindu dispositions.[22] A religiously fractious anti-colonial movement and the eventual Partition of British India into separate Indian and Pakistani nation-states ended the idea of Hindustan as a political territory. But even if Hindustan as a political territory had become unattainable in the twentieth century, Hindustan as a soundscape remained a lived reality. A soundscape, writes Emily Thompson, drawing on Murray Schafer's earlier work, is an "auditory landscape," and like a landscape it is "simultaneously a physical environment and a way of perceiving that environment."[23] Even as governments actively sought to mold national soundscapes and embraced hyper-nationalist and majoritarian radio campaigns, radio stations like Radio Ceylon and the AIR Urdu Service, as well as Axis Radio stations during World War II, effectively kept alive the idea of a united India as they created aural landscapes. These projects were fragile—and they were not always progressive or interested in emancipatory political ideas—but their resistance to nationalist and imperial agendas did enable the survival of a shared regional identity.

The concept of soundscape certainly can help us understand how radio challenged nationalist conceptions of space, but it can be insufficient for analyzing the power of sound as a means of resistance. The concept does not, for example, adequately capture the affective power and influence of programs like *Āvāz De Kahāṅ Hai* (Call to me. Where are you?), during which radio broadcasters performed emotional letters from listeners in India and Pakistan, quite literally calling on listeners on both sides of the divide to tune in to each other's voices. That is because the power of these "aural productions and performances" lay not only in the ways in which they created space, but also in the ways they deployed space. As the ethnomusicologist Alex Chávez argues, referring to the experience of Mexican immigrants in the United States and their musical performances, "People carry locations with them, here and there." To make sense of these broadcasts and aural performances, like Chávez, I locate the effect of sounds in the bodies of listeners. "The audible force of the message is received in the body," and the aural performance of these letters "touches—both materially and emotively—those whom it surrounds in the moment, those who are listening; . . . as it reaches out, crosses, pulling in those far away (separated by borders) fulfilling desires for intimacy."[24]

My own work on South Asia draws inspiration from Chávez's ethnography, which attends to how sound and the particular bonds it enables can help individuals contest immigration policies and negotiate a sense of belonging that defies government's agendas. Yet as Chávez notes, to account for these experiences, we must first renounce artificial divisions between the "material or sonorous aspects and the immaterial, agentive or political meanings of sound." We must acknowledge that "material textures of sounds" exist "in culturally-specific—and therefore subjectively—affective terms."[25]

Radio Resonance

To account for the ways in which radio created affective links in the bodies of listeners that could defy state agendas, policies, and borders, I pay careful attention to how people *listened* to radio, arguing for a more expansive definition of what it means *to listen*. When I first began this project, I was baffled by an apparent contradiction. In the 1940s, in a population nearing four hundred million, the number of radio receivers in colonial India hardly broke two hundred thousand, at least according to official statistics.[26] As I discovered, several factors contributed to low ownership rates of receivers during World War II, including their high cost and shortages related to war. Highest among these reasons for low ownership was the British administration's initial reluctance to invest in broadcasting infrastructure. Yet despite the fact that so few had access to radios, British colonial administrators were obsessed with "the effects" of Axis radio broadcasts on Indian audiences.[27] I first encountered what I later came to call "radio resonance" in colonial officers' anxious descriptions of damaging "rumors" that were "directly traceable to enemy radio."[28] I again found resonance in the descriptions of "Bose rumors" that surrounded Subhas Chandra Bose's various radio addresses during World War II from Germany, Japan, and Southeast Asia.

I employ the concept of "radio resonance" to account for ways that conversation, rumor, and gossip can intensify, expand, and enrich what is being broadcast and to account for the affective bonds this "talk" could create. In sound studies, resonance has been an important and recurring idea used in various ways. Veit Erlmann, for example, uses the term in a rather broad sense to refer to the "extension of the hearing body into the self-aware subject."[29] In *Nazi Soundscapes*, Carolyn Birdsall, writing about Germany, uses the term "affirmative resonance" to "refer to a practice or event when a group of people communally create sounds that resonate in a space, thus reinforcing the legitimacy of their group and identity patterns."[30] This definition is probably the closest to my own use of resonance, except that in Birdsall's definition, the "affirmative" response and its public performance en masse is crucial. In contrast, I focus on how resonance could be gradual, how broadcasts could spur discussion over time, and I give special attention to how radio resonance could operate through secretive and sometimes subversive networks.

Even if we consider collective listening practices and assume as many as a hundred people listened to a single receiver, it would have been physically impossible for more than a minuscule percentage of the population in colonial India to hear Subhas Chandra Bose's voice during World War II. To put this in perspective, one poll reported that 79 percent of the U.S. population heard Franklin Delano Roosevelt's "Day of Infamy" speech on the radio following Japan's bombing of Pearl Harbor.[31] It would be easy to dismiss Bose's radio voice as unimportant, but his mounting popularity in India during the war and British administrators' deep concerns about his broadcasts suggest otherwise. What quickly became clear is that whereas in the United States politicians like Franklin Delano Roosevelt could expect a large percentage of the population to tune in to their radio addresses, in India, Bose had to rely on the strength of oral networks of communication to carry his radio message forward. As a broadcaster, Bose consciously nurtured an on-air persona that invited gossip-like conversation in ways that profoundly shaped not only his political career but also his polemic afterlife and that helped inspire his many so-called reappearances after his death.

Radio resonance continued to be important even as the availability of affordable battery-operated transistors ensured that many more people could tune in to radio broadcasts. I encountered radio resonance again while studying Radio Ceylon's popular Hindi film-song programs. Key to the success of Radio Ceylon's *Geetmala* was the fact that the program encouraged listeners' active participation and conversation. Listeners discussed the songs' rankings and sang the winning tunes in college "canteens" and private homes. In fact, this book's title evolved from a conversation with Ameen Sayani in which he described how "the talk" that surrounded his program ensured that this music reached "millions."[32] Although very different in content, the "talk" about *Geetmala*'s competition was not categorically different from the rumors and gossip that surrounded Bose's broadcasts. The ways in which radio programs' influence resonated beyond the reach of receivers is a key theme of this book. Radio, I demonstrate, was not only *listened* to but also *talked* about—and that conversation was not supplementary but central to the medium's reception.

Aural/Oral

To a certain degree, all media depend on a kind of resonance. After all, people have long discussed printed material or talked about movies. Even social media depends on word of mouth. I am, however, specifically interested in the way in which radio's particular forms and its aurality enabled its resonance. For example, Axis radio news, which relied on spoken word, was especially prone to rumor and conversation. The immediacy of the speech, the emotions, and the tone that only the individual human voice could convey, as well as the ephemerality of radio broadcasts (once heard, radio news could not be accessed again on later days), all made possible the marriage of rumor and radio. Similarly, Radio Ceylon's Hindi film-related programs enabled films to circulate aurally.

Although it might appear that accounting for radio resonance is a straightforward exercise, taking this concept seriously invites us to rethink foundational ideas of sound studies. In particular, it invites us to suspend binary understanding of "the oral" and "the aural." Jonathan Sterne, for example, has shown that the invention of sound reproduction technologies necessitated the separation of the ear and the mouth.[33] To physically reproduce sound, inventors had to first think of sound and voice as experienced in the ear rather than emanating from the mouth, as others had. Before the nineteenth century, "theories of sound took the voice and the mouth, or music and a particular instrument (such as the violin), as the ideal-typical for the analysis, description, and modeling of sonic phenomena." In contrast, the "new sciences of sound," understood sound itself, "irrespective of the source" as the "general category or object."[34] In this way, at least in scientific discourse "the ear displaced the mouth"[35] in attempts to reproduce sound technologically because, as Kate Lacey explains, "it was now possible to treat sound as a phenomenon that excites the sensation of hearing."[36] These findings spurred the growth of the field of sound studies, encouraging scholars to explore aural traditions—and to approach listening and sound as culturally constructed practices and entities. Interestingly, however, these findings inadvertently produced their own kind of ontological shift, promoting the binary categorization of "aural/ear/hearing/listening" and "oral/ mouth/talking" and obscuring important ways in which sound reproduction technologies reached larger publics though oral networks. Focusing on twentieth-century South Asia, this book reveals that the interdependence of the ear and the mouth continued in the age of sound reproduction technologies. In fact, radio's newly found influence in India during World War II was possible only because the medium was *talked about* in addition to being *listened to*.[37]

In arguing for the importance of radio resonance, the book highlights radio's relationship to oral forms of communication against a well-established tradition in radio studies of thinking about radio alongside (or in opposition to) written and print traditions. Certainly, in South Asia as elsewhere, radio interacted with the written word. Listeners' diaries, song booklets, publications, newspapers, and letters expanded radio's reach. However, these records are best read as rare written transcripts of a much larger conversation *about* and *around* radio that formed a crucial aspect of the medium's reception.[38] While some scholars of radio have certainly noted radio's connection to oral traditions, particularly those focusing on nonwhite communities, I place radio resonance not on the periphery, but at the very center, arguing that *to talk* was *to listen.*

Following Gavin Steingo and Jim Sykes's call to decolonize sound studies, I do not "demarcate" South Asia "as a space for sonic difference," but instead I strive to "develop a new cartography of modernity for sound studies."[39] Attention to radio's connection to oral networks of communication, can help us understand the medium's influence in other regions, including the Global North, even as it decenters a certain kind of western experience of sound reproduction technologies. Consider, for example, Charles de Gaulle's famous *L'Appel du 18 juin* (Appeal of June 18) speech to Vichy France, delivered from the Broadcasting House in London following German's forces occupation during World War II. Derek Valliant and others have questioned the importance of this broadcast, despite its wide memorialization, because, at the time, audiences in France would have been too preoccupied with the occupation to tune in to the BBC.[40] Valliant and others might be right that the reception of Gaulle's radio speech was limited, but that does not necessarily mean the speech was not influential or pivotal. Again, we must focus on not only who or how many people listened to original broadcasts but also on how radio broadcasts *resonated* over time.

Toward an Interdisciplinary Radio History

One of the challenges I have faced while pursuing this interdisciplinary project is convincing historians that radio history *is* history—that the study of media is not ancillary or complementary, but rather is essential to our understanding of the past. Radio broadcasting (and more generally, the politics of sound that surrounded this technology) was vital to the subjects that have long concerned historians of twentieth-century South Asia: anticolonialism, decolonization, Partition, independence, and postcolonial state building.[41]

Radio sources allow us to reconsider the standard periodization of South Asian political history. Radio boomed in South Asia during a time of protracted political turmoil—from the 1940s to the 1970s. During this period, British rule came to an end and separate Indian and Pakistani nation-states were born as the subcontinent was immersed in a wave of communal violence.[42] *Radio for the Millions* highlights the significant continuity between colonial and postcolonial radio, presenting empire and nation not as opposite entities, but as by-products of each other, intimately intertwined.[43] Both colonial and postcolonial governments owned and managed some of the same national networks. At the same time, listeners also tuned in to foreign radio stations that challenged the agendas of colonial and nationalist radio programming. Until the 1980s, with the growth of local FM broadcasting, the basic structure of radio broadcasting in postindependence India and Pakistan mirrored its colonial predecessor, even as listening and broadcasting practices evolved.[44]

In addition to highlighting important continuities, *Radio for the Millions*, shifts attention away from a historiographical preoccupation with the "unfurling of national flags,"[45] during the 1947 Independence and the 1971 War, which resulted in Bangladesh's (East Pakistan) independence. Instead, I frame World War II and the 1965 Indo-Pakistan War as watershed moments in the region's history. In part I, I join a small group of scholars who are challenging Eurocentric histories of World War II that ignore South Asia as well as nationalist histories that overlook the global war's influence on the region.[46] I demonstrate how the war forged radio broadcasting infrastructures and listening cultures in the subcontinent. Part I also departs from a straightforward narrative that privileges Gandhi's nonviolent campaign and the Indian National Congress. Instead, by focusing on the history of radio, I show how pro-Axis ideas, namely support for Japan and Germany and sympathy for fascism, also formed part of the Indian anticolonial movement.[47]

In part III, I turn to the 1965 Indo-Pakistan War, mostly understood as a minor and inconsequential military clash between the two newly founded countries. I argue that the war—and in particular Radio Pakistan's broadcasts during the war—set the stage for the breakup of Pakistan that was to follow in 1971 and for the failure of Pakistan as a Muslim homeland.[48]

Yet if *Radio for the Millions* asks historians of the subcontinent to take media history seriously, it also encourages media studies scholars to engage historical works—that is, to use them not as mere "historical" background but to engage with the arguments and methods they present. *Radio for the Millions* seeks to demonstrate that historical methods as well as the field's predilections, including a commitment to intense archival work and preference for studying longer periods of time in a single narrative and for valuing contextualization over theorization, can offer a fresh understanding of media's place in individual lives and societies.[49]

Beyond chronology and periodization, this study contests the partitioning of scholarship, along national lines, that has mirrored the 1947 Partition of the subcontinent. *Radio for the Millions* takes into account developments and incorporates a rich collection of sources (in Hindi and Urdu) from both India and Pakistan (and to a lesser degree Sri Lanka as well).[50] In pursuing this research, I followed the radio's waves whose boundaries were not determined by the physical borders imposed by newly formed governments but rather by the strength of transmitters and radio receivers and by the preferences of listeners.[51] Attention to sound makes it clear that the two countries' shared history and culture did not end at Partition.[52]

Radio for the Millions demonstrates that while radio did not bring down imperial or national states or demolish physical borders, it did provide genuine opportunities for listeners and broadcasters to challenge these political structures in their everyday lives, at least until the early 1980s. Radio's sounds empowered listeners and broadcasters, as Chávez put it, "to go on pushing and creating, and pulling at the real and metaphorical edges of the nation-states."[53] It is this constant pushing and pulling that I chose to center in this narrative, not because they were always fully successful, but rather because the pushing and pulling enabled a way of living, of existing, and of belonging that formed an essential aspect of people's everyday lives. If these *"sounds of crossing* take place out of necessity, always" as Chávez notes,[54] they are also "uninhibited by the telos of realization," to borrow J. Daniel Elam's phrasing, and it is our duty to study them in that spirit.[55] One place where this most clearly manifests itself is in the survival of Hindustani on the radio airwaves, long after governments and even writers and readers had declared it "dead."

The "Ideology of Hindustani": Beyond the Hindi-Urdu Binary

Radio for the Millions seeks to move beyond binary understandings of Hindi and Urdu. Some define Hindustani as "a colloquial mix of Hindi and Urdu."[56] This definition, however, has many problems, and one is that nobody seems to agree on what that mixture actually entails, on the precise combination of Sanskrit-origin and Perso-Arabic-origins that it requires. I approach Hindustani as contemporaries did: as a "utopian symbol"—a "point of desire."[57] During the height of the nationalist movement, "the ideology of the Hindustani language" offered Mohandas K. Gandhi, Subhas Chandra Bose, and other leaders committed to Hindu-Muslim unity a way to transcend the sticky problem of language and religious identity. More than a language, Hindustani was an ideology and linguistic commitment to an anticommunal agenda. Moreover, Hindustani was a "utopian symbol" not only because it was free of religious affiliations but also because it promised to be a lingua franca that would connect speakers of other regional languages without threatening regional tongues and identities.

In the 1930s, British administrators argued that radio in Hindustani offered the best way to reach the "masses of India." One government official explained: "two thirds of the native population can understand, even if it cannot speak, Hindustani." Referencing radio broadcasts specifically, he assured his coworkers that Hindustani was "propitious" for a "large-scale" campaign.[58] British attempts to broadcast in Hindustani were, as we will see in chapter 1, ultimately marred by controversy, and after independence, the governments of India and Pakistan promoted Hindi and Urdu, respectively, as emphatically national languages through the medium of radio. If, however, we tune in to the competing voices transmitted through the ether—to the stations that challenged imperial and national agendas—we can "hear" how Hindustani not only remained alive well after Partition but also continued to thrive on alternative channels.

During World War II, Axis radio stations effectively harnessed Hindustani's lingua franca status as they promoted a pro-Axis fascist-inflected form of Indian nationalism on the airwaves. In later years, Radio Ceylon successfully broadcast in a simple version of Hindustani to attract a larger, transnational audience. Moreover, the AIR Urdu Service, inaugurated in 1965, although technically aimed at Pakistani audiences fluent in Urdu, embraced a version of Urdu that leaned close to Hindustani. Hoping to appeal to listeners in India, who might not have been familiar with more difficult Persian or Arabic vocabulary, broadcasters embraced the "ideology of Hindustani." Although these three radio networks and services had different politics and agendas, they were able to effectively deploy Hindustani as a lingua franca in part because they lay outside the jurisdiction of imperial and national governments (with the exception of the AIR Urdu Service).

Radio, being an aural medium, could avoid controversies and linguistic barriers of script that literature, for example, could not. Script is undeniably the most discernible religious or "communal" marker of these languages. On the air, broadcasters could also implement a more colloquial form of speech that was not nearly as marked as the higher registers of literary Hindi and Urdu. Perhaps most important, radio listeners did not necessarily need to understand everything broadcasters said on the air to get the gist of the programs and to enjoy them. The written word often lacked that same kind of versatility.

My focus on Hindi-Urdu radio follows a transnational narrative centered in North India and Pakistan. Although the book's narrative certainly spills outward to eastern and western India, where Hindi and Urdu are well understood, *Radio for the Millions* privileges a certain type of North Indian Hindi-Urdu milieu. Cognizant of this fact, I decided against a book title that claims all of South Asia in favor of one that owns its linguistic limitations. Similarly, I am also wary of narratives that present Hindustani as a linguistic panacea for the subcontinent's ills, as some accounts of the Hindustani language tend to do so. The "ideology of Hindustani" also can be deeply hegemonic. After all, South Asia is a richly linguistic diverse region, home to several hundred languages, and the search for a North Indian lingua franca inevitably stifled regional tongues.

Moreover, Hindustani's versatility, although anticommunal, was not always harnessed for emancipatory political projects. The sections on World War II explore how Axis radio broadcasters ultimately used Hindustani to promote a fascist-inflected militant form of Indian nationalism during World War II that could be extremely misogynistic. Radio Ceylon's embrace of Hindustani was motivated by profit-driven enterprise, even if the listeners and broadcasters did not wish to perceive it in this way. Jayson Beaster-Jones's comments regarding the production of Hindi film songs apply to commercial radio programs as well. Although "success may be measured in a number of different ways" for those who had money invested, "the bottom line [was] the bottom line."[59]

Scholarship on South Asian Radio and Film

Scholarship on radio in South Asia is surprisingly thin; however, in the past decades, interest in radio has been growing, particularly from the colonial period and, more recently, also from the postindependence period.[60] Recent works on Hindi film songs have begun to specifically consider radio and cinema's important symbiotic relationship.[61] Vebhuti Duggal examines how *farmāïś* (song-request radio programs) shaped radio-listening cultures, and Ravikant's bilingual scholarship (in Hindi and English) considers how cinema circulates through other mediums, including print, the internet, and radio.[62] These and other exciting and emerging studies on film came to the study of radio through their concern with film and film music, and they often take on cinema studies or an ethnomusicology approach. My approach is different. I study radio and film's relationship within the larger history of South Asian radio, analyzing film-song radio programs alongside other radio genres, and I remain explicitly in conversation with the broader historiography of the subcontinent.

We should reflect on why scholarship on radio in South Asia is thin, particularly compared with the now deep vein of scholarly publications on South Asian cinema. The difficulty of accessing sources has made it more challenging to study radio, but the historical timing of the medium also has played a role. Radio's reign as the leading medium of mass communication in South Asia, like elsewhere, was rather short. Radio was preceded by silent cinema, shared the limelight with the talkies, and was eclipsed by the rise of television in South Asia in the 1980s. Radio, in many ways, is the forgotten middle child. The most important reason behind radio's relative scholarly neglect, however, is also the most compelling argument for its study. Radio in South Asia has suffered from a somewhat unconscious predisposition by scholars of media history to deny aural experiences the prestige and importance granted to visual experiences.[63]

This neglect of radio by scholars of cinema is not a minor oversight. Throughout most of South Asian cinema's lifetime, and particularly before the proliferation of television in the subcontinent in the early 1980s, watching a movie was, for most cinema fans, a planned and rare event. In contrast, listening to radio programs about film, in particular listening to Hindi film songs, was a daily occurrence. This is clear in the experience of the seventy-plus-year-olds Srikant Patel and his wife, Saroj Patel, from Sangli in Maharashtra, India, whom I met in Radio Ceylon's studios (now Sri Lanka Broadcasting Corporation) in Colombo in the summer of 2013. The couple traveled all the way to Sri Lanka with their son to visit the studios of what was once their favorite radio station. This was the couple's first and probably only trip outside of India. As a teenager in the 1950s, Srikant Patel listened to the radio every day. By contrast, he remembers seeing no more than three films at the movie theater. Radio provided many opportunities for audiences to hear films, and this aural encounter was in many cases the *main* way—and in some cases the *only* way—that people experienced films. In conversation with the rich vein of scholarship on South Asian film, this study argues for the vital role of radio in forging the region's cinematic culture.

Radio Moments

Radio for the Millions consists of three parts, with two chapters each, covering the three moments: World War II, the difficult first decade of independence, and the 1965 Indo-Pakistan War and its aftermath. The first chapter in each of these three sections analyzes the different governments' broadcasting aims and policies, and the second discusses the most significant challenges to those policies.

Set during the last decades of British rule, chapter 1, "News on the AIR," argues that the outbreak of war transformed radio's place in Indian society. Before the war, the British administration, eager to keep anticolonial leaders off the airwaves, avoided political broadcasts of all kinds and provided only meager funding for radio broadcasting. After the outbreak of World War II, and largely in response to the growing popularity of German and Italian radio propaganda on the shortwave, the colonial government reversed direction and funneled funds into the national network: AIR. Chapter 1 also analyzes radio and rumor's symbiotic relationship: news first heard on the radio traveled by word of mouth in India, lending local significance to far-flung military and political developments around the world and enabling radio's influence to reach beyond those individuals with access to a receiver. Radio's relationship to rumor ensured that India became a "radio-aware" society long before it had high radio-ownership rates.

Turning to the second half of the war, chapter 2, "Netaji's 'Quisling Radio,'" offers a detailed discussion of the radio broadcasts of the Indian revolutionary and Axis-sympathizer Subhas Chandra Bose. Bose's radio station(s), Azad Hind (Free India), which aired first from Germany and later from Singapore, Burma, and Japan, became British radio's most prominent rival in India. Bose was the only major Indian anticolonial leader who effectively brought his message to the airwaves, and during the height of the war, he embraced the radio as a medium of resistance against colonial rule. Whereas previous studies have tended to deemphasize Bose's ties to Nazism, this chapter places him at the very center of the dissemination of Axis propaganda in India.[64] Bose's use of radio inevitably ties him to the Fascist governments that sponsored him. The chapter ends with an analysis of a series of rumors that claimed Bose was living in Russia in the 1960s and that his voice could still be heard on the radio (Bose was killed in a plane accident in 1945). Bose's life and afterlife, the chapter concludes, were intimately tied to his media: radio and rumor.

Chapter 3, "The 'Sound Standards' of a New India," chronicles AIR's social uplift programs of the early 1950s and 1960s and the redefinition of Indian citizenship in auditory terms in the first decade of independence. The minister of information and broadcasting, B. V. Keskar, an Indian classical music enthusiast, filled broadcasting hours with classical music programs and invited musicians trained at renowned academies to AIR's studios to perform and record. Keskar also ordered that AIR stations stop broadcasting Hindi film songs altogether. The chapter argues that in the wake of independence, AIR sought to orchestrate a soundscape for the Indian nation through the medium of radio. In their attempts to train the ears of radio audiences and forge what I call "citizen-listeners," they also refined the meaning of citizenship in auditory terms. Chapter 3 also questions the commitment to secularism of the government of India's first prime minister, Jawaharlal Nehru, as it demonstrates how AIR, led by Keskar, promoted anti-Muslim and caste-ist (discriminatory on the basis of caste) campaigns during the decade following independence.

Frustrated by AIR's programs, listeners in India turned their dials to Radio Ceylon. Chapter 4, "Radio Ceylon, King of the Airwaves," first traces the origins of this station to a military transmitter brought to Ceylon during World War II by the British Army. It then considers Radio Ceylon's Hindi film-song programs, which began in the 1950s. The station not only made this music widely available on the radio but also influenced the way listeners experienced film songs, encouraging them to decouple songs from films; to develop personal relationships with singers; and, most important, to integrate film songs into their daily lives. Throughout this chapter, I highlight the transnational collaborative nature of Radio Ceylon, paying careful attention to the ways in which songs and voices circulated beyond national borders—from Ceylon to India and Pakistan, where Radio Ceylon was widely popular.

Focusing on radio drama, chapter 5, "Radio Pakistan's Seventeen Days of Drama," chronicles Radio Pakistan's broadcasts during the seventeen-day-long 1965 Indo-Pakistan War. The Pakistani network aired nearly round-the-clock programming—mostly in Urdu—that created an atmosphere of intense national pride in cities in West Pakistan (contemporary Pakistan). Radio plays such as *Nidā-e-Haq* (Voice of truth) were especially effective in rallying support for the war and inciting anti-Indian sentiments. The chapter also studies the actor-singer Nur Jehan's performance on the air by bringing attention to the important gender dynamics of the radio campaign, where female voices performed supporting roles in what was presented as a verbal match between men. The 1965 war aggravated the growing hostility between the eastern and western wings of Pakistan. By drawing the circle of nationalism closer around West Pakistan and by posing Urdu as the language of Pakistan, against Bengali, spoken by the eastern wing, the 1965 radio war set the stage for the breakup of Pakistan in 1971.

Although the 1965 radio campaign initially appeared successful, it too had to contend with persistent rivalries. Shortly after the end of the 1965 war, and largely in response to Radio Pakistan's broadcasts, AIR inaugurated a new radio service. The service targeted Urdu-knowing audiences in West Pakistan, but it quickly gained popularity in North India as well, where Urdu was widely understood. The Urdu Service aired news, music, and radio plays, but at the heart of the service were letters from fans on both sides of the border sharing pre-Partition memories. Focusing on the role of letters and in particular broadcasters' dramatic performances of these letters, chapter 6, "The AIR Urdu Service's Letters of Longing," demonstrates how this radio service enabled listeners and broadcasters to build links across what had become an increasingly impenetrable border. The chapter also addresses the limitations of the Urdu Service. The nostalgia and sentimentalism that AIR Urdu broadcasters fostered through their various programs might have created cross-border links, but ultimately it did not result in any form of social action. Moreover, AIR's Urdu Service helped cast Urdu (and to a certain extent Hindustani as well) into what I call a "language of nostalgia," ensuring that Urdu and Hindustani in postindependence India became associated with bygone pre-Partition days.

Radio Archives and Sources

Radio for the Millions draws on more than a decade of research in India, Pakistan, Sri Lanka, the United States, and the United Kingdom. It relies on a rich collection of unconventional and difficult-to-locate sources, including official government documents, broadcast recordings, letters to radio stations, diaries, and more than eighty oral interviews with broadcasters and dedicated listeners. My commitment to this recovery of sources is not just method; it is also argument. The decolonization of sound studies and particularly scholarship on radio must begin with a commitment to collecting and accessing sources outside of Europe and North America and in vernacular languages.

In South Asia, as in many regions of the world, radio as an object of historical inquiry poses rather serious challenges. Scarcity of sources and barriers to access are the first and most important challenges. Radio stations, throughout the subcontinent, were at best lackadaisical about archiving materials, both recordings and radio-related documents, and at worst, impervious to serious archiving projects. For the most part, radio stations' archival collections consist of recordings with what broadcasters call "high shelf value." In other words, stations archived broadcasts that they could replay. This means that while gramophone records, radio drama, and politicians' speeches during special occasions tended to be archived (and now are being digitized), the bulk of daily radio programs, such as news bulletins, music competitions, listeners' letters, and song-request cards, were much less likely to survive. Moreover, radio stations, less accustomed to scholarship than traditional libraries and archives, lack a protocol for research. This, in some instances, makes accessing material easier, but it also can render material completely inaccessible.

Accessibility of government documents was another challenge. Government documents during the decades of British rule in South Asia are for the most part plentiful and accessible. In contrast, many government-related documents from post-1947, both in India and Pakistan, remain off limits to scholars. My approach in pursuing this project was to follow radio's traces, wherever they would take me, including to more than two dozen archives and libraries scattered throughout India, Pakistan, Sri Lanka, the United Kingdom, and the United States. I combined research in various government archives with careful readings of broadcast transcripts and radio-related paraphernalia, including memoirs by listeners and broadcasters, diaries, newspaper clippings, and letters to the radio stations by listeners.

A key important resource is the several dozen detailed oral history interviews that I conducted over many years with radio veterans in India, Pakistan, Sri Lanka, and the United States. In conducting and analyzing these interviews, I benefited from the outstanding oral histories on the Indian Partition. In particular, I found Amber Abbas's recent work with Aligarh Muslim University students helpful. She reads testimonies as "oral geographies" that expose "a history of social and spatial disruption." Even though Aligarh students did not experience physical violence, interviews reveal their "place" in India remained under threat after the Partition.[65] In the absence of an extensive centralized radio archive, these interviews enabled me to get a sense of important events and to develop a chronological and geographical framework for this study.[66] Also, many broadcasters I interviewed shared newspaper clippings about their radio programs, letters from listeners, handwritten transcripts of broadcasts, and even recordings.[67]

If the first challenge to studying radio is the scarcity of sources, another challenge, paradoxically, is abundance. In the rare cases that daily recordings were preserved, the amount of material available can be overwhelming. The 1965 war archive in Radio Pakistan's Islamabad station contains thousands of hours of material on spools that I could not possibly analyze during my visit. The challenge then was how to decide what to listen to. I selected for close readings the material that I knew, based on prior interviews with broadcasters as well as from newspaper publications, had been especially important during the war. Because there are practically no published works on this conflict, to get a grasp of the historical context of the war, I complemented my readings of Radio Pakistan's recording collections with documents about the war from U.S. State Department records found at the Lyndon B. Johnson Library in Austin, Texas.

I faced a similar overabundance when reviewing the thousands of daily transcripts of Axis broadcasts, from Japan, Japanese-occupied Southeast Asia, and Germany, at the National Archives of India. My approach in this regard was similar. To identify some of the main themes of Axis propaganda, I selected moments during World War II that I knew were important—the Quit India movement, the Fall of Singapore, and the Cripps Mission—for which I could do detailed analysis of transcripts and juxtapose these analyses alongside more distant readings of other broadcast transcripts.

It is not just my collection of a diverse array of sources, but also my "reading" of written and aural sources that merits further discussion. Taking a cue from subaltern studies scholarship, I trace rumors of radio broadcasts in British colonial records and read them against the grain.[68] When analyzing radio drama, I draw on radio drama works to "read" sounds so as to "hear" the ways in which radio molds the imagination.[69] In the chapter on Radio Ceylon, I recreate Hindi film-song programs that went on live and were never recorded through the careful juxtaposition of radio schedules, broadcaster memoirs, oral interviews, and listeners' letters to radio stations alongside existing recordings of Hindi film songs. As such, *Radio for the Millions* can be read as a meditation on how we might recover fragments of an aural past when sources are limited. At the same time, I remain cognizant of Sterne's warnings about the excavation of an aural past. With dutiful work, we might be able to recover traces of past aural experiences, but we cannot presume to know with any kind of exactitude what it meant to listen at the time.[70] Like Santanu Das's *India, Empire, and First World War Culture*, "the impulses of this study are both analytic and recuperative."[71] But at a deeper level, this study also seeks to capture what Raymond Williams calls "structures of feeling" associated with radio broadcasts. These structures include "elements of impulse, restraint and tone; specifically affective elements of consciousness and relationships: not feeling against thought, but thought as felt and feeling as thought; practical consciousness of a present kind."[72] In my readings of broadcast sounds, I hope to have captured at least some of what Das describes as "texture of experience" and to have remained "alert to their sensuous and affective dimension."[73]

One final point: the sources I have gathered made it possible for me to approach the study of radio from several angles. Some chapters are more concerned with governments' policies toward radio, whereas others focus on radio content. When sources permit, I also analyze listeners' reactions to broadcasts. Although I agree with Neil Verma that radio studies scholars have for far too long ignored the "actual sound" of programs, I do not believe that radio's institutions, its audiences, or its sounds can be easily separated or that that separation is always necessary or productive.[74] Close readings of radio programs can—with some conjecture and careful extrapolation, of course—help us better understand the experience of listening to the radio in late colonial and early postcolonial South Asia. In the following pages, I tune in to a radio history in the hopes that it might enable us to hear the story of the Indian subcontinent at the crossroads of the empire in a new tune.

PART I

RADIO NEWS AND WORLD WAR II

CHAPTER 1

NEWS ON THE AIR

On September 3, 1939, the British viceroy of India, the marquess of Linlithgow, declared war on Germany on India's behalf. One man, who called himself the "Bengali observer," recorded his impressions of the general atmosphere in Calcutta in the month immediately following the controversial declaration of war. He did not write about the viceroy's refusal to consult with elected Indian officials before declaring India belligerent, nor did he write about the newly elected Congress ministries' resignations following the declaration of war.[1] Instead, the Bengali observer wrote about how friends and acquaintances in his native city of Calcutta experienced the war through their radio receivers. The outbreak of war, the Bengali observer explained, had spawned an unprecedented interest in foreign radio news programs. Foreign stations—at the time, most prominently German radio—aired news programs in Indian languages, particularly Hindustani. Eager to learn more about the war, listeners in his city, the Bengali observer noted, tuned in to foreign and pro-Axis broadcasts with great interest.[2]

In the wake of the declaration of war, the British administration instituted stricter censorship on newspapers and specifically clamped down on pro-Axis publications.[3] Colonial administrations, however, could do little to stop people from listening to Axis radio programs. One distressed administrator wrote: "The German broadcasts are known to be full of lies but everyone listens to them with great interest and they inevitably have an effect."[4] Axis radio announcers routinely and intentionally exaggerated the truth, withheld crucial information, and broadcast downright false stories, both about the global war and about developments in India. British officials in India were not particularly surprised that German stations manipulated the truth. After all, the Nazi government had long thrived on manipulating the press. But they were alarmed by the degree of interest that people in India showed in these broadcasts and by the speed with which news heard on the radio traveled far beyond the reach of radio receivers.

To broadcast to India, the Nazi government recruited a small group of Indian-born translators, scriptwriters, and newsreaders. Broadcasting mostly in Hindustani, these announcers spoke to Indian audiences as members of the resistance, promising that simply by tuning in to Axis radio, they were part of a radical revolutionary anticolonial community on the airwaves. Axis radio announcers blended anticolonial rhetoric with blatantly false pro-fascist and anti-Semitic comments and conspiracy theories. Echoing techniques of aural propaganda used on German audiences, Axis radio aimed at Indian listeners sought to make Indians into what Carolyn Birdsall calls "earwitness participants" of a revolutionary aural community.[5] While witnessing, having knowledge of an event or change through personal experience, has been "conceived in terms of the eyewitness, with the two words almost used interchangeably," Birdsall argues for the alternative concept of "the earwitness" that accounts for the "cultural manifestations of sound and listening."[6] Thinking about earwitnesses and earwitnessing also can help us make sense of the importance of Axis radio broadcasts in India.

In response to German radio broadcasts and their perceived popularity with Indian audiences, British colonial government made the first genuine, albeit belated and haphazard, attempt to reach the general population through the medium of radio. Before the outbreak of war, the British colonial administration, eager to keep anticolonial leaders off the airwaves, placed strict restrictions on political broadcasts of all kinds and provided only meager funding for radio broadcasting. The necessities of the war and the perceived popularity of Axis broadcasts, however, forced the British colonial administration to change course and rapidly invest in broadcasting, especially news bulletins and news commentary. It was in response to the war that the government developed the national broadcasting network: All India Radio (AIR).

In conversation with emerging scholarship on World War II in South Asia, in part I (chapters 1 and 2), I demonstrate how World War II forged radio broadcasting infrastructures as well as fashioned listening cultures. Here, I join a group of committed scholars challenging both Eurocentric histories of World War II that ignore South Asia as well as histories of the region that overlook the global war.[7] Chapter 1 focuses on the first half of the war and analyzes both Axis broadcasts and the British administration's interpretations and responses to those broadcasts. Chapter 2 turns to the second half of the war and to the radio broadcasts of the Indian revolutionary and Axis-sympathizer Subhas Chandra

Bose. Bose's radio station(s), Azad Hind (Free India), aired first from Germany and later from Singapore, Burma, and Japan and became British radio's most prominent rival in India.

In both chapters, I analyze radio's important relationship to rumor and consider how radio's ties to rumor challenge our understanding of the medium and listening cultures more broadly. Colonial administrators repeatedly complained about rumors traceable to radio broadcasts. For example, in December 1940, one British official explained: "A croup [sic] of rumors has been generated, in many cases directly traceable to enemy broadcasts . . . [and] in some parts of the country they have disturbed the confidence of the people and led to such signs of nervousness."[8] On one hand, accounts of radio rumors echo an older and well-documented colonial understanding of Indian society as naïve and prone to misinformation.[9] On the other hand, these accounts reveal how radio integrated itself and expanded on already robust oral networks of communication. For various reasons, including wartime shortages of receivers, but more important, because of the British administration's prior unwillingness to invest in radio, radio receivers' ownership rates in India during World War II were abysmally low.[10] Yet accounts of rumors traceable to radio broadcasts suggest that radio's influence reached beyond individuals with access to receivers. This invites scholars of radio to consider how listening and talking can be intrinsically linked. After all, as Luise White notes, one of the distinguishing features of rumors is that listeners and talkers can blend into each other and it is in "their exchange and evaluation that [rumors] take on sophisticated analysis."[11] Birdsall, in her analysis of sound in Nazi Germany, emphasizes the importance of Nazi sounds' physical presence in urban spaces, whereas I show that "earwitness" listeners need not have physically "tuned in" to broadcasts. They could become "earwitness" participants by engaging in the rumors and talk that surrounded these broadcasts.

I also employ the concept of "radio resonance" to account for radio's influence in the region. In wartime India, news that was first heard on the radio traveled by word of mouth to cities, towns, and villages, lending local significance to far-flung military and political developments. Just as scholars of South Asia have convincingly argued that the strength and resilience of oral networks of communication made India a "literacy-aware" society long before it achieved high levels of literacy, I posit that oral networks of communication made India a "radio-aware" society long before it had high radio-ownership rates.[12]

This chapter opens with a brief outline of the early history of radio in the subcontinent and then traces the institutional history of the national broadcasting network: AIR. I demonstrate that the colonial government became involved in broadcasting half-heartedly. First, it was cajoled by radio sellers to take over failed private broadcasting initiatives and later took to broadcasting to prevent anticolonial leaders from doing so. I then consider the war's outbreak as a key turning point in radio's history in the subcontinent. In the final section, I analyze Axis radio broadcasts and consider their effects on both the local population and on the British administration's attitudes toward radio.

Broadcast Beginnings: Indian Broadcasting Corporation

John Reith was the iconic founding director of the British Broadcasting Corporation (BBC). Reith liked to fantasize about what radio could do for India's millions. He wrote letter after letter to the government of India urging administrators to inaugurate a public broadcasting service in the country.[13] It is not hard to imagine why Reith was so enthusiastic about bringing radio to India. Orientalist accounts about the parochialism, illiteracy, and so-called backwardness of India's population, then estimated at 300 million, provided an exemplary template for idealistic early radio visionaries to dream big.[14]

To Reith's frustration and disappointment, the colonial administration showed little interest in financing a broadcasting scheme. The administration cited financial restraints. Indeed, transmitters were expensive and so was their maintenance. Yet behind the British administration's unwillingness to invest in radio broadcasting lay a deep-seated fear that the medium could easily be used against colonial government. The anticolonial movement had gained new steam. Mohandas K. Gandhi returned to India from South Africa in 1915 and quickly emerged as the charismatic leader of a growing and increasingly vociferous Indian anticolonial movement.[15] As Joselyn Zivin notes, for the colonial government of India, "the possibility that the government's opponents might control the ether seemed, if not exactly an immediate concern," then certainly "a potentially catastrophic" prospect. The British had reason enough to worry about any kind of "association of radio with mass politics."[16]

The administration's unwillingness to invest in broadcasting did not tamp down all efforts to bring broadcasting to India. Instead, it inspired some important private enterprises. A group of Indian and British entrepreneurs in 1926 pooled enough funds to purchase two medium-wave transmitters and managed to convince the central government to protect the company's monopoly for five years. This would be sufficient time, the investors believed, to build an adequate infrastructure and a loyal listenership in colonial India. They called their company the Indian Broadcasting Company (IBC). Its Bombay station aired its first broadcast on July 1927 and its Calcutta station in August of the same year.[17] The IBC broadcast mostly in English and catered to the upper echelon of Indian society, making little effort to reach the "Indian masses" that Reith had insisted radio was especially suited to serve. The IBC even secured an agreement with the Performing Rights Society of London, a society that represented the rights of artists, to broadcast recordings of the society's concerts.[18]

Within months of its inauguration, the IBC faced serious financial difficulties. The company relied solely on fees from licenses and import taxes, but it did not collect enough revenue to cover the station's operating costs.[19] The IBC announced it would cease its services in February 1930.[20] Radio vendors, both English and Indian, immediately protested that the imminent closing of the IBC would be the deathblow to their business, which they had started with the government's blessing back in 1927.[21] Radio vendors, among them both Indian and British businessmen, persuaded the reluctant viceroy to purchase the IBC's stations in Calcutta and Bombay, and the two stations resumed broadcasting on April 1, 1930, under the new name of the Indian State Broadcasting Service (ISBS). Thus, under these inauspicious circumstances, state-controlled radio in India came into effect. The colonial government, however, refused to divert any more public funds to broadcasting. To pay for the cost of running the two stations, it raised import taxes on radio receivers to 50 percent.[22] This meant that fewer people could purchase the now-even-more-expensive radio receivers.[23]

In reality, the government of India, particularly the viceroy, Lord Irwin, would have been content to let the medium die a slow death. When Eric Dunstan, the IBC's director, asked the viceroy for financial assistance, the viceroy remarked, "It cannot be said that broadcasting is, under existing conditions, of immense strategic importance in India."[24] Behind the viceroy's hesitance lay a looming fear that by building up a broadcasting organization, the colonial government might just be creating a mouthpiece for the anticolonial movement.

The following year, however, radio in India received a much-needed boost from an unforeseen source. In September 1932, the BBC Empire Services inaugurated services on the shortwave.[25] In a broadcast, King George V explained that the BBC Empire Services, which broadcast in English, targeted "men and women, so cut off by the snow, the desert, or the sea, that only [a] voice out of the air can reach them."[26] Within weeks, the BBC Empire Service gained loyal followers not only among the British community in India, but also among some English-speaking upper-class Indians.[27] While a detailed study of the BBC Empire Services is outside the scope of this study, it is not hard to imagine why this service outdid the struggling ISBS, which catered to the same kind of elite listeners in India. The Empire Services, with studios in the heart of London, employed more experienced broadcasters and put out many more hours of programing than the ISBS. More important, as one administrator and fan explained, the Empire Services provided a "sentimental link" between residents in the overseas dependencies and the mother country.[28] Despite the exorbitant 50 percent import tax on radio apparatuses, within a period of less than two years, the number of licenses in India doubled. By 1934, there were twenty-five thousand registered licenses in India.[29]

Once more, radio vendors persuaded the still-hesitant colonial government to become further involved in radio broadcasting.[30] Vendors argued that the rising revenue from license fees and import taxes, fueled by the sudden increase in sales of radio receivers in India, should be used to develop the broadcasting infrastructure in the subcontinent. The new viceroy of India, Lord Willingdon, in January 1934, reluctantly conceded to the vendors' demands. Willingdon set aside a modest budget of two and a half lakh rupees to build a radio station in New Delhi and wrote to John Reith in London to send a radio expert trained by the BBC to India to become India's first controller of broadcasting.[31] Trapped between the enthusiasm for the Empire Service among a privileged elite and a tacit fear that the medium could be used against the administration, public broadcasting in India was born.

One more point is crucial: the colonial government's initial refusal to fund large projects and bring transmitters to India slowed the medium's development in the region as a government-run pan-Indian infrastructure. This lack of government support, however, simultaneously enabled local and small-scale broadcasting projects. A number of private radio clubs, run mostly by local Indian entrepreneurs and music enthusiasts, sprouted in various urban centers in the mid-1920s, including Bombay, Calcutta, and Madras. The clubs used low-power transmitters, which could be heard only within a few miles' radius and, for the most part, broadcast what were then called "gramophone concerts."[32] Although small-scale and short-lived experiments, these radio clubs whetted listeners' appetite for music on the radio.[33] Moreover, as I further describe in this chapter, many radio clubs were later integrated into the national public broadcasting network.

Similarly, a group of idealistic British officers and army officials inaugurated a handful of experimental village broadcasting projects in various rural areas.[34] Like the radio clubs, these experiments relied on the dedication of a few committed individuals, mostly retired British administrators, with a lofty understanding of what radio could do for India's rural populations. These projects remained small and faced a variety of problems, including developing interesting programming for rural audiences. While most of these programs fizzled out, some, like the radio clubs, became part of the national broadcasting network.[35]

All India Radio and Lionel Fielden

Following pressure from radio vendors to expand the broadcasting network, the viceroy of India asked John Reith to help him identify "the best man possible" to lead the development of broadcasting in India.[36] (There were certainly well-accomplished women broadcasters in the BBC, even in those early years, but Willingdon requested a man for this post.) Reith was so excited that the government of India had finally shown an interest in radio that, according to his autobiography, he considered volunteering to go to India himself. But, bogged down with responsibilities in England, he ultimately decided against the idea.[37]

Ian Stephens from the Indian Home Department, a right-hand man of the viceroy, had insisted that this post should be offered to a "concealed die-hard" imperialist, who would protect the interests of the British Empire in India. The man Reith selected, Lionel Fielden, a forty-one-year-old broadcaster from the BBC Talks, hardly fit that bill.[38] During his time in India, Fielden managed to rile up his coworkers by breaking just about every unspoken rule of European life in India. He did not make an effort to conceal his homosexuality or his dislike for the well-established patterns of white colonial society in India.[39] He stayed away from clubs, avoided summer vacations in hill stations, and refused to live in British quarters.[40] Most important, he openly supported the nationalist movement. Within months of his arrival, he had reached out to M. K. Gandhi, Jawaharlal Nehru, and activist and poet Sarojini Naidu.[41]

Yet despite Fielden's anticolonial leanings, he served the empire rather well—perhaps better than he later would have liked to admit. His arrival in India marked a new stage for radio, one that was above all characterized by the centralization of radio broadcasting. It was Fielden who renamed the national network, All India Radio, and assigned its catchy and rather appropriate acronym AIR. The name, which to this day remains in use, became official on June 8, 1936.[42] In the years to come, Fielden toiled to ensure that the organization lived up to its new name. He integrated independent broadcasting projects, including surviving radio clubs and some rural broadcasting schemes, into the national network.[43] Moreover, despite having access to limited funds, Fielden oversaw the erection of new stations in strategic urban centers. These included Lucknow, Trichinopoly (now Tiruchirappalli), and Dacca (now Dhaka, Bangladesh) and the significant expansion of existing stations, including the Delhi and Lahore stations.[44]

Fielden improved AIR's infrastructure but struggled to improve and expand programming. As Fielden later admitted, he simply lacked the cultural understanding and language skills (other than English, he spoke no Indian languages) to develop effective programming.[45] He was, however, successful in recruiting writers to AIR, including the Bukhari brothers, Zulfiqar Bukhari and Patras Bukhari, two well-known writers and enthusiasts of Urdu.[46] With Fielden as director, the famous Urdu writer, Saadat Hasan Manto, also regularly wrote plays for AIR, as did the Hindi and Urdu writer Reoti Saran Chandra and many others.[47] Fielden and the Bukhari brothers also recruited musicians to come to AIR—particularly women from the *tawaif* (a type of female performer who excelled in music, dance, and poetry) tradition.[48] Overall, in this early period, AIR struggled to develop content, and radio therefore remained a limited and largely untapped medium in colonial India.

Part of the problem was that the colonial government continued to place rigid restrictions on what material could be broadcast. The government prohibited members or representatives of any political party from speaking on the radio.[49] To cover up what was clearly an illiberal policy that restricted freedom of speech, the government of India also banned any kind of political material from the airwaves. This meant that the colonial government could not advertise the "benefits of the Empire" on the air just as nationalists could not criticize colonial rule.[50] Under these constraints, AIR could broadcast only educational and entertainment programs. In the heated political atmosphere that characterized India in the mid-1930s, AIR's radio educational and civic programs must have seemed comically banal to those who cared to tune in. At the height of the nationalist movement, AIR broadcast a debate between two Muslims on the question, "Should cars be used instead of bullock carts?" and a discussion in English by Miss Norah Hill titled, "Round India with [the] Red Cross."[51] The outbreak of the war and the popularity of German and other Axis radio soon changed all of this.

Berlin Calling and Nazi Earwitnesses

As the Bengali observer at the beginning of this chapter noted, Axis radio broadcast became a sensation in India within weeks of the war's outbreak.[52] The government was quick to take notice of the new trend. As early as December 1939, just two months after the viceroy had declared war on India's behalf, colonial officers throughout India exchanged anxious telegrams discussing the sudden popularity of the shortwave radio news programs from Germany. The governor of the North-West Frontier Province, the region of British India that was closest to Europe and from where the colonial administration expected an invasion, explained to his superiors in Delhi: "It is remarkable how much attention appears to [be given to] daily broadcast from Germany."[53] Similarly, a colonial officer reporting from Jodhpur in the western region of Rajputana remarked: "A considerable number of owners of wireless receiver sets tune in to broadcasts from Berlin every day."[54] To an already distraught British administration in India, struggling to cope with the new demands of the global war and with an ever-strengthening anticolonial movement, Nazi radio in Hindustani seemed to have emerged from nowhere and to have quickly developed a loyal Indian following. Berlin's efforts to broadcast to India, however, fit well within the Nazi government's approach to broadcasting and propaganda more generally.

In *Nazi Soundscapes*, Carolyn Birdsall discusses the "disciplinary functions of listening (and eavesdropping) as well as the sonic dimensions to exclusion and violence" in Nazi Germany.[55] Nazi-era appropriation of "sound and sound technology," Birdsall argues, helped transform ordinary Germans into "earwitness" participants in the experience of a "national community." In conversation with earlier scholarship on Nazism and radio, Birdsall notes that radio was the center of this larger campaign.[56] The radio had played a crucial role in helping

Germans "adjust to new racial identities," "believe in the necessity of war," and "accept the dynamic of unconditional destruction."[57]

The Nazi government exported their radio campaign abroad and specifically targeted populations in British colonies and territories, hoping to erode trust in the colonial administration and consequently hurt the British government. The better known of these services is the Arabic-language shortwave service, which targeted audiences in the Middle East and North Africa.[58] What is less known, however, is that around the same time, the German Foreign Office also inaugurated a shortwave broadcasting service to India. To reach Indian audiences, the German Foreign Office made use of a shortwave transmitter in the occupied Netherlands town of Huizen, which the Dutch government had used to broadcast to the Dutch East Indies, now Indonesia. In this way, the Nazis capitalized on existing European colonial infrastructure to broadcast to British colonies.[59]

British officials were surprised by the attention that Axis radio broadcasts were getting but were quick to point out that the key to the service's allure with Indian audiences was Nazi radio's alleged support of the growing and strengthening anticolonial movement. One officer explained that the service's main attraction was its presentation of "England as the ruthless oppressor" and "Germany as a friend of India."[60] Of course, German radio's message was profoundly contradictory. The Nazi government not only had imperial ambitions of its own but also deemed Indians biologically inferior. Yet what seems to have made this contradictory message if not entirely believable, at least plausible, was that German radio employed Indian voices.

To broadcast to India, the Nazi government recruited a small group of translators, scriptwriters, and newsreaders, many of whom were students in German universities.[61] On the airwaves, these Indian-born broadcasters (all of them, it appears, men) addressed listeners using terms such as "brothers in India," presenting themselves as exiled anticolonial activists. Some listeners would have been aware of the important Indo-German connection that had flourished in Germany a few decades earlier. In the 1920s, Berlin became a hub of anti-imperialists activity. Many Indian nationalists built links to Germany, among them communist leaders, such as M. N. Roy and Virendranath Chattopadhyaya, who spent formative years in Germany. Even the future first prime minister of India, Jawaharlal Nehru, made enduring political connections in Berlin when he visited in 1926. Although most broadcasts do not appear to reference these connections explicitly, there is little doubt that at least some listeners would have been aware and that this could have increased their interest in the broadcasts.[62]

Axis radio announcers spoke to Indian audiences as potential members of the resistance. Broadcasters promised that by merely tuning in to Axis radio, they became part of a revolutionary anticolonial community on the airwaves. Moreover, from the very beginning, German shortwave service announcers aligned themselves with the Indian National Congress, the leading anticolonial political organization in India, and with M. K. Gandhi's campaign. In reality, neither Gandhi nor other prominent Congress leaders would have endorsed statements made by this radio service, starting with its pro-fascist and anti-Semitic messages. Yet by alleging support to Gandhi and the Congress, Axis radio managed to bring anticolonialism and politics more broadly to the Indian airwaves. Like in Germany, these radio programs sought to create listeners into "earwitness" participants of a particular type of revolutionary aural community.

The British administration acknowledged that the German service's alleged support of the anticolonial movement was a huge part of its appeal, but it stopped short of admitting that the administration's efforts to keep anticolonial leaders off the airwaves had opened up the space for German shortwave radio. British officials had placed strict restrictions on political discussions on AIR, whether pro-empire or nationalist, making people hungry for radio news. Moreover, the censorship of newspapers during the war also added to Axis radio's allure.

After the outbreak of the war in 1939, the colonial government reenacted the Defense India Rules Act of 1915, which gave British authorities at all levels of government almost unlimited ability to censor newspapers.[63] During the first years of the war, central, provincial, and local government officials opted for what were "less blatant methods of control," but as the war turned in Japan's favor, the government moved to more invasive censorship methods.[64] Government officials actively punished and even shut down newspapers that dared to reproduce pro-Axis views, and they also punished those who exposed the "brutality" and "inefficiency" of the British administration.[65] The constricted political coverage in print conjoined with AIR's own restrictions on political discussions pushed more Indian listeners to turn to Axis-affiliated channels.

Germany, however, was not the only Axis country to broadcast to India. The Italian government also sponsored a shortwave radio service called Radio Himalaya. A Punjabi man named Iqbal Shedai managed this station and was likely the service's primary voice. Unlike the German broadcasts, which offered a constant stream of broadcast news for several hours, Radio Himalaya does not appear to have had a consistent schedule.[66] Moreover, whereas German news broadcasts were carefully edited and well organized (even if they were incendiary and often untruthful), Radio Himalaya's broadcasts were unpolished and disorganized.

Japan also began broadcasting regularly to India—primarily in Hindustani as well, but it was only after Subhas Chandra Bose took over the leadership of the Indian National Army in 1943 that the British government gave Japanese radio serious consideration. In this chapter, I prioritize discussing the German service, while explaining how Italian and later Japanese broadcasts buttressed this service.[67]

"Clear Hindustani Mixed with a Few Hindi Words"

Language was a crucial component of Axis radio's presence in India, and for the most part, the German shortwave service to India broadcast in Hindustani. Concerned about the growing popularity of this service, the British government hired radio monitors to simultaneously transcribe, translate, and prepare weekly summaries of radio broadcasts, which colonial officers would then read and analyze. These verbatim translations and summaries are a rich resource and tell us a great deal about the content of broadcasts—the topics they discuss, their tone, and the ways they evoke emotion. Unfortunately, however, they tell us very little about the word choice, syntax, and pronunciation of announcers because they are English renderings.

One British official remarked that Berlin-based announcers spoke in "clear Hindustani, mixed with a few Hindi words." What did this officer mean by such a statement? Is the reference to "mixed" meant to evoke the idea of Hindustani as the "point of desire" I describe in the introduction?[68] Even more important, what did this officer mean by the term "clear"? Clear in what way and to whom? Perhaps he meant that broadcasters spoke in a way that would have been accessible not only to those in Hindi-Urdu speaking regions, but also to nonnative speakers of Hindustani, in particular, to speakers of related languages, such as Punjabi, Bengali, Marathi, and Gujarati. After all, one of the main attractions of Hindustani and the reason why major Congress leaders, including Gandhi, Nehru, and Bose, had supported it as a national language was its accessibility throughout western and eastern India.[69] Axis radio, at least according to government sources, seemed to have successfully capitalized on that.

Another British official remarked that the "Berlin style" was popular with Indian listeners because it was "independent and [did] not constantly give the *impression of translation*."[70] Was this officer trying to tell us that the Axis radio reflected the way people *actually* spoke? After all, the search for Hindustani had long been a search for a spoken vernacular. Of course, without any available recordings of broadcasts or transcriptions in the original language, our analysis of the language of broadcasts remains necessarily speculative. We cannot say with any kind of certainty how Axis radio in Hindustani *sounded*. What we do know with certainty is that the British administration believed that Berlin was doing something *right* when it came to language. As I will elaborate further in this chapter, the perceived success of German radio ultimately pushed the British administration to scramble for an effective language to address Indian audiences and to search, ultimately unsuccessfully, for its own version of Hindustani.

Content: Axis Radio Themes and Incendiary Topics

Axis radio programs consisted of a combination of short news bulletins, mostly about the global war, but also about developments in India, followed by longer impassioned scripted talks. These talks addressed the history of British imperialism, the global war, and the Indian anticolonial movement alongside current events. Sometimes broadcasters provided poignant and historically accurate critiques of imperialism and the politics of the war. Other times, they exaggerated, spun, or twisted events and developments. In what follows, I focus on a few themes of Axis radio, with special attention to German broadcasts, but also taking into account the Italian service and the burgeoning Japanese service. One thing that is notable is that Axis radio favored topics that were already circulating in India, some openly endorsed by leading activists and others attended to less openly.[71]

The evils of British imperialism were the most important topic of Axis radio. Almost every single talk in one way or another reminded Indian audiences that British imperialism had impoverished India and had enriched Britain: "Alas! Britain has reduced India to abject poverty during the past two hundred years."[72] Announcers equated imperialism with slavery, referring to British rule of India as "centuries-old slavery."[73] Broadcasters also carefully and methodologically debunked myths about the so-called benefits of British rule long endorsed by the colonial administration: "the British often claim that they are ruling over India for the benefit of the Indians, and in order to civilize them." Their only intention is to "plunder India."[74] As we might expect, announcers chose particularly incendiary topics that could easily evoke emotion. For example, the Jallianwala Bagh massacre, during which a British general ordered the massacre of more than one thousand unarmed Indian civilians at a religious gathering, was a commonly cited event on Axis radio. Announcers, hoping to fire up listeners, reminded their audience—and were not incorrect in doing so—that the British administration had willingly and purposely engaged in mass murder. This discourse was by no means unusual in anticolonial circles. Gandhi himself often spoke about the Jallianwala Bagh massacre as did a number of other leaders, even those who might have not supported the Indian National Congress. What was different was the kind of crudeness that Axis radio embraced in its broadcasting and the deliberately incendiary tone it took on.

If the British Empire's crimes were the Axis radio's main topic, the United States' alleged imperialist ambitions in India trailed not far behind. As early as November 1941, German broadcasters warned Indian listeners that the United States had imperial ambitions in India.[75] U.S. politicians, Berlin-based announcers explained, "expressed sympathy for India" only because Americans "want to capture [Britain's] possessions."[76] German broadcasts frequently noted that the

United States had clear financial interests in India: "Roosevelt was ensuring the U.S. commercial interests by investing capital in Indian industries."[77] Axis announcers repeatedly warned Indian listeners that the United States was every bit as dangerous and hurtful to India as was Britain.

Another staple theme of Axis radio, particularly during the first half of the war, was the notion that the global war was an opportunity for the Indian nationalist movement. Announcers urged Indian audiences to "strike when the iron was hot." "Indians should sacrifice their all to see India free since the present opportunity seldom repeats itself," said one broadcaster.[78] Another one suggested: "It is the duty of the Indians to take advantage of the present unique opportunity"[79] and advised audiences to "take advantage of this *golden opportunity, and liberate your motherland*."[80]

With the same passion with which broadcasters asked listeners to act swiftly, they also named and shamed prominent Indians who supported the British war cause. For example, German radio aired a talk called "A Few Words Addressed to Sir Feroz Khan Noon." The announcer called Feroz Khan, a military adviser who had joined Churchill's cabinet and was critical of Congress's opposition to the viceroy's declaration of war, a hireling and traitor to the nation.[81] The message was clear: to support Britain in the war cause was to collaborate with the enemy.

How the British depended on and exploited Indian *sepoys* (soldiers) was also an important and recurring hot-button topic, which too explored themes of collaboration with the empire. During World War II, the Indian army expanded dramatically and became the largest volunteer army in history, with more than 2.5 million Indian soldiers serving in all theaters of the war. The notion of a "volunteer army" was, of course, problematic. Hoping to increase enrollment, the British actively recruited outside the so-called martial races, the communities that the British had deemed biologically apt for combat, and loosened weight and health restrictions for enrollment. The result was that many men joined the army out of dire economic necessity. The army meant guaranteed daily meals and consistent, although still meager, income for their struggling families. German radio tapped this issue and argued, not inaccurately, that Britain was essentially sacrificing Indian men's lives to ensure the British Empire's survival.[82] Axis radio also placed the issue of mercenary Indian soldiers fighting for the British Empire in the context of a longer history of British imperialism and its reliance on the Indian army, reminding listeners that Indian soldiers had fought in World War I and that their "only reward" for their "sacrifices" had been "oppression."[83]

If the idea of the Indian sepoy serving as a human shield for the British Empire was an incendiary topic aiming to arouse anger and distrust in listeners, British racism against Indians was another one. In April 1940, Radio Himalaya explained: "However much you may protest, you will remain dark-skinned.

King George, Lord Linlithgow and others might give you promises that you will become white, but you should remember that these are all foul play."[84] Even in its awkwardly translated form, we can hear the crudeness, sarcasm, and, more important, the provocative tone of the original broadcast. Similarly, in January 1942, as the Japanese accumulated victories against Allied powers, German radio explained the situation in terms of race: "[The British] are ashamed of admitting that the Japanese are dealing heavy blows on the white-skinned people and inflicting defeats after defeats on them."[85]

Fascism and Anti-Semitism in Axis Propaganda

The German service to India blended anticolonial rhetoric, which was some-times truthful and other times offered exaggerated critiques of British rule, with blatantly false pro-fascist and anti-Semitic comments and conspiracy the-ories.[86] Broadcasters also spent a lot of time contradicting and disproving what they called "false reports" about the situation in Germany and about Hitler's policies against Jews.[87] One broadcaster explained: "The British only wanted to represent Hitler as a savage and Germany as an oppressed and weak country."[88] The message of Axis radio was clear-cut: reports about atrocities in Germany sought to discredit Britain's rival and betrayed a deep-seated fear of Germany's rise in Europe. Moreover, much like Nazi propaganda directed at domestic audiences, this Hindustani-language service also blamed Jews for disturbances in Germany. Hitler's government, Indian announcers told Indian audiences again and again, had had no choice but to take action against Jews, who were determined to harm Germany: "If you are sure that a person or several persons are bent on setting your house on fire, . . . will you not fight in self-defense or will you use no weapon if you are forced to fight?"[89]

Moreover, as we would expect, this service also pushed typical anti-Semitic tropes about Jews allegedly controlling financial institutions, the press, and the film industry.[90] Axis radio also stressed that Germans and Indians were both victims of wrongdoings perpetrated by the Jews and the British.[91] One broad-caster noted: "The Jews and the British had oppressed the German people and sought their destruction and obliteration, just like the British had sucked India dry through nearly 300 years of imperialism."[92] Sometimes the analogies of British and Jewish enemies and German and Indian victims were conflated. Toward the end of the war, a German shortwave announcer blamed not only the British but also Jews for the spread of famine in East India: "Famine in India is Jew ingenuity"; Jews "buy grains wholesale and export it."[93] In this way, Axis propaganda blended anticolonialism with fascist anti-Semitic rhetoric.

Finally, Axis propaganda's patriarchal and misogynistic comments deserve our attention. On one occasion, German radio reported that the British were actively recruiting Indian women for the battlefield. The broadcaster noted: "They have been sacrificing Indians to save themselves. Now they want to sacrifice Indian women too."[94] I wish to draw attention not only to the obvious falsity of the statement (there is no record that the British had intentions of drafting Indian women for combat) but also to the patriarchal anger this statement sought to evoke. These kinds of false, but highly provocative, broadcasts were particularly effective because they incited conversation and traveled well by word of mouth. Regardless of whether or not listeners believed them, it was difficult to not have an opinion about them and to not "talk" about them.[95]

It was not, however, Axis radio's anti-Semitic messages, false statements about Germany, or alleged support for the anticolonial movement that troubled British administrators. Rather, what concerned them the most was Axis radio's penchant for airing clearly false and misleading reports about the global war and about the political situation in India.

British officials, for example, complained that German radio did not admit to the losses in Stalingrad and told Indian audiences that Germany would win, even as the German Army prepared to retreat, and that German radio exaggerated the extent of unrest in India (see figure 1.1). One appalled British officer noted that during a "relatively tranquil week" in India, German radio falsely reported that there was "rebellious activity on the frontier," that "labour [was] in violent revolt," and "the viceroy's train [was] guarded by 49 men with machine guns as he [left] Delhi on tour."[96] "There has been no abatement in the stream of falsehood and exaggeration issuing from Berlin," wrote an alarmed British colonial officer in India in 1940.[97] As I further elaborate in chapter 3, particularly during the Quit India movement, when Gandhi called for the immediate departure of the British, Berlin-based announcers exaggerated the extent of the uprising against the British in the hopes of further inciting rebellion and eroding trust in the British administration's ability to contain conflict.

Concern about German radio's misinformation and their possible effect on Indian audiences inspired what appears to be one of the first studies of radio audiences in India. In May 1940, AIR personnel interviewed 12,507 listeners in major cities, including Bombay, Delhi, Lahore, Lucknow, and Calcutta, in the hopes of better understanding people's listening habits. I have not been able to find questionnaires or the participants' responses or any other statistical data derived from this research. What we do know is that researchers ultimately concluded that German broadcasts in Hindustani and English were "widely listened to" but that "belief in their truthfulness varied."[98] In other words, listening to Axis radio did not necessarily translate into believing it. This study, however, did little to ease British officials' concerns. As previously noted, one administrator remarked: "The German broadcasts are known to be full of lies but everyone listens to them with great interest and

HERE are two of the false statements which have come over the enemy radio. You know now that they are absurd, but at the time you may have believed them. Don't be fooled by what the enemy says — his purpose is to mislead you.

"THE SINKING AND DESTROYING OF THE WHOLE OF BRITISH SHIPPING WILL BECOME A MATTER OF TWO MONTHS."

— GERMAN BROADCAST, 7-8-1940.

"IT IS RIDICULOUS TO SUGGEST THAT NEW ARMIES ARE WAITING TO BE THROWN INTO THE BATTLE. THE RUSSIANS ARE UNABLE TO DO ANY SUCH THING."

— GERMAN BROADCAST, 28-10-1941.

1.1 Advertisement from an undated supplement to the *Indian Listener*, a magazine distributed free of cost to all holders of radio receiver licenses. Based on the content and its placement in the archive, it is likely to have been published sometime in late 1941.

Source: All India Radio Library, New Delhi.

they undoubtedly *have an effect*."[99] But as officials struggled to make sense of what precisely "the effect" of German broadcasts was, they grappled with fundamental questions about radio reception: What was it like to listen to Axis radio? Who could tune in to Axis radio?

German Lies, Indian Rumors, and Radio Resonance

Sources on how Indian listeners perceived Axis radio are limited. This is because radio everywhere has a peculiar ability to disappear from the archive, but also because in wartime India, listening to the Axis radio was a clandestine activity. Krishna Bose, who was eleven years old when the war broke out and resided in Calcutta, remembered that her parents would close all the windows and doors before turning on the radio to Axis broadcasts.[100] She had little recollection of the broadcasts' actual content at the time of the interview, but more than half a century later, she still remembered that that listening to Axis radio felt like a fugitive act. This is hardly surprising given the British administration's many efforts to discourage listeners from tuning in to Axis broadcasts and their various attempts to criminalize listening to Axis radio. For example, on December 1940, months after Viceroy Linlithgow's declaration of war, the administration passed an order that forbade holders of commercial radio licenses from playing Axis radio programs in any business premises.[101] A few months later, the administration prohibited *all* owners of radio receivers from playing enemy broadcasts in public spaces, including in shops, bazaars, places of worship, or even verandas, where the sound of the radio could easily reach the streets or neighboring homes.[102]

How did Axis radio sound? In the absence of firsthand accounts of reception, handwritten notes and typed transcriptions of Axis radio put together by Indian translators and transcribers working for the colonial administration provide important clues into the listening experience: "For the first eight minutes the station could not be located."[103] "The broadcast is unintelligible due to strong atmospherics and persistent whistling." "For about 16 minutes the stations was inaudible . . . only the words 'dear Indians' could be heard clearly. At about 8:11 the station came through."[104] "The remainder" of the broadcast "was only partly audible."[105] Shortwave reception was inconsistent and unreliable. Even trained radio monitors with access to state-of-the-art receivers had to constantly fiddle with the radio knobs to locate radio stations and make them clear. Static and interruption thus became part of listening experiences.

At the same time, radio monitors' comments also suggest that listeners did not have to hear an entire program to get the gist of its message and to be able to pass it on. One monitor explained: "A considerable deterioration in reception has resulted in an extremely dull week, but there was enough material to indicate certain points."[106] This helps explain why Axis radio was so repetitive. Axis broadcasters did not expect listeners to be able to tune in to all or even most programs. Instead, broadcasters expected listeners to catch bits and fragments of their broadcast material—incendiary comments, observations, and accusations—and then to talk to family and friends about what they had heard. The repetitive and abrasive nature of Axis radio was not merely aesthetic or political; it also served another purpose: exaggerations, provocative comments, insinuations, and personal attacks invited conversation and traveled well by word of mouth.

During World War II, only a tiny fraction of the Indian population owned radio receivers.[107] According to one survey, there were one hundred and sixty thousand registered licenses in 1943 in a population of approximately three hundred million.[108] Despite the various rural initiatives, the presence of radio was even less common in rural areas, as most radio receivers required electricity, which was still unavailable in most rural areas. As expected, British officers did not trust radio license statistics and for good reason. First, many radio owners intentionally did not register their receivers to avoid paying the designated fees.[109] More important, however, the British administration also understood that counting the number of receivers was a poor way to gauge the size of audiences because collective and public listening practices were widespread in India. Yet even when we take into account these practices, the reality is that only a tiny percentage of the population could have physically heard sounds emanating from a radio.

The British government came to believe that Axis radio, whether heard and discussed in large gatherings or in private homes, was the source of rapidly spreading and destructive rumors.[110] Of course, the colonial government's accounts of rumors took on a paternalistic tone and relied on stereotypes about Indians' predisposition to believe fantastic and untrue stories.[111] Consider, for example, a cartoon strip published in the *Indian Listener*, AIR's official English-language magazine, in June 1942. A man named Prasad and his wife learn from a radio broadcast that their city would soon be attacked. Prasad sells his possessions in haste and leaves the city immediately. While he awaits the catastrophe away from home, Prasad begins to run out of money and his wife resents him (see figure 1.2). In a cartoon published a month later in the same publication, a man learns that the British government plans to close all private shops in his town. In a panic, he sells his shop for a lot less than it is worth only to learn a few months later that the whole affair turned out to be a lie spread by "enemy radio" propaganda (see figure 1.3). These cartoons are clear examples of colonial publicity and they speak to the colonial biases and anxieties and to the colonial administration's fixation with German radio's growing popularity in India. These cartoons, however, also help us understand how radio broadcasting, a technology not yet accessible to most of the population, could have played an important role in the everyday lives of people and could have contributed to the changing political understanding of the war in colonial India. The cartoons quite literally depict how information heard on the radio traveled by word of mouth. In the first image, Prasad repeats what he just heard on the radio, ensuring that the radio message will reach others. In the second image, the man learns of the government's projects from a friend who heard the announcement on the radio and told him.

In his study of nineteenth-century information systems, Christopher Bayly argues that India was a "literacy-aware" society long before its literacy rate was

1.2 Supplement to the *Indian Listener*, June 7, 1942. Note how this cartoon depicts the "dangers" of listening to enemy radio stations.

Source: All India Radio Library, New Delhi.

1.3 Supplement to the *Indian Listener*, July 22, 1942. Note how this cartoon depicts how radio news traveled by word-of-mouth.

Source: All India Radio Library, New Delhi.

comparable to Europe or the Americas. "Awareness of the uses of literacy" in India, Bayly notes, "spread much further" and was more influential "than the number of formal literates suggests."[112] Similarly, British accounts of rumors traceable to radio broadcast (as depicted in the two cartoon strips in figures 1.2 and 1.3) demonstrate that India became a "radio-aware" society during World War II, despite low ownership rates.[113]

"Rumors Directly Traceable to Enemy Broadcasts"

The literature on rumor in colonial India is rich and highlights the importance of rumor as a means of "insurgent communication."[114] Using the example of the 1857 rebellion, Ranajit Guha explains that the "unfounded and unverifiable reports about cartridges greased with animal fat, flour polluted by bone meal, and forcible conversion to Christianity" served as the "trigger and mobilizer" for revolt against the colonial administration among both soldiers and civilians.[115] Guha demonstrates how these incendiary stories could serve both as message and as medium because it was precisely the alarmist and sensational nature of the information that enabled their quick dissemination.[116] Similarly, the incendiary nature of Axis radio broadcasts served a specific communicative purpose: it furthered the distribution of radio news by inviting audiences to talk about it.

It is here that the notion of radio resonance proves useful. Radio is widely understood as a broadcast medium that distributes or "broadly casts" information using sound waves. Yet colonial officers' concern with the spread of rumors "directly traceable to radio broadcasts" suggests that radio's power in wartime India lay not so much in its ability to "broadcast" information, but rather in its ability to trigger discussion about that information. Radio's form, its ephemerality (listeners could not access recordings again) and its aurality, was important to this process as it made radio news's transmission by word of mouth all the more natural. Rumor is, as Guha nicely puts it, "spoken utterance par excellence," and so was radio. News heard on the radio was therefore particularly well suited to travel by word of mouth.

Taking radio's relationship to rumor seriously also helps us understand how radio during World War II forged a sense of community. Anjan Ghosh explains that rumor "engages in a dual task." Rumor "subverts authority of the dominant power," and "enhances the unity of the rebels by creating a community of believers."[117] This cohesiveness based on shared witnessing experiences is similar to what Birdsall in her study of "Nazi sounds" refers to as becoming an "earwitness." Like in Nazi Germany, in colonial India, radio broadcasts were sought to create a particular shared sonic encounter. Yet whereas Birdsall underscores the physical act of listening to radio broadcasts, in colonial India, earwitness participants need not physically "tune in." They could become earwitness participants by engaging in the rumors and talk that surrounded Axis broadcasts.[118]

The British colonial administration, however, interpreted matters differently. Administrators did not see the spread of radio-related rumors as emblematic of how the medium worked. Instead, they saw rumors as a distinctly Indian disease, false radio news from Axis countries as the original source of infection, and "truthful" British news as the only plausible treatment to a rapidly spreading illness.[119]

All India Radio Responds to World War II

An addendum published in the *Indian Listener* targeting the British community in India as well as English-speaking elite Indians, nicely demonstrates the British strategy to respond to Axis news. As shown in figure 1.4, the note occupying an entire page explained:

> News these days is varied and fluctuates like a woman's temper! And it does seem a little hard that the regiment of servants have to pick up odd scraps of news, from whoever throws to them, and often enough the mischievous rumour-monger is able to give full play to his talents.
>
> There is however a way of dealing with this danger. The A.I.R. broadcasts from Delhi in Hindustani from 6:40 p.m. to 6:45 p.m.—an hour carefully chosen so as not to coincide with the busy time of a servant in the average home in India. We earnestly request you to co-operate by putting on your wireless at this time, and inviting your servants to listen to an elementary news in a nutshell.[120]

In addition to betraying obvious sexism and classism, this note lucidly explains how the British sought to solve the current crises: truthful news.[121] If the British government had been suspicious of radio and hesitant to engage with political topics, the popularity, or at least the perceived popularity, of Axis radio and the demands of the global war, jolted the British administration out of its indifference to radio broadcasting. As the war progressed, the government of India turned to radio with new funds and personnel and began to assiduously cultivate an Indian audience.[122]

As previously discussed, Lionel Fielden had already inadvertently built the infrastructure that allowed AIR to respond to the war. He left India in 1940 to rejoin the BBC and was not able to see the fruition of his work with AIR. (Given Fielden's strong anticolonial leanings, that might have been for the better.)[123] Patras Bukhari, the director of the Delhi station and also a renowned Urdu writer, took over Fielden's post and remained in charge of AIR from war through India's independence and Partition.[124] As I elaborate in a later section, Patras Bukhari's ascendance in AIR became the source of a long

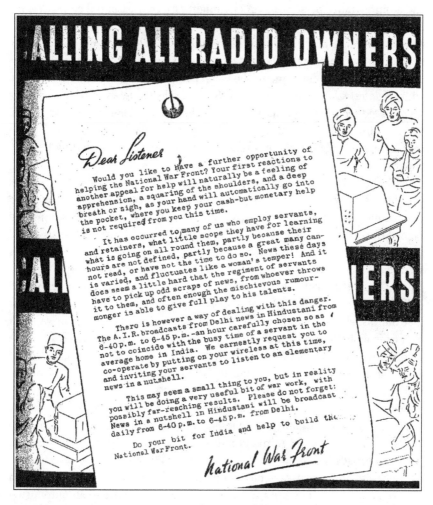

1.4 Advertisement from an undated supplement to the *Indian Listener* calling radio owners to allow servants to listen to the radio. Based on the context and placement in the archive, it likely was published in late 1941.

Source: All India Radio Library, New Delhi.

drawn-out language controversy, but it was ultimately under his leadership that AIR responded to the war.

Although the colonial government certainly would have approved funds for new stations, wartime restrictions made it difficult to transport transmitters to India. Instead, AIR used resources to improve existing stations. Over the course of the war, AIR more than doubled its staff. By 1942, it employed nine hundred workers, including announcers, editors, writers, translators, engineers, and administrative personnel.[125] As we might expect, the Central News Organization (CNO), a centralized radio news body originally set up by Fielden that edited, translated, and distributed news bulletins to all AIR radio stations, saw great expansion during the war. In October 1939, one month after the viceroy of India declared war on Germany, the CNO inaugurated news studios, complete with the latest sound equipment.[126] CNO staff selected news provided by news agencies, edited the stories, and translated them into various Indian languages. Bulletins in Hindustani and English took precedence, but the CNO also put together news bulletins in other regional Indian languages, including Bengali, Gujarati, Marathi, Tamil, Telugu, and Pashto.[127]

AIR also sought to increase its news broadcasts by expanding its contracts with news services. The Home Department made a special request to Reuters to provide more news and "interpretive comment."[128] Also, during the summer of 1940, AIR contracted the services of the United Press of India, an Indian-based news organization that collected news of national importance.[129] This news service covered negotiations between Indian leaders and the British government. Given the British government's previous unwillingness to report on political matters, the new interest in broadcast politics is revealing.[130] It is clear that the British felt that above all, they needed to invest in more news, both about the global war and about developments in India, to effectively compete with the Axis radio broadcasts. Referring specifically to radio news, a colonial administrator explained to his colleagues in London that the outbreak of war had created a "demand for news."[131]

Increasing the number of news bulletins, the colonial government quickly learned, would not be sufficient. One British officer explained "the main trouble" was that British programs broadcast "purely news items," whereas the "German broadcasts commented on most items."[132] What this officer seems to have been saying is that Axis radio's opinionated hot-button-topic style was a lot more appealing than AIR's sober news style. In response to an outpouring of similar remarks, in succeeding months, AIR staff toiled to increase war commentary and opinion programs. For example, a program called *Jag Bītī* (world news) explained "the main events of the past week" to listeners. The purpose of this program was to provide the necessary background information to help listeners make sense of the news bulletins.[133] One officer, probably more wishfully than truthfully, remarked that "during the last few weeks the Delhi Province has been largely free of disturbing rumors regarding the war which appear to have been common in other parts of India, and I believe that this is due in no small measure to the broadcasting schemes."[134]

AIR also put out radio programs that directly responded to Axis radio broadcasts. In May 1940, AIR inaugurated *Berlin Kī Xabar* (Berlin News). This Hindustani-language program discussed news from German broadcasts and pointed out biases and fallacies. *Berlin Kī Xabar* aired from the Delhi, Bombay,

Lahore, and Lucknow stations. In August 1940, the Calcutta station inaugurated a Bengali version of the program and a Marathi version went on the air shortly thereafter.[135] There was some debate within AIR circles regarding the effectiveness of these types of counterpropaganda programs. Some sensed, and perhaps were ultimately right, that programs like *Berlin Kī Xabar* were counterproductive because they inadvertently encouraged Indian listeners to tune in to enemy wavelengths.

Following the outbreak of the war, however, AIR toiled to bring more Indian voices to the airwaves. As expected, most Indians who agreed to speak on AIR disagreed with the Congress's criticism of the viceroy's declaration of war on India's behalf. For example, AIR devoted the week of June 11, 1940, to programs related to Italy's participation in the war and "the collapse of the French army." Among the notable speakers featured that week were Sikandar Hayat Khan, a Punjabi politician who later opposed Gandhi's Quit India movement, and Sir Cowasji Jehangir, a prominent member of the Bombay Parsi community who a decade earlier had openly clashed with the Congress's two most respected Parsi members, Dadabhai Naoroji and Pherozeshah Mehta, and who openly supported the viceroy's declaration of war.[136]

Hindi and Urdu on the AIR

Yet as AIR expanded its vernacular programming, it could not avoid being hobbled by language controversies that were then engulfing the subcontinent. In particular, AIR became the target of a growing and strengthening literary movement that claimed a "pure" form of Hindi devoid of Persian- and Arabic-origin words, which featured prominently in spoken Hindustani.[137] As Francesca Orsini demonstrates in her study of the Hindi literary movement, by the 1940s, this movement had built a significant public sphere and developed a strong and resonant voice. Supporters of the Hindi movement specifically accused AIR of having a Muslim bias and claimed that AIR's Hindustani leaned heavily toward Urdu. Writing in the *Modern Review*, one critic remarked: "All India Radio under the direction of those who are in control . . . [has] made efforts to strangle Hindi language and culture, and to give a fillip to Urdu and Islamic culture."[138]

As this comment makes clear, a great deal of the criticism revolved around issues of personnel. Shortly after his arrival in India, Fielden hired two upperclass Muslim brothers, Patras Bukhari and Zulfiqar Ali Bukhari. The elder of the brothers, Patras, had been a professor of English at the Government College of Lahore and also was a relatively well-known satirical Urdu writer.[139] The younger brother, Zulfiqar Ali, had been a translator for the army and also was an Urdu literature enthusiast who had shown great interest in theater and acting.[140] Fielden and Zulfiqar Bukhari were close friends. Some believed that the

Bukhari brothers had used their closeness to Fielden to promote Urdu (and Muslims) at the expense of Hindi (and Hindus) at AIR.[141]

In reality, as Emily Rook-Koepsel perceptively explains, Patras Bukhari, the elder of the brothers, had been rather wary of the idea of AIR promoting a single national tongue from the beginning. Instead, he argued that to serve India's diverse population, local broadcasters had to have significant control over individual stations. He actively campaigned for a decentralized programming system that privileged regional languages and local dialects.[142] At the same time, Patras Bukhari, in accordance with most members of the Congress, including Gandhi, believed that if AIR had to favor a national language of sorts, Hindustani should be that language.[143] Moreover, as earlier noted, the pressure of the war and the success, or the perceived success, of the Hindustani-language Axis radio programs had pushed the administration to try to find its own version of Hindustani.

Most important, however, is that Patras Bukhari did not dodge the controversy regarding AIR's version of Hindustani and the station's preference for Muslim writers. He responded to the accusations of Muslim/Urdu bias in AIR by trying to create a less religiously marked inclusive form of Hindustani and, more important, by actively bringing renowned Hindi writers to AIR. He called for conversations on AIR about what Hindustani could and should be. He recruited S. H. Vatsyayan "Agyeya" and Chiragh Hasan Hasrat, Hindi and Urdu authors, respectively, to make a lexicon of Hindustani that would be appropriate for newscasts and, in particular, for commonly used English words. As David Lelyveld writes, the "Hindi poet made a list of Hindi equivalents and the Urdu essayist made a list of Urdu counterparts. Then the two sat down and worked out a compromise based on what they considered most common and, if possible, neutral."[144] This ambitious project took five years to complete and did little to ease the erupting controversy. Ultimately, the project fizzled out and the ambitiously inclusive Hindustani dictionary was never implemented.[145]

In addition, Patras Bukhari brought representatives of the Hindi Sāhitya Sammelan (Hindi Literature Convention) and the Anjuman-e-Taraqqī Urdu (Organization for the Advancement of Urdu), the leading organizations for the advancement of Hindi and Urdu literature, respectively, to weigh in on the matter.[146] He organized a series of radio talks under the title "What Is Hindustani?" Among the invited guests were Rajendra Prasad, the future president of independent India; Acharya Narendra Deva, a leading socialist politician; and Maulvi Abdul Haq, a longtime leader from the Anjuman-e-Taraqqī Urdu.[147] In the end, meetings and deliberations did little to ease the controversy that surrounded AIR's pro-Muslim reputation because the problem had never been that AIR's Hindustani was illegitimate or not inclusive enough. The problem all along had been that the very idea of Hindustani as a national language was losing valence in the changing political environment that moved toward Partition and called for clearly marked religious and linguistic identities.[148] Hindustani no longer had a place in the national radio network and Patras Bukhari—and earlier his brother, Zulfiqar Ali Bukhari, as well—had been targeted and ultimately pushed out *because* they were Muslim and prominent Urdu writers.[149] New dictionaries and discussions about language could not have stopped that.[150]

In 1946, Sardar Vallabhbhai Patel was appointed to lead the interim Information and Broadcasting Ministry. Patel, considered one of the most communalist Congress leaders of India, actively pushed policies that hurt Muslim communities and repeatedly doubted Muslims' loyalty to India in the years following independence.[151] Patel officially eliminated Hindustani broadcasting in favor of separate Hindi and Urdu programs, ensuring that AIR's linguistic partitioning preceded the subcontinent's partition.[152]

It is clear that AIR, as a government institution in India, could not escape the controversy over language and identity erupting in the subcontinent. In contrast, German radio was able to effectively take advantage of Hindustani's lingua franca status to reach a widespread population in northern, eastern, and western India who could understand, if not necessarily speak, Hindustani.

Conclusion

I wish to end with three brief anecdotes that illustrate the ways in which radio's important relationship to World War II was clear to contemporaries. In her memoirs of her life in colonial India and her later immigration to Pakistan, Moiz Fatima writes: "World War II had started, so radio had reached our home. We all sat in front of the radio, listening to news, heard songs [*Dūsrī jang-e azīm shurū ho cukī thī lehāzā hamāre ghar radīo ā cukā thā. ham sab radio ke āge baiṭh kar xabreṅ sunte, gāne sunte*]." What is noteworthy about this account is the way in which Moiz, somewhat unconsciously, associates radio's presence with the war's outbreak.[153] Similarly, in an oral interview a British tea plantation owner unconsciously turned to radio when asked to describe his experience of the war in Cochin, India. "It was not until just before the outbreak of the 1939 war that the real breakthrough in radio came. . . . Getting direct news in this way everyday was a great boom. We remember vividly the ups and downs of the fortunes of the war."[154] I find, however, an anecdote shared by historian Janam Mukherjee about his own father's memories most revealing. Following the bombing of Pearl Harbor, Mukherjee's grandfather sent his family who lived in Calcutta to the countryside. In preparation for the trip, Mukherjee's father, then eleven years old, built a radio from cardboard. The carboard radio, writes Mukherjee, looked so realistic that the young boy was "not the only one who was surprised" when the radio produced no actual sound.[155] The boy's enthusiasm for radio is emblematic of the medium's role during World War II.

It also shows how radio could have a consistent and vital presence during wartime India even as ownership rates remained low. After all, the cardboard radio might have not emanated sound per se, but it clearly spurred conversation about radio broadcasts and contributed to the radio resonance that was so vital to the medium.

In this chapter, I have argued that the war was a pivotal moment that engendered long-term effects on the broadcasting infrastructure and, more important, on listening cultures. British India had a comparatively weak radio infrastructure before World War II. Eager to keep the increasingly vociferous nationalist leaders off the airwaves, the colonial government restricted political broadcasts and provided meager funding to the national radio network. After the outbreak of the war and largely in response to the influx of Axis radio propaganda in Indian languages and the spread of "rumors directly traceable to enemy broadcasts," the colonial government mobilized radio in what turned out to be a belated and haphazard attempt to garner Indian support for Allied forces.[156] In the succeeding chapter, I focus on the second half of the war and provide a detailed analysis of the Indian revolutionary and Axis-sympathizer Subhas Chandra Bose's radio broadcasts from Germany and later Southeast Asia. By listening to these broadcasts—as well as "the talk" that surrounded these broadcasts—many Indians were able to question British accounts of events and, as the Bengali observer invoked in the chapter's opening explained, "draw their own conclusions."[157]

CHAPTER 2

NETAJI'S "QUISLING RADIO"

The *Newsweek* cover story of November 21, 1943, "Axis Propaganda
Barrage Badgers Britain on India," had a sonorous appeal. It read:
"Out of the ether a chilling voice whistled. Dial twirlers, halting
at a German beam, caught the cold fury of a man who had spent more than
a dozen years in empire prisons."[1] The *Newsweek* reporter, who clearly wished
to appeal to readers' ears, was referring to an Indian leftist revolutionary, then
residing in Germany, in a language that was as tuneful as it was condemna-
tory: "This voice belonged to Subhas Chandra Bose, the most implacable
British-hater of all Hindu radical leaders, now a prized specimen in Hitler's
covey of Quislings."[2]

Bose, a well-known left-leaning anticolonial leader, had been living in Berlin
since 1941, after permanently parting ways with his colleagues in the Indian
National Congress and escaping house arrest in Calcutta.[3] With Nazi sponsorship, Bose trained a legion of Indian prisoners of war (POWs) captured by
Axis armies in the campaigns in Africa and the Middle East and managed a
shortwave radio station aimed at audiences in India.[4] Like most British and U.S.
publications, *Newsweek* played up Bose's alliance with the Nazis, denying him
any agency and painting him as a demonic radical. What makes this particular article stand out is its attention to Bose's voice and its sensibility to sound.
The author alluded to a central, yet surprisingly understudied, angle of Bose's
anticolonial career: during World War II, Bose, to his followers and opponents
in British-ruled India, was first and foremost a radio voice.

Echoing the *Newsweek* article's attention to sound, this chapter seeks to "dis-
entangle the discursive threads" of Bose's life and legacy through an in-depth

study of Bose's radio persona.[5] Although both Bose and, more generally, South Asia are largely absent from global histories of World War II, Bose is actually one of the most intriguing wartime characters.[6] Hoping to overthrow the British colonial yoke, Bose made a problematic strategic alliance with the Axis powers, flouting not only the colonial administration in India, but also Gandhi's pacifist anticolonial campaign. As the war shifted east, Bose, with Hitler's blessing, left Berlin in 1943 to lead yet another army of liberation in Japanese-occupied Singapore. During the final year of the war, his Indian National Army (INA), alongside Japanese armies, fought (and lost) against Allied forces in northeastern India.

Bose's afterlife is even more captivating. Three days after Japan's surrender, Bose died in a plane crash on his way to Taiwan. Immediately after the war, the British tried and indicted three of Bose's INA officers for treason. Overwhelmed by the popular outcry in India, which included support for Bose and his INA, the British administration remitted the officers' sentences and released them to crowds chanting "*Jai Hind*" (Victory to India). In the decades to come, fantastic stories circulated throughout India that Bose was still alive. Some claimed that India's first prime minister, Jawaharlal Nehru, who had been critical of Bose's Axis alliance during the war, was preventing Bose's return to India.[7] After all, Bose, proponents of this theory remarked, not necessarily inaccurately, was the only Indian politician with a large enough popular following to pose a serious challenge to Nehru's uncontested leadership of newly independent India.

Today in India, Bose is not remembered as a quisling. On the contrary, he is depicted as a brave national hero. The Kolkata international airport, one of India's major international airports, bears his name, and his birth anniversary is widely celebrated in both his native Bengal and throughout India. *Jai Hind* can be heard in parades and on TV shows and can be seen on Twitter accounts.[8]

Set during the war years, but focusing on the second half of the war, which constitutes the peak of Bose's career, this chapter tunes in to Bose's radio campaign as it unfolded on the airwaves. My attention to Bose's radio persona might be unconventional, at least in the context of scholarship on Bose, but it is very much true to the historical moment. Despite their memorialization in postcolonial India, neither of Bose's armies posed a significant military threat to the British rule. In the end, Bose's Indian Legion in Nazi-occupied Europe, which had by some estimates about three thousand soldiers, turned out to be a mostly inconsequential military enterprise, which Bose ultimately abandoned when he left Berlin. Despite having high aspirations, Bose's INA, which at its peak boasted an estimated fifty thousand soldiers, including volunteers and Indian POWs who renounced their loyalty to the British crown, faced bitter defeat in northeastern India during the last year of the war.[9] In contrast, as a radio broadcaster, Bose, I argue, proved transformative. He was the only major

Indian anticolonial leader who effectively brought his message to the airwaves, and during the height of the war, he embraced the radio as a medium of resistance against colonial rule.[10]

A study of Bose's radio campaign provides an excellent example of how the medium of radio during the height of World War II contested the British colonial government. Moreover, a study of Bose's persona also casts doubt on a narrative, both popular and scholarly, that distances Bose from Nazism and fascism.[11] In the pages that follow, I show how Bose's voice circulated in the context of Axis propaganda and how the militant form of nationalism that he embraced on the air echoed some of Axis radio propaganda's key themes. In this way, the chapter demonstrates that Bose's ties to Nazism and fascism were stronger than historians have acknowledged and makes clear how a detailed study of radio can help us revise accepted narratives.

Along the way, the chapter also compares Bose's radio persona to the U.S. "radio president," Franklin Delano Roosevelt (FDR). The comparison is apt despite the two men's unequal access to power (Bose was a fugitive anticolonial leader; FDR was president of the United States, soon to be the leading political power in the world) because the notion of FDR as a "consummate radio performer" has shaped scholarship on radio and politics.[12] FDR's speaking style, Bruce Lenthall argues, was at the heart of his performance. By speaking as an ordinary man, as the "friend next door," FDR created a sense of "ethereal intimacy" with listeners.[13] In conversation with this scholarship on radio, I demonstrate that Bose was a radio performer too, who like FDR sought to create intimacy, albeit in different ways. Bose's broadcasts allow us to rethink our understanding of how radio broadcasters connected with audiences and to consider how radio resonance, and specifically radio's ties to rumor and gossip, created affective bonds that enabled the spread of this leader's political message.

Bose in Germany

Bose reached Germany in April 1941, following his escape from house arrest in Calcutta under the noses of an entourage of guards. He undertook an extraordinary fugitive trip to Afghanistan by train, foot, and, at least according to one account, even mule.[14] Once in Kabul, Bose first tried to contact the Soviet ambassador, but he had better reception in the German embassy. Bose explained to German officers that he wanted to go to Berlin to promote India's freedom. The German Foreign Office did its own investigation and concluded that Bose was a "very vain and pushy character," but invited the Bengali activist to Berlin nonetheless.[15] What biographies of Bose do not mention is that, by then, Germany had already inaugurated a radio service to India in Indian languages (see chapter 1). The German Foreign Office likely deemed that Bose could prove an important asset to this growing publicity service. Bose, now disguised as an Italian ambassadorial messenger and bearing an Italian passport that identified him as Orlando Mazzota, made his way to the German capital.

Bose was no stranger to Germany or Europe. A decade earlier, Bose had traveled throughout Europe meeting journalists, government leaders, and diplomats, as well as Indians residing in Europe, effectively taking on the role of an ambassador of the nationalist movement.[16] Having spent almost half a decade in Europe in the 1930s, Bose was well aware of the rise of fascism. His position toward fascism was at best ambivalent and at worst warm. He did not condemn the persecution of Jews in any of his private correspondence from Vienna and on at least one occasion praised Mussolini.[17] During his last trip to Europe, Bose's private life had undergone important changes. He met Emilie Schenkl, an Austrian woman whom he had hired to help him prepare a book manuscript and whom he later married and had a daughter with during the war.[18] One of the first things Bose did after reaching Berlin was to write to Schenkl in Vienna: "You might be surprised to get this letter" and to know that "I am writing from Berlin."[19]

Bose had grand plans for his stay in Nazi Germany: he wanted to form a government-in-exile in Berlin, but to his disappointment, Hitler, who expressed disdain for the Indian anticolonial movement, had little interest in propping up Bose's campaign.[20] The German government, however, did help Bose recruit soldiers for his Indian Legion among POWs stationed in Europe. Axis armies had taken between fifteen and seventeen thousand Indian soldiers in their campaigns around the Mediterranean.[21] With German support, Bose hoped to lead an army of liberation that would march across the Soviet Union and Afghanistan into India. Bose's plan was ambitious and, in many ways, impractical, but he was neither the first nor the only person to come up with the idea. During World War I, members of the Ghadar Party had made similar plans that, for a variety of reasons, were never carried out.[22] In the end, however, the Indian POWs were reluctant to renounce their loyalty to the British crown, and after several months of work, his team had managed to recruit only a few thousand soldiers from the more than fifteen thousand POWs.[23]

In Berlin, Bose ultimately had more success with his publicity work. With the financial support of the Nazi government, Bose, in November 1941, formally inaugurated the Free India Center, an organization whose main aim was to promote Indian nationalism in Nazi Germany.[24] The center hosted talks about Indian nationalism, literature, and culture and put out a German and English magazine called *Azad Hind* (Free India).[25] The center also celebrated a longer history of Indo-German connections, featuring, for example, talks on German philology related to India and also celebrating anticolonial leaders' ties to Germany.[26] It was, however, the center's broadcasting venture that proved most influential.

Bose called his radio station Azad Hind Radio. According to his associates, the station's first broadcast aired in October 1941.[27] Just three months later, the station boasted more than twenty broadcasters, many of them Indian students in Germany, and it beamed three hours of news bulletins and commentary a day, primarily in Hindustani and English, but also in several Indian languages, including Bengali, Persian, Tamil, Telugu, and Pashto. The choice of Hindustani as a primary broadcast language is no surprise. German shortwave radio already had been broadcasting rather successfully in Hindustani. Moreover, although a native speaker of Bengali, when leading the Indian National Congress, Bose had passionately campaigned for Hindustani as a national tongue.[28] To avoid any kind of religious connotations to the Devanagari and Nastaliq scripts, Bose had argued that Hindustani should be written in Roman script, against Gandhi who advocated the use of both scripts in all government documents.[29] By broadcasting in various Indian languages, but privileging Hindustani, Azad Hind Radio ascribed to what I described earlier as the "ideology of Hindustani," that is, the aspirational idea that Hindustani could be a language free of religious affiliations and a lingua franca that could connect speakers of other regional languages (see the introduction).

Like other Axis programs aimed at Indian audiences, Azad Hind focused on news and news commentary, but at least one account claims that the station also occasionally aired music broadcasts. According to this account, Azad Hind's employees, who were living in the heart of Germany and had limited access to Indian music, developed a creative method: they recorded BBC Indian music programs directly from their own radio receivers, changed the announcements, and then rebroadcast the reworked music programs back to India.[30] I have found no transcripts explaining what type of music the station broadcast. These music broadcasts, if they were indeed broadcast, likely consisted of gramophone records, including film songs, as well as popular semiclassical music, such as the songs of Gauhar Jaan, which were then widely available on gramophone records.[31]

During the station's first months, Bose chose not to speak on the airwaves. His biographers maintain that there were two reasons for Bose's "radio silence." First, Bose did not wish to reveal his location to British intelligence, which he believed was still searching for him.[32] Second, Bose did not want to make his alliance with Nazi Germany public until Hitler first made an official declaration in support of the Indian independence movement.[33]

How was Azad Hind different from the German service described in the previous chapter? What was Azad Hind Radio's relationship to the German government and to the existing German shortwave radio service to India? One of Azad Hind's employees, Mukund Vyas, claimed that Azad Hind was an independent service. The German government, Vyas explains, provided broadcasting staff with daily news summaries of events from various Axis-supporting news agencies. Azad Hind's radio personnel selected stories, translated them into Indian languages, and added interpretive comments. Vyas explained in his memoirs that with the exception of some early "pin-pricks and minor irritations," the Nazi government "maintained a policy of non-interference" and let Indian broadcasters say what they wished on the airwaves.[34] Vyas goes as far as to maintain that the broadcasting staff of Azad Hind Radio "not infrequently reproduced Allied claims" and ignored "German counterclaims."[35] Romain Hayes in his analysis of Bose's years in Germany also makes the point that the station and the center were able to maintain significant independence from Nazi directives.[36]

Monitoring reports and transcripts commissioned by the British government of India, however, tell a rather different story. British radio monitors did not list Azad Hind Radio as a separate service. Most broadcasts from Germany were labeled generically as "German radio in Indian languages." How might we read this discrepancy in the sources? The reality was that even if Azad Hind was an independent service, it would have been difficult for most radio listeners in India to actually distinguish between these services.[37] As detailed in the previous chapter, shortwave reception was characteristically unreliable and unpredictable. Radio listeners had to fiddle with their radio knobs to find stations and to readjust them mid-service. Moreover, audibility was another key problem. Even radio monitors with access to the best equipment often complained of "whistling" and "atmospherics."[38] Yet if British colonial sources suggest that Azad Hind Radio did not join the airwaves with a big splash, and the station's voices might have been lost among the greater cacophony of Axis broadcasts, the same sources indicate that Bose's first radio broadcast certainly received separate attention.

Listening to Bose's Radio Voice

In February 1942, Japanese armies took control of Singapore, an island off the southern tip of the Malay Peninsula, which had long been a stronghold of the British Empire in Asia. Winston Churchill famously described the Fall of Singapore as "the worst disaster" in British military history.[39] Britain's losses in Singapore changed the stakes of the war for India; the war had now effectively reached India's doorstep. From Berlin, Bose seized the moment. On February 19, 1942, Bose took to the radio for the first time: "This is Subhas Chandra Bose speaking to you over Azad Hind Radio. . . . For about [a] year I have waited in silence and patience for the march of events. And the hour has struck, I come forward to speak."[40]

This was the first time Bose spoke publicly since he went underground after his remarkable escape from his Calcutta home in the winter of 1941. His very presence on the airwaves was evidence that "a new world order" was evolving—that Britain's hegemonic power was under serious threat.[41] Bose was quite aware of the symbolic meaning of his presence on the airwaves and the ways in which it undermined the British Empire. Here was a man long hunted by British officers, who had endured long stints in British prisons, speaking confidently and freely from the heart of Berlin, assuring fellow Indians and anticolonial leaders that the British Empire's days were now numbered. "The fall of Singapore is an auspicious event which bears for India the promise of life and freedom," Bose told Indian audiences during that first speech.[42] As the historian Yasmin Khan perceptively notes, Bose speeches sought to "simpli[fy] the task ahead," encouraging listeners to "relish the breakdown of the old status quo," to hail Britain's losses, and to celebrate Japan's wins.[43]

To accomplish this, Bose took great pains to explain his position on the war, in particular his alliance with Axis governments in the simplest terms possible. He asked listeners in India to reconsider the conventional understanding of India's enemies and friends. Britain, he argued, was India's most formidable enemy. "The British Empire was born of robbery and greed and thrives on injustice and oppression."[44] Bose explained to listeners that an Allied victory in this global conflict would mean the continuation of the British Empire and the "perpetuation of [India's] slavery."[45] Therefore, supporting Britain and the Allies was equivalent to supporting "the enemy."[46] In turn, Bose argued "that the enemies of British Imperialism are [India's] friends and allies" as it is ultimately "in their interest to see the British Empire broken up, and India once again free."[47] In his various speeches, Bose asked Indian listeners to ignore the internal politics of Axis countries and to instead focus on what these countries could do for India: "Do not be carried away by ideological considerations; do not bother about the internal politics of other countries, which is no concern of ours. Believe me when I say that the enemies of British imperialism are our friends and allies."[48]

As described in the previous chapter, the idea that Axis powers supported Indian independence had been the basic premise of Axis radio propaganda beamed to India since the early months of the war. Again and again, Axis announcers had expressed loyalty to Gandhi and to the growing Indian anticolonial movement. Bose's voice, however, brought new life to an already important service. Bose was not just an ordinary Indian voice on the airwaves. He was a well-known anticolonial leader, one known for his unapologetic critique and shrewd defiance of British imperialism. The British administration was quick to take notice of Bose's radio voice. One officer remarked: "[Bose] is now being used to broadcast from North Germany; but his political career in India was a failure, and his voice will add little force to the clamor with which Axis stations attempt to corrupt Indian opinion."[49] The officer's overconfident remarks and self-conscious attention to Bose's "failed" career betrays a growing colonial anxiety about the Indian anticolonial leader's presence on the airwaves.

This raises the ever-crucial question of reception. Who heard Bose's radio voice? Leading anticolonial leaders certainly heard his voice. Nehru, who was a staunch antifascist, was quick to make clear his disapproval of Bose's alliance with Hitler and Axis countries more generally.[50] Gandhi, who frequently voiced his dislike for modern media, primarily film, likely did not physically hear Bose's voice on a radio receiver, but he surely knew what Bose had said on the radio.[51] In fact, Maulana Abul Kalam Azad, then president of Congress, was convinced that Bose's addresses from Germany spurred Gandhi to take on a more radical campaign and to call for the Quit India movement in the summer of 1942.[52] The radio enabled Bose to remain in conversation with major antico-lonial Indian leaders and to weigh in on domestic matters that concerned him from thousands of kilometers away.[53] Ordinary people surely took notice of Bose's opinions regarding high politics negotiations. For example, Gupta Sen, a devout follower of Bose, more than fifty years later, remembered the Bengali leader's broadcasts on the radio regarding the famous Shimla conference of 1945, a meeting in which the viceroy and political leaders convened to agree on a self-government plan. Sen noted that Bose, while thousands of miles far from the negotiation, had participated in these meetings through the radio and had made clear to the Indian public his opinions.[54] But what can we concretely say about the ordinary Indian women and men whom Bose invoked in his various speeches; who among them heard Bose's voice?

As detailed in the previous chapter, for a variety of reasons, not least among them the British administration's fears that anticolonial leaders would take over the medium, radio ownership rates in colonial India were very low. One report by All India Radio (AIR) noted that in January 1943 there were 179,000 regis-tered licensed receiver sets in India in a population of more than three hun-dred million.[55] Even if we account for the many unlicensed receivers and for widespread collective listening practices and assume that as many as a hundred people listened to a single receiver, it would have been physically impossible for more than a small percentage of the urban population to hear Bose's voice on the radio.[56] Moreover, those who were able to tune in necessarily did so clandestinely as the government forbid and even punished those who dared to tune in to Axis radio stations.[57] Krishna Bose, who decades later married Sisir Bose (Subhas Chandra Bose's nephew), for example, recounts in an interview that listening to Bose's speeches on the radio "was very dangerous treason so that one had to be very careful."[58] Tuning in, she explains, felt like a fugitive and clandestine activity. Yet as detailed in chapter 1, colonial anxiety about "rumors" directly traceable to enemy broadcasts points to how radio integrated itself and expanded on existing networks of oral communication and demon-strates that radio's influence extended well beyond those who could (and dared to) tune in to Axis radio. What this means is that, whereas politicians like FDR could safely expect a large percentage of their constituency to tune in to their radio addresses, Bose had to rely on the strength of oral networks of communications to carry his radio message forward.[59]

Aware of the limited number of radios in India but also of the colonial government's strict censorship of printed media, Bose used the medium of radio wisely and strategically, encouraging discussion about him and about the content of his broadcasts. Consider, for example, Bose's broadcasts during the Bengal famine. The devastating human-made famine engulfed the rural regions of Bengal and, at that point in the war, claimed, by some estimates, as many as four million lives from starvation and related disease.[60] The British had made every effort to contain news of the famine not only for fear that it would encourage hoarding but also to conceal the administration's own culpability in the crisis.[61] In contrast, Axis radio announcers began reporting on the crisis as early as 1942. In August 1943, Bose broadcast a proposal to send one hundred thousand tons of rice to Bengal to help ease the effect of the famine in his native province. From Rangoon, Bose said: "100,000 tons of rice are waiting to be transported from Burma to relieve hunger in India." He asked the viceroy of India, by then Lord Wavell, to accept the offer: "At the moment when the British Government expresses its willingness to accept this delivery, the name of the harbor as well as the authorities who will hand over the rice will be named."[62]

Surely, Bose must have known that the British administration would not accept his offer. That, however, was beside the point. Bose's offer of rice—made *on* the radio—was a blatant and poignant critique of the administration's inefficacy at dealing with the food crisis and was meant to spur conversation among his followers and opponents. Bose's announcement intended to create room for interpretation and enable conversation and speculation. At this, Bose's announcement appears to have been effective. A few days later, British intelligence reports made note of the spread of the "latest Bose rumor" regarding his rice offer.[63]

Expanding on the notion of radio resonance, I want to also consider gossip as a useful analytical tool for understanding how radio, and more specifically Bose's voice, reached Indian audiences in wartime India. If rumors can lack active interlocutors, gossip speaks specifically to the ways in which people conferred, exchanged information, and were emotionally invested in these exchanges. As Patricia Meyer Spacks notes, what is particular about gossip is that it enables participants to engage in "emotional speculation."[64] Gossip has a kind of affective power that reels us in and forces us to take matters personally. As a broadcaster, Bose carefully nurtured a media persona that invited gossip-like conversation and emotional speculation. He encouraged people to talk not only about his campaign but also about him, to evaluate, to judge, and to discuss his own persona, to welcome him into the intimacy of their lives. For example, in June 1942, Bose noted: "After this long, laborious, and critical study of world-affairs, there is not the slightest possibility of being misled or misguided in *my judgment*. I should also like to add that whatever I have done since leaving home, or whatever I may do in the future, has been—and will be—done with the sole purpose of bringing about the speedy emancipation of my country."[65] In this speech, Bose, of course, was trying to convince his listeners that he was not a puppet of the Nazi government—that his opinions were his own. He was also, however, actively inviting conversation about his persona, and his judgment, encouraging his followers (and opponents) to weigh in, to discuss the matter—to judge for themselves.

Of course, part of what was going on is that the secretiveness that surrounded Bose's career as a fugitive anticolonial leader constantly on the run created the perfect fertile ground for gossip. His incredible escape from house arrest, his secretive trip across the world, and his surreptitious appearance on the radio following the Fall of Singapore were all fertile territory for speculation, as was later his appearance in Japan and Southeast Asia and the inexplicable plane accident in which he lost his life. After all, gossip and secrecy are intrinsically related and feed on one another. But as a broadcaster addressing his audience on the air, Bose milked these so-called open secrets about his life and career, relishing them and encouraging his listeners to do the same. This was not a coincidence but part of Bose's attempt to actively make use of radio resonance—to ensure that his message on the radio could reach beyond radio receivers.

In some ways, Bose's use of media has interesting parallels to Bhagat Singh's, an Indian anticolonial leader whose execution by the British government at the age of twenty-three, following acts of violence against British officials, made him a popular hero. In her enigmatic study of Singh's short but deeply influential anticolonial career, Maclean argues that Singh consciously used imagery to craft narratives about his campaign. The immense popularity of Singh's image, she argues, was not a natural or expected development, but "part of a sophisticated media campaign carried out over a two-year period."[66] Bose's radio voice too was part of a sophisticated campaign that, like Singh's, sought to delegitimize British rule.

Most telling, perhaps, was Bose's dramatic response to news of his death. On March 12, 1942, the BBC (and it appears AIR as well) falsely announced that Bose had died in a plane crash on his way to a conference in Tokyo.[67] Bose heard the announcement of his death on the airwaves. Two days later, he took to the radio: "This is Subhas Chandra Bose who is still alive speaking to you over Azad Hind Radio." He remarked: "The latest report about my death is perhaps an instance of wishful thinking."[68] Gandhi had already sent his condolences to Bose's mother via telegraph: "The whole nation mourns with you the death of your son. I share your sorrow to the full."[69] The British's false announcement and Bose's epic response on the radio were fertile territory for gossip-like discussion. It is precisely this kind of fascination that Khan refers to when she writes that the Indian public "watch[ed] [Bose's] every move with the glee of a cinema audience."[70] People in India, however, could not have possibly "watched" Bose. Aside from the battleground in northeastern India, Bose did not set foot in mainland India after his escape from house arrest that January night in 1941.

Bose's followers were also unlikely to read his speeches in printed form. As Sanjoy Bhattacharya and Devika Sethi have pointed out, while local and regional officials had been somewhat hesitant to take on aggressive print censorship policies during the first two years of the war, after December 1941, officials shed all hesitation, actively punishing newspapers, arresting journalists, and closing down small presses whom they deemed in violation of Defense of India Rules.[71] Moreover, the central government explicitly banned the reproduction of Axis broadcasts in print.[72] This meant that printed copies of Bose's broadcasts would not have been easily available during the years of the war, at least not in the open market.[73] Moreover, it also appears that the government tried to clamp down the circulation of the image of Bose's face. At least one account notes that a group of students was arrested in Bombay in 1942 for printing posters "bearing the picture of Subhas Chandra Bose."[74] During the war, Bose was quite literally nowhere to "be seen." Some heard his voice on the radio and many more learned about Bose and his campaign in discussions of his broadcasts.

Listening as Defiance

Bose promoted radio as a form of defiance against the British government. On the airwaves, he spoke to his audience as potential members of the resistance, promising that simply by tuning in to his voice and to Axis radio, they were part of a revolutionary community. Bose, however, also encouraged listeners to tune in to "enemy" radio stations, in particular to AIR and to the BBC, which he mockingly called "Anti-India Radio" and "Bluff and Bluster Corporation," respectively. Both stations, Bose argued, not inaccurately, were British-run and aired news from a British imperial perspective. In his various speeches, Bose encouraged what I call "listening as defiance," that is listening to British-run radio for cues that would help supporters of the anticolonial movement better understand the colonial government's intentions and strategies.[75] For example, in June 1943, Bose noted in a radio speech: "If one were to listen to the broadcasts from England after the campaign in Tunisia . . . one would think that the Anglo-American forces have already won the war."[76] In reality, Bose explained, the Allied forces were as far from winning the war in 1943 as they were in 1940. What these "propaganda tactics" reveal, Bose told Indian listeners, is that the Allied countries "badly need some success."[77] Listening in this manner was not a weapon of the weak, but rather a form of understanding and defying the enemy by using his words against him.

Bose was not the only one to approach listening to colonial radio in this way. In his fascinating account of the Algerian revolution, Frantz Fanon explains that during the revolution Algerians tuned in to French colonial radio stations in addition to revolutionary stations to better understand "the enemy." Fanon argues that listening to the French radio during the revolution constituted a form of active defiance of colonial power. This was precisely how Bose understood the power of radio: that it could at once serve as the voice of revolution but that it also enabled revolutionaries to, quite literally, *hear* the enemy.[78] For both Fanon and Bose, using radio as a means of defiance required a specific form of listening—that is, listening "in between lines."

For example, Bose paid close attention to the tone and character of British broadcasts and encouraged his listeners to do the same. After tuning in to the Lord Wavell speech on AIR in June 1945, Bose explained to his listeners: "The manner and tone of the Viceroy's speech gave one the impression that he himself had very little hope that nationalists in India would accept this offer."[79] By carefully listening to British broadcasts against the grain, Bose maintained, Indians could better understand British intentions.

Bose himself was an avid radio listener. In fact, he had been a devout radio listener long before he became a broadcaster. During the weeks following the outbreak of the war and the Indian viceroy's controversial declaration of war, Bose, like many others in India, closely followed radio broadcasts from Axis and Allied stations. In fact, the excuse that his younger and more technology-savvy nephew, Sisir Bose, was helping Bose tune in to stations from across the globe allowed the two to spend many hours together planning an escape route without eliciting suspicion from either British spies or from nosy relatives, whom they preferred to keep uninformed about their plans.[80]

After Bose left India for Europe, he listened to the radio zealously. Mukund R. Vyas, one of Bose's closest associates in Berlin, described Bose's passion for radio news in the following way: "I have yet to come across a person so devoted to radio news and commentaries."[81] Bose knew the schedules of various stations by heart, and he never missed a transmission he deemed important. Even in the battlefield in Burma, when Bose clearly had many more pressing concerns, he followed radio news and reports closely. British intelligence records revealed that Bose hired a soldier named Tara Chand to listen to radio day and night and to prepare detailed summaries of transmissions. Bose later read and analyzed Chand's radio reports.[82]

As a devoted radio listener, Bose believed in the power of radio to get his messages across. He chose his words cautiously and meticulously curated a radio persona. In their studies of Bhagat Singh's media campaigns, both J. Daniel Elam and Kama Maclean argue that Singh's sophisticated media campaign was possible because Singh had "an extraordinary awareness of visuality" and its affective powers.[83] We can make a similar argument regarding Bose's uses of radio. In the ways he encouraged gossip and emotional speculation about himself and about his campaign and actively helped create a narrative of himself through his broadcasts, Bose, like Singh, exhibited a particular "appreciation for the affective."[84] Careful attention to Bose's radio voice during the Quit India movement can help us understand how he consciously molded his radio persona as well as how Bose's voice circulated in the larger context of Axis radio propaganda to India.

Voice of India/Voice for India: Axis Radio and Quit India

On August 8, 1942, Gandhi delivered a speech in Bombay demanding that the British "quit India" once and for all, inaugurating what later came to be known as the Quit India movement. Within hours of Gandhi's speech, the British government put most leading Congress leaders behind bars and the movement quickly spilled out of Gandhi's and Congress's leadership control. With no central headship, local politicians and leaders took the lead as protestors burned police stations, raided post offices, destroyed railways, and targeted British administrators.

Scholarship on the Quit India movement is somewhat divided. Some scholars argue that the movement paved the way for the eventual British withdrawal. Others maintain that Quit India might have weakened the anticolonial movement because the British government was able to curb rebellion and reaffirm its power.[85] What most scholars agree on, however, is that Quit India "turned the political fortunes of the Congress." As Raghavan notes: "The party was forced to cool its heels in prison for the remainder of the war" enabling other actors previously on the fringes of the anticolonial movement and sometimes at odds with Congress to "mobilize their own base of support."[86] Bose was among them and during Quit India, like during the entire course of the war, he relied on the radio to carry his message forward.

As the historian Romain Hayes notes, Bose was taken aback by the "intensity of the uprising" as he did not expect "anything of this magnitude."[87] Yet on the airwaves, Bose spoke almost as if Gandhi had just handed him the relay stick of the anticolonial movement.[88] He read Quit India as an affirmation of his own military campaign and as evidence that India was indeed ready for a major armed revolution. "The people today are spontaneously passing on from passive resistance to active fighting."[89] Bose explained: "The younger generation in India has learned from the experience of the last twenty years that, while passive resistance can hold up or paralyze a foreign administration, it cannot overthrow or expel it without the use of physical force."[90] He gave precise instructions to followers in India on how to protest the administration: "organize processions for entering and occupying government institutions—law-courts, secretariat buildings, etc., with a view to rendering all work impossible there."[91] Taking on a commanding tone, he spoke, despite being thousands of miles away, as if he himself was one of the organizers: "Activities should be shifted from place to place if necessary in order to avoid being crushed."[92]

Yet even as he presented himself as a leader of the Quit India movement, Bose did not entirely abandon his "objective outsider" position. He informed Indian listeners of how the outside world "saw" and "heard" events in India: "friends, . . . you will certainly feel encouraged to hear that India today [is] on the front-page of the world press and Indian reports [are] the most interesting items of radio broadcasts all over the world."[93] Outside of India, and particularly in Germany, Bose told Indian listeners that Quit India was on everybody's lips. This dual role of both an insider and outsider to Indian politics had been a crucial aspect of Bose's radio persona since his first broadcast.

Bose was the only Indian anticolonial who was able to successfully take his message to the airwaves, and he gladly owned the role of an ambassador of the anticolonial movement on the radio. He announced: "The voice of these freedom-loving Indians cannot cross the frontiers of that country."[94] Hence, "my task is to keep the outside world informed of all the facts of the Indian situation."[95] Despite being thousands of miles away, Bose, on the airwaves, effectively represented the anticolonial movement—he spoke *for* India. This was not without irony given Bose's dramatic break with Gandhi and with other leading Indian National Congress colleagues in 1939.

At the same time, place was an important and recurring theme in Bose's various speeches. Bose often began his speeches by reminding listeners of his location and of the places he had traveled, first in Europe and later in Southeast Asia. For example, in June 1942, Bose began a broadcast in the following manner: "About five weeks ago I addressed you last over the radio. . . . Since then, I have travelled quite a lot and I am now in the very heart of Germany. Through the courtesy of the Berlin Short Wave Station, I therefore desire to address you again on the present international crisis."[96] Bose speaking on the shortwave could have, if not fully conceal, certainly played down his location. He chose to do the opposite. Place was an important theme in Bose's speeches because he believed his position—outside of India—validated his political stance on the war. In August 1942, Bose told audiences: "I have seen with *my own eyes* and have heard with *my own ears*. I am therefore able to form an impartial and objective opinion as to what is happening."[97] Whereas other anticolonial politicians were languishing in jail in India, Bose explained, he had traveled to Germany and had been able to gain personal knowledge of world affairs. He therefore was in a position to assess and judge the Axis leaders' true intentions. Bose reassured listeners: "from my *intimate knowledge* of these three nations,

I can assert . . . that they have nothing but sympathy and goodwill for India and for Indian independence."[98] Here, by emphasizing his location, Bose was effectively placing his voice outside of India. In this way, on the airwaves, Bose could simultaneously speak *for* India and *to* India. He was both a knowledgeable insider and an unbiased outsider.

During Quit India, Bose more emphatically embraced this duo role of insider/outsider, as he adopted a more dramatic tone than in the past. Bose reassured listeners their "blood" dignified their fight: "Freedom cannot be won without shedding the blood of martyrs. . . . It is the baptism of blood, which gives a nation the strength to achieve liberty and to preserve it."[99] When in Southeast Asia, Bose and his team employed the popular slogan "*Tum mujhe xūn do, main tumhen āzādī dūṅgā*" (Give me blood, I will give you freedom), which even today remains in circulation. Bose's references to blood were meant to emphasize his own belief that India needed armed revolution, but they also echoed the "rhetoric of death and sacrifice" in Axis propaganda to India. German announcers reminded listeners that Britain had "Indian blood" on its hands: "The British carried out the massacre of the Indians at Amritsar in 1919, of the Moplas in 1920, at Lahore in 1930, and then at many other places. The British dyed their hands with the blood of the *Khaksars*."[100] Earlier Italian-based announcers had also referenced blood: "Germany and Italy have never oppressed the Indians or sucked their blood like leeches. . . . It is the British, who though they profess to be fighting for 'Liberty and Democracy' have been sucking India's life-blood like vampires."[101] And, of course, the theme of blood, the blood that united the Aryan nation as well as the blood that Germany should shed in the nation's service—was a staple in domestic Nazi propaganda and fascism more generally.

Bose's speeches also echoed key messages of other Axis propaganda. For example, on the airwaves Bose articulated a noncommunal message, denouncing any kind of religious nationalism. Bose's anticommunal stance certainly reflected his own opinions, principles, and convictions. Throughout his career, he remained staunchly committed to an intrareligious understanding and was remarkably successful at promoting religious harmony among soldiers and supporters of the INA in Southeast Asia. Bose's anticommunal message, however, also aligned with a key theme of Axis radio.[102] Axis radio announcers had used communalism as an opportunity to hammer down the British administration for fostering religious divisions in India. For example, one broadcaster from Tokyo remarked: "[The] British, with their Satanic policy of 'divide and rule,' played us one against each other and so it is only in our unhappy India that religion is being prostituted by its communal leaders to serve their selfish gains."[103]

Similarly, Bose's support for Gandhi on the airwaves, particularly during Quit India, echoed Axis radio's unwavering backing of Gandhi.[104] In his radio addresses, Bose downplayed his previous rivalry with the revered Indian leader.

On Gandhi's birthday, Bose remarked: "Gandhi's service to the cause of India's freedom are [*sic*] unique and unparalleled."[105] Gandhi, he argued, had not only taught Indians "national self-respect and self-confidence" but also "set the stage" for "the final struggle for liberty—the last war of independence" that he, Bose, ultimately would lead.[106] Bose's vociferous support of Gandhi on the radio, particularly during Quit India was strategic and aimed at gaining supporters. It is also, however, a reminder that the Indian National Congress did not have a complete monopoly on the anticolonial narrative or even on Gandhi himself. As K. A. Abbas, then a journalist with *Bombay Chronicle* noted, different and often contradictory views about what the anticolonial movement should be could coexist.[107] Someone who was an avid Gandhi supporter and believer in nonviolence also could regularly and enthusiastically tune in to Axis radio and to the gossip and rumor that surrounded it. As Abbas nicely put it, this kind of cohabitation of seemingly contradictory ideas, sometimes within the same individuals, "was [a] peculiarity of the national movement."[108]

In addition to Bose, his associates in Berlin took an active role during the Quit India movement. Azad Hind inaugurated two new radio stations: Radio Waziristan and Congress Radio. These were a type of counterfeit radio station during which broadcasters lied about their location and claimed they were broadcasting from India. Radio Waziristan, also known as Azad Muslim Radio, targeted Indian Muslims. Berlin-based announcers claimed to be in Waziristan, near the Indian border with Afghanistan. The station put out daily fifteen-minute-long broadcasts, which, for the most part, seem to have consisted of updates about rebellions happening throughout India and provocative political talks that revolved around two main points: (1) Britain is Islam's enemy and (2) Indian Muslims should reject communalism and rally with other religious communities. Radio Waziristan tried to accomplish a difficult thing: to celebrate a pan-Muslim identity, while simultaneously convincing Indian Muslims to ally with other religious groups, namely Hindus and Sikhs, in driving the British out of India.[109]

The underlying purpose of this station seems to have been to encourage Muslims to join Quit India demonstrations. Muslims had not been active during the Quit India movement, in great part because the Muslim League had opposed Gandhi's call for total mobilization. As Pandey notes, Quit India confirmed that there had been a significant Muslim drift away from the Congress. Like other Axis broadcasts, Radio Waziristan's talks were as incendiary as they were misleading: "The British are interested in Gandhijis' death";[110] "The Allied powers are bent upon finishing Islam from the face of the earth";[111] and "It is the religious duty of every Musalman to kill the British wherever they are found."[112] Surely, not everybody that tuned in or heard about these broadcasts believed that the British planned to kill Gandhi, just as many likely were not convinced that Muslims had a religious duty to kill British people. But as argued in the previous chapter, incendiary comments are particularly good at catching listeners' attention and spurring conversation.

The second Berlin-based counterfeit radio station was called Congress Radio.[113] Like Radio Waziristan, Congress Radio aired news and updates about the Quit India movement and was intentionally incendiary. One common technique employed by this station during the uprising was to shame those who did not support the movement. For example, on October 19, 1942, the station ardently criticized C. Rajagopalachari for describing Quit India as a "movement of destruction." Rajagopalachari was a longtime supporter of Gandhi's campaign but had publicly opposed the Quit India movement.[114]

Interestingly, a Congress Radio station also was broadcasting from a low-power transmitter in Bombay during the Quit India movement. The station, which was run by a group of young students, was on the air for a little longer than two months (from August to October 1942), when the local police confiscated the transmitter and arrested its organizers and broadcasters.[115] Unlike Axis shortwave radio and unlike Bose, these Bombay-based broadcasters, did not voice support for Germany and Japan. What is clear is that even if Congress Radio operated on low-power transmitters and had limited reception in the city, this station contributed to the clamor—on and off the airwaves—that characterized the Quit India uprising. Moreover, it also is likely that listeners, both monitors and ordinary listeners, confused this genuinely local station for the German-based station falsely claiming to be broadcasting from India and vice versa.

K. A. Abbas shared an interesting anecdote that sheds light on the reception of Bose's radio voice and more generally on Axis radio during wartime India. During a Communist Party meeting, his friends discussed a "new" Congress Radio on the air. They claimed that the station was yet another counterfeit station operating from Germany, Italy, or Japan and could not be based in India. Abbas noted: "I was not in a position to contradict them or to say that I had just come from this secret radio station and that it was a stone's throw away from the Communist Party."[116] Notably, the confusion that surrounded the two Congress Radio stations and other Axis-counterfeit stations reveals not only that radio in wartime India incited gossip as British colonial sources claim but also that the stations themselves mirrored the dynamics of gossip and rumor.

Similarly, one British soldier stationed in India who was unusually interested in understanding the local *māhol* (atmosphere) came to believe that the Japanese and Bose were leading the entire Quit India movement via shortwave radio. "There is no doubt at all that some of this is directly led by Jap agents, and the Jap wireless (with Bose from Berlin) is giving *precise* instructions to the angry congressmen."[117] The young British soldier was wrong about Bose leading the uprising, but it is not hard to imagine why he might have felt this way. It was in this context of confusion on the airwaves that Bose's voice circulated during Quit India and during the war more generally.

The British colonial government made use of the Indian Army, which consisted mostly of Indian soldiers and had grown dramatically during the war, to quell uprisings. By late October 1942, Axis radio stations had changed their strategy. They had stopped broadcasting news of uprisings and stopped urging people to join revolts. Instead, Axis stations reported on the cruelty of the British response. Indeed, as one Berlin-based announcer noted, the British did not hesitate to use *"lathis,* revolvers, machine-guns and tear-gas" against protestors.[118] The government's response to the movement was as cruel as it had been swift. Axis radio accounts, however, also were laden with exaggeration. Announcers stressed that the British not only committed atrocities against Indians but also enjoyed performing them.[119] One announcer noted: "Members of the House of Commons expressed *pleasure and satisfaction* when Amery declared that British planes were used for bombing and machine-gunning unarmed Indian demonstrators."[120]

The emphasis on British cruelty in Axis broadcasts during Quit India had another, perhaps less obvious purpose—that is, to shift attention away from reports of Nazi crimes. An announcer speaking from a branch Azad Hind stated: "The British never tired of condemning Nazi methods, but they forget their own atrocious deeds in India. India is, indeed, a vast concentration camp. Indian patriots have been incarcerated, their only crime being that they love their country." The announcer concluded: "This is how the British treat Indians and still they condemn similar methods adopted by others."[121] In his own speeches, Bose did not employ terms such as "concentration camps" to describe British oppression of India, but he did engage similar techniques. He asked listeners to focus on British atrocities and to ignore the internal policies of Axis governments.

Intimacy and Affect in "Stump Speeches" and Fireside Chats: A Radio Campaign from Southeast Asia

By the end of 1942, Bose had already made plans to leave Germany for good. He knew all too well that an invasion from the western frontier of India—across the Soviet Union—with the Indian Legion would be impossible. During Bose's only meeting with Hitler, the Nazi leader recommended that Bose travel by submarine to Japan and agreed to assist with arrangements. Bose's staff recorded a few speeches that they broadcast in his absence. Following a grueling nine-month submarine trip on June 21, 1943, Bose once more took to the air, shocking both his countrymen and the British administration: "Countrymen and friends, in April you last heard my voice over another radio in another part of the world. Now, I am in Tokyo."[122] News of Bose's address from Tokyo and trip to Japan quickly spread. C. K. Narayanswami, a noted journalist and leftist politician, in an oral interview remembered how excited he was to learn Bose had reached Tokyo. Narayanswami was arrested during the war for his anticolonial activities and was in prison when Bose reached Tokyo. "We had, in the meantime, the very exciting news of Subhash Chandra Bose's escape from India and his activities in Berlin. Then *we heard* of his presence in Tokyo."[123] While Narayanswami's account doesn't mention radio (and radios were almost surely not available in prison), his reference to "hearing" about Bose reaching Tokyo is interesting. Narayanswami associates, in a rather unconscious manner, the act of listening/hearing with the Bengali leader and points to the ways in which information about Bose's whereabouts and specifically reaching Japan traveled quickly.

As he had done from Berlin, in Asia, Bose continued to preach for the liberation of India with Axis assistance and insisted that the Axis powers were India's friends. Now broadcasting from Asia, Bose embraced a pan-Asian ideology: "India and Japan have in the past been found by deep cultural ties that are about twenty centuries old." It "is certain," he explained, "that once India is free these ties will be revived and strengthened."[124] He tiptoed around the issue of Japan's invasion of China: "It is true that the Indian view on Japan underwent some change following the Chinese affair. But after the beginning of the great East Asia war the situation has become different." He concluded in a straightforward manner: "Today, Japan is waging war against our common enemy; Chunking has joined our enemies."[125]

With Japan's blessing, Bose took over the INA, a regiment of Indian British Army soldiers that had been captured by Japanese forces in Singapore. Rash Behari Bose (no relation to Subhas Chandra Bose), a Bengali revolutionary who had been living in Japan for about a decade, had managed to convince the Japanese government to allow him to organize an army with new Indian POWs captured in Singapore. Subhas Chandra Bose, a decade younger than Behari Bose, and by now, in part thanks to his radio addresses, a rather well-known figure, inserted life into the INA at a critical moment. If Bose had faced difficulty convincing Indian soldiers in India to defect, the task proved much easier in Southeast Asia. In particular, Bose was successful at convincing Indian civilians residing in Malaysia and Singapore to join his army and to financially support his campaign.[126] As Yasmin Khan notes: "The strength of the INA was undoubtedly built on the bedrock of local support from Indian residents in Malaya."[127] At its peak, the INA constituted an impressive fifty thousand soldiers, who had sworn allegiance to the Japanese emperor.[128]

To ensure that news of his military campaign in Southeast Asia reached India, Bose continued to rely on the medium of radio.[129] He delivered several speeches himself, but also relegated a great deal to his associates. For example, Lakshmi Sahgal, an INA female officer who led a women's brigade known as the Rani of Jhansi, spoke on the radio: "The voice of a woman . . . may come as a surprise to you. But remember this. Ours is no Mercenary Army. Ours is an Army of liberation." She remarked: "The present world situation has given us Indians in East Asia this long awaited opportunity, and we are determined to make the fullest possible use of it."[130] The INA also had a musical ensemble made up of soldier musicians.[131] British monitoring reports include specific details of INA songs, suggesting that the songs were also broadcast on the radio. Tunes in Hindustani, such as "Āzād kareṅge" (We will liberate) and "Āzādī khel mat samjho" (Freedom is no children's play), likely aimed to boost the morale of INA soldiers, while also spreading the INA's message on the airwaves.[132]

Azad Hind Radio branches opened first in Singapore and later in Burma as well. When Bose traveled to Tokyo, Bangkok, and Saigon, he also broadcast from shortwave stations in these cities. As the war progressed, he became more comfortable with the microphone. Although there are few recorded versions of Bose's speeches, a marked difference is evident between a recording in Hindustani delivered in 1938 as president of Congress, and his recorded address in Singapore in 1943, when he accepted leadership of the INA.[133] In the former recorded speech, Bose reads from a script, makes pauses in awkward moments, and even appears to struggle with some phrases in Hindustani. In the later recording, we hear a confident voice, accustomed to the microphone, speaking, it appears, extemporaneously in fluent Hindustani.[134] Toward the end of the war, when broadcasting from Burma in 1944, Bose described his surroundings in more vivid ways than before: "Here the weather is very pleasant and very agreeable. A feeling of supreme optimism pervades the whole atmosphere despite the boastful propaganda that the enemies have been indulging in for a long time and despite the occasional appearance of enemy airplanes."[135] Bose, however, never quite abandoned the more typical militaristic "style of the stump speech."[136]

A brief comparison with the U.S. president whose radio addresses during the Great Depression and World War II shaped a generation of scholarship on radio is useful. Although not immediately apparent, FDR and Bose had a great deal in common. Both men's careers and public personas were intimately tied to the medium of radio. The two turned to radio in an effort to build a direct connection to the public. FDR, who first began broadcasting during the Great Depression, used the radio to circumvent the written news press, which he deeply distrusted. Similarly, through his radio address, Bose was able not only to circumvent British accounts of the war, as presented in the written press, which was heavily censored by the colonial administration during the war, but also to contest the British-run radio stations, including AIR and the BBC.

FDR's success as a broadcaster, writes Bruce Lenthall, can be linked to the president's speaking style. On the air, he spoke not as a leader, but as a friend next door, and he sought to create a sense of intimacy with his constituents over the radio.[137] Intimacy, writes Alex Chávez, "is achieved by surpassing the self, where one's own body engages in ecstatic communication with another or many others, allowing for a type of communion, often realized along unknown paths that release the self from the enclosures of scarcity and utility."[138]

FDR's personable style and down-to-earth voice allowed him to create that type of communion with listeners. John Durham Peters has convincingly argued that "securing the mainstream acceptance for radio required means to close the obvious gaps of distance, disembodiment, and dissemination."[139] He notes: "Intimate sound spaces, domestic genres, cozy speech styles, and radio personalities . . . all helped bridge the address gap."[140]

As a broadcaster, Bose never fully embraced the warm and friendly style that was characteristic of FDR's fireside chats, but he did seek to develop intimacy, to build a type of communion with his listeners.[141] Bose did that, however, by encouraging gossip and emotional speculation about his persona—by turning to radio resonance. For example, broadcasting in 1943, Bose told radio audiences that his trip from Berlin to Tokyo had been a "slap in the face" of the British government. He argued that the latest AIR broadcast claiming that he had left Berlin because of differences with the German government was a "pathetic attempt to conceal the British government's embarrassment at being unable to stop *one man* from traveling across the world."[142] The emphasis on "one man" is crucial. Bose turns the discussion back to himself and cues into a sensational and dramatic element, nourishing and personalizing the conversation.[143] Comments about the British announcement of his death as "wishful thinking" and even the broadcast about sending rice from Japanese-occupied Burma are examples of a conscious attempt to create an intimate form of politics through radio resonance. Moreover, the significance of Bose's broadcasting from Burma would have not been lost on listeners (and talkers) back in India. The British government had exiled Bose to Burma in the 1920s for his revolutionary activities; he now spoke from Burma as a free man.[144]

The British response to the "intimate talk" and "gossip" of Bose is also interesting and revealing.[145] By the time Bose began broadcasting from Japanese-occupied Southeast Asia, AIR had developed detailed guidelines about how to respond directly to the Indian leader's growing popularity. To discredit Bose, the guidelines note that AIR should first and foremost criticize Japan's ambition in the region and stress that "Bose and his INA are propaganda stunts which deceive no one in India, however much they may deceive the Japanese and those Indians overseas misguided enough to believe in Bose." Most interestingly, however, the guidelines also recommended that announcers directly attack Bose's "character" and that they expose him as "selfish and ambitious" and willing to "sacrifice all other interests to satisfy his ambitions."[146]

Gossip in Life and Death

As late as 1944, in the face of Allied victories and Axis losses, Bose remained optimistic on the airwaves. In the summer of 1944, when it became clear that

Germany's surrender was imminent, Bose announced on the radio: "I want to repeat again that the Indian situation is independent of the European situation. No matter what happens in Europe in the future, the Indian people have a God-sent opportunity for achieving their liberation."[147] In the same speech, he also offered words of praise for the defeated German Führer, even as the world began to learn of the sheer extent of his crimes: "The courage, tenacity and fortitude with which the armed forces of Germany fought till the moment of Herr Hitler's death must compel the admiration of the whole world."[148] As late as 1944, in Southeast Asia and no longer financially dependent on Nazi sponsorship, Bose continued to show his support for Hitler on the airwaves. As the U.S. armies made advances in Asia, Bose continued to reassure Indian listeners that Japan would win. "The Americans will go on nibbling at the outer circle," but Japan will go on "maintaining her hold over the inner circle, until American morale ultimately begins to crack."[149] Regarding the INA, Bose acknowledged losses and difficulties, but he continued to deliver inspirational speeches: "It will be a long and hard struggle. . . . But we shall fight more bravely than the British and their mercenaries can."[150] Bose's righteous tone reflected his understanding that the INA did not pose a legitimate military threat to the British armies, but that the army's existence did endanger the legitimacy of the empire: "We have the consciousness that we are fighting for justice—for Truth—and for our birthright of liberty."[151]

The INA fought alongside the Imperial Japanese Army in northeastern India and faced bitter defeat. From Singapore, Bose announced his army's defeat on the radio, blaming it on the monsoon. He promised, however, to return to India and continue the fight before long. "My own plan is clear." I will "go on fighting with the Azad Hind Fauj to the last man and to the last drop of our blood."[152] Japan's surrender on August 15, 1945, after the United States dropped atomic bombs on the Japanese cities of Nagasaki and Hiroshima, took Bose, like many others throughout the world, by surprise. Bose fled to Taipei, Taiwan, then still held by Japanese forces, but his airplane malfunctioned and crashed. Bose suffered severe burns and succumbed to his wounds in a hospital on August 18, 1945. Five days later, the Domei agency of Japan announced Bose's death, and soon thereafter several other radio stations, including AIR, did so as well.[153]

Back in India news of Bose's untimely death was met with profound disbelief. Gandhi made no secret that he did not believe Bose had died in the plane crash. He told a group of workers: "I believe Subhas Bose is still alive and hiding somewhere."[154] Many in India shared Gandhi's suspicion that Bose had yet again managed to deceive the British administration and had faked his own death (figure 2.1). This theory would have seemed reasonable given Bose's series of famous escapes. Even the British were suspicious and ordered two extensive investigations to ensure that Bose was, as one British officer put it, "actually and permanently dead."[155] British inquirers concluded that Bose had succumbed to injuries endured in a plane crash.

2.1 Picture from a 1946 calendar depicting a "live" Bose dressed in uniform standing next to his grave.

Source: Cornell University Poster Collection.

British fears that Bose was not "permanently dead," however, turned out to be correct in unanticipated ways. The colonial government's administration tried INA soldiers, who were returning home after the war's end. In what was surely one of the colonial government's worst publicity gaffes, the colonial government, in a trial in the Red Fort of Delhi, convicted three INA officers, a Hindu, a Muslim, and a Sikh. Their choice of men and location (the Red Fort was the main residence of the Mughal dynasty until 1856) provided the perfect opportunity for the Indian public to rally in defense of the INA and of Bose's larger campaign. As Krishna Bose nicely put it, the INA trials made "the saga of Subhas Chandra Bose burst into life."[156] Bose's voice could no longer be heard on the airwaves, but in the months of the trial, Bose's image, which had been mostly absent during the war, began to proliferate throughout India, with posters and images celebrating him as a national hero (figures 2.2 and 2.3). In addition, with print censorship rules loosened after the end of the war, Bose's

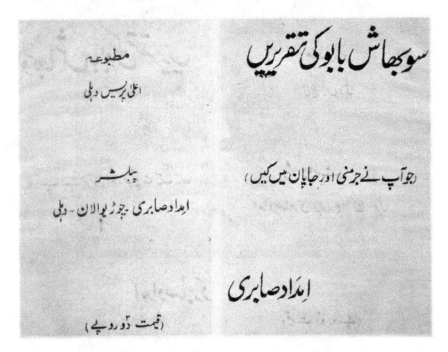

2.2A AND 2.2B Subhas Chandra Bose's radio speeches were published in a collection entitled *Subhas Bābū Kī Taqrīreṅ; Jo Āpne Germany Aur Japan Meṅ Kīṅ* (Subhas Babu's Speeches; The Ones You Made in Germany and Japan). (a) Book cover of the collection. (b) Image of a garlanded Bose above the three INA trials soldiers, which nicely depicts the way in which Bose's presence could be felt during the trials. The book, which cost two rupees, lacks a publication date, but the epilogue makes it clear that it was published during the INA trials.

Source: Subhas Bābū Kī Taqrīreṅ (Ālā Press, Delhi). Edited by Imdad Sabri.

2.2B (*Continued*)

2.3 Poster published in 1946 featuring an interesting aural component. The words "*Chalo Dilli* [Let's go to Delhi/Onward to Delhi]" emanate from Bose's trumpet. It is almost as if the poster depicts the ways in which Bose's voice remained in the air even after his radio voice could no longer be heard in the airwaves.

Source: Cornell University Poster Collection.

radio speeches (translated to various Indian languages) began to circulate in books and magazines alongside reports of the INA trials.[157] If Bose's radio voice could not be heard on the radio receivers in the aftermath of the war, print copies of his speeches and images of his face now ensured that his voice continued to circulate (and be read and heard), offering further proof of how radio worked alongside other print and oral media. What was clear to the British administration and to the general public is that if Bose had lost in the battle-field, the INA trials proved that the Bengali Axis-sympathizing leader clearly won on the propaganda front. Moreover, the INA trials, the public outrage, and likely also the circulation of Bose's printed speeches, added to the growing feeling that Bose was still alive, beliefs that did not subside after independence.[158]

Nearly a decade after independence in 1947, Jawaharlal Nehru's government instituted a formal inquiry committee into Bose's death. The committee's extensive report corroborated the British administration's earlier findings that Bose had died shortly after his plane crashed, but this did little to mitigate the feeling that Bose was still alive. In fact, newly released documents have shown that even Nehru might not have been fully convinced that Bose was "permanently dead." Nehru's government spied on the Bose family for two decades, and the spying, some claim, is evidence that Nehru suspected Bose might return at any moment.[159]

In the 1960s, rumors about Bose's whereabouts intensified. A story circulated throughout India that Bose had become a *sanyasi* (an aesthetic) and that he was residing in the Shaulmari Ashram in West Bengal. Another story that also made rounds in the early 1960s was that Bose was living in a prison in Siberia. Perhaps most interesting and relevant to our study is the narrative about Bose speaking from Radio Moscow after Indian and Pakistani leaders signed a cease-fire agreement in Tashkent, ending the 1965 Indo-Pakistan War. At least one version of the story noted that Bose had announced the beginning of the Third World War on the radio. The rumor was so widespread and believed that the parliament organized its own investigation in the matter.[160]

In his biography of Subhas Chandra Bose, the historian Sugata Bose argues that the "many attempts to resurrect" Bose and the rumors about his return testify to "continuing charisma" of "the unifying and selfless Indian leader."[161] Scholars of rumor, however, have warned us that when it comes to rumors, things tend to be much more complicated. "Charisma" and "selflessness" alone cannot explain the emergence and circulation of such stories. Rumors, they note, speak to hidden truths and anxieties about societies.[162] The story about Bose's voice appearing on the radio during the Tashkent agreement appears to reflect apprehension specific to the 1965 Indo-Pakistan war, namely the prospect of never-ending war between India and Pakistan (see chapters 5 and 6). Clearly, there is much work to be done on the meanings of rumors and conspiracy theories about Bose's resurrection, and much of it is beyond the scope of this limited study on radio. What I wish to emphasize here is the important link between Bose's radio persona and the Indian public's refusal to believe news of his death in the decades to come. The gossip and rumor that have characterized Bose's afterlife are not categorically different from the gossip and rumor that surrounded his radio voice during the years of the war.

To make this point, I want to briefly return to the British officer's inquiry into whether Bose was "*permanently* dead."[163] On one hand, the officer's comment referenced the fact that the government had once erroneously announced Bose's death on the radio as well as Bose's aptitude for deceiving the British administration. On the other hand, the phrase "permanently dead" also alluded to the idea that Bose had not been entirely alive during the years of the war. After all, with the exception of a battle in the northeast, he did not return to continental India after his legendary escape from house arrest in 1941. During the peak of his career, Bose had "lived" through his radio voice, which had been heard only by some, invoked by many more, and, like the gossip that surrounded it, always had an ephemeral and somewhat ghostly quality. In other words, one way in which we can read the officer's comment about permanence and death is by pointing out that gossip and rumor were not just central to Bose's afterlife. They were central to his wartime career—they were part and parcel of Bose's primary publicity medium, the radio. And in wartime India, radio (and the gossip and rumor that surrounded it), like Bose himself, had an ethereal quality.

Conclusion

A study of Bose's radio persona demonstrates how the medium of radio during the peak of World War II contested the colonial government's account of events and threatened its legitimacy. Despite colonial officers' efforts to keep the Indian nationalists off the airwaves, Bose, broadcasting from Germany and Southeast Asia, promoted radio as a form of resistance and defiance against the British government.

In closing, I wish to directly address the two central questions that have guided my analysis thus far. What does the study of Bose's radio persona tell us about how the medium of radio reached audiences? What does it tell us about Bose's own political career? Regarding the first question, Bose's radio persona forces us to take seriously the role of rumor and gossip and to reconsider how the medium of radio reached audiences—how it connected with listeners. If FDR successfully created intimacy with listeners through a down-to-earth friendly speaking style, Bose harnessed intimacy with followers in India by encouraging people to *talk*. This has important implications for our understanding of the medium of radio and how it connects with audiences. Bose was able to build affective bonds with his audience by harnessing the power of radio resonance—that is, by encouraging his listeners and followers to talk and gossip about his career and his persona.

In addressing the second question, we must remember that most biographies of Bose, scholarly and popular, play down his ties to fascist governments. They have done so by emphasizing Bose's long anticolonial career, effectively shifting the focus away from his more problematic wartime activities, as well as by presenting Bose's alliance with the Axis as purely opportunistic and ultimately inconsequential to his nationalist message and to its reception. A study of Bose's radio voice demonstrates that such suppositions are at best disingenuous and at worst manipulative. Bose's radio persona, as well as the rumors and gossip that surrounded his voice and shaped his afterlife in the decades to come, cannot be separated from the larger context of Axis propaganda to India during World War II. Axis radio praised authoritarianism, broadcast outright false news, and spurted anti-Semitic messages, while simultaneously pronouncing loyalty to Gandhi's anticolonial movement. This doesn't necessarily make Bose into a quisling or a full-blown collaborator as the previously quoted *Newsweek* reporter purports, but it does cast serious doubt on a narrative committed to *seeing* Bose solely as "his majesty's opponent." In so doing, it points to the important ways in which a history of radio, and sound more generally, retunes our understanding of South Asian history.

Chapters 1 and 2 trace the changing course of radio during World War II and reveal how the medium integrated itself into existing oral networks of communication. Both chapters demonstrate that radio ultimately escaped British control. At the same time, however, the wartime policies of the colonial administration had important long-term effects. During the war, the colonial government developed a national radio network. This set the stage for how leaders of the newly independent countries of India and Pakistan would attempt to foster allegiances to governments and fashion national identities through state-run broadcasting networks in the decades to come.

PART II

MUSIC AND POSTINDEPENDENCE RADIO

CHAPTER 3

THE "SOUND STANDARDS" OF
A NEW INDIA

In October 1952, B. V. Keskar, the newly appointed minister of information and broadcasting and de facto head of the national radio network, All India Radio (AIR), took to the airwaves to address the public's disconcerting taste for Hindi film songs. These songs, he remarked, are "becoming more and more vulgar and their tunes are concocted [of] irrational cocktails of western dance tunes."[1] At the time, AIR's various radio stations dedicated a few peak hours daily to film-song broadcasts. The "predominance of these songs," Keskar explained in another radio broadcast, "is slowly eliminating light music of various types and throttling its future growth."[2] Less than two months after joining the ministry, Keskar ordered that AIR stations stop broadcasting Hindi film songs altogether, inaugurating what became a contentious, if unofficial, ban on film songs over the national radio network, which lasted nearly half a decade.[3]

Film scholars reference Keskar's diatribe against film music as an example of the kind of widespread stigma and severe censorship that the film industry endured in its early decades.[4] In a 2007 interview, the eminent Hindi broadcaster Ameen Sayani joked that Keskar had some "strange ideas" about "how pure and good and totally traditional we should be."[5] Sayani, half in jest, suggested that the minister could have greatly benefited from the guidance of a professional psychiatrist; how could one conceive of banning the now evergreen Hindi film songs of the 1950s from the national radio network?[6] Still, accounts of Keskar's tirade against film songs—popular and scholarly alike—rarely address the broader implications of Keskar's policies. Following Ravikant's call to consider the ban in the larger context of the "official national aesthetic," I investigate the broader and long-term consequences of AIR's reforms.[7]

Keskar's reforms followed the British departure from India in August 1947 and the violent Partition of the Indian subcontinent into separate Indian and Pakistani states. The broadcasting network that the British colonial government developed during World War II in a belated and haphazard attempt to garner Indian support for the Allied cause was also partitioned into two separate networks: AIR and Radio Pakistan. In the decades following independence and Partition, both networks attempted to fashion national identities through the medium of radio. In part II, employing Keskar's controversial reforms as a moment of departure, I focus specifically on the role of music in radio broadcasts. The current chapter analyzes Keskar's social uplift programs in the early 1950s and 1960s, paying close attention to the campaign to promote Indian classical music traditions as a new "national" culture among the "masses of India." In chapter 4, I analyze Radio Ceylon's film-song programs and explain how and why a commercial station located on the nearby island of Ceylon (now Sri Lanka) effectively side-stepped the Indian government's agenda and fostered a shared aural culture across the newly formed Indo-Pakistan border.

During his decade-long tenure as minister of information and broadcasting (1952–1962), B. V. Keskar spearheaded reforms to AIR's musical and linguistic programming as well as the institution's structure and personnel. Keskar filled broadcasting hours with classical music programming, inviting musicians trained at renowned academies to AIR's studios to perform and record, while simultaneously ordering that all AIR stations cease the broadcast of film songs altogether. The ultimate goal of these reforms was not merely to transform AIR, but rather to transform the auditory experiences of the citizens of the newly independent nation. In the wake of independence, Keskar and his supporters, I argue, sought to orchestrate a soundscape for the Indian nation through the medium of radio.[8] As it sought to train the ears of radio audiences and forge what I call citizen-listeners, the campaign refined the meaning of citizenship in auditory terms.

Classical music was the focus of Keskar's elaborate and ambitious campaign and, accordingly, is the focus of this chapter. Keskar had trained in the classical vocal tradition of *Dhrupad* (a genre of music) in Benares but had long given up singing in favor of a career in politics. He was the main architect and the driving force behind AIR's reform campaign, but he received support from prominent musicians, such as Krishna Ratanjankar, principal of the Bhatkhande Music Institute in Lucknow, and Sumati Mutatkar, a renowned vocalist and later professor at the University of Delhi; from AIR employees; and, perhaps most important, from government administrators. Rajendra Prasad, president of India from 1950 to 1962, not only provided bureaucratic support for AIR reforms but also took to the radio to endorse them.[9] The prime minister of

India, Jawaharlal Nehru, was not as proactive as the president in showing support for AIR's reforms. Yet Keskar's continued tenure as minister of information and broadcasting (Keskar was minister throughout most of Nehru's term) attests to Nehru's faith in Keskar's work and is evidence of the prime minister's implicit support.[10]

Moreover, as David Lelyveld has pointed out, Keskar's vision for AIR as a "central government monopoly that would play a leading role in integrating Indian culture and raising standards" went hand in hand with the basic principles of Nehruvian socialism. Named after the country's first prime minister Jawaharlal Nehru, Nehruvian socialism describes a "mixed economy," in which the central government controls major industries.[11] Keskar's faith in the technology of radio and its ability to reform the Indian soundscape mirrored the prime minister's faith in science and technology as a means for national development.[12] Similarly, although Keskar's dislike for Hindi film songs certainly reflects his own musical taste, it also echoes a socialist-leaning government's discomfort with the idea that culture can be created in the marketplace.[13] Most important, just as fostering national unity was a primary concern of Nehru's government, AIR's campaign promised to spread a national culture by ensuring that all citizens remained, quite literally, tuned in to the same wavelength.

A close analysis of AIR's campaign, therefore, also forces us to rethink common assumptions about Nehru's government, in particular about its proclaimed commitment to secularism and inclusivity. AIR's cultural uplift campaign defined the terms of national integration in communal terms. Not only did AIR's campaign link classical music to the revival of an imagined ancient Hinduism and favor Hindu musicians over Muslim, it also promoted a Sanskritized version of Hindi—devoid of Arabic- and Persian-origin (read Muslim) words—as India's national language. As I show in this chapter, musical and linguistic reforms were deeply linked.

In recent years, scholars of Indian politics have argued that the Indian government defined citizenship not as a set of legal rights, but rather as a "learning activity or an ongoing process of acquiring skills and attributes."[14] As such, the newly formed Indian government shifted the responsibility of citizenship to its constituents, asking them to learn (and to enact) their citizenship, rather than promising to protect a set of inalienable privileges. Absent from this excellent and influential body of scholarship is an analysis of how sound and music shaped this new understanding of early citizenship in postcolonial India. Similarly, although scholars of sound have investigated radio's and music's relationship to a collective identity throughout the world in great detail, citizenship and its relationship to soundscapes remains a fairly unexplored topic, but it is one to which scholars have begun to turn to in recent years.[15] Ana Maria Ochoa Gautier, writing about colonial Latin America, for example, demonstrates how debates "on the value of indigenous languages also provoked the invocation of

Spanish as the transcendental condition for the theologico-political definition of citizenship."[16] Similarly, Rebecca Scales's work on radio in interwar France demonstrates how heated discussions in the parliament and in the press about "radio's ability to reintegrate veterans of the First World War into civil society" points to a new understanding of radio listening as a "practice of citizenship."[17] Here, focusing on South Asia and on a later period and expanding on Srirupa Roy's conclusions about citizenship being a learned activity, I show how Keskar's radio campaign sought to create "national" sounds and to mold Indian citizen-listeners who could appreciate these sounds.

Administrators and broadcasters at AIR assumed that citizen-listeners would be "docile" and "impressionable."[18] Radio listeners, however, proved to be quite the opposite. They protested against AIR's music broadcasts unleashing what became an ardent debate over film songs, their propriety, and their relationship to national consciousness. The criticism of AIR broadcasts and the debate over film songs and radio broadcasts constituted a form of radio resonance, as they are clear examples of how listeners "talk" about radio. Whereas the radio resonance of Axis radio broadcasts increased interest in Axis radio stations and amplified their message, vocal critiques of AIR's programming ultimately moved listeners away from AIR's programs. Encouraged by these discussions, radio listeners abandoned the government-run radio station and turned their dials to foreign radio stations, whose broadcasts better suited their musical tastes. I argue that notwithstanding the Indian government's aggressive campaign to reform listening practices and to orchestrate a national soundscape, radio, and music, ultimately, sound itself remained outside the state's grip.

This chapter opens with a brief discussion of the contested idea of classicism in Indian music and then turns to Keskar's understanding of Indian classical music and his aspirations for its revival. I consider how ideas about music, sound, and radio's distinctive faculties justified and informed AIR's cultural uplift campaign. My focus is on government policies and rhetoric as opposed to the more in-depth analysis of broadcast material found in other chapters. As I show in the pages that follow, the government's policies and rhetoric and the debates that surrounded them are deeply revealing of the politics of the sound that characterized the time. In a subsequent section, I outline AIR's reforms, focusing on music programming and linguistic policies. I analyze how Keskar and his supporters imagined citizenship as an auditory practice. The chapter closes by explaining the challenges to AIR's ambitious campaign. I demonstrate that the campaign had long-lasting effects but ultimately failed to contain its citizens' auditory experiences.

Defining Classical Music

In his many radio speeches, Keskar remarked that his main objective as minister of information and broadcasting was to usher in a revival of Indian classical music traditions through the medium of radio. But what exactly is Indian classical music? One answer is that Indian classical music consists of two largely separate musical traditions: the Hindustani in the north and the Carnatic in the south. The two traditions have "highly developed theories, musical forms, performance contexts, and stylistic lineages that pass on practical knowledge orally."[19] Scholars of Indian musical traditions, however, have arduously debated the meaning of the term "classical" in the Indian context. "The word 'classical,' " Katherine Schofield writes, is "multivalent and slippery"; the label, once used to refer to literature or material artifacts from ancient Rome and Greece, bears an obvious Eurocentric overtone.[20]

Indeed, a number of recent works have argued that the very notion of "classical music" in India emerged under the shadow of British colonialism. Amanda Weidman argues that not only discourses about Carnatic music in South India but also "the very sound and practice of music" were produced "in and through the colonial encounter."[21] Similarly, in an earlier publication, Janaki Bakhle maintains that Hindustani music in North India transformed from being an "unmarked practice" in the eighteenth century to being marked as classical music in the twentieth. Bakhle also maintains that "colonialism marked the ideological epistemological beginnings" of this important change.[22]

Disagreeing with both scholars, Schofield maintains that "many of the shifts marked out by the most recent scholarship as uniquely a product of the British colonial moment" were actually "foreshadowed in a much earlier process of veneration, canonization, standardization, and systematization" in the Mughal courts.[23] For example, Mughal court audiences and musicians regarded Hindustani classical music genres like *Khayāl* and *Dhrupad* as "elite" and "refined" long before the advent of British colonialism in the subcontinent.[24] Regardless of whether Indian classical music underwent a "process of classification" in the Mughal period, during the late colonial period, or both, it is clear that by the 1950s a notion of "classical" or "art" music had been established— however fluid, inconsistent, and even contradictory that idea might have been. Keskar believed that radio had the power to bring that form of classical or art music to the "masses" of India.[25]

The Ghost of Music Past

Keskar's radio campaign was as ambitious as it was elitist. It sought to bring high culture to what he called "the mass of the people."[26] Keskar, however, did acknowledge the difficulties and contradictions within such a project. He explained: "It is natural that the section of the society with higher emotional development and education enjoys and appreciates the more developed and more abstract type of music."[27] He went on to explain that not all people share the same musical sensibilities: "The more developed people, who read and write . . . require a more complex vehicle to express" their thoughts and ideas.[28] Keskar, however, had unyielding faith in the power of the medium of radio to influence society, and he believed that radio would "lift" the "sound standards" of the newly formed country.[29]

Keskar's campaign, however, was as much about rescuing classical music as it was about rescuing listeners from their unfit musical sensibilities, habits, and tastes. Almost without fail, Keskar began discussions on Indian classical music with a melodramatic description of its dire current state: "Classical music is in the doldrums"; "Music is an orphan wandering aimlessly for help";[30] "As things stand today, music has been left to itself to drift with the stream or sink."[31] His analysis of the causes of music's unfortunate condition followed a complex trajectory borrowed from a nationalist and communalist narrative about India's pre-Islamic past.[32]

Keskar, like many other Hindu nationalists, sought to revive an imagined "golden Hindu age." He described the revival of classical music as a return to an unadulterated past and blamed Muslims—both patrons of music and musicians—for classical music's decline. In the pre-Islamic past, Keskar argued, music had been intimately woven into religious life: "In the temples and in worship music was a vital medium. It was considered to be one of the most sublime ways of attaining God. Some of the greatest musicians were saints."[33] He also professed, without providing any evidence, that "in ancient times in every family[,] instruction in music was a must while giving education to children."[34]

Muslim rule in India, Keskar claimed, corrupted that pristine "Hindu" musical tradition because Islam frowns upon music and discourages adherents from listening to music and from playing it. Even though many Muslim rulers had been generous patrons of music, under their benefaction, the meaning of music changed. In Mughal courts, Keskar argued, music became the purview of "dancing girls, prostitutes, and their circle of pimps."[35] Under Muslim rule, music in India went from being a source of divine inspiration and worship for the middle classes to becoming a means of entertainment, often of questionable nature, for the rich and powerful. Keskar argued that "respectable" North Indian Hindus, eager to preserve their piety, had no choice but to turn away from music. Strategically absent from Keskar's speeches are the various ways Muslim musicians, not only in India but throughout the world, have used music as a source of spiritual inspiration.

Islamic rule, the minister of information and broadcasting explained, did not penetrate nearly as deeply in the south as it did in the north. Safe from Muslim influence, he argued, Carnatic music enjoyed an "uninterrupted flow of old tradition."[36] The result was that in the south, music retained its respectability and continued to be intimately associated with Hindu religious life. This, however, also meant that the spread of Islam in the north had another unfortunate consequence: it created an artificial rift between northern and southern styles of music. Because of Muslim influence, Keskar insisted, music in these two regions grew apart and Carnatic and Hindustani music eventually became two separate systems.[37] He maintained that Islam, therefore, not only had corrupted and desacralized musical practices but also had partitioned India's musical heritage.

The British, Keskar asserted, "are the most unmusical people."[38] Unlike Muslim rulers, the British did not actively try to impose their own musical preference on Indian society in great part because they had no "taste" for music whatsoever.[39] Indian musical traditions remained safe from European influence, but in the absence of interest or patronage, music "dried up," surviving only in the courts of princely states throughout India.[40] Rulers of states, such as Gwalior, Baroda, and Indore, saved this art from complete extinction. Eventually, however, these princely rulers too began to imitate British ways and showed less and less interest in music.[41] The problem, Keskar explained, was that the unmusical British colonial rulers had caused even greater harm than initially was apparent: they had trained a "new generation" of Indian elite in British ways, with no interest or background in their country's musical traditions. The Indian elite's plan for the new India, therefore, had no room for music.

Music's story, Keskar maintained, was not all doom and gloom. In the early twentieth century, an important movement arose to restore music's due place in society, championed by two men: Vishnu Bhatkhande and Vishnu Paluskar.[42] These two reformers labored to reestablish music's respectability. They achieved some degree of success in popularizing music among respectable, upper-caste families, particularly, although not only, in their native Maharashtra (also Keskar's native region). Keskar admired these reformers' work and borrowed their ideas, convictions, and even rhetorical techniques. He believed, however, that their campaigns had achieved limited success. Bhatkhande and Paluskar had influenced middle-class women and men and had convinced them that Hindustani music was as "highly intellectual and respectable as any other branch of art and learning."[43] The masses of India, Keskar argued, sadly remained mostly ignorant of Indian classical music traditions. Radio, Keskar repeatedly preached, would bring classical music to the common people and restore classical music's lost glory.[44]

The Power of Music

To justify his campaign, Keskar insisted that music was different from any other art. Music, he explained, "regulates the orderly expression of the primeval emotional forces."[45] He linked music to the emotional, irrational, and even primeval qualities of humans. Music, he argued, was not just a matter of personal taste or refinement; it was "the language of expressing emotions."[46]

In his interpretation of music's powers, Keskar clearly drew on an understanding of human senses—namely, sight and hearing—as inherently separate and belonging to opposing domains. Jonathan Sterne famously coined the term "audio-visual litany" to refer to the idea that "vision is about exteriority, hearing about interiority. Vision is objective. Hearing is affective, emotional, subjective and so on."[47] In recent years sound studies scholars have, as Judith Coffin nicely puts it, "shredded the binary logic" that associates hearing with emotions and interiority and seeing with objectivity.[48] These scholars have demonstrated that these ideas have long been exagerated, not only by historical actors but also by academics who have bolstered assertations about the distinctive qualities of sounds.[49] I am less interested in proving or disproving ideas about the unique qualities of sound and music than I am in understanding their historical significance *within* the subcontinent and, most important, in tracing *how* these ideas informed and validated AIR's social uplift campaign of the 1950s.

Ideas about music's intrinsic powers bear a strong cultural resonance with historical documents of the subcontinent. Texts such as the *Nāṭyaśāstra*, composed sometime between the first and fifth centuries and significantly expanded in later centuries, provide a detailed theoretical account of music and other arts' effect on the emotions.[50] Similarly, Indo-Persian treatises from the eighteenth century discuss the power of music to move emotions in extensive detail. In Mughal courts, music was widely believed to "arouse tranquility, melancholy, longing" and to produce "truth, discernment, and even enlightenment in the seeker of righteousness."[51] In equal measure, Mughal writings also cautioned listeners about music's potential dangers. Music of the wrong kind or from the wrong sort of source, they noted, could make men of influence lose foresight and, consequently, squander their wealth and political power. In these texts, music is likened to a courtesan, whose beauty had a hypnotic and magnetic power that could sway even the most unyielding of men.[52] Certainly, much remains to be done on perceptions of music's power in the Indian context and how these changed over time. But it is clear that the claim by some sound studies scholars that the "audio-visual litany" is somehow a Judeo-Christian construction requires some serious rethinking.[53] For our purposes, what I wish to emphasize is that, exaggerated or not, notions of music's extraordinary power to move emotions and to govern so-called interiors had a strong cultural resonance in the Indian subcontinent and, in the 1950s, ideas about music's extraordinary powers both informed and justified AIR's reforms.

Rajendra Prasad, then president of India, remarked in a radio broadcast in November 1958 that "the question whether music is a means of human welfare or just an end in itself[, a] source of comfort only to the singer[,] is not quite relevant for us because the effect of music on man and human society is there for anyone to see."[54] An acoustic analogy would have served Prasad better, but he still succeeded in making his main point: music affects individuals and societies in ways that are difficult to pinpoint, but that are nonetheless every bit as real. Music's power, he argued, was all the more resilient precisely because it affected people in ways that they could not fully comprehend or control. Debating the power of music and its effect on human beings, Prasad argued, was beside the point. He noted, we must "accept the power that music wields and then try to cultivate it for recreation and edification according to the requirements of the individual and the human society."[55] Prasad implied, if not quite stated, that the government, as a benefactor and protector of its citizens, should become involved in musical matters. Keskar, however, was much more explicit than the president and asserted that the government of the newly formed nation of India must "step in" and "support the evolution of sound standards."[56]

If music was linked to the individual's soul, Keskar argued, it also was related to the nation's psyche. A newly formed country must pay especial attention to music: the "absence of this important aspect of a plan for a new society can only result in making the society defective and weak in its most important aspect[s], i.e. emotional and moral."[57] It is noteworthy that the language Keskar and his supporters embraced to justify and explain AIR's reforms resembles the language of nineteenth-century Colombian reformers, who, like Keskar in the mid-twentieth century, were deeply concerned with the soul of their nation in the making. As Ochoa Gautier notes, these reformers and government officials came to believe that "music" was essential to the "edification of the citizen"[58] and that music was a "standard bearer for an ethical training."[59] Ochoa Gautier's research demonstrates the central role that ideas about music and the powers lawmakers attached to it played during a turning point in Colombian history. Similarly, in midcentury India, also a turning point following independence from British rule, ideas about the power of music and its relationship to citizenship played a crucial role.[60]

Although music was vital to all nations, Keskar argued, it was even more important to India. Music was one of the few arts that was "100 percent Indian" and had survived centuries of unadulterated British imperialism.[61] Recent scholarship has turned this generalization on its head, demonstrating that colonialism in fact did engender important changes in musical traditions.[62] Keskar and his supporters, however, were correct in pointing out that western classical music had not made inroads in Indian society as deeply as it had in other regions of the world. Only a small fraction of the English-educated Indian population listened to and appreciated western classical music.[63] Hindustani and Carnatic classical music's resilience in the face of an all-pervasive colonialism, Keskar believed (along with many in and out of the Indian government), should be a source of national pride and justified government intervention in musical matters.

Programs and Reforms

Ideas about the power of radio to influence individuals and societies were as important to AIR's cultural uplift campaign as were conceptions of music and sound's special faculties. Keskar theorized the power of radio in terms of what this medium could do for music. "Radio," he explained in a broadcast address to the nation, "stands for music."[64] Keskar envisioned the national broadcasting institution as a patron of Indian music—ironically, not very different from the Mughal courts he so ardently criticized. As a government-run institution, AIR not only would provide financial support for musicians and offer a platform for their performances but also would dictate standards and reform musical tastes.[65]

To become the "greatest patron of music in the world," Keskar believed AIR first needed to build a strong and centralized radio network. By the 1950s, Indian government officials took it for granted that a government-run and government-funded radio network constituted the best way to make use of the technology of radio. Yet AIR's structure was in many ways a colonial vestige.[66] The British colonial government had been fearful of any kind of commercial broadcasting not least because it feared that anticolonial leaders would take control of the medium and use it to campaign against British rule (for information on how the outbreak of World War II and the popularity of Axis propaganda spurred AIR's development, see chapter 1).[67] After independence, Nehru's socialist-leaning government eliminated any possibility of ever considering a private broadcasting system or even a government-supported independent broadcasting company on par with the BBC.

Moreover, as minister of information and broadcasting, Sardar Vallabhbhai Patel played a major role integrating princely states into the Indian union (sometimes through diplomacy and many other times by force) and with equal zest incorporated radio stations from former princely states into a national broadcasting network.[68] When he joined Nehru's administration in 1952, Keskar continued his predecessors' efforts, both British and Indian, to centralize radio broadcasting in India.

Keskar, like many in Nehruvian government, invoked the language of scarcity as justification for centralization: "In order to utilize our resources to the best advantage it is necessary to rationalize and restrict the number of stations to the minimum and try to give through them programs of better quality to the listening public."[69] Keskar used government funds to increase the number of broadcast hours and to purchase more powerful transmitters that would widen existing stations' reach and was hesitant to open new radio stations. Keskar even ordered the closure of a radio station in Aurangabad, a city in his native state of Maharashtra, arguing that the larger Bombay station could cover the region's needs. Aurangabad residents, protesting the closure of their local station, wrote to the prime minister demanding government support for local programming.[70] Their complaints, however, fell on deaf ears not least because Keskar's centralization policies aligned with Nehru's belief in a strong central government.[71]

Keskar most actively encouraged the centralization of music production. He recruited top artists from across the country and brought them to the Delhi station. Under his leadership, the Delhi AIR station transformed into a national music production center that provided recorded programs to smaller regional radio stations. Most important, Keskar also inaugurated a number of influential national musical programs, which were produced in Delhi and relayed to other locations.

The most famous of these programs was the *National Programme for Music*, an hour-long radio program that featured the country's top Hindustani and Carnatic musicians during weekend nights, then (and still) a peak listening time. The program was recorded in Delhi and relayed to other regional stations. AIR staff encouraged Carnatic and Hindustani musicians to perform on the same evening. Keskar hoped AIR, as a patron of classical music, would help bring Carnatic and Hindustani music traditions "nearer [to] each other" and ensure that these traditions could "march together."[72]

Musicians from both Carnatic and Hindustani traditions came to regard performing in the *National Programme* as a major badge of honor, and many classical music enthusiasts became devout followers of the program. AIR staff took great care to select the performers and the pieces featured in the program but made little effort to connect with audiences. The *National Programme*, as a result, never acquired a significant following among nonspecialist audiences, and musicians were aware of the program's limited reach. Daniel Neuman conducted fieldwork in the Delhi AIR station in the 1960s and noted that a popular saying among musicians was that "fewer than 1 percent of the listening public tune[d] to the *National Programme*."[73]

Large instrumental ensembles were not part of either the Hindustani or the Carnatic musical traditions, but Keskar believed that India needed to have its own national orchestra and that AIR should be its patron. Before Keskar's appointment, AIR had two small instrumental ensembles, a Hindustani and a Carnatic one. These ensembles formed part of the External Service Division, a subsection of AIR that prepared broadcasts for foreign audiences. After becoming minister of information and broadcasting, Keskar shifted the ensembles out of the somewhat neglected foreign services department to the up-and-coming New Delhi radio station. He combined the two separate groups into a single orchestra and made Ravi Shankar and T. K. Jayarama Iyer codirectors. Ravi Shankar had by then trained with the renowned court musician Alauddin Khan for several years and had established himself as one of the nation's top sitar players.[74] Jayarama Iyer, also a recognized musician in South India, directed the Carnatic ensemble. Keskar trusted that these two celebrated musicians representing northern and southern styles of music would work together toward creating a national music. Keskar named the orchestra Vādya Vrinda, a Sanskrit neologism meaning instrumental group, and reserved several hours a week of programming for the orchestra's performances. By the end of 1952, Vādya Vrinda had twenty-eight members, including a few western-trained musicians who played woodwind or string instruments.[75] Vādya Vrinda musicians read music from notations and conductors directed musicians with hand gestures, despite the fact that neither practice was standard in Hindustani or Carnatic musical circles.[76] Keskar and his team acknowledged their departure from tradition, but they promised radio audiences that Vādya Vrinda's music would "retain an Indian character."[77] Most famously, some of Ravi Shankar's earliest experiments with fusing western and Hindustani classical music took place in the renowned "studio number one" of AIR's Delhi station, where he spent countless hours practicing with the national orchestra.[78] Undeniably, Vādya Vrinda was a fascinating enterprise that merits its own study. What I wish to emphasize, however, is that Vādya Vrinda exemplifies Keskar's contradictory desire to at once prove that Indian music was on par with the so-called western tradition and at the same time protect Indian music—its musicians and listeners—from too much "foreign" influence.

In addition to ensuring that AIR would support and offer a platform to the nation's most talented musicians through Vādya Vrinda and the *National Programme*, Keskar also wanted AIR to encourage budding musicians. To this end, he established several amateur music competitions and inaugurated beginners' music lessons and music appreciation programs for uninitiated listeners. In these programs, music teachers—usually trained in formal music academies—taught radio audiences the rudimentary concepts of Hindustani and Carnatic classical music.[79]

Keskar, however, paid attention not only to musical programming but also, as David Lelyveld notes, to the "kind of people" that worked at AIR. He recruited directors of music academies and appointed them to AIR's top posts. He, for example, appointed Krishna Ratanjankar to direct the broadcast of classical music at AIR.[80] Ratanjankar had been the first principal of the Marris College of Music in Lucknow and was a student and protégé of the music reformer Vishnu Bhatkhande. Ratanjankar, with Keskar's backing, inaugurated a new audition system that required, among other things, that musicians have knowledge of musical theory. This requirement put many hereditary musicians—who had learned music orally through the more traditional *gurū-śiṣya* (apprentice system) and who had little or no knowledge of musical theory—at a serious disadvantage. The system was clearly meant to favor musicians trained in professional academies, who were more often than not Hindu, upper-caste, and middle class. As Max Katz notes, musical academies' goal of "liberation of knowledge from hereditary musicians" had created institutional structures that put Muslim musicians, trained in a kinship-oriented apprentice system, at a great disadvantage.[81]

Keskar's policies did not go unchallenged. Some, in and out of music circles, accused Keskar of showing preference for upper-caste Maharastrian Hindu musicians. P. N. Rajbhoj, a representative of the Schedule Castes Federation, pointed out in a public parliamentary hearing that members of scheduled castes were not encouraged to participate in AIR music programs.[82] The Bharatiya Sangeet Kalakar Mandal, a musical organization led by the renowned Hindustani classical musician Mogubai Kurdikar, led a protest against AIR's audition policies, which Kurdikar argued discriminated against musicians trained in the apprentice system.[83] The matter became so heated that it reached the prime minister's desk. Keskar felt compelled to defend AIR's hiring policies to Nehru himself: "Whether in U.P. [Uttar Pradesh], Madhya Pradesh[,] or Punjab, the important musical educational institutions are guided and directed by eminent Maharashtrians for the simple reason that other persons are not available for that purpose." Keskar went on to explain: "The Muslim musicians whose number[s] are dwindling suffer under the handicap of illiteracy and they are not, therefore, capable of doing general cultural work [with the] exception [of] giving music performances."[84] Creating music, Keskar therefore concluded, was not enough. Musicians also had to conduct "cultural work" and that meant promoting classical music as a respectable middle-class and, to a large extent, an upper-caste Hindu profession.

Samācār meṅ hindī sunīe (Now Listen to the Hindi in News)

Keskar's communalism is also evident in AIR's language policies. As minister of information and broadcasting, Keskar carried on Sardar Vallabhbhai Patel's language policies. Patel, considered to be one of the most communalist leaders of the new India, actively pushed policies that hurt Muslim communities.[85] Patel simultaneously headed the Departments of Home Affairs and Information and Broadcasting before the official departure of the British as part of an interim government. Arguably, Patel's most influential broadcasting policy was eliminating Hindustani broadcasting in favor of separate Hindi and Urdu programs. Patel ensured that AIR's linguistic partitioning preceded the subcontinent's partition.[86] As we might expect, Hindi broadcasts took precedence, with only a few stations broadcasting programs in Urdu.[87] Moreover, under Patel's leadership, the controller of broadcasting, Ahmed Shah Bukhari (commonly known as Patras Bukhari), who was not only Muslim but also a prominent Urdu writer, faced heavy censure. Patras Bukhari eventually migrated to

Pakistan, it appears at least in part because of the pressure he felt at AIR, giving up his career in broadcasting altogether and taking up a teaching position in the Government College in Lahore (see chapter 1).[88]

As AIR became more centralized and more programs were produced in Delhi and relayed to regional stations under Keskar, Hindi broadcasting in non-Hindi-speaking areas increased in the first decades of independence.[89] During Keskar's tenure, however, it was the type of Hindi that became a major point of controversy and, in particular, the Hindi of news bulletins. Hindi bulletins had to be concise, could not use colloquial language, and were the furthest away from spoken language. Under Keskar's tenure, Hindi news bulletins became increasingly Sanskritized, as writers bent over backward to avoid the more colloquially used Persian- and Arabic-origin words. One newspaper account explained: "News bulletins in Hindi have become increasingly difficult to understand" because they are "embellished with Sanskrit terminology." The critic went on to explain that "the educated Hindi scholar may find much praise in the elaboration of the language, and in the occasionally painful dexterity of the harassed news readers in pronouncing difficult obsolete words," but the "the poor listener" was unable understand "the state of the world around him, which, incidentally[, was] the reason why he listen[ed] to news bulletins."[90] Hindi news bulletins started with the following phrase: "*hindī meṅ samācār sunīe*" (Now listen to *news* in Hindi). Radio listeners would joke that a more appropriate introduction would be "*samācār meṅ hindī sunīe*" (Now listen to the *Hindi* in news) to emphasize that the awkwardness and difficulty of the language was the most distinctive part of the broadcast.[91]

In the early 1960s, shortly after leaving the Ministry of Information and Broadcasting, Keskar wrote to Nehru to absolve himself of any wrongdoing: "I am not the author of A.I.R.'s Hindi. It was started long before me. Certainly[,] a great deal of expansion took place while I was there for 10 years but a large part was due to expansion of A.I.R.'s network."[92] Indeed, Keskar might not have initiated AIR's language reforms, and ultimately, his predecessor, Patel, bore greater responsibility for linguistic reforms at AIR. The initiative to promote Sanskritized Hindi as a national language through the medium of radio, however, had much in common and was deeply tied to the campaign to promote classical music among the "masses of the people."[93] Ultimately, they both sought to create an appropriately "national" soundscape and to mold proper citizens.

Citizen-Listeners

How did Keskar and others at AIR conceive of the listeners they sought to reach through their radio broadcasts? In writings and broadcasts, he spoke about the importance of listeners: "Music lives and flourishes on listeners"; "The listener is the basic unit on which the edifice of music is built"; "The knowledgeable listener who fully understands the beauty and fine points of the art . . . makes for musical progress and builds up the sound tradition."[94] On several occasions, Keskar explained that a music tradition needed first and foremost "discernable listeners" (by which he meant discerning listeners) who not only could tell a good performance from a bad one, but also whose passion for good music would inspire musicians to improve their performance. The ultimate goal of AIR's uplift campaign, therefore, was to create a society of perceptive classical music enthusiasts.

By this time AIR had access to some statistics about radio audiences. One report by the Ministry of Information and Broadcasting estimated that by 1954, there were 759,643 registered receiver licenses in India.[95] Keskar and others at AIR had reason enough to distrust these reports because, among other things, they failed to account for collective listening practices, then (as now) prevalent in India. Keskar seemed little interested in appraising available statistics of listening audiences. His understanding of audiences was based on a broad vision of the polity. He and his associates at AIR conceived of radio audiences as neither individual listeners nor an organized public, but rather as citizens of the newly formed nation-state—that is, as citizen-listeners.

In recent years, scholars of South Asia have argued for rethinking the importance of citizenship in newly independent India. For example, in a recent study about food and citizenship, Benjamin Siegel maintains that "India's leadership proposed a vision of citizenship wherein rights derived from the completion of responsibilities and wherein preferences were to be subsumed in the name of development."[96] In a similar vein, Roy has argued that "in marked contrast with the liberal-democratic norm [of] autonomous citizen[ship]" in postcolonial India, citizenship was defined not as "an already-possessed right or claim that could be exercised in the present," but rather as a "learning activity or an ongoing process of acquiring skills and attributes."[97] A common thread in these works on citizenship is the idea of the citizen as a learner and the state as educator. Keskar too imagined radio audiences as learners "in need of the state's tutelage."[98] Listeners, he remarked, "have developed unmusical manners and attitudes which do not help in creating the proper atmosphere for appreciating music."[99] As the national radio network, AIR's primary task, Keskar explained, was to train listeners to unlearn their bad habits and to ensure that they knew how to properly appreciate Indian classical music traditions.

Hindi Film Songs and Recalcitrant Radio Listeners

Keskar is remembered less for his gargantuan efforts to promote classical music than for his prolonged and tenacious campaign against Hindi film songs.

What often goes unstated is that Keskar joined the Ministry of Information and Broadcasting at an important turning point in the history of film music. Jason Beaster-Jones notes: "One of the primary distinctive features of the Hindi film" is the "inclusion" of film songs. "These song picturizations have been an element of Hindi film since the advent of sound in cinema."[100] Early film songs, like early films, borrowed heavily from various Indian theater song numbers, which in turn drew on Hindustani musical traditions.[101] Musicologists remark that, whereas film songs of the 1930s were "stylistically virtually indistinguishable" from theater song numbers, by the 1940s, film songs had achieved some degree of independence. And by the 1950s, film songs had effectively become a separate genre altogether.[102]

Changes in presentation, voice, instrumentation, and lyrics marked this important transformation. For example, film songs from the 1940s were less likely to include an *ālāp*, a vocal unmetered improvised section that precedes classical and various theatrical music performances.[103] Around this time, vocalists also adopted a "soft" and "narrow" "crooning style," which musicologists have argued was more "appropriate for the microphone" than the loud, open-throated, sometimes coarse, vocal singing style of theater artists.[104] By the late 1940s and early 1950s, instrumental interludes of film songs became longer and more grandiose. Singers joked that in the past musical interludes were meant to give them a chance to catch their breath, whereas now they sang to give the instrumentalists a break from playing.[105] Finally, as Keskar repeatedly pointed out in his various speeches, film songs during this time also began to incorporate a number of so-called foreign elements. For example, even though Hindustani classical music does not traditionally employ harmony, by the 1950s, nearly all Hindi film songs incorporated some form of harmony.[106] Electronic effects, such as echo and artificial reverberation, gave film songs a "new studio-produced 'glossy'" feel that helped listeners instantly identify them as a distinct genre.[107]

Keskar criticized the elements that musicologists describe as marking film songs as a separate genre, particularly their willingness to borrow from non-Indian music traditions. As mentioned earlier, in one radio address, Keskar described Hindi film songs as "concocted [of] irrational cocktails of western dance tunes."[108] In addition to the music, however, the language of Hindi film songs likely also contributed to Keskar's distaste for these songs. As scholars have pointed out, Hindi films also could be called Hindustani film songs because they consciously employed a syncretic language.[109] Some Hindi film songs, however, drew extensively on Urdu poetic traditions and perhaps more accurately could be called Urdu songs.[110] I have not found specific critiques by Keskar or others at AIR about the language of Hindi film songs and their association with Urdu, which by then had become the national language of Pakistan. It is not unlikely that Keskar, who clearly supported Patel's policies against Urdu-language radio programming and promoted AIR's Sanskritized

Hindi, also might have disliked film songs for their association with Urdu literary genres.

Notably, at the same time, Keskar's distaste of film songs had much to do with a wide-ranging stigma toward the film industry, still prevalent in Keskar's time and particularly among his generation. It was common at the time to typecast the film industry and especially female performers as lewd and vulgar.[111] Manishitha Dass has shown that cinema in the colonial period was a site of "demotic" danger. She argues that conceptualizations of film audiences in colonial India demonstrated the friction between idealized visions of cinema as a sort of democratizing power because of its ability to reach those outside of the "lettered city" and anxieties of cinema as a polluting force that ultimately was harmful to the "body politic" because it was deemed unrefined and even lewd.[112] Anxieties about film actresses and actors, and consequently about films as well, being vulgar and therefore harmful to the audiences and to the nation as a whole persisted in the postcolonial period. It is thus not surprising that, at least during the early years of Keskar's tenure as minister of information and broadcasting, some applauded his condemnation of the film industry. One man from Bombay wrote to the film magazine *Movie Times* to congratulate the new minister for having the courage to openly condemn the "low moral tone" of the Bombay film industry.[113] Watching a film, this decrier bemoaned, was "a painful experience" because films were "cheap, sexy, degrading and humiliating."[114] But, at least in public forums, Keskar's most pressing critique of film songs was not that they were "degrading" or "sexy," but that they had veered too far from Indian classical music traditions. It is "difficult," he noted in a broadcast inauguration speech, to "call any such mixture by the name of composition."[115]

One of Keskar's first actions as minister was to place a strict quota on AIR's film-song broadcasts. Programming schedules demonstrate that before Keskar's appointment, most AIR radio stations had dedicated several hours a day to film-song broadcasts. Keskar ordered that film songs make up no more than 10 percent of the national network's music programming and set up a film-music censorship committee to screen film songs.[116] Filmmakers were particularly angered by this decision because it meant that film music now had to endure two stages of government censorship: first, film songs had to meet the approval of the Central Board of Film Censors, which screened the entire film including its songs, and second, film songs now had to pass AIR's own music censorship board.

When Keskar announced one more modification to AIR's policies, the film industry retaliated. The norm at AIR had long been that before or after playing a film song, broadcasters announced the name of the film in which the song originally had appeared. Keskar argued these announcements amounted to free publicity for films and thus violated AIR's commitment to noncommercial broadcasting. As a result, Keskar ordered that all music show hosts stop announcing the names of films in their programs and maintained that this decision was justified. AIR, he argued, was a public institution and could not provide publicity for a commercial industry.[117] Keskar's comments against film songs' commerciality were not idiosyncratic, but rather reflected a socialist-leaning government's uneasiness with the idea that culture could somehow be marketable and profitable.

Shortly thereafter, the president of the Indian Motion Picture Production Association (IMPPA) called an extraordinary meeting to discuss the new reform. He maintained that out of "sheer self-respect," if nothing else, Indian filmmakers must once and for all cut all ties to AIR. He noted that if AIR was unwilling to accurately credit film songs, then the national broadcasting organization should not play them at all.[118] Keskar responded to IMPPA's announcement by refusing to play these songs on the national radio network.

AIR's diatribe against film songs unleashed an ardent debate over these songs, their propriety, and their relationship to national consciousness. Keskar's biggest quandary with film songs was they had lost ties with the region's traditional music. Some radio listeners shared Keskar's concern. M. C. Zainul Hussain addressed film-music directors in an editorial note: "Why stoop so low and copy music of other lands when we are fortunate [to have] an excellent base in our various ragas for compositions?"[119] In a similar vein, K. Ahmed from Hyderabad wrote to the *Movie Times* to complain that many new Hindi film songs were but a "cheap copy" of Hollywood tunes.[120] Ahmed felt especially frustrated because directors like Naushad, Ramchandra, and S. D. Burman clearly had the knowledge and musical training to compose film songs that remained true to the basic principles of India's classical traditions, but they stubbornly refused to do so.[121]

Many within the film industry also held similar trepidations about film music's growing westernization. In the month following AIR's ban, editorials by music directors discussing their music filled the pages of film magazines and newspapers. For example, R. C. Boral, a veteran in the field, wrote an editorial in *Filmfare*, wary of the growing westernization of film songs. He explained that it was a good thing that music directors were now aware of the musical traditions of other regions, and he praised directors' willingness to experiment. He insisted, however, that they should "remain true to [Indian] soil, where there is abundance of material to draw from and give forth rich and glorious melodies that can be found in the vast storehouse of our 'shastric' and folk music."[122] Boral shared Keskar's concern that the growing popularity of film songs ultimately threatened Indian classical traditions and remarked that "the present trend will extinguish Indian melodies."[123] Moreover, filmmakers, many of whom were deeply affected by the ban, also participated in this debate through the medium they knew best: film. It is not a coincidence that during Keskar's tenure, three major films that chronicled the lives of classical musicians made it to the big screens: *Baiju Bāvrā*, *Shabāb*, and *Basant Bahār*.[124]

While some listeners were receptive to Keskar's complaints about westernization of film music, few agreed with AIR's ban. Keskar justified his controversial ban on film music by arguing that AIR, the national broadcasting station, had a special responsibility to uplift the masses. Listeners, however, turned Keskar's logic on its head and began to define film music as the music of the masses or the music of the common people.[125] The opinion pages of film magazines from the early 1950s point to a different understanding of the value of film music framed in opposition to AIR reforms that warrants attention. A listener from Bombay wrote to the *Movie Times* to explain her dissatisfaction with AIR's new policies: "A large section of the *masses*" purchases radios "only [to] hear a variety of film music without undergoing extra cost." Implicit in her letter is the idea that by banning Hindi film songs, AIR was not uplifting the masses as the minister and his supporters claimed, but rather denying them the right to listen to the music they liked. One listener with a good sense of humor accused Keskar and his supporters of engaging in an "orgy of self-righteous[ness]." But perhaps most revealing is a letter in *Filmfare* penned in 1952, the year that Keskar inaugurated AIR's reform. "Music in India was largely confined to the temple and the palace before the advent of films. The films brought music to the common man," explained one dissatisfied listener writing to the magazine.[126] In reality, nonelites in India had had access to music long before the advent of films. However, this listener's point is nonetheless important because it demonstrates how listeners, largely in response to AIR's ban, began to describe film songs as the music of the "common man." As another listener remarked in the editorial page of *Filmfare*, "the versatility of film music and its appeal to all segments of society explains its continuing popularity and establishes its significance as a *mass-art*."[127] In perhaps the most vivid editorial I have encountered, a listener explained that following "a hard-day's toil the common man cannot listen to classical music even if it is forced into his ears." She remarked: "Classical music is for those whose dogs take bread and butter, but not for *the public*."[128]

Listeners clearly made up the strongest voice against AIR's social uplift program, but Keskar did face resistance from some elite members of the Indian government. For example, Harindranath Chattopadhyaya, a poet and musician member of the parliament, ardently criticized B. V. Keskar's handling of AIR during a public parliamentary hearing in April 1954. Others in the parliament, however, came to Keskar's defense, among them Pandit Balkrishna Sharma, a representative from the Uttar Pradesh, and R. Velayudhan from Tranvancore-Cochin. That afternoon the parliament voted to fund AIR's reforms.[129]

The ardent debate over film songs, their propriety, and their relationship to national consciousness that unleashed following AIR's unofficial ban of film songs constituted a form of radio resonance. After all, the opinions of radio listeners printed in film magazines as well as transcripts of parliamentary debates are written evidence of what was clearly part of a larger conversation about radio and specifically about AIR's radio music programming. Similarly, critiques of AIR's unintelligible Hindi-language news bulletins were also a form of radio resonance because they, too, are examples of how people "talked" about radio. Yet whereas the radio resonance of Axis broadcasts in World War II increased interest in Axis radio stations and ultimately increased their popular ambit, critiques of AIR's programming moved listeners away from the government station. As I further describe in the next section and in chapter 4, these discussions encouraged listeners to stop tuning in to AIR altogether and to instead tune in to radio stations whose musical preferences better suited their tastes.

All India Radio's "Sweet" Music

Keskar and his supporters did not turn a deaf ear to the criticisms of its programs, and in particular to listeners' complaints that classical music programs were not of interest to the common listener. AIR inaugurated "light music production units" in various stations to compose and record film-like songs. AIR called this alternate film-music Sugam Sangīt, which roughly translates to "easy," "sweet," "light," or even "melodious" music. These songs, Keskar explained, would be simple and easy to put to memory, but they would avoid the many flaws of film songs, namely westernized tunes and erotic or meaningless lyrics. Ironically, AIR recruited artists from the film industry to work in the station to make the songs more attractive to a popular audience.[130] The famous music director Anil Biswas, who had long been critical of the film industry's embrace of European musical elements, worked for AIR and composed tunes for Sugam Sangīt.

A radio critic who wrote a weekly column for *The Statesman* and called himself Vigilante wrote extensively about Sugam Sangīt. His critical columns are one of the few available accounts of this ambitious AIR production. Vigilante wrote that AIR had inaugurated this new scheme with a "fanfare of trumpets," but that ultimately, Sugam Sangīt proved to be a great disappointment.[131] Vigilante criticized the "monotony" of the compositions and the "paucity" of the singers.[132] On one rare occasion, he remarked that the song "Ītnī dūr kinārā" (A shore/edge so far) was "the right type" because it had "simple, effective words" and it was "sang [sic] in a pleasant manner."[133] No other Sugam Sangīt composition merited his praise. In a series of weekly columns, he explained that film music had a "certain attraction and thrill for the ordinary listener" that AIR had been unable to replicate. Sugam Sangīt tunes, he explained, certainly had "praiseworthy" motifs and strove to "improve the morals," but they were not "food for love." Vigilante asserted that, compared with film songs, Sugam Sangīt compositions sounded "crude" and "amateurish."[134]

Even while congratulating the staff of these music units for "achieving a fair amount of success," Sumati Mutatkar, the director of music at AIR and a renowned Hindustani classical musician, acknowledged that Sugam Sangīt's songs simply could not compete with film songs. Mutatkar explained: "While listening to a film song out of its context the listeners visualize the situation and this adds great charm and appeal to the song." Vigilante was a lot blunter: the AIR program "makes the listener yawn and stretch his hands towards the knob."[135]

Indeed, many listeners in India dissatisfied with AIR programming refused to tune in and instead searched for other radio stations. In the wake of AIR's controversy over programming, Radio Ceylon, a commercial radio station in the nearby country of Ceylon (now Sri Lanka) that broadcast mostly film songs, rose to prominence. One AIR employee commented on a popular saying that circulated in the 1950s that nine out of ten receivers were tuned to Radio Ceylon and the tenth was out of service.[136]

As AIR lost audiences to Radio Ceylon, some within AIR tried to convince Keskar to pull back on its policies. The poet Narendra Sharma asked Keskar to reintroduce film songs to the national network.[137] Facing shrinking audiences and ardent criticisms, Keskar finally relented in October 1957 and began rolling back his aggressive reform. That year AIR inaugurated Vividh Bharti, a variety music station based in Bombay that included film songs in its programs. But by then, Radio Ceylon had reached immense popularity in India and beyond. Moreover, AIR, even as it began to retract many of Keskar's policies, never quite shed the paternalistic ethos forged to a great extent during this time.[138]

Conclusion

By charting a set of ambitious reforms to the Indian national broadcasting network and carefully tuning in to their communal undertones, in this chapter, I question long-held assumptions about the secularism and inclusivity of Nehru's administration. More important, I also demonstrate that conceptions of citizenship in newly independent India were closely linked to notions of aurality and invite scholars studying music, sound, and soundscapes in other regions to more seriously consider sound's relationship to notions of citizenship.[139]

AIR's cultural uplift campaign sought to forge a soundscape for the new nation and to educate and, more important, to discipline citizen-listeners. Keskar, and others at AIR, conceived of citizen-listeners as docile; listeners, however, proved to be quite the opposite. Dissatisfied with AIR's programming, listeners criticized the station's programming in the pages of film magazines and in everyday discussions. Most notably, they protested AIR's reforms by turning the knobs of their radios away from the Indian government-run network and by tuning in to foreign and commercial stations, whose choice of music better fit their musical tastes. In this way, these recalcitrant radio listeners ensured that radio, music, and sound itself ultimately escaped the state's grip.

CHAPTER 4

RADIO CEYLON, KING OF THE AIRWAVES

In the summer of 1944, largely in response to newspaper reports, the British government ordered an investigation into the low morale and poor working conditions of British soldiers stationed in South and Southeast Asia. The official report, prepared in November 1944, concluded that soldiers were, indeed, suffering from low morale and made several recommendations. These included improving medical facilities and providing larger beer and cigarette rations and better radio programs.[1] In response to the specific recommendations regarding radio broadcasting, the War Office, which handled military-related logistics, came up with an ambitious plan: setting up a transmitter in Delhi that would be powerful enough to reach British soldiers anywhere the war in Asia would take them.[2] The War Office surmised that access to radio, in particular, listening to "authentic news from home" and enjoying the latest musical hits, would offer disillusioned British soldiers a much-needed "link home," and would boost soldiers' morale.[3] That summer, the War Office asked the Marconi Company to construct a state-of-the-art one-hundred-kilowatt shortwave transmitter—about as powerful as possible then—and initiated the complicated arrangements to ship the transmitter, which took up an entire room, to the Indian capital.[4]

Louis Mountbatten, a media-savvy individual, famous for his skill at public relations and tendency for showmanship, immediately took an interest in the ambitious radio project and its Marconi-built transmitter. Mountbatten is best known in the Indian subcontinent for his role as the last British viceroy of India.[5] His decision to hasten the British retreat from the subcontinent in

1947, many historians believe, contributed to the turmoil that followed independence.[6] Yet for the history of radio and music, it was Mountbatten's prior, lesser-known military post as the supreme commander of the South East Asia Command (SEAC) that proved most influential.[7] To sidestep the bureaucracy of the colonial government of India and the growing anticolonial movement, Mountbatten decided to shift his command offices to the nearby island of Ceylon.[8] He then lobbied hard and succeeded in bringing the Marconi transmitter to the island instead of India as originally planned and set up a brand-new station in Ceylon exclusively for British soldiers. He called the station Radio SEAC, after his command's initials.[9]

Ultimately, Radio SEAC did not turn out to be the prominent military radio station Mountbatten had envisioned. A dock strike and other war-related hindrances set back the transmitter's arrival. It was not until May 1946 that the famed and powerful Marconi transmitter finally aired its first broadcast from Ceylon.[10] By then, the war had been over for more than a year, and Mountbatten was making plans to leave the island.[11] It was in the 1950s and afterward that the military transmitter, now in the hands of the independent Ceylonese movement, finally reached its full potential. Shortly after the country's independence in 1948, Ceylon launched a Hindi-language commercial service targeting listeners in newly independent India and Pakistan. The station, however, rose to fame toward the end of 1952 when, as detailed in the previous chapter, All India Radio (AIR) inaugurated an ambitious set of reforms. In the wake of these reforms, Radio Ceylon began broadcasting Hindi film-song programs and quickly began to garner a loyal audience in newly independent India and Pakistan. In the decades to come, Radio Ceylon and the film industry in Bombay developed an important reciprocal commercial relationship. Film producers provided the music that helped Radio Ceylon attract listeners and sponsors to its Hindi-language programs. Radio Ceylon broadcasters, in turn, not only made these songs widely available on the airwaves but also developed programs that consciously fostered listeners' active participation in radio programs.

What Mountbatten could not have possibly known in the summer of 1944 was that shifting his command from India to Ceylon and bringing the transmitter to the island would have such important consequences for the history of sound and radio in the Indian subcontinent. In the postindependence period, Radio Ceylon—its broadcasters and listeners—was able to effectively contest the independent Indian government's ambitious reforms to create loyal citizen-listeners because Radio Ceylon, located in the neighboring nation-state island of Ceylon (now Sri Lanka), lay outside the Indian government's jurisdiction, both physically and administratively. Moreover, by cultivating audiences in Pakistan in addition to India, Radio Ceylon broadcasters also indirectly challenged the Pakistani state's efforts to mold a new national culture disconnected from India.

My moment of departure in this chapter, like in the previous one, is AIR's infamous ban of Hindi film songs, which began in 1952 and officially ended half a decade later in 1957. However, I move backward in time—to World War II and to Ceylon's independence in 1948—to make sense of the station's origins as a military wartime radio station, and I move forward in time—to the late 1950s and 1960s—to account for the long-term influence of Radio Ceylon's programs. Even after AIR reinstituted Hindi film-song broadcasts (first in 1957), these broadcasts went out on medium-wave transmitters and their reception was accordingly limited, at least initially. In contrast, Radio Ceylon's wide-reaching shortwave transmitter, which could be heard throughout India and Pakistan, continued to promote a shared culture on the airwaves across state-imposed borders.

Throughout this chapter, I highlight the transnational collaborative nature of Radio Ceylon, paying careful attention to how songs and voices circulated beyond national borders—from Ceylon to India and Pakistan. I also account for technologies' porous borders. After all, Radio Ceylon's productions are an excellent example of what scholars of media have called media convergence or transmedia. Henry Jenkins explains in his paradigm-shifting work that "convergence culture" is composed of (1) "media industry cooperation," (2) "the ensuring of movement of content . . . across media platforms," and (3) "audiences that traverse and participate in this movement."[12] Radio Ceylon—including its broadcasters and producers as well as its radio productions and audiences—constitutes an early example of this development still largely "viewed as contemporary phenomena."[13] Yet while I trace this exchange across various media—radio, film, and gramophone records—my focus remains on audiences' aural experience of films and in placing that sonic experience in the larger context of the Indian subcontinent's cultural and political history.[14] Specifically, I argue that Radio Ceylon helped forged an "aural *filmi* culture" across the borders of postindependence South Asia that was committed to the "ideology of Hindustani" and that enabled the survival of the idea of Hindustan, a religiously inclusive homeland and a regional identity, as a soundscape. Unlike AIR's didactic music programs analyzed in the preceding chapter, Radio Ceylon's programs created a transnational audience and challenged state polices by deliberately fostering listening audiences' active participation in programs and by embracing radio resonance's power. A significant part of the programs' appeal and reason for success, I demonstrate, is that broadcasters developed what media theorist John Durham Peters calls "formats of virtual participation for the absent," that is, broadcasting techniques that encouraged listeners to participate in radio programs.[15] Moreover, these programs also encouraged listeners to develop what Jonathan Sterne calls "audile techniques," which is a systematic and learned form of listening to Hindi film-song radio programs.[16] In the pages that follow, I show how broadcasters trained listeners to decouple songs from films, to recognize the voices of playback singers' and music composers' styles, and to associate personal characteristics to singers and composers.

This chapter has two parts. In the first, I ask how and why a radio station based in Ceylon, a non-Hindi-Urdu-speaking region, came to host an immensely popular commercial station providing a Hindi-Urdu-language service aimed at Indian and Pakistani audiences. In the second part, I turn to the broadcast content, beginning with language. This station's broadcasters, I argue, adhered to what I described earlier as the "ideology of Hindustani" and in this way indirectly challenged both the Indian and Pakistani state policies. I then offer close readings of Radio Ceylon's Hindi film-song programs, including the legendary *Geetmala* program described in the book's introduction. I show that it was through these participatory "formats of communication with the absent" and "audile techniques" that Radio Ceylon was able to forge a transnational aural *filmi* culture and to keep alive the ideology of Hindustani and the notion of Hindustan as a soundscape.

Independent Ceylon's Commercial Radio

When Ceylon gained independence in 1948, the British closed down Mountbatten's Radio SEAC but left behind the powerful military transmitter on the island (see figure 4.1).[17] As soon as British officials learned of the Ceylonese government's desire to use the transmitter for commercial broadcasting, they began to regret letting the broadcasting equipment "out [of their] hands."[18] One alarmed officer noted: "I did not realize what a wide area Radio SEAC

4.1 Radio SEAC transmitter in Ekala, near Colombo (undated, but likely from the late 1940s).

Source: National Archives of Sri Lanka.

can cover." The transmitter's broadcast can "reach into Iraq and to the east to almost the whole of China. It can, of course, reach all the parts of India with great clarity."[19] British officials were particularly worried that U.S. businesses could take advantage and advertise their products on the airwaves "with serious consequences to United Kingdom markets."[20] Moreover, commercial broadcasting *"across frontiers"* they noted, could have unexpected political consequences. "The danger here is that the government may not stop at ordinary commercial broadcasting—toothpaste, magazines, etc.—but might sell time to political bodies, e.g. Hindus and Moslems."[21] As detailed in chapter 1, the fear that native politicians would exploit radio facilities had long worried colonial officials. Now, in a changed political world following the end of colonial rule in South Asia, British officials had few options. The size of the equipment made it impossible to disassemble and ship back to England, and they could do little to stop the independent Ceylonese government from venturing into commercial broadcasting. In March 1949, the former military transmitter, despite British discomfort, aired its first broadcast as Radio Ceylon.[22]

From the beginning, Radio Ceylon involved a complex system of transnational collaboration. Immediately after independence, Ceylonese politicians reached out to the Australian government for assistance with launching a commercial station on Radio SEAC's premises. Australia had developed a unique hybrid system of broadcasting that combined commercial and public service radio. As part of a foreign aid program called Plan Colombo, the Australian government sent out one of their best radio experts to Ceylon. Clifford Dodd, an Australian broadcaster and administrator with more than two decades of experience in commercial radio, became Radio Ceylon's first director of commercial broadcasting in 1948 (see figure 4.2).[23]

Under Dodd's influence, Ceylon adopted an Australian-style mixed broadcasting system.[24] The Ceylonese government managed two separate radio networks: the National Network and the Commercial Service. The National Network relied on government funds, targeted Ceylonese audiences, and aired educational programs. The Commercial Service put out entertainment programs and relied almost exclusively on commercial sponsors for financial support. The Ceylonese government owned and managed both networks, and income from commercial broadcasting—at least in principle, if not always in practice—offset expenses from the public service network.[25] The present study concerns only Radio Ceylon's commercial branch and, more specifically, the commercial service aimed at populations in India and Pakistan, called "India Beam" and later "India-Pakistan Beam." Broadcasters and listeners in India and Pakistan, however, used the generic term "Radio Ceylon" to refer to this service exclusively, and I have done the same in this book.

Much like the Australian commercial radio stations where Dodd had worked, Radio Ceylon's India-Pakistan Beam originally featured music from

4.2 Clifford Dodd at work in his office in Colombo (undated).

Source: National Archives of Sri Lanka.

the United States. For example, a program called *Fran Warren Sings* show-cased the young American female singer's most popular numbers. A program titled *Negro Spirituals* likely replicated the same racist dynamics of the U.S. radio shows that featured African American music. Other more generic sounding musical programs, such as *It's Dance Time, My Songs for You*, and *Singing Americans*, played the latest musical numbers from the United States.[26] All of Radio Ceylon's early programs were in English, a language that only a privileged fraction of the populations of India and Pakistan could understand.

In late 1951, Radio Ceylon began to experiment with Hindi-language transmissions. It is unclear what triggered this important change. What appears to have happened is that Dodd and others at Radio Ceylon sensed that broadcasting in Indian languages and particularly in Hindi, the unofficial national language of India, would attract larger audiences in the subcontinent than English-language programs. The station's first attempts at broadcasting in Indian languages, however, were rather unambitious. Radio Ceylon hired two women originally from India residing in Colombo to host two weekly Hindi-language programs, Vimla and Kamini Ganjwar, later known as the Ganjwar sisters, who aired a number of Hindi film-song programs. Their choice of music, however, does not appear to have been particularly strategic. They likely played Hindi film songs because this was one genre of Indian music readily available on gramophone records at the time.[27]

Radio Ceylon's timing, however, could not have been better. A year after Radio Ceylon started its modest Hindi-language transmissions, AIR stations ceased the broadcast of film songs (see chapter 3). Moreover, one reason why Radio Ceylon was able to quickly garner an audience is that listeners in colonial India had already been conditioned to tune in to the foreign shortwave station during World War II. Listeners throughout the subcontinent had turned their receiver knobs in search of alternative radio stations on the shortwave (see chapters 1 and 2). Many in colonial India had tuned in to Axis radio broadcasts and specifically to Subhas Chandra Bose's broadcasts (and to gossip and discussion about them) to question British accounts of the so-called good war. During the postindependence era, listeners drew on this important radio-listening practice, and once more fiddled with their dials in search of alternative music programs that better suited their musical tastes.

Some tuned in to Radio Goa's transmissions. Goa was a Portuguese colony and its radio station, which was not part of the AIR network, continued to play Hindi film songs. Listeners in Punjab and along the western coast were able to tune in to Radio Pakistan's Karachi and Lahore stations.[28] Radio Pakistan would soon also censor songs from films produced in India as part of a nationalist agenda, not unlike AIR's campaign (see chapters 5 and 6). In this early period, however, Radio Pakistan aired film songs, although not without some restrictions. According to broadcasters, Radio Pakistan during this period avoided playing songs that referenced Hindu mythology or Hinduism in any way.[29] Goan and Pakistani stations were certainly a good option for listeners dissatisfied with AIR's programming, but these stations used low-power transmitters and could be heard only in nearby areas. In contrast, the broadcasts from the Marconi transmitter Mountbatten had brought to Ceylon reached throughout most of India and Pakistan. As mentioned in the book's opening anecdote, one enthusiastic listener in Bombay spoke for many when he wrote to *Movie Times* in February 1953 to express his satisfaction with Radio Ceylon's new Hindi film-song programs. "The change" in programming, he remarked, "is most welcomed."[30]

In addition to radio listeners, Indian film producers too "welcomed" Radio Ceylon's new film-song programs and began regularly mailing gramophone records of new (and sometimes also old) productions to Radio Ceylon's Colombo studios. It was this practice that enabled Radio Ceylon to build a substantial Hindi film-song gramophone library, which broadcasters used in their many Hindi film-song programs. To this day, Radio Ceylon houses what is perhaps the most extensive and complete collection of gramophone records of Indian and Pakistani film songs in the world.[31] This library enabled Radio Ceylon to foster a shared aural culture on the airwaves in the decades following the physical partition (see figure 4.3) as well as enabled Radio Ceylon's transmedia productions.

4.3 Radio Ceylon Hindi film-song gramophone library with Jyoti Parmar, now a Hindi-language broadcaster with Sri Lanka Broadcasting Corporation.

Source: Photo by author.

Notably, royalties do not seem to have been an issue of discussion in this early period, as producers were likely eager to have their music broadcast on the radio. In the late 1960s, however, filmmakers did demand royalties for their songs and, at one point, even threatened to take legal action against Radio Ceylon if the institution did not properly remunerate them.[32]

Radio Ceylon's Sponsored and Sustenance Programs

Back in Colombo, Dodd and his team quickly noticed that AIR's gargantuan reforms, particularly the controversial ban on Hindi film songs, presented a rare opportunity for their station and toiled to make use of it. The Radio Ceylon team, however, faced one major difficulty: how could Dodd and his mostly Sinhala-speaking staff recruit sponsors with an interest in advertising their products to Indian audiences?[33] Radio advertising was a fairly new concept in India, and after the carnage of Partition, which devastated the region's social and economic infrastructure, few businesses wanted to experiment with new forms of advertising. Moreover, Nehru's socialist-leaning government placed strict restrictions on foreign exchange. This meant that Indian businesses had to apply for special permission from the reserve bank to pay for Radio Ceylon's sponsored programs.[34]

Dodd connected with Daniel Molina, a U.S.-born entrepreneur based in Bombay with advertising experience.[35] Molina recruited foreign companies with Indian offices that could bypass the Indian government's restrictions on foreign exchange. Molina managed to convince CIBA, a Swiss chemical company with an Indian branch, to experiment in radio advertising. CIBA sponsored many of Radio Ceylon's pioneering Hindi programs, including the super-hit program *Binaca Geetmala*. Soon other businesses followed CIBA's lead. Britannia Biscuit Corporation, Jay Engineers Works, and Boots Pure Drug Company were among the first companies to advertise their products on Radio Ceylon.[36] Although more research would be required to better assess the profitability of advertising on the radio in this early period, CIBA's and other companies' continued sponsorship of programs suggests that it was a worthwhile investment.

Molina and his associates also began to venture into programming and established a programing branch, which they called Radio Enterprise Services (RES).[37] Hamid Sayani, who already was an established AIR broadcaster and a fairly known voice in India, became RES's first director of programming. Incidentally, Hamid Sayani was also the legendary Hindi broadcaster Ameen Sayani's elder brother and introduced the then still teen-aged Ameen to the art and craft of radio broadcasting.[38]

Magnetic tape copies of RES's programs traveled every week—over the newly operating airlines—from Bombay to Radio Ceylon's Colombo-based studios and were broadcast to India and Pakistan with its powerful former military transmitter. At first, Radio Advertising Services staff recorded programs in a small studio at St. Xavier's College in Bombay. In later years, the company shifted to the heart of the commercial district of Colaba in Bombay, in front of the renowned Regal Cinema. During the peak of Radio Ceylon's popularity, RES occupied the entire floor of the building and commanded a strong presence in the Bombay film world.

Back in Colombo, Dodd put as much enthusiasm into developing a solid Hindi branch in Colombo as he did into building links to India and the Bombay film industry. Clifford Dodd recruited broadcasters from India with experience in either Hindi broadcasting or the film industry. These broadcasters became the hosts of what later came to be known as "sustenance programs." These were Hindi film-music programs that went out live from the Colombo studios and that relied on the stations' extensive Hindi film-song gramophone library. RES's sponsored programs provided the income on which Radio Ceylon subsisted, whereas sustenance programs filled the majority of Radio Ceylon's broadcast hours.[39] This meant that what listeners in India and Pakistan understood as Radio Ceylon's Hindi Service in reality was the combined work of two independent organizations: a commercial radio station owned by the Sri Lankan government and Daniel Molina's private advertising company based in Bombay. Staff from these two organizations worked closely together, but Radio Advertising Services never maintained official ties to Ceylon's government.[40]

It was Radio Ceylon's transnational networks that enabled music and voices to move beyond national borders. The station was owned by the Ceylon government but was managed by an Australian director. A U.S.-born business owner based in Bombay recruited sponsors for the station's varied programs, while Indian broadcasters, some based in Bombay and others in Colombo, anchored Radio Ceylon's various programs. Most important, Radio Ceylon's audiences also crossed borders. In addition to India, the station developed a strong and loyal following in Pakistan.

Pakistani film magazines' references to Radio Ceylon offer important evidence of Radio Ceylon's listenership in Pakistan. In December 1957, for example, one listener discovered that the Pakistani-made film *Bedārī* (Awakening, 1956) was a copy of the earlier released Indian film *Jāgritī* (Awakening, 1954) after listening to *Jāgritī*'s songs on Radio Ceylon's programs.[41] Although the availability of Indian films and film songs in Pakistan changed depending on the status of its relationship to India, Radio Ceylon consistently made old and new Indian-made film songs available on the airwaves for Pakistani listeners. In the years following the 1965 Indo-Pakistan War, when the Pakistani government officially banned the screening of all Indian films as well as the broadcasting of their songs on Radio Pakistan, listeners simply continued to tune in to Radio Ceylon. One listener writing to the Pakistan-based film magazine *Eastern Film* warned the government that their attempts to stop Pakistani listeners from enjoying Indian film songs was futile because "more and more listeners have started tuning to Radio Ceylon."[42]

It is not clear whether or not other sponsoring companies like CIBA actively advertised in Pakistan in addition to India.[43] Yet regardless of sponsors' interest in the Pakistani market, there is little doubt that Radio Ceylon broadcasters were quite interested in and committed to nurturing audiences in Pakistan. In interviews, Radio Ceylon broadcasters all have noted that they received mail from Pakistani listeners.[44] Manohar Mahajan, for example, in his account of Radio Ceylon, *Yādein Radio Ceylon Kī*, includes fan letters from Pakistani listeners, alongside mail from listeners in India. Moreover, programming schedules reveal that in the 1960s, Radio Ceylon began to air programs that exclusively featured film songs from Pakistani-made films. These programs were likely meant to please Pakistani listeners as well as to introduce listeners in India to film songs from the neighboring nation.[45]

Most telling is that when Ameen Sayani visited Pakistan for the first time in May 2007, Radio Ceylon fans gathered in the Arts Council auditorium in Karachi to finally "see" the man whose voice they knew so well. That night when he replayed clips from his old radio programs, some members of the audience cheered enthusiastically and others quietly shed tears, overwhelmed by nostalgia. Newspaper reports of the event, like the audience in the Arts Council auditorium, celebrated Sayani both as an eminent voice that had long been part of the Pakistani soundscape, as well as a shared legacy with neighboring India and a symbol of a surviving shared culture nearly a half-century after Partition (figure 4.4). *Express*, for example, wrote that Ameen Sayani "ties India and Pakistan together," and *QVS Audio Video* noted that "radio was still waiting for a voice artist like Sayani."[46]

4.4A, 4.4B, AND 4.4C Newspaper clippings of Ameen Sayani's 2007 visit to Pakistan. (a) The caption reads: "Ameen Sayani Ek Muddat Tak Muhabbat Kī Mālā Bunte Rahe" (For Such a Long Time, Ameen Sayani Knitted a Garland of Love), *Gateway*, May 9, 2007. (b) "Amin Sayani Overwhelmed by City's Love" (newspaper unknown). (c) The caption reads: "Pāk Bhārat Dostī Mazbūt Rište Meṅ Bandh Jāe: Ameen Sayani" (Ameen Sayani: May India and Pakistan Build a Strong Relationship), *Express*, May 8, 2007.

Source: Newspaper clippings of Ameen Sayani's visit to Pakistan, courtesy of Sultan Ahmad Arshad.

Amin Sayani overwhelmed by city's love

By Shanaz Ramzi

AFTER quite a few futile attempts in the past, Karachi finally succeeded in playing host to the legendary broadcaster, Amin Sayani, whose dream it was to visit the city where his childhood friends live.

And he reportedly relished every minute of it. Invited by his friend, Sultan Arshad of Amateurs' Melodies Group, Ameen Sayani's week-long trip was filled with love, adulation and action.

On his very first night here the 75-year old veteran radio compere was invited to the residence of Sultana Siddiqui, president of HUM TV, where he was introduced to a varied group of people including television and film personalities, journalists and members from the corporate sector. Sayani, whose voice is every bit as mesmerising as it was way back in the '50s, regaled the guests with anecdotes from his 45 year career as a Geetmala broadcaster.

The following day, between lunch at the channel and dinner at a friend's place, Sayani met members of the press at a special briefing arranged for the purpose, and answered their eager queries. The next day was the much-awaited tribute programme

Visitors' Log

held in his honour for which Ameen Sayani had been especially invited. Singers belonging to Amateurs' Melodies Group sang hit Indian film songs from 1954 to 1969 which

had been selected by the Geetmala host himself and the latter entertained the audience with bits of information about himself and his long association with the programme.

However, probably the funniest comment made by the man who was "totally floored" by the love shown for him in Pakistan was that he was impressed by Karachi's cleanliness!

Actor Nadeem who was also present in the audience was requested to say a few words about the electronic media giant. He not only obliged, but at Sayani's request also sang a vintage Indian film song. Many in the audience could be seen nostalgically humming along with the singers on the stage.

Much of Sunday was spent with old friends and in sight-seeing, as indeed were Sayani's last two days here. He also managed to take out time for a television interview to be aired on Sunday, and for an interview on FM89, not to forget a high tea hosted by a local club. Judging by the standing ovation Ameen Sayani received at the tribute programme and the affection showered on him, one feels that he is surely going to try and visit Karachi once again.

4.4B *(Continued)*

پاک بھارت دوستی مضبوط رشتہ میں بندھ جائے: امین سیانی

میری خواہش ہے افغانستان، سری لنکا، مالدیب اور ہم سب ایک اتحاد کی مثال قائم کریں

گیتا کا گیت مالا اور ریڈیو سیلون سے شہرت حاصل کرنے والے معروف براڈ کاسٹر کا تقریب سے خطاب

کراچی (کلچرل رپورٹ) امین سیانی کا نام گیت مالا کے حوالے سے اور ریڈیو سیلون کی وجہ سے زبردست شہرت کا حامل ہے۔ امین سیانی پہلی بار پاکستان آئے تو ہم ٹی وی کے مہمان بنے۔ ان کی جانب سے گزشتہ روز کراچی میں ان کے ساتھ ایک نشت کا اہتمام کیا گیا ٹی وی کی چیئرپرسن سلطانہ صدیقی نے خیر مقدم کیا اور ان کی ریڈیو کے حوالے سے شاندار خدمات پر سراہا۔ اس موقع پر صحافیوں سے گفتگو کرتے ہوئے امین سیانی نے کہا کہ ریڈیو سیلون سے گیت مالا نے انہیں اس قدر شہرت دی کہ آج تک میں اس سحر سے نکل سکا۔ اردو ہندی الفاظ کی آمیزش سے ان کے انداز میں نکھار آیا اور یہ میں نے کیبر داس سے سیکھا۔ میں سات

سال کی عمر میں ریڈیو سے وابستہ ہوا، 9 ممالک میں صداکاری کی اور 9000 ہزار کمرشل پروگرام کئے۔ امین سیانی نے کہا آج ایف ایم ریڈیو پر ایک ہی انداز کے کمپیر ہیں۔ انھوں نے کہا میں پہلی بار پاکستان آیا ہوں مجھے یہاں پر لوگوں سے مل کر بہت خوشی ہوئی میری خواہش ہے کہ پاکستان اور بھارت کے درمیان نہ صرف دوستی بلکہ ایسے مضبوط رشتہ بھی قائم ہو جائیں جو دنیا کے لیے ایک مثال بن جائیں بلکہ میری تو خواہش ہے ہم، ہم جیسے افغانستان، سری لنکا، مالدیب ہم سب ایک یونی کی مثال قائم کریں، اس موقع پر اطہر وقار عظیم نے انکشاف کیا کہ امین سیانی کا شمار دنیا کے پانچ بہتر ریڈیو براڈ کاسٹر میں ہوتا ہے۔

4.4C *(Continued)*

Radio Ceylon and the Ideology of Hindustani

Language was a key aspect of Radio Ceylon and Ameen Sayani's appeal. Radio Ceylon broadcasters hailed from India and, for the most part, called the language they spoke on the airwaves Hindi. Radio Ceylon employees, however, adhered to what I described earlier as "the ideology of Hindustani." They strove to speak a language free of religious affiliations that could connect speakers of other regional languages, without threatening regional identities. In so doing, they defied both the Indian and Pakistani governments' linguistic policies, which promoted Hindi and Urdu, respectively, as national languages.

Radio Ceylon's linguistic preferences were influenced by the film industry, whose song productions the station aired. Radio Ceylon's decision to use Hindustani needs to be analyzed in the context of this important transmedia relationship between radio and film. The Hindi film industry in Bombay consciously subscribed to the ideology of Hindustani. Madhumita Lahiri explains it well when she writes that in postindependence India and Pakistan, "Hindustani does not persist in literary publications, legal records, or elementary school textbooks, yet it can be found in one large, populist realm: that of the Bollywood cinema."[47] Hindustani also remained well and alive on the airwaves. For the Bombay film industry, employing Hindustani was a commercial decision as much as it was a political one. The versatility and widespread intelligibility of Hindustani allowed the film industry to access a large and diverse audience.[48] Similarly, Radio Ceylon's use of Hindustani was a commercial decision, but one that was ultimately successful because it capitalized and expanded on already existing linguistic connections. By employing a simple version of Hindustani, Radio Ceylon broadcasters were able to reach a diverse population—spread throughout northern, eastern, and western India as well as throughout most parts of Pakistan—that could understand, if not necessarily always speak, Hindustani.[49]

Again, Radio Ceylon's timing was crucial. It was under the British that AIR first instituted separate Hindi and Urdu programs and officially eliminated Hindustani broadcasting. During B. V. Keskar's tenure, however, AIR's Hindi became a matter of contentious debate (as outlined in chapter 3). Hindi news bulletins became increasingly Sanskritized and employed what many felt was an extremely clumsy and forced language. In broadcasting in Hindustani and embracing the ideology of Hindustani, Radio Ceylon directly defied AIR's and the Indian government's policies. Radio Ceylon's success, therefore, needs to be understood in the context of Keskar's reforms. Listeners welcomed Radio Ceylon's accessible language just as they had welcomed the stations' Hindi film-song broadcasts. Radio Ceylon's policies, however, also challenged the Pakistani government's stance that a version of Urdu, divorced from Hindi and free of Sanskrit loan words, should be the national language of the newly independent Pakistan.

Ameen Sayani's linguistic history and approach to language is most reveal-ing.[50] The language Sayani spoke on the air was consciously neither Muslim nor Hindu. For example, in *Geetmala*, he often used the greeting *ādāb*, which can be associated with North Indian Muslims, and he unashamedly quoted from Urdu couplets in his programs.[51] At the same time, Ameen Sayani was perfectly comfortable employing words much closer to the Hindi spectrum in his pro-grams, such as the word *kāryakram* (program).[52]

Interestingly, Ameen Sayani was not a native speaker of Hindi, Urdu, or Hindustani. He grew up in a Gujarati-speaking Muslim household and attended an English-language boarding school. In a number of interviews, Sayani described his plunge into Hindi broadcasting as purely accidental. He was still in his teens when a senior announcer asked him to read a Hindi-language com-mercial because the permanent voice artist did not arrive in time. The pro-ducer liked Sayani's voice and invited him to host a new Hindi program. Ameen Sayani's older brother, however, advised him against anchoring a program in a language Ameen was clearly not comfortable speaking. The young Ameen Sayani, however, was eager to prove himself as a broadcaster in his own right and ignored his elder brother's advice. The fact that Sayani was not a native speaker of Hindi, however, seems to have ultimately worked in his favor. On the air, Sayani consciously adopted a simple manner of speech that nonnative speakers of Hindi, including his own family members, could easily understand.[53]

Radio Ceylon broadcasters were able to adhere to the ideology of Hindustani because the station, located in Ceylon, lay outside the jurisdiction of both the Indian and Pakistani governments and could freely ignore the linguistic policies (and politics) of both governments, but also because radio is an aural medium. It was much easier for broadcasters to embrace Hindustani in spoken broad-casts than it would have been in written form because they could avoid issues of script. Also, on the airwaves, broadcasters could deploy a more colloquial form of speech that was not nearly as marked as the higher registers of literary Hindi and Urdu, which borrow from Sanskrit and Arabic or Persian, respectively.[54] Hindi film-song programs, which tended to be colloquial and somewhat infor-mal, were particularly propitious for this. Perhaps most important, radio listen-ers did not necessarily need to understand everything broadcasters said on the air to enjoy the music and to get the gist of broadcasters' announcements.[55]

Radio Receivers

Timing was important in regards to another important matter. Radio Ceylon's birth and growth concurred with the increasing availability of radios in the subcontinent. Following the lift of production restrictions worldwide after the end of World War II, and the consequential increase of radio manufacturing around the world, high-quality valve radio receivers became more affordable and accessible throughout the Indian subcontinent. It is difficult to find reliable statistics of radio receiver ownership in the subcontinent. The Indian and Pakistani government's statistics are unreliable because a large percentage of radio owners did not register their sets to avoid yearly registration fees, just as they had done during World War II.[56] Nonetheless, the abundance of radio ads in newspapers and magazines as well as the proliferation of ads for radio repair services suggest that radio receivers became more widespread in the years following the war (see figures 4.5a and 4.5b).

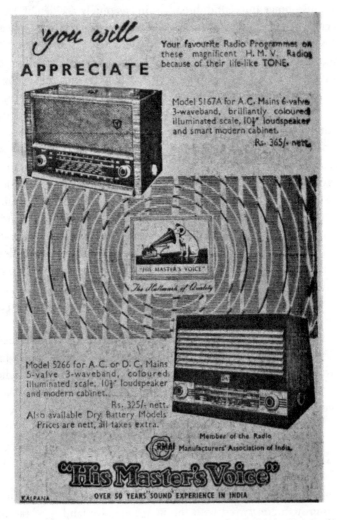

4.5A AND 4.5B Advertisements for high-quality valve radios published in the film magazine *Screen*. (a) His Master's Voice and (b) Ecko.

Source: Screen, November 10, 1959. National Film Archives of India.

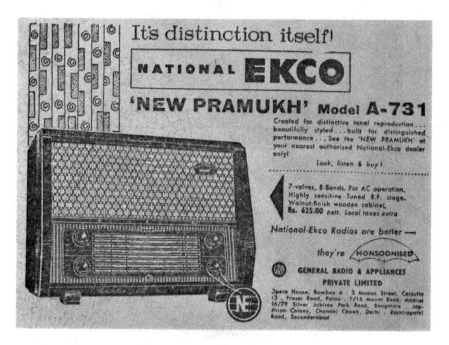

It's distinction itself!

NATIONAL **EKCO**

'NEW PRAMUKH' Model A-731

Created for distinctive tonal reproduction...
beautifully styled...built for distinguished
performance...See the 'NEW PRAMUKH' at
your nearest authorised National-Ekco dealer
only!

Look, listen & buy!

7-valves, 8-Bands. For AC operation.
Highly sensitive Tuned R.F. stage.
Walnut-finish wooden cabinet,
Rs. 625.00 nett. Local taxes extra

National-Ekco Radios are better —

they're MONSOONISED

GENERAL RADIO & APPLIANCES
PRIVATE LIMITED

Opera House, Bombay 4 . 3 Madan Street, Calcutta
13 . Frazer Road, Patna . 1/18 Mount Road, Madras
16/79 Silver Jubilee Park Road, Bangalore . Jag-
dhian Colony, Chandni Chowk, Delhi . Rashtrapathi
Road, Secunderabad

4.5B (*Continued*)

More important, however, the growing availability of cheap battery-operated transistors ensured that many more music fans could tune in to radio programs. As Vebhuti Duggal's research has revealed, a large underground industry of cheap transistors sprouted in India after independence. Locally produced receivers likely became available as early as the 1950s when Radio Ceylon's first Indian-language programs aired, but the industry boomed in the next decade alongside the Ceylon-based radio station.[57] Because producers operated underground to avoid regulation and taxation, it is hard to determine sales numbers, but again the proliferation of ads for these transistors in newspapers and magazines as well as listeners' own testimonies point to their importance and growing presence (figure 4.6).[58]

In most places of the world, the growth of the transistor contributed to a more individualized form of radio listening, but in South Asia, transistors were at the center of the public and quasi-public listening experience. As Duggal demonstrates, "listening to the radio particularly the Hindi film song was not based on a quiet, completive listening, driven by the norms of fidelity; rather . . . the norm here was the *aesthetic of loudness*."[59] It is particularly telling, she notes, that ads for these locally produced transistors emphasized their loudness as their main attraction. This means that even as radios and transistors became more widely available, the public and collective listening practices that had been so important

4.6 Advertisement for NEC transistor radios. Similar transistors were made in Pakistan (see chapter 6).

Source: Times of India, May 27, 1951. Image published with permission of ProQuest LLC.

during World War II remained the norm, with roadside restaurants, chai stands, and *pān* shops serving as gathering grounds for radio listening.[60] This is in part, as I will elaborate in later sections, because the audile techniques broadcasters promoted in their programs depended on collective listening practices. Even private homes, Duggal perceptively argues, were often not places of individualized private listening, but rather gathering grounds for families, friends, and, above all, for groups of women to tune in to radio programs. The "aesthetic of loudness" was part of the radio listening experience within the home.[61]

The wider availability of radio receivers, both valve radios and transistors, broadcasters' conscious embrace of Hindustani, and the station's powerful military transmitter enabled Radio Ceylon to access a large, diverse, and transnational audience. It was through a specific set of participatory broadcasting techniques, however, that broadcasters were able to engage listening audiences and forge a transnational "aural *filmi* culture" that centered on not just Hindi film songs but also on a broader aural experience of films. In my subsequent analysis of Radio Ceylon's programs, I unpack these broadcasting techniques.

Geetmala's Resonance

Binaca Geetmala was the station's iconic radio program and one of the many RES productions whose recordings made the weekly airplane trip from Bombay to Colombo. Binaca was the name of a brand of toothpaste and toiletries owned by CIBA, the sponsoring company, and the composite word *Geetmala* means "garland of songs" or "chain of songs." Ameen Sayani was the program's host.[62]

"*Geetmala* was a strange story,"[63] Sayani remarked when discussing the humble beginnings of this radio show that went on to conquer millions of hearts. In 1951, CIBA was sponsoring a fairly successful English-language hit-parade program on Radio Ceylon. By the early 1950s, hit-parade programs, which ranked songs based on popularity as determined by sales, playtime, or listeners' requests, had become commonplace in the United States and parts of Europe and Latin America, but they were new to the Indian subcontinent. As Radio Ceylon had begun to experiment with Hindi-language programs, CIBA decided to try out a Hindi film-song version of its current English-language program. *Geetmala*'s original format was straightforward: Sayani played a selection of popular film songs and asked listeners to rank songs in order of popularity and to mail in their lists to the company's offices. By compiling listeners' rankings, Sayani made a final hit-parade list, which he announced in the succeeding program. Listeners whose own rankings coincided with the final hit parade shared a modest monetary prize.[64]

Geetmala first aired in 1952 and became an instant hit. Sayani maintains that by the end of 1953, *Geetmala* was receiving an average of sixty-five thousand letters a week from listeners participating in the competition. To reduce the young broadcaster's workload, RES cut out the competition portion of the show and based songs' rankings solely on gramophone record sales. Initially, the company consulted with the top eight music shops in India, but gradually it increased the number of shops. At its peak, *Geetmala* incorporated sales data from more than forty shops from metropolitan Indian cities.[65]

As I explain elsewhere, *Geetmala*'s ranking system was not perfectly democratic because, more than accurately representing listeners' musical preferences, it helped create them.[66] The reality is that only a tiny percentage of the population in India and Pakistan could afford to buy new records week after week. In these early years, one record could fit two songs, and the average film in the early 1950s had anywhere from five to fifteen songs. Moreover, the final hit-parade list did not consider record sales from Pakistan, in part because the availability of Hindi film-song gramophone records in Pakistan depended on current government policies toward imports from India. This meant that only a small percentage of *Geetmala*'s audience actually had any significant role in the rankings. But the program's main attraction—and surely part of the secret of its success—was that it made its listeners feel as if they did in fact take part in the competition.

Sayani developed the concept of *sangīt sīṛhī* (musical ladder) and every week described how songs moved up and down this ladder. He invited listeners to anticipate songs' rankings and to root for their favorite songs and encouraged them to take the competition seriously. To add pomp to the transmissions, he played a concert of trumpets when revealing the name of the top song of the week at the end of the program. Wednesday nights quickly became *Geetmala*'s nights, with people gathering outside *pān* shops, restaurants, and private homes to listen in.[67] Sayani built up curiosity and excitement in all his weekly programs, but for many, *Geetmala*'s yearly program was the most thrilling radio program of the year. During the end of the year program, Sayani announced the top songs of the year based on yearly statistics CIBA's team had collected.[68]

In her study of listening practices and the Hindi film song, Duggal points to the importance of "aural overflow" in these public listening settings.[69] The sound of film songs emanating from receivers, both transistors and valve radios alike, would reach even those who might not be consciously tuning in. Duggal notes that chai shop and *pān* shop owners used radio to attract clients. Yet even as *Geetmala* fostered large crowds of intended and unintended listeners, the key to *Geetmala*'s success was that the *sangīt sīṛhī* traveled well by word of mouth and could reach those who might not have heard the radio program. This is where the idea of radio resonance becomes relevant. News about which songs had topped *Geetmala* during a particular week became the so-called talk of the town.[70] Moreover, these songs were more likely to be sung in public and private settings. In this way, someone who might not have heard the program could easily learn about the song rankings in discussion as well as become familiar with the winning songs' tunes and lyrics, and even their corresponding films. Sultan Arshad Ahmad from Karachi, Pakistan, a devout fan of the program, remembers discussing *Geetmala*'s popularity lists in his college canteen and arguing for hours with his classmates about whether or not the rankings were adequate. Many of his friends who could not tune in to the program still learned about the song rankings in these canteen discussions.[71] *Geetmala* nicely shows that radio's strong links to oral communication networks that had been so important during World War II not only continued in the postindependence period but also formed a key aspect of the program's cross-border success. After all, the "talk" about *Geetmala* in school canteens in Karachi that Ahmad describes was not categorically different from the "rumors directly traceable to enemy broadcasts" that had greatly worried British officers during the global war.

Ameen Sayani's "musical ladder" also depended on a similar type of "emotional speculation" and personal involvement that had been so important to Bose's radio persona during the war. *Geetmala*'s listeners became so deeply invested in film-song competitions that many kept detailed records of each week's listings. For example, J. J. Kulkarni from Sholapur, Maharashtra, kept a diary every week from 1957 until 1962, in which he carefully noted down the names of the songs that topped *Binaca Geetmala* (figure 4.7).[72]

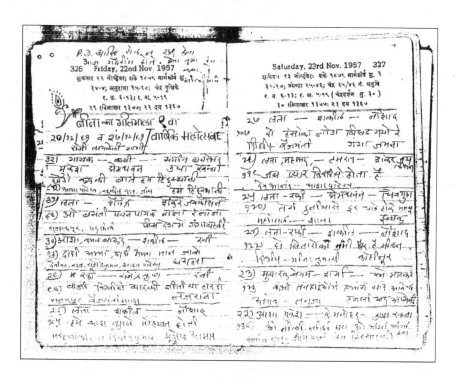

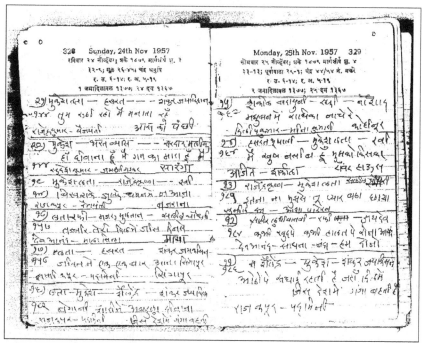

4.7 Two pages from J. J. Kulkarni's diary. He lists the songs that topped *Binaca Geetmala*. Kulkarni sent copies of the first twenty pages of this diary to Dalbir Singh Parmar, a Hindi broadcaster based in Colombo.

Source: Courtesy of Jyoti Parmar, Dalbir Singh Parmar personal papers.

Most impressively, Anil Bhargava, for four decades, diligently recorded all the songs that made it onto the show as well as any changes that the program underwent during the forty-plus years on the air. Based on these detailed notes, Bhargava wrote a book called *Binaca* Geetmala *Kā Surīlā Safar* (*Geetmala's* melodious journey), one of the richest resources about *Geetmala* available, and an important source for this and other studies on the radio program.[73]

These diaries are a rich resource that not only make clear the importance of *Geetmala* but also demonstrate how radio and Hindi film songs effectively seeped into the rhythm of everyday life. For several decades, every week Bhargava, Kulkarni, and many others like them sat down to meticulously write down the results of the program. The diaries also point to an important relationship between radio listening and writing. The practice of writing— particularly writing letters to radio stations, but also, as in the case of *Geetmala*, writing notes about programs for personal use—formed an important aspect of the radio-listening experience, a topic I cover in greater detail in chapter 6. However, while writing practices are clearly important, these personal diaries are first and foremost rare written transcriptions of a much larger and widespread conversation about *Geetmala's* own song rankings.[74] The diaries are what Lisa Gitelman has called "legible representation of an aural experience."[75] They are a written record not only of the sounds listeners heard emanating from their receivers but also of their radio resonance—that is, of the broader discussion that surrounded those broadcasts.

If the rumors "directly traceable to enemy broadcasts" of World War II were characterized by their fragmentary and scattered nature, these *Geetmala* diaries reveal how orderly, planned, and, most important, thorough Radio Ceylon's resonance was. Unlike the Axis radio programs, which relied on what was essentially a patchy, if still effective, form of resonance, Ameen Sayani and other Radio Ceylon broadcasters developed programs that made use of resonance in more systematized ways. Radio clubs constitute another example of the ways in which Radio Ceylon and, in particular, *Geetmala* encouraged resonance.

Geetmala's Radio Clubs

For the most part, people listened to *Geetmala* and to Radio Ceylon collectively in restaurants, *pān* shops and chai stands, and at large family gatherings. Aware of the importance of these listening practices and hoping to further capitalize on them, Radio Ceylon broadcasters came up with the idea of forming *radio śrotā sangh* (radio listening clubs). Members of radio clubs would gather in homes or public spaces once a week to listen to *Geetmala* and would vote for their favorite songs. The president or leader of the radio club counted the votes every week and mailed results to Radio Ceylon's staff. At first, *Geetmala* had ten to fifteen registered listening clubs, but according to Sayani's team, during the peak of its popularity, Radio Ceylon would receive mail from about four hundred radio clubs.[76]

Although Sayani maintains that CIBA sometimes used statistics from these clubs to check gramophone record sales data and flag any major discrepancies, I have found no concrete evidence that club members' votes actually swayed *Geetmala*'s hit-parade lists in a significant way. Moreover, in interviews, CIBA personnel have noted that to keep the system as fair as possible and to avoid controversy, the company, for the most part, relied on gramophone record sales data.[77] What appears to have been happening is that the radio clubs' real purpose was to increase listeners' interest in and dedication to the radio program as well as encourage further conversation about the program's results and ultimately to create radio resonance. And, in this respect, radio clubs were remarkably successful.

Members assigned a great deal of importance to radio clubs. They held weekly gatherings, printed special letterhead paper and envelopes, and made seals with the names of their listeners' clubs. Duggal's research has shown that by the 1970s some radio clubs began putting out their own publications, which included short essays on radio, film songs, and cinema, as well was short stories, poems, and jokes. These later radio clubs were no longer exclusively for *Geetmala* or for Radio Ceylon, as listeners tuned in to a variety of radio programs, including AIR's Vividh Bharti's programs.[78] Unfortunately, we have less information about *Geetmala*'s earlier radio clubs because neither Radio Ceylon nor Sayani kept copies of the program's earlier correspondence. But when Sayani briefly revived *Geetmala* in the late 2000s, he and his son Rajil Sayani kept some of the correspondence they received. Although from a later period, these letters do give us a sense of the kind of weight that listeners attached to the radio clubs and how these clubs helped expand the popular ambit of both radio and film songs, further promoting listeners' active participation. Consider, for example, the stamp and letterhead from the Manihari Radio club, which as its name suggested, was located in Manihari, a small town in the state of Bihar (figure 4.8). Sayani and other broadcasters assured me that this practice was also common during *Geetmala*'s earlier years. The professionalism evident in the letterhead, which includes a photograph of its president, makes clear the importance that *Geetmala* listeners attached to clubs.

Moreover, as part of an effort to revive the program in 2000, Rajil Sayani also compiled a list of about four hundred radio clubs based on records his father had kept since the 1950s. Unfortunately, this list does not include the dates when these clubs were first founded or the dates when they stopped sending mail. The list, however, does offer some insight into the composition of radio clubs.[79] For example, many electronic shops, or electrical shops as they are normally called, registered their own radio clubs and invited people to join

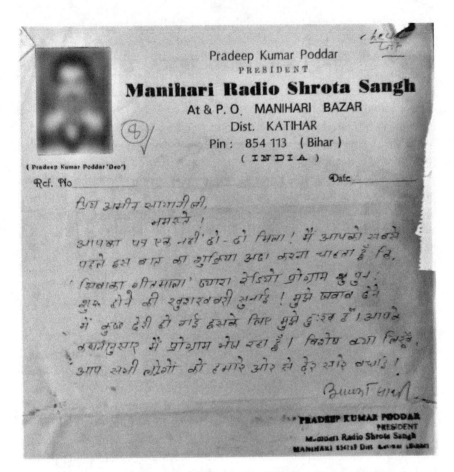

4.8 Letter to Ameen Sayani from a listener named Pradeep Kumar Poddar, who was president of his radio club. Note the custom-made letterhead and the stamp.

Source: Courtesy of Ameen and Rajil Sayani.

and come to listen to programs in their shops. Deepak Electronics in Jodhpur registered a club, as did Sameer Audio Store in Bombay. As Duggal has perceptively noted, in addition to *pān* shops and restaurants, electrical shops were also key gathering grounds for listening to radio.[80] It is no surprise then that electrical shops would sponsor radio clubs, likely in the hopes that some of its members eventually would purchase their own radios. Additionally, some extended families started their own radio clubs, such as the Dakliya Family from Jodhpur Rajasthan. College students founded radio clubs as well. For instance, the Bihar Agricultural College had its own club. Some clubs were limited to listeners of age-groups, such as the youth radio listeners clubs in Belgaum, Karnataka.

Finally, there were radio clubs whose members likely had little else in common other than a love of music, such as the Ajnabī Radio Śrotā Sangh (Strangers' radio club) in Bhagalpur Bihar. One would hope that over the years, members of this so-called strangers' club became friends.[81]

Geetmala was Radio Ceylon's most iconic and enduring program and its analysis offers insight into radio's modes of engagement with audiences and the continued importance of radio resonance. I now turn to the somewhat forgotten Hindi film-song "sustenance programs," which filled the majority of Radio Ceylon's broadcast hours. These programs went out live from Radio Ceylon's Colombo studios and relied on the station's extensive gramophone library, which included new and old Hindi film songs. Although Radio Ceylon's sustenance programs for the most part featured songs from Indian-made films, these programs likely occasionally included songs from the emergent Pakistani film industry.[82] In developing sustenance programs, Radio Ceylon broadcasters made use of "formats of virtual participation for the absent,"[83] as they encouraged listeners to acquire what Jonathan Sterne calls "audile techniques" (i.e., methodical and learned forms of listening).[84] Broadcasters trained listeners to decouple songs from films, to recognize the voices of playback singers and music composers' styles, and to associate personal characteristics with singers and composers. Yet if AIR's didactic programs during Keskar's tenure treated listeners as docile and impressionable, Radio Ceylon programs sought to do the opposite: they fostered listeners' active participation in radio programs, even as they promoted these audile techniques.

Songs Decoupled and Recoupled

One of the most obvious yet surprisingly unacknowledged features of Hindi film-song radio programs is that these programs decoupled songs from the films in which they originally appeared. This is an important and powerful practice, which grants songs a certain kind of independence from films. Admittedly, radio was neither the only, nor the first, technology to detach songs from films. Gramophone records had made songs available separate from films several decades before radio. More important, as scholars of Hindi film have long argued, song pamphlets, which helped film and music fans put songs to memory, preceded both the gramophone and the radio.[85] Finally, at the center of all these technologies was the human voice, which brought film songs to homes and bazaars, and expanded the ambit of film songs' reach. A close analysis of Radio Ceylon's sustenance programs makes radio's unique role in decoupling songs from films clear. Beyond physically separating aural songs from visual films, Radio Ceylon broadcasters designed film-song programs with formats that deliberately encouraged listeners to imagine songs as separate entities by grouping songs based on their qualities, rather than on the films in which they originally had appeared.[86] This decoupling process was at the heart of Radio Ceylon's transmedia productions and was a crucial aspect of the transnational aural *filmi* culture Radio Ceylon helped create.

Consider, for example, a program called *Śīrṣak Sangīt* (Title songs). The original program, which was first inaugurated in the 1950s, had a straightforward format. The broadcaster selected a title word each week and played songs whose first two lines included this word. So, for example, if the broadcaster selected the word *duniyā*, which means "world," he would only play songs whose opening lines included the word *duniyā*, such as the song "Yeh duniyā yeh mehfil mere kām kī nahīṅ" (This world, this gathering, is not for me). While hosting the program, the broadcaster would encourage listeners to participate in the program by asking them to predict, from the comfort of their own homes, the songs he would select during the course of the program. This constituted a key part of the appeal of *Śīrṣak Sangīt* and many other Radio Ceylon programs that through their specific formats encouraged listeners' responsiveness and active participation.[87]

The program *Anokhe Bol* (Unusual words) also grouped songs based on characteristics of the songs, as it exclusively featured film songs that contained meaningless words, such as the much praised and still very popular song "Īnā mīnā ḍīkā," from the film *Āśā* (Hope) and the song "Aplam caplam chaplai re" from the film *Āzād* (Freedom).[88] Incidentally, *Anokhe Bol* also celebrated an aspect of film songs that film-music critics, including B. V. Keskar, repeatedly condemned. The use of meaningless phrases, in the eyes (or ears) of critics, was proof of film music's degradation. For example, a staunch supporter of Keskar's campaign wrote the *Movie Times* to complain about Hindi film songs' lyrics: "Some of our song writers can also take the credit for having introduced a strange new language in our songs." Their poor use of language, this critic explained, proves "the utter bankruptcy of our song writers."[89] One of the aims of Sugam Sangīt or "light music production units" (described in chapter 3) was to write meaningful lyrics with "simple and effective words" that could forge ideal citizen-listeners.[90] With programs such as *Anokhe Bol*, which celebrated the Hindi film songs' "unusual words," Radio Ceylon's early broadcasters responded to the Indian government's critiques of film songs, providing yet another example of how Radio Ceylon developed in opposition to AIR's policies.

A few other sustenance programs also challenged AIR's critiques of film songs while at the same time encouraging the songs' independence from films. For example, the program *Sargam* (Musical scale) celebrated film music's classical roots by featuring film songs that were close to the Hindustani classical tradition, such as the songs of the acclaimed film *Baiju Bāvrā* (Crazy Baiju,

1952). During the course of this program, the assigned broadcasters announced the raga on which the selected song was based and made note of the director's and singer's musical training. A program called *Sandeš Gītvāle* (Musical messages) also might have been a sort of rebuttal to the all-too-familiar criticism that films and their music were amoral. The announcer aired songs that had similar moral messages or lessons, talked about the chosen songs' shared message, and discussed the message's relevance to people's personal lives. Programs such as *Sandeš Gītvāle* (Musical message), *Šīršak Sangīt* (Title songs), *Anokhe Bol* (Unusual words), and *Sargam* (Musical scale) challenged AIR policies and rhetoric while encouraging listeners to think of film songs as independent units and to attach characteristics to film songs that extended well beyond the visual cinematic context. The process of decoupling, however, was never straightforward or uncomplicated. Broadcasters developed programs that consciously encouraged songs' independence from films, but they also simultaneously cashed in on songs' intrinsic attachment to motion pictures.[91] In this way, Radio Ceylon contributed to what Anna Morcom has called "the double lives" of Hindi film songs—that is, the peculiar ability of songs to circulate freely outside the cinema while remaining attached to the films in which they originally appeared.[92] What I wish to stress is that the "ease with which songs [could] be extricated from films" and then simultaneously linked back to films was not merely an aesthetic or technical aspect of the Hindi cinema, but rather was one that required the active training of film-song listeners. By promoting film songs' independence from films in some programs and actively linking songs to films in other programs, Radio Ceylon broadcasters forged this binary set of characteristics as they taught listeners to listen in a particular way.

Consider, for example, a sustenance program called *Drišya Aur Gīt* (Scene and song), which applied the following format: listeners mailed in short written descriptions of a film scene preceding a song, the broadcaster read listeners' written descriptions, interjected a few comments, and then played the corresponding songs. The program encouraged listeners to visualize film scenes and connect songs to their original productions. The most involved listeners would mail their own description of songs, which broadcasters would later read on the airwaves.[93] In the age before television and video players, when most people could not watch a film a second or third time without having to pay for a movie ticket, *Drišya Aur Gīt* helped listeners relive movie-going experiences. In some cases, programs like *Drišya Aur Gīt* were the primary way in which film lovers, who for whatever reason could not see a film in the cinema, could "see" the scenes associated with film songs. Moreover, as Ravikant points out, for many listeners, watching the actual film could sometimes be a disappointing experience because listening to the song and imagining the scene offered its own type of excitement.[94] Programs like *Drišya Aur Gīt* enabled radio listeners to experience film scenes aurally. It is, for example, telling that descriptions of Indian films in the editorial pages of the Pakistani film magazines often revolve around film songs.[95]

By far, the programs that most actively pegged songs to films were publicity programs for newly released films. These programs, which were produced and recorded in Bombay by RES personnel, functioned as aural trailers for films. They included the film's songs, which were the primary component of film publicity programs, as well as brief descriptions of the film's basic story line and short clips of the film's dialogue. Radio Ceylon's programming schedules reveal that at least a couple hours a week were set aside for these film advertisement programs.[96] Radio's role in publicizing films, and for that matter Hindi film songs' role in advertising films, constitute fascinating topics that could easily fill the pages of a separate study. For example, film-producing companies released soundtracks before films, and film songs circulated on the radio before visual versions of these were available in movie theaters. Consider, for example, an ad for the film *Cār Darveš* published in the *Times of India* in March 1964 (see figure 4.9). The main selling point for the film in this ad is that its songs are "popular and in demand" on Radio Ceylon, pointing to the ways in which the aural experience of film—through radio—could be even more important than the visual experience in a cinema hall. Indeed, as Corey Creekmur points out, "the assumption that Bombay films are constructed as plots that get 'interrupted' by songs, or, in the preferred terms of contemporary theory, that the film are narratives disrupted by spectacle may simply get things backwards."[97] Interestingly, the ad also nicely highlights the importance of radio's resonance as it remarks that songs heard on the radio are "lovingly hummed in every home," suggesting the ways in which radio broadcasts expanded beyond the reach of radio receivers.

I cannot do full justice to the important commercial and financial relationship between film and radio in this study. But I do wish to draw attention to a couple of things regarding these radio publicity programs that clarify Radio Ceylon's role in forging an aural *filmi* culture.[98] First, film publicity programs actively linked songs to films and promoted film songs' double lives. Second, for some listeners these publicity programs were the only way in which they became familiar with films' plots and characters, particularly before the advent of television. As mentioned earlier, watching a film in the cinema in the 1950s and 1960s would have been a special and planned event for most. In contrast, learning about a particular film's plot, hearing its songs, and becoming familiar with its actors would have been a daily occurrence for radio listeners. This aural experience of films, which involved the active coupling and decoupling of songs and films, was not incidental or supplementary, but rather often was the most important way in which many in India and Pakistan experienced Hindi films.

4.9 Advertisement for *Char Dervesh* in *Times of India*, March 8, 1964. Notice how the selling point of this film is that its songs are heard on Radio Ceylon.

Source: Image published with permission of ProQuest LLC.

Making Friends with Playback Singers

If the double lives of Hindi film songs is their most important feature, then playback singing is second.[99] Playback singing too has important ties to radio, and specifically to Radio Ceylon. Playback singers record songs for use in films, but they do not appear in the film; instead, actors or actresses lip-sync songs in film scenes. In the 1930s, most Hindi film actors sang their own songs, but by the mid-1940s, professional playback singers interpreted the majority of film songs. The term "playback system" is commonly used in the subcontinent to reference the fact that a handful of playback singers came to dominate the Hindi film industry for nearly four decades, from the late 1940s until the late 1980s.[100]

Lata Mangeshkar, and to a lesser extent her younger sister Asha Bhosle, monopolized female Hindi playback singing for nearly four decades. Lata and Asha, as they commonly are known in the subcontinent, outdid earlier female singing stars, including Getta Dutt, Suraiya, and Nur Jehan.[101] The monopoly in male playback singing, although less extreme, was no less significant, with singers such as Mohammed Rafi, Kishore Kumar, Mukesh, and Talat Mahmood "lending their voices" to nearly every major Hindi film actor for several decades.[102]

Neepa Majumdar explains the importance of the playback system by means of comparison. Hollywood musicals of the 1950s and Hindi films of roughly the same time period actually used similar musical technologies. Both cinemas paired "ideal voices" to "ideal bodies" and simultaneously appealed to two "sets of pleasure, the aural and the visual."[103] These two film cultures, however, attached different meaning to the "voice-body" duo. Hollywood's audiences expected an actual match between the body and the singing voice, and directors went through significant ordeals to conceal their different origins. It is telling, Majumdar writes, that Audrey Hepburn was denied an academy award nomination for her performance in the film *My Fair Lady* when it became public knowledge that she did not sing her own songs.[104] In contrast, by the late 1950s, Hindi film audiences not only accepted the "mismatch of the body and the voice" but also, in some cases, even considered this disparity part of the film's allure.[105]

Majumdar's compelling analysis forces us to rethink the importance of the voice and body combination in Indian cinema, but it does not explain *how* playback singers became celebrities. An analysis of how radio and playback singing, two technologies of the disembodied voice, worked together can unravel radio's crucial role in molding an aural cinematic culture. Radio Ceylon broadcasters, through specific sets of broadcasting techniques and radio programs, helped tailor audiences' tastes toward the voices and styles of a few select playback singers and encouraged listeners to develop affective relationships with playback singers.

Let's begin with the program *Āj Ke Kalākār* (Contemporary artists), which had a simple format: the announcer chose a singer every week and played a selection of her film songs and, when available, also played some non-film songs she might have sung before or after joining the film industry. In between songs, the broadcaster briefly commented on the chosen artist's singing career as well as on her or his personal life.[106] For example, during a forty-five-minute episode dedicated to the renowned playback singer Talat Mahmood, the announcer would play two or three of Mahmood's film songs, one or two *ğazals* (a musical and poetic genre) that Mahmood recorded outside the film industry, and perhaps also one of the Bengali songs he had sung during his years in Calcutta. In between songs, the broadcaster would brief listeners on Mahmood's singing career, covering his early work in Bengali film, his shift to Bombay, and his short flirtation with acting. To liven up the show a bit, the announcer also would discuss details from Mahmood's personal life. He could have talked, for example, about Mahmood's childhood in Lucknow and mentioned his parents' initial opposition to their son's musical predisposition. A singing career, they believed, was unsuitable for a young, respectable Muslim man. In this manner, *Āj Ke Kalākar* circulated what Majumdar calls "extra-textual knowledge" of singers' lives and careers and encouraged audiences to associate "moral and emotional" traits with playback singers' disembodied voices (see figure 4.10).[107]

An advertisement for Murphy radio, published in the *Movie Times* in 1952, offers a remarkable visual representation of radio's role in promoting playback singers' celebrity status. Talat Mahmood poses next to a radio set, drawing attention to the symbiotic relationship that developed between radio and playback singing. Note that, at the time this ad was printed, AIR had just stopped broadcasting film songs. To listen to Talat Mahmood's film songs, radio listeners would have had to tune in to Radio Ceylon's programs.

The program *Kal Aur Āj* (Yesterday and today), which was essentially a more sophisticated version of *Āj Ke Kalākar*, also promoted playback singers' celebrity status, but did so in a different way. The program applied the following format: the broadcasters selected a singer for each week's show and played songs from that singer's past films as well as from recent productions. The broadcaster then would encourage listeners to track changes in playback singers' voices.[108] In this way, *Kal Aur Āj*, like many of Radio Ceylon's productions, promoted what Majumdar calls "voice recognizability"—that is, listeners' ability to recognize and immediately identify playback singers' voices. An important characteristic of the playback system is that, whereas actors and actresses had to retire when their youth began to fade, singers continued to have commercial success over several decades.[109] *Kal Aur Āj* not only celebrated this unusual aspect of the "playback star system" but also actively encouraged listeners to listen for it.[110] Gopal Sharma, the Radio Ceylon broadcaster who first came up with the original idea for this program, and who served as its host for the majority of the program's life, explained in an interview that he designed this program to encourage listeners to listen closely to playback singers' voices and styles.[111] The "encouragement" that Sharma described is a perfect example of the kinds of audile techniques Radio Ceylon fostered.

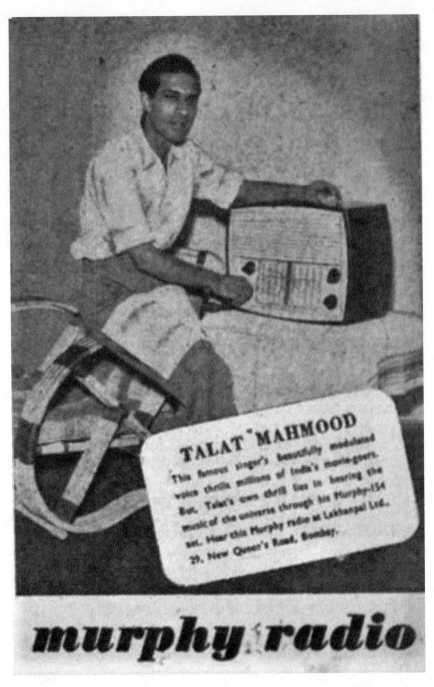

4.10 Advertisement for Murphy radios published in the film magazine *Movie Times* in 1952. Talat Mahmood poses next to a radio set, drawing attention to the symbiotic relationship that developed between radio and playback singing.

Source: *Movie Times* 3, no. 1 (1952): 24. National Film Archive of India.

Another one of Sharma's signature productions was a program called *Badalte Hūe Sāthī* (Changing partners). The program featured "film-song duets," that is, film songs performed by two playback singers, usually a female and male singer. For example, on a particular day, the program could open with the duet "Tasvīr terī dil meṅ jis din se basā lī hai" (Since the day I have had your picture in my heart) sung by Lata Mangeshkar and Mohammed Rafi. The next number then featured Mohammed Rafi and Geeta Dutt's "Aye dil hai muśkil jīnā yahaṅ zarā haṭ ke zarā bac ke" (Oh heart, it is difficult to live here, move carefully), and the one after that featured Geeta Dutt and somebody else. The idea was that singers would quite literally change partners after every song. But the trick was that the program always had to end with the singer whose voice had inaugurated that evening's show. Audience participation was a key aspect of this program. Sharma would ask listeners to anticipate which duet would follow the one he was currently playing. More involved listeners would mail their own lists of possible duet sets to the show, and Sharma occasionally played their selections on his shows and acknowledged the involved listener's contributions on the air.[112]

In addition to encouraging playback singers' stardom, Radio Ceylon also contributed to music directors' celebrity status in important ways. As noted earlier, in the Hindi cinema context, music composers are commonly referred to as music directors. Music directors gained celebrity status around the same time as playback singers started to become household names.[113] *Āj Ke Kalākār* also featured the works of music directors and shared tidbits about their lives and careers. For example, a program about the composer Hemant Kumar, would feature some of his most famous compositions, discuss his transition from playback singing to music director, and discuss his musical training.[114]

Radio Ceylon, through its various "formats of virtual communication" and by encouraging "audile techniques" encouraged listeners to develop affective bonds with playback singers and music directors. These bonds were an essential aspect of the "aural *filmi* culture" that Radio Ceylon helped forge. A picture of a *pān* vendor in present-day Kolkata perhaps best illustrates this point. Amid the various addictive products displayed in the shop—cigarettes, soft drinks, and all the necessary ingredients for making *pān*—are various pictures and news clippings of the vendor's favorite singer, Mohammed Rafi. The décor of his tiny shop, where he spends many hours a day, is illustrative of the important affective bonds that radio helped develop (see figure 4.11).

A Musical Feud

This chapter explained how and why a Ceylon-based former military radio station broadcasting in Hindustani and aimed at audiences in India and Pakistan

4.11 A *pānwālā* in Kolkata.

Source: Courtesy of Suboor Usmani.

"conquered the airwaves." Radio Ceylon rose to fame in the wake of AIR's reforms and the minister of information and broadcasting's diatribe against Hindi film songs. Radio Ceylon's broadcasting techniques, unlike AIR's didactic music programs, fostered listening audiences' active participation in programs, effectively promoted "audile techniques," and made active use of radio resonance's power. In so doing, Radio Ceylon was able to forge a transnational aural *filmi* culture that actively contested the state borders of 1947 and that promoted shared culture across national borders.

By 1957, B. V. Keskar relented on his tirade against film music when he half-heartedly inaugurated Vividh Bharti, a variety music station that broadcast film-song programs. Ten years later, following Radio Ceylon's continual expansion and growing popularity, Vividh Bharti too began to air commercial programs emulating Radio Ceylon styles and its "format of communication with the absent."[115] As Vividh Bharti grew in the decades to come, its broadcasters promoted an aural *filmi* experience in competition with and alongside Radio Ceylon.[116] By the mid-1970s, Radio Ceylon's transmitter had deteriorated significantly, and Vividh Bharti's programs began to win audiences from

4.12 Poster advertisement for the film *Baiju Bāvrā*. Notice how prominently the film's songs feature in this ad.

Source: National Film Archive of India.

the Ceylon-based station. By then, the Indian government, and especially the Ministry of Information and Broadcasting, had come nearly full circle with its anti-Hindi-film-song stance and had begun to embrace these songs as a sort of national culture.

Certainly a longer story could be told of how the Indian government through Vividh Bharti and other initiatives sought to co-opt the aural *filmi* culture that Radio Ceylon pioneered. Yet a couple of things remain clear: Vividh Bharti's growing popularity could not erase an earlier history. The aural *filmi* culture that Radio Ceylon built consciously challenged the nation-state borders of 1947 and enabled the growth of a shared aural culture. This is part of the reason why Hindi film songs in Pakistan remain a crucial aspect of popular culture, even as the Pakistani government restricted access to Indian-made films. More important, however, is that Radio Ceylon sustained the idea of the Indian subcontinent as a homeland for people of all faiths by building a transnational soundscape. And it did so in direct opposition to the Indian government's radio reforms outlined in the previous chapter.

I close our discussion of Radio Ceylon by returning to the film *Baiju Bāvrā*, whose song "Tū Ganga kī mouj, maiṅ Jamuna kā dhārā" (You are the wave of the River Ganga, I am the current of the River Jamuna) I referenced in the book's opening vignette. The film *Baiju Bāvrā*, set during the reign of the Mughal emperor Akbar, juxtaposes the lives of two musicians: Baijnath (Baiju for short), the talented son of a poor folk singer, and Tansen, a celebrated royal court musician. During the film's climax, Baijnath and Tansen are caught in a musical feud that the aesthete emperor presides over. The emperor has vowed to execute the weaker performer. First released in 1952, *Baiju Bāvrā*, like its songs, indirectly addresses the politics of sound that engulfed the subcontinent during the first decade of independence (figure 4.12). The two dueling musicians could very well be compared to two radio networks: AIR and Radio Ceylon. Much like Baijnath and Tansen, AIR and Radio Ceylon were competitors, not for the ears of a music-loving emperor but for the soundscape of an independent India. During the film's conclusion, however, neither musician faces that tragic fate because their music, which enchants not only the royal court but also the film's listening audiences, emerges as the only possible winner of the challenge. AIR and Radio Ceylon's own feud ended in a similar manner. Ultimately, it is the music that emerged triumphant.

PART III

DRAMATIC RADIO
AND THE 1965
INDO-PAKISTAN WAR

CHAPTER 5

RADIO PAKISTAN'S SEVENTEEN DAYS OF DRAMA

On the morning of September 6, 1965, the Indian army bombed a canal near the Wagah border. The explosion was audible in parts of Lahore but, in the following weeks, many in Pakistan— especially in the cities of Lahore and Karachi—heard the "sounds of war" through their radio receivers. Within hours of the Indian army offensive, Radio Pakistan inaugurated an intensive "morale-raising" campaign. Radio stations throughout Pakistan aired continuous news updates as well as artistic programs, including patriotic *mušāirā* (poetry recital gatherings), music programs, and dramatic productions.

The Indian army's offensive followed a series of military skirmishes between the Indian and Pakistani armies that had begun nine months earlier.[1] Although the two countries did not officially declare war, the various clashes between the Indian and Pakistani armies in 1965—starting in February 1965 in the Rann of Kutch and concluding with the Soviet Union–sponsored ceasefire signed in Tashkent by President Ayub Khan and Prime Minister Lal Bahadur Shastri in February 1966—came to be known as the 1965 Indo-Pakistan War. For broadcasters and radio listeners in Pakistan, however, the war lasted seventeen days: it began on the morning of September 6, 1965, with the Indian army attack in Lahore and ended with the United Nations–sponsored ceasefire agreement on September 22, 1965. More than during any other armed conflict in Pakistan's history, radio was the primary medium for shaping most urban Pakistanis' experience of the conflict with India.[2] These so-called seventeen days of war are the subject of this chapter, and the war's ideology, aftermath, and larger significance are the subject of part III.[3]

Drawing on a collection of recordings in Islamabad and published transcripts of broadcasts, this chapter demonstrates how an intense radio programming campaign that lasted a mere seventeen days effectively transformed an otherwise minor military conflict into a significant cultural and political event.[4] Chapter 6 turns to the war's aftermath and explains how an Indian-based radio service, inaugurated shortly after the war's end, contested the war's ideology in the decades that followed. In both chapters, I focus on what I call "dramatic radio," which includes radio plays, but, as I outline in chapter 6, also dramatic interpretations of listeners' letters to the radio stations.

In my understanding of the 1965 war as an event, I rely on Paddy Scannell's perception of events as purposeful creations. An event, Scannell writes, has "forestructure that is realized . . . as it unfolds, as it takes place as it is meant to take place." Naturally, events don't always work out as planned, but they are "invested with a set of expectations (however great or small)."[5] In this chapter, I analyze how the "sounds of war" were created. I do so, however, "with an ear towards" the medium-specific techniques and conventions that broadcasters and performers used to embed meaning and ceremony in the military clash in Punjab.[6] In particular, I am interested in how radio reels in listeners, carries them over long distances, mobilizes many voices, and makes those voices appear to be a harmonious chorus. Close analysis of the broadcast material moves us even closer to the historical moment and the soundscape of war. Expanding on Scannell's analysis, I demonstrate, that it was not that there was disparity between the "actual" scale of the event and what radio or the media hype made of it, but rather that that the media hype *was* the event. It is revealing, for example, that many radio listeners described the singers, writers, and artists that participated in Radio Pakistan's campaigns as soldiers and weapons. One listener explained: "We felt that Pakistan's army was attacking the enemy with bombs and airplanes and every night a writer through his art was beating India's strategies."[7] In conversation with works on radio drama in the United States, in particular Neil Verma's *Theater of the Mind*, I listen to the ways in which Radio Pakistan's broadcasters staged a soundscape of war.[8] In this chapter, more than any of the previous ones, the act of physically listening to the broadcast material takes precedence, and in my analysis of the war, I foreground the actual broadcast material. The wider accessibility of radio receivers and the availability of transistors as well as the sheer intensity of the event ensured that many more listeners tuned in to radio broadcasts. But even then, radio resonance continued to play a crucial role because the conversations that Radio Pakistan fostered during the seventeen days of war contributed to the soundscape of war.

Across the border, All India Radio (AIR) responded to the crisis as well, but its wartime programming was not nearly as extensive or enthusiastic as Radio Pakistan's coverage.[9] More important, whereas Radio Pakistan archived recordings of programming during the war, AIR, for the most part, did not. This, of course, tells us a great deal about the different meanings that government

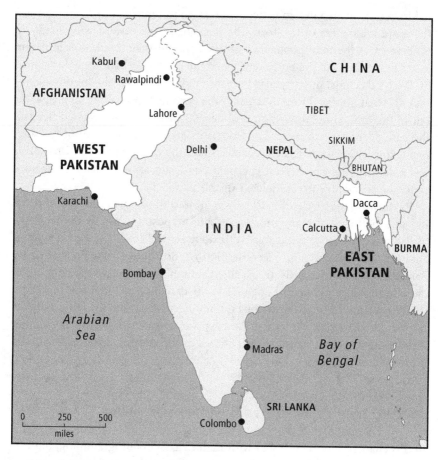

5.1 Map of East and West Pakistan, 1965.

Source: Map by Erin Greb.

organizations attached to the war and its auditory component.[10] In India, the 1965 war was a territorial dispute with a recalcitrant neighboring nation. In Pakistan, the war was a moment when nationalist energies were mobilized.

Finally, this chapter considers Radio Pakistan campaign's successes and failures. During the war, Radio Pakistan's broadcasts succeeded in galvanizing audiences in major metropolitan centers in West Pakistan, particularly in the cities of Lahore and Karachi. If listeners resisted AIR reforms in the 1950s, listeners in Pakistan supported and actively participated in Radio Pakistan's radio war. Radio Pakistan's seventeen days of war, I argue, won immediate success only to politically backfire in the near future.

The war did little to fix the country's internal problems and, in fact, further aggravated hostility between the eastern and western wings (see figure 5.1).

Pakistan was divided in two noncontiguous wings separated by more than two thousand kilometers of territory. The Bengalis in the eastern wing made up 60 percent of the total population of Pakistan, but they faced discrimination in the upper levels of the bureaucracy and the military, which were dominated by West Pakistanis, in particular Punjabis and Muhājir (Urdu-speaking communities that migrated from India after the Partition). Moreover, language was one of the most contentious points of debate. East Pakistanis wanted Bengali, the native language of most East Pakistanis and more than half of the total population of Pakistan, to be an official state language on par with Urdu. This was a demand for which West Pakistani politicians at best made conciliatory concessions and at worst completely dismissed.[11]

By drawing the circle of nationalism around the Punjab, the site of fighting and the focus of many broadcasts, and by posing Urdu as the language of Pakistan, the 1965 "radio war" ultimately set the stage for the breakup of Pakistan and East Pakistan succession in 1971. So although the story of Radio Pakistan's war campaign is an excellent example of how governments used radio to mobilize nationalist energies in the early postcolonial era, this radio war also brings to light the serious limitations that nationalist radio projects faced in South Asia. Ultimately, the 1965 war reveals the fault lines running through South Asian nationalisms, as well as the endurance of transnational listening audiences.

The 1965 Indo-Pakistan War in Historical Context

In this chapter, I am concerned with Radio Pakistan's programming, but it is important to first place the 1965 war—and its broadcasts—in the context of a longer history of hostility between the two newly formed countries. At its core, the 1965 war was a territorial dispute dating back to pre-independence days. Mohammed Ali Jinnah and others in the Muslim League wholeheartedly believed that the princely state of Kashmir belonged in Pakistan because the majority of this state's population was Muslim. When Kashmir's monarch, Maharaja Hari Singh (who was Hindu) showed signs that he might join India, the Pakistani government sent a covert military operation to the region. In response, Indian prime minister Jawaharlal Nehru then sent the Indian army to Kashmir. This military dispute between India and Pakistan, which came to be known as the First Kashmir War (the 1965 war became the second) ended with a United Nations–sponsored ceasefire that allotted more than 60 percent of Kashmir to India.[12]

As the Cold War unfolded, Pakistani leaders—most prominently General Ayub Khan, who became head of state in 1958 following a military coup— warmed up to the United States.[13] Ayub Khan reckoned that befriending the

United States would help Pakistan gain international support for its claim over Kashmir. More important, Ayub Khan hoped (and was right) that the United States would build up Pakistan's army.[14] Ayub Khan's plans, however, began to go awry in the early 1960s, when the United States leaned closer to India, hoping to check China's growing power in the region. President John F. Kennedy tried to reassure the then very anxious Ayub Khan that whatever assistance the United States would give to India would be used only against the Chinese. Kennedy's assurances, however, were to no avail.[15] The 1965 Indo-Pakistan War arose in the context of this now strained U.S.-Pakistan relationship.

In February 1965, Indian and Pakistani armies had a skirmish in the Rann of Kutch, a swampy and mostly uninhabitable territory near the Gujarat border. According to U.S. State Department analysts, the Pakistani army purposefully provoked the Indian army by occupying Indian territory, but the details of this skirmish remain unclear to this day. In June 1965, British prime minister Harold Wilson successfully persuaded India and Pakistan to end hostilities.[16]

Within months, however, trouble arose in Kashmir; rebels raided roads linking Kashmir to other major North Indian cities.[17] Khan, after some heavy pressure, acknowledged to U.S. officials that he had sent Pakistani soldiers to Kashmir disguised as civilians.[18] He did not, however, make that information available to the Pakistani public or even to many of his close associates. Radio Pakistan broadcasters have suggested that, at the time, they were not aware of the Pakistani army's complicity in the upheaval in Kashmir or the Rann of Kutch. Although it is impossible to verify broadcasters' claims, it is true that Pakistan's complicity in Kashmir and the Rann of Kutch did not become public knowledge until decades later, when Ayub Khan's close associates published tell-all accounts.[19]

On the morning of September 6, the Indian army retaliated and launched a military attack near the Lahore border.[20] The attack took both the Pakistani military, then preoccupied with the fighting in Kashmir and Kutch, and the Lahore public by surprise.[21] Radio Pakistan's seventeen days of war began immediately after.

Making a Radio War

Within hours of the Indian army attack near the Punjab border, Ayub Khan took to the airwaves. "Pakistanis now face a major test," he told radio audiences. "This morning the Indian army attacked Pakistan from Lahore."[22] Making no mention of the previous skirmishes in Kashmir and Kutch, Khan went on to explain the significance of the occurrence, relying on conspiracy theories about Indian rulers' deep-seated hatred toward Pakistan. "For the past eighteen years," Khan told listeners, Indian politicians "have been preparing for war against Pakistan." Ayub Khan claimed that the very existence of Pakistan was under threat and urged them to draw strength from their faith: "The Indian rulers, perhaps, do not know who they face. Faith and belief are in our hearts." Pakistan will win, Ayub Khan assured his listeners, because "the words, 'there is no God but Allah and Muhammad is his messenger' echo in the hearts of Pakistan's people." Ayub Khan concluded: "We will not sit in a peace until we once and for all silence the enemy's canons."[23] Immediately after Ayub Khan's speech, Radio Pakistan's nine stations suspended normal services and replaced scheduled programs with rolling continual news, discussion, patriotic music performances, poetry recitals, and radio plays for and about the current military conflict.[24]

Broadcasters—including news anchors, program managers, and station directors—contributed above and beyond the call of duty. For instance, Azam Khan, the music director of the Lahore station, remembers sleeping in the basement, skipping meals, and surviving off peanuts and *gur* (a kind of molasses) during the "days of war."[25] Broadcasters' memories recounted a half-century later are colored, of course, by nostalgia. Radio Pakistan employees were officially government employees and would have had no choice but to support Ayub Khan's undertakings or risk losing their jobs. That said, more than the broadcasters' sentimental stories of the war, the sheer amount of original material produced during this remarkably short period, as evidenced by the war archive in Islamabad, suggests that many broadcasters did indeed give their time and energy willingly and enthusiastically.[26]

Moreover, the 1965 war presented a marvelous opportunity for broadcasters, singers, writers, and poets to shine in the public light. Many seized the moment. For example, Shakeel Ahmad, a newsreader from Lahore station, gained unprecedented fame after the 1965 war. His dramatic style of reading, which included fast delivery with abrupt, but carefully selected, pauses and clear and deliberate enunciation became iconic during the war and its aftermath. In the years to come, broadcasters in both India and Pakistan came to mimic his style. The broadcaster Mirza Sultan Beg, also from the Lahore station, likewise gained considerable fame during the war through his talk show *Nizamuddin*, which aired from the Lahore station. Beg played the character Nizamuddin and shared personal experiences about the soldiers fighting in the war, whom he claimed to have interviewed in-person on the actual battlefield. Although Beg had worked in radio for twenty-one years, his performance during the war, at least one account noted, was the highlight of his career.[27]

Not only Radio Pakistan's broadcasters, but also singers and writers, some of whom were not employed or directly associated with Radio Pakistan, also stepped into the spotlight during the war. The story of the singer and actress Nur Jehan's decision to volunteer to sing during the war is perhaps best known. She phoned the Lahore radio station from her home immediately after she heard Ayub Khan's broadcast and offered to sing on the radio. The station director did not believe it was her speaking until Nur Jehan showed up the next day, allegedly in a white sari.[28] Mehdi Hassan, who by 1965 had already gained considerable fame through his enchanting *ǧazal* performances, composed and sang several patriotic songs from the Karachi station. Mehdi Hassan and Nur Jehan performed in both Urdu and Punjabi. Other singers whose voices reverberated during the "seventeen days of drama" include Zarina Agha, Umeed Ali Khan, Gulzar Ahmad, and Khurshid Begum.[29]

Writers and poets were also active during the radio campaign. Well-known poets, including Ahmad Nadim Qasmi, Mukhtar Siddiqui, Safdar Mir, Ada Jafri, Himayat Ali Shair, Mustafa Zaidi, Shafi Aqeel, Jaun Elia, and Kishwar Naheed, composed and recited poetry supporting the Pakistani army.[30] Radio Pakistan aired many live *mušāirā*, mostly in Urdu but also in Punjabi, Pashto, Sindhi, and Baloch. In addition, poets also organized more informal "war" *mušāirā* in private living rooms, school auditoriums, and press clubs. Some of these private *mušāirā* were recorded and later broadcast on the radio.[31]

The Urdu critic C. M. Naim, in an in-depth study of the 1965 Urdu war poetry, concludes that among literary circles in Pakistan during the war "the opinion was nearly unanimous" that writers must defend "their country by means of their writings."[32] Some poets, however, chose not to participate. Most notably the prominent leftist Urdu poet, Faiz Ahmad Faiz, remained silent during the war, most likely for political reasons. Similarly, the renowned Urdu poet Josh Malihabadi, who had long been critical of the Pakistani government and its anti-India stance, did not participate in war *mušāirā*.[33]

Many amateur singers and poets also contributed to the radio campaign. The Karachi station, for example, actively encouraged student groups to perform on the radio during the seventeen days of war. A singing group from the Government College for Women performed several songs in the Karachi station. Mehdi Hassan accompanied this all-female singing group as the leading voice. The Jinnah College for Women, NED Engineering College, and Islamia College for Women also performed patriotic songs on the radio.[34]

It is crucial to mention that not all of Radio Pakistan's stations responded equally to the crisis. The Lahore station, closest to the site of fighting, followed by the Karachi and Rawalpindi (then the provisional capital) radio stations were the most active. Radio Pakistan's stations at the time were not well connected. Stations could share speeches and news bulletins over the telephone, but they could not simultaneously broadcast longer plays or song programs for which sound quality mattered greatly. The Lahore and the Karachi stations managed to share some productions by sending recordings using a rushed postage system during the days of war, but correspondence with other radio stations was difficult and cumbersome.[35]

Not only did the Lahore radio station remain most active during the war, but it was also the focal point of many productions from other cities, as it had been the site of the Indian military attack. Many poems, songs, and plays were addressed to Punjab, or more specifically to Lahore, and either consciously or unconsciously promoted a Punjabi-centric form of nationalism. For instance, an ensemble from the Government College for Women performed an Urdu song titled "Xittā-e-Lahore tere jāṅ nisāroṅ ko salām" (Region of Lahore, I salute those [soldiers] who readily sacrifice their lives for you) from the Lahore station. The poet John Elia penned the lyrics to the song "Lahore sar-baland hai, Lahore zindābād" (Mighty Lahore, long live Lahore).[36] Also, the radio drama, *Maulvī jī*, which I analyze in more detail in succeeding pages, most likely aired from the Karachi station but was set in a village near Lahore. In this way, the war promoted a Punjabi-centric form of nationalism that would have serious consequences in the years to come.

It is also crucial to note the importance of the radio transistors presence in Pakistan to the seventeen days of war. Film magazines and newspapers, for example, widely advertised battery-operated transistors, including cheaper Pakistan-assembled transistors (figure 5.2).[37] Although I have not been able to find specific statistics, ads, as well Radio Pakistan's own accounts, do suggest that transistors were already available in 1965 and many more Pakistanis had access to radio, particularly in urban centers like Lahore and Karachi (figure 5.3).[38]

In this chapter, I pay special attention to the "actual sounds of radio," providing close readings of war productions. Yet radio resonance remained important during this period as the radio war's success hinged on the wider conversation and excitement that radio broadcasts spurred. The power of Nur Jehan's songs addressed to male soldiers and generals is that they were easy to put to memory and to sing in private and public spaces. Similarly, the racy plots of plays like *Nidā-e-Haq* (Voice of truth) and their memorable characters invited discussions.

Nur Jehan's War Songs and Radio's "Liveness"

Nur Jehan's war songs are the most celebrated items of the war and have best survived the test of time. Ask anybody in Pakistan, young or old, what she knows about the 1965 war, and she is likely to talk about Nur Jehan's memorable radio performance. She might even hum one of Jehan's tunes, which are still traded in MP3 and CD form in Pakistan's many media bazaars and are widely available on the internet.[39] Despite the focus on her in popular memory, Jehan's singular extraordinary performance during the war was the result

5.2 Advertisement for a popular transistor brand in *Eastern Film*, an English-language film magazine, from 1966.

Source: University of Texas at Austin Collection.

of an entire broadcasting team's effort. Among them was the music producer Azam Khan, the poet Sufi Tabbassum, who wrote many of the lyrics of her war songs, and a group of dedicated musicians from Radio Pakistan's Lahore radio station, which included Nazim Ali (*bansuri*), Sadiq Mandu (*tabla*), and Faizi Sahab (*sarod*).[40]

In his retelling of events Azam Khan notes that shortly after Nur Jehan called the radio station and volunteered to sing, the station director took him aside and gave him one assignment: make sure Nur Jehan records one new song every day. Composing a song is a creative endeavor that can take weeks,

5.3 Advertisement for the *Naǧmā* (song) transistor, printed in *Eastern Film* in 1968. The interesting aspect of this advertisement is that it advertises this radio as ideal for working people but is printed in an English-language magazine for a clearly elite audience. The intent appears to be to convince elite Pakistanis to purchase this transmitter for the people working in their home.

Source: University of Texas at Austin Collection.

sometimes months. Azam Khan, however, came remarkably close to achieving his goal; he oversaw the production of twelve songs during the seventeen days of war.[41]

On September 8, just two days after the Indian army's attack on Punjab, Nur Jehan performed the original Punjabi song "Mereyā ḍhol sipāhiyā tenuṅ rabb diyāṅ rakkhāṅ" (My beloved soldier, may God guard you) on the radio. The song, penned by Sufi Tabassum and composed by Azam Khan and Nur Jehan, was dedicated to the lower-rank soldiers fighting on the front against India. Azam Khan remembers that that evening the phone would not stop ringing. People called to congratulate Nur Jehan on her performance and to request that the station replay the song again and again. In the days to come, many listeners also mailed suggestions for song lyrics for Nur Jehan to interpret.[42] A few days later, largely in response to requests that Nur Jehan also sing for army officers and generals who, like lower-rank soldiers, put their lives on the line, Sufi Tabassum wrote the lyrics to the Punjabi song "Merā māhī chhail chhabīlā hāye nī karnail nī, jarnail nī" (My splendid beloved, oh colonel, oh general).[43] The song was dedicated to the high-ranking officers leading the attack against India.

Nur Jehan's persona was almost as important as the songs she performed. She was thirty-nine years old in 1965, and by then, had built an extraordinary career that had spanned several media: from theater to film / ("talkies") to radio. Nur Jehan was no symbol of female purity or homely Pakistani values. On the contrary, she was known for her sensuality, which unfortunately many described as promiscuity. Nur Jehan's first husband, Shaukat Hussain Rizvi, wrote a scathing memoir of their life together criticizing her "lowly" origins and accusing her of having multiple affairs while they were married.[44] Similarly, the renowned Urdu short-story writer Saadat Hasan Manto, acclaimed by many for his insightful writing about women, in a posthumously published memoir, wrote that the singer-actress drank alcohol and had a way with men. Manto ultimately concluded that the renowned singer-actress clearly exemplified all the qualities of her "lowly" class.[45] As an example of Nur Jehan's questionable character, Manto wrote that Nur Jehan once wore a šalvār-qamīz (shirt and pant ensemble) made of net material that exposed her body when the sun rays hit at a particular angle. Manto, however, did not write why he had waited for the sun to hit at that particular angle.[46]

Nur Jehan was born Allah Wasai, to a musically and artistically inclined Punjabi family of humble means in 1926. As a young child, she traveled with her family from her hometown of Qasur in Punjab to the province's capital, Lahore, where she and her sisters performed in plays. In later years, she moved to Calcutta and finally to Bombay, following the film and theater industries.[47] She became a household name in her twenties after her performance in the extremely successful film *Xāndān*, released in 1942. A journalist and long-time fan of the actress-singer, Khalid Hassan, however, believes it was the less well-known film *Zīnat*, released three years after *Xāndān*, that first showcased Nur Jehan's musical talent. In a *qawwali* number, her voice, Hassan remarks, was "like a flame leaping out."[48] Indeed, musicologists have noted that it was Nur Jehan who pioneered the high-pitched, crooning singing style highly suited for the age of sound reproduction technologies, the same style that the playback singer Lata Mangeshkar perfected and widely popularized in later years.[49]

After Partition, Nur Jehan migrated to Pakistan. With her departure from India, Nur Jehan left the field open for Lata and her younger sister, Asha Bhosle, to dominate the Bombay film industry's music scene. In Pakistan, Nur Jehan found her own, if indeed very different, voice and musical success. During the 1965 war, she seized the moment, and her voice then indisputably "leapt out like flame."

Even in Pakistan and away from the Indian film industry, Nur Jehan remained in competition with the younger Lata in India. During the Independence Day celebration in 1962, Lata had performed the song "Ai mere vatan ke logoṅ, zarā āṅkh meṅ bhar lo pānī" (Oh my countrymen, bring tears to your eyes), which honored the Indian soldiers who died in the Indo-China War of 1962. The renowned film-music composer Ramachandra composed the tune, which is widely believed to have brought Prime Minister Nehru to tears. Nur Jehan's performance in September 1965, while much more extensive than Lata's prior performance, must have felt, at least to some, like a rebuttal of some sort.

As Neepa Majumdar has pointed out, Lata's star persona is defined precisely "by the absence of physical beauty and glamour" and, in many instances, seemed completely desexualized.[50] In contrast, Nur Jehan's flirtatious songs addressed to male soldiers promoted a kind of romance not only between the actress and soldiers but also between Nur Jehan and her listening public. Nur Jehan's 1965 war songs had a subtle but powerful message: India might have the stoic and asexual Lata to urge India to mourn martyred soldiers in a war it had clearly lost, but Pakistan had the fiery and sensual Nur Jehan, whose voice inspired soldiers and generals to fight fearlessly and, most important, to win.[51]

Moreover, the "liveness" (the feeling that the event is taking place "live" and was not prerecorded) of Nur Jehan's performance on the radio was a key part of its appeal. In her own retelling of the war days, Nur Jehan explained the significance of her live radio performances (figure 5.4). "When I sang 'Mereyā ḍhol sipāhiyā,' it was not pre-recorded. I sang it straight into the microphone and it went out live because the tape recorder was not working. It was [a] very poignant moment for me, and I cried a lot."[52] Even when prerecorded, her songs also directly or indirectly commented on current news. This helped give the war radio programming a "real time feel" and promoted the feeling of "liveness," which was crucial in instigating an emotional response from the audience. For instance, Nur Jehan recorded the original Punjabi song "Merā sohṇā she- har kasūr nī hoyā duniyā vicc mašhūr nī" (My beautiful city of Qasur is now famous through the world) shortly after listeners learned that the Indian and

اے وطن کے سجیلے جوانو

میرے نغمے تمھارے لئے ہیں

Noor Jehan the darling of our soldiers on front.

5.4 Nur Jehan performing for Radio Pakistan, *Eastern Film*, 1966.

Source: University of Texas at Austin Collection.

Pakistani armies had fought in the town of Qasur, which was incidentally Nur Jehan's birthplace. As John Durham Peters points out, many of the most successful radio performers "exploited liveness" to "cut through the public anxiety about fakery and duplication in the radio world." The performance of "liveness" enabled a "token of the live body" to "extend across the waves to assure truthfulness."[53] By emphasizing the "liveness" of her life persona, Nur Jehan sought to convey to audiences a sense of authenticity.

Although the act of listening to Nur Jehan's voice live was important, radio resonance continued to play a role during the war. Part of the reason for Nur Jehan's fame and success is that the songs' influence extended outside the reach of radio receivers. Although most accounts emphasize the act of listening to the radio, it is clear that Nur Jehan's songs were sung and enjoyed in family gatherings. Her remarkable performance was also the source of conversation and praise during the days of war.[54] As the music director, Azam Khan, explained to me in an interview, even those who might not have physically heard Nur Jehan's voice, for one reason or another, could not possibly miss "the talk" about her live performance on the air. Nur Jehan won the Pride of Performance award not just because her singing was superb, as Khan noted, but also because of the sheer attention her performance on the radio received and the excitement it spurred.[55]

Nur Jehan's songs played an important role in galvanizing support for the war, especially in the cities of Lahore and Karachi. Her songs in Punjabi and Urdu, like many of the 1965 war broadcasts, endorsed a Punjabi-centric type of nationalism that helped draw the circle of Pakistani nationalism closer to Punjab. As I further explain later in this chapter, in later years, a movement emerged that posed Punjabi against Urdu and argued that Punjabi's literary and cultural heritage had been repressed by Urdu. Punjabi literary figures contended that Punjabis had all too readily "relinquished their language" in favor of Urdu and "ensure[d] their dominance in state administration and other positions of authority."[56] This movement, known as the Punjabiyat, gained strength during the 1980s. During the 1965 war, however, Urdu and Punjabi were not set against each other but rather complemented each other.

Radio Pakistan's "Theater of the Mind"

Drama production, like songs, also helped galvanize listeners during Radio Pakistan's seventeen days of war. These productions drew on what was by then a well-established tradition of radio drama. By the time of the 1965 war, radio drama in Pakistan had emerged as an independent genre with a distinct aesthetic aural experience. Broadcasters and writers had developed a set of sound techniques and writing conventions that aurally conveyed "space, time, movement, and emotion."[57] The Lahore and Karachi radio stations in particular were centers of radio drama production and attracted high-profile writers, such as Rafi Pir, Imtiaz Ali Taj, Ashfaq Ahmad, and Intizar Hussain among others.[58] Radio Pakistan also attracted and formed talented actors, such as Mohni Hameed, Parveen Akhtar, Aqeel Ahmad, Khurshid Shahid, Mirza Sultan Beg, Sultan Khoosat, and Zia Mohyeddin. Radio Pakistan produced plays in various regional languages, but Urdu and, to a lesser extent Punjabi, took the lead.

Much work can be done on Urdu radio drama in the subcontinent—the genre's development, its aesthetic contributions, and its relationship to other traditions, such as stage drama and film.[59] Both AIR and Radio Pakistan produced radio plays in the decades following independence, but this genre seems to have flourished in Pakistan more than in India partly because the lucrative Bombay film industry attracted India's best writers, producers, and actors. In contrast, Pakistan's nascent and not nearly as economically successful film industry left more room for radio drama to prosper. During the 1965 Indo-Pakistan War, radio producers, writers, and actors showcased their skills and talents.

Existing radio serials, such as Intizar Hussain's *Mīyāṅ Ke Yahāṅ* (Mian's place), which broadcast from the Karachi station, and Ashfaq Ahmad's *Talqeen Shah*, which aired from the Lahore station, continued to play during normal programming hours. Writers and producers, however, improvised new episodes that addressed the current military crisis.[60] *Talqeen Shah*, in particular, attended to the military conflict in a rather creative way.[61] During the days of war, the main character, Talqeen Shah, played by Ashfaq Ahmad, had a few brawls with a hostile neighbor named Hashmi, who had stolen a flower vase from Talqeen Shah's house. Hashmi Sahab now claimed he was the rightful owner of the vase. Hashmi had become friends with a young man called John Hussain, who eagerly supported Hashmi's sneaky moves. The flower vase represented Kashmir, which was famous for its scenic landscapes, Hashmi represented Prime Minister Shastri, and John Hussain represented U.S. president Lyndon B. Johnson.

Radio Pakistan also aired a number of plays exclusively produced for the war. In the following pages, I offer close readings of two such dramatic productions. In my readings of these plays, I draw on theoretical devices and vocabulary recently developed by scholars of radio drama that help us "hear" how these productions were able to transform a minor military conflict into a significant event and how they sought to create citizen-listeners.

Maulvī jī and Audioposition

The play *Maulvī jī* is a short radio drama produced and aired during the 1965 war. It was likely replayed after the war as well. The catalog does not list the station that broadcast the play, but the play's location in the archive as well the cast suggest that the play first aired from Karachi.[62] The play is set in an unnamed Pakistani village. The narrator and main actor is a young girl named Billo, who, based on her voice and speech pattern, we can estimate is between eight and twelve years old. Billo narrates the story of her village Maulvi's (Islamic preacher) tragic martyrdom. The play's appeal, however, is not its plot, but rather its sound techniques—the way in which the play, through sound, is available to convey place and space and consequently to evoke emotion in listeners. In my reading of this play, I pay special attention to what Neil Verma calls "audioposition"— that is, the listeners' point of view in the radio plays—and how such position helps evoke emotion.[63] Listening for audioposition constitutes one way of examining how this 1965 war radio play *resonated* with listeners.

The first scene opens with a long flute solo that slowly fades as Billo's equally melodic voice takes center stage. In her village, Billo explains, only boys can go to school, but her schoolmaster father tutors her in the evenings. She knows how to read and recently completed her first Urdu book. She recites one of her favorite prayers from the book. She evokes the sounds of her village life: the call of the vegetable seller, who visits her home every afternoon, the tinkling of the bulls' bells announcing their return from the fields just when the sun begins to set, and the ducks' squawking and splashing in the nearby ponds. But she holds religious sounds dearest to her heart—two in particular: the sound of schoolboys' voices praying in the morning assembly and the sound of the Maulvi's *azān* calling devotees to prayer five times a day.

We, the listeners, are "positioned" in proximity to Billo. She doesn't speak to us. Instead, she speaks to herself, and we can hear her thoughts because we are "positioned" in her mind. September 6, Billo explains, began like every other day, with the sweet sound of the Maulvi's *azān* calling devotees to prayer at the break of dawn. Like every other day, Billo gets out of bed as soon as she hears the *azān* and runs to the rooftop of her house to watch the village men making their way to the mosque. Today, however, something is amiss; in the background, Billo can decipher (as we can also) a soft, muffled rumble. This low growl soon turns into an awesome roar. It is now that we the listeners realize that this play reenacts the Indian army attack near the Punjab border. The play, as we would expect, also purports the Pakistani government's stance that the Indian raid near Lahore was completely unexpected and unjustified and that more than a military strike, it was an attack on Pakistan's very identity—a threat to the country's existence and, consequently, an attack on Islam itself.

In the next scene, our audioposition changes abruptly from Billo's mind to inside the village mosque. We hear the deep and aged voice of the village Maulvi: "I will not abandon my mosque, . . . take the women and children to safety," followed by the unidentified voices of men, one after another: "I will not abandon the house of God"; "I also will not abandon the house of God"; "I too will not abandon the house of God." A chorus of male voices follows: "We will not leave the house of God." The voices of the unidentified men in the mosque and the voice of Maulvi seem to revolve around us. In this, we, the listeners, are neither closer to nor farther from anybody, but we seem to inhabit a kind of abstract space, where we do not hear voices from their own locations, but from where the voices come to us.

Verma calls this kind of sequence, where voices "leap from one mike to another 'objectively' arraying the world before us, kaleidosonic audioposition."[64] He writes that dramatists from the United States in the 1930s used this technique to introduce listeners to varied perspectives and to take them on tours across the country. *Maulvī jī* does not go that far, but in the mosque scene, the listeners are positioned in a neutral space—at an equal distance from all characters, which, indeed, is quite different from the space listeners inhabit in earlier scenes when they are coupled with Billo's mind.

Another abrupt scene change returns us to Billo's mind. Unlike stage drama or even film in which frequent scene changes can be cumbersome, radio plays often include many abrupt scene changes with minimal segues. Listeners in 1960s Pakistan, familiar with this artistic genre, would have been well accustomed to quickly adjusting to the changing audio scenario. From the rooftop of her house, Billo hears an explosion (and so do we). She then describes how the mosque's tall minar dramatically falls to the ground, signifying an assault on Islam. A group of uniformed soldiers wearing shoes, Billo also informs us, rampage the mosque immediately after the minar's dramatic fall.

Once again, our audioposition shifts to the mosque. "You've dishonored the house of God," the Maulvi defiantly tells the soldiers. One soldier yells at the Maulvi: "Stop this nonsense, and tell us where the Pakistani army is hiding." We hear gunshots and then briefly return to Billo's mind. Her voice breaks as she realizes that the Indian soldier just killed the Maulvi. The sight of his red blood spreading on the mosque's white marble floor, she remarks, is as awe-inspiring as it is devastating. We once more return to the mosque and hear the voices of the village men chanting one after another: "Maulvi ji has become a martyr," "I will protect the house of Allah," "I am a pillar of the mosque." Then a chorus follows: "We are all a pillar of the mosque"; "Our house is the house of God."

In these concluding scenes, kaleidosonic audioposition conveys a sense of comradeship or brotherhood—a feeling that we, the listeners, are all in this together. It is also telling, for example, that it is not Pakistani soldiers whose voices we hear at the end of this play, but ordinary village men, first chanting one after another, and finally chanting in unison, giving the feeling of a unified chorus in which many voices might participate.[65] Throughout this play, the careful juxtaposing of intimate and kaleidosonic audioposition allows listeners to feel both a personal and an intimate connection with Billo as well as a sense of comradeship with strangers, making the war at once an intimate and collective experience.

Nidā-e-Haq: A Tale of Transmission

The dramatic production that stole the limelight during the seventeen days of war was a sketch radio drama serial written by the film writer Naseer Anwar called *Nidā-e-Haq* (Voice of truth) that aired from the Lahore radio station every evening at nine o'clock.[66] The play features two male characters, Mian and Mahashay, who represent Pakistan and India, respectively. The two men discuss the ongoing military conflict between India and Pakistan. In this way, the show effectively thematizes communication between two warring nations.

The terms *miyāṅ* and *mahāšae* are respectful titles of address for men, similar to the English-language titles "sir" or "Mr." *Mahāšae* is a Sanskrit-origin word with the suffix "maha" meaning great. The word *miyāṅ* has a more Muslim orientation, but it is not an explicitly Islamic term of address. A schoolmaster, regardless of his religious identity, might be addressed as *miyāṅ*, as could a husband or, in some cases, even a father. In the play, however, Mahashay is unequivocally Hindu and Indian; Mian is Muslim and Pakistani (see figure 5.5).

5.5 Aqeel Ahmad (Mahashay) and S. A. Amīn (Mian) in the Lahore radio station studio during a recording of *Nidā-e-Haq*.

Source: *Roznāmā Anjān,* January 3, 1966. Courtesy of Azam Khan.

As one newspaper review of the play remarked, "Mahashey was greedy, fraud; he was a betrayer, and a living emblem of deceit." Mian, in contrast, "had Pakistan's dignified and respected personality; he was the voice of truth."[67]

A strong gendered dynamic is also at play here. By employing male voices, *Nidā-e-Haq* presents the 1965 Indo-Pakistan War as a dispute between men. Female voices, including the melodious voice of Nur Jehan, certainly could cheer men on the battlefield. Moreover, female characters, like the young and innocent Billo in *Maulvī jī* were personally affected by the war. *Nidā*, however, makes it clear that the actual fighting—verbal as much as physical—was a man's domain. Female voices perform supporting roles, serving as a chorus in what was essentially a verbal match between men. Turning to Adriana Cavarero's analysis of the relationships among gender, voice, and embodiment can be helpful. Cavarero explains: "Symptomatically, the symbolic patriarchal order that identified the masculine with reason and the feminine with the body is precisely an order that privileges the semantic with respect to the vocal." In other words, "woman sings, man thinks."[68] During the 1965 war, men thought/deliberated/spoke/fought while women, and in particular Nur Jehan, sang—playing a supportive and ultimately physical role. The story of the 1965 radio war therefore offers further evidence of the ways in which radio reinforced prejudices against women's voices, even as it celebrated women's voices. I offer further evidence of Christine Ehrick's argument that radio helped anchor prejudices "against the female voice in the public arena" even as it applauded and celebrated the presence of women on the airwaves.[69]

Nidā's episodes are somewhere between twenty and twenty-five minutes. Recurring themes and jokes as well as references to previous episodes, give this production dramatic coherence, but the program does not have a narrative line that carries listeners from one episode to the next. Like many radio serials, *Nidā* has an improvised feeling and lacks the "glossy" finish of shorter dramatic productions like *Maulvī jī*. It might be perhaps most accurately referred to as a play sketch. Moreover, while the plot of *Maulvī jī* is a serious martyrdom meant to bring listeners to tears, *Nidā* is meant to be funny and derives humor from the litany of stereotypes about Hindus and Hinduism that it enacts. If we had to compare *Nidā* to a play familiar to radio studies scholars, *Amos 'n' Andy* (which aired from 1943 to 1955) is perhaps the most appropriate.[70]

Nidā hopes to bring Pakistani audiences together through shared laughter. Makeen Ahsan Kaleem, when commenting about this play's appeal a few years after its production, wrote: "During the time of the war everybody felt a weight, and in those days it was difficult to find an opportunity to laugh, *Nidā* would take us to the world of laughter."[71] Humor has long been an important aspect of propaganda. In a study of radio propaganda in the United States during World War II, Gerd Horten notes that "sugar-coated messages through humor" was almost always preferable to "straight propaganda," not only because humor made propaganda more digestible but also because laughter encourages "social cohesion and cross-cultural and cross-class harmony."[72]

Moreover, *Nidā* is dialogue rich. For the listener, the play's challenge—and its appeal—is to decode the characters' complex conversations, grasp the double meaning of phrases, and understand the many inside jokes. If, in *Maulvī jī*, space and sound are vital and intimacy is created through careful "positioning" of the listener, in *Nidā*, it is speech that takes center stage. In fact, we can say that the way messages are "transmitted" and "received" is the play's central motif.[73]

For the first three episodes of the play, Mian and Mahashay are pseudo-narrators. They do not speak *to* each other as much they speak *at* each other. In the third episode, the format of the program changes altogether, and Mian and Mahashay engage in what we might describe as a pure form of dialogue; they say exactly what they feel and think without any kind of filter. This unmediated dialogue not only brings the characters closer to one another, but also brings listeners closer to them. Through Mian and Mahashay's frank and unmediated conversations, we get to know their personalities, opinions, and quirks, and come to imagine them as singular representatives of what was a thoroughly ideological caricature of different national and religious personalities. As listeners, we are positioned somewhere in between the two characters and remain there throughout the serial. In this way, the play is able to create the impression that we, the listeners, are prying into a private conversation.

Mian and Mahashay's unmediated dialogue also serves another important purpose: it makes it easier for Radio Pakistan to voice a litany of abuses against Hindus without necessarily taking responsibility for them. It is telling that Mahashay (the Hindu character), and not Mian, makes most of the derogatory comments about Hinduism and Hindu.

For example, Mahashay tells us that Hindus are most comfortable in subservient roles. In nearly every episode, Mahashay addresses Mian as *maharaj*, a term of honor meaning king or ruler. Mahashay also tells us that for millennia, Hindus "have been worshiping every incarnation of power."[74] In one episode, Mahashay explains, "We have always been servants. Mountbatten has made us into a boss, but we just can't get rid of our servant scars."[75] Mahashay explains that the Vedas, which he describes as Holy Scriptures, encourage and reward cowardly behavior and condone violence against non-Hindus.[76] Crucial to this episode is that by putting the Hindu-bashing abuses in Mahashay's mouth and couching them in the context of a truthful, unfiltered conversation, the play's author, Naseer Anwar, and his production team, make the abuses not only seem less virulent but also more plausible. This method also enables the production team to push the idea that Hindus have a religious duty to hate Muslims. Mahashey tells audiences: "It is written in the Vedas . . . that Hindus must kill nonbelievers."[77]

Finally, the dialogue format also enables Radio Pakistan to present the Pakistani government's stance on a number of political issues in a casual manner, distracting audiences from the obvious fact that *Nidā* is straight government propaganda. Mahashay explains that Indian politicians refuse to let Kashmiris decide their own fate for no reason other than being greedy. In one episode, Mahashay tells Mian, "Maharaj, well you are right that India had borrowed Kashmir, but this impounded item's time has run out. We just can't return it now." In turn, Mian again tells us that Kashmiris wish to join the Pakistani union and oppose Indian rule on all accounts. The play also makes it clear that the Pakistani government will not budge on the issue of Kashmir until Indian politicians allow a plebiscite in that state.

After Kashmir, the second most important theme in the play is that India's secularism is a hoax. In a number of episodes, Mian and Mahashay discuss the misfortune of other minority groups—in particular, Sikhs, Christians, and low-caste Hindus. For instance, in one episode, Mian asks Mahashay: "Why is there not a single Sikh representative in the Indian parliament?" Mahashay answers without the least bit of hesitation: "Why would India's Hindu leaders want a Sikh representative?"[78] In another episode Mian confronts Mahashay: "The entire world knows that Indian politicians have destroyed mosques, *gurūdūāre* [place of worship for Sikhs], and churches." Mahashay responds: "Oh Maharaj, those mosques, *gurūdūāre*, and churches became Hindu temples. So what is the difference? In the end, we all worship [the Hindu God] Ram (*Bhagvān kī pūjā—Rām kī pūjā*)."[79] Unsurprisingly, Pakistan's own internal problems are absent from the narrative—in particular, East Pakistan's growing discontent with West Pakistani dominance in the government bureaucracy and in the military.

Mian and Mahashay also discuss U.S. policies in the region. As detailed earlier, the 1965 war emerged in the context of a strained U.S.-Pakistan relationship. Pakistani politicians, in particular, were angry that the United States provided military help to India during a military dispute with China in 1962. In *Nidā*, Mahashay admits that Indian politicians, smitten with the United States, are given access to weapons that they could later use against Pakistan. Mahashay goes as far as to claim that India lost the war against China in 1962 on purpose to ensure that the U.S. army would continue to provide military aid to India.[80] As we might expect, Mian and Mahashay make absolutely no mention of Pakistan's prior alliance with the United States, nor do they mention the aid the U.S. government provided to the Pakistani military.

Finally, Mahashay and Mian discuss the ongoing food crisis in India. In 1965, India experienced a bad monsoon, and grain production in the country fell significantly. The Indian government feared a famine would soon follow.[81] Naseer Anwar uses the metaphor of food in two ways. First, the metaphor suggests that Indian politicians have a total disregard for the welfare of the Indian public. While gluttonous politicians gobble down food, the Indian people starve. Second, the metaphor of hunger and food helps portray Indians—soldiers and civilians alike—as physically weak and ultimately uncourageous. In one episode, where Naseer Anwar showcased his aptitude with language, Mahashay explains that Prime Minister Lal Bahadur Shastri asked his fellow citizens to grow grains and vegetables in their own homes. Shastri even recommended that people start planting mustard seeds on their palms (*hathelī par sarsoṅ jamānā*), which is an aphorism that means to attempt the impossible. In rapid-fire delivery style, Mian tells us that the Indian prime minister asked his people to extract oil from those mustard seeds and to use that same oil to massage their heads and to regain some strength so that they could be ready to fight Pakistan.[82]

Language as Transmission

As we might expect, *Nidā* conflates language with religion in the most overt possible manner. In the absence of visual clues, the characters' diction becomes the most important signifier of communal identity. We know that Mahashay is Hindu because he speaks "Hindi" and uses Sanskrit-derived words, and we know that Mian is Muslim because he speaks polished "Urdu" and not only employs Arabic- and Persian-origin words, but also pronounces them correctly. As Urdu speakers put it, Mian's "*sheens*" and "*qafs*" were impeccable.

Still, it is notable that at no point do the characters have trouble communicating. Mahashay sprinkles in a few difficult Sanskrit words here and there, but that does not stop Mian from perfectly understanding what Mahashay has to say. Nor does it stop Mahashay from conveying the program's message to the Urdu- and Punjabi-speaking audience in Lahore and Karachi. Indeed, the play's writer, Naseer Anwar, received a great deal of praise for his command of Hindi. For instance, Rais Ahmad, a Pakistani listener and fan of this program, explained: "The strangeness of the language did not make it difficult to listen to it and enjoy it. On the contrary, it made it more enjoyable."[83] Another listener remarked: "From the program you could tell that the writer was very aware of Hindu traditions. The language was beautiful, and I wanted it to last longer."[84] Intizar Hussain, a celebrated Urdu writer, explained in an article: "The Hindi that Nazir Anwar would write—now nobody else can do."[85] Most interesting, in *Nidā*, the demarcation of linguistic and national difference between Urdu and Hindi hinges upon the audience's familiarity with Hindi. It is noteworthy that the strongest expressions of Urdu-Hindi hostility, and in this case, Indian-Pakistani hostility in the 1965 war, depend on the intimate familiarity of Hindi. In *Nidā*, the listeners' audioposition, between the two main characters, Mian and Mahashay, creates a feeling that we are listening in or prying into a private conversation. That prying, however, depends on intelligibility between the two characters and between the audience and the characters.

Naseer Anwar also uses language to demonstrate Mian's cultural and linguistic superiority. Ultimately, *Nidā* is a linguistic feud between Mahashay

(India) and Mian (Pakistan), and in every episode, Mian wins the battle of the tongue. Mahashay mispronounces the first name of India's own vice president calling him "Jakir instead of Zakir." Mahashay cannot even say the name of the region that he claims rightfully belongs to India. Again and again, Mahashay says "Kasmir" instead of "Kashmir." It is clear that these are not just mispronunciations but rather are markers of Urdu-speakers' linguistic superiority.

What goes unspoken, but is impossible to miss, is that *Nidā* is deeply invested in presenting Urdu as *the sole* and rightful national language of Pakistan, countering East Pakistan's claims that Bengali should be a joint national language. Herein lies what was perhaps *Nidā's* most important message. In the play, Mian repeatedly tells radio listeners: "This is the voice of Pakistan." Mian's statement echoes the first governor-general of Pakistan, Mohammed Ali Jinnah's, infamous address in Dhaka: "Let me be clear to you that the state language of Pakistan is going to be Urdu with no other language. Anyone who tries to mislead you is really the enemy of Pakistan."[86]

The introduction to a printed edition of the program includes a long section with listener responses. These, of course, had been carefully selected and include only responses by listeners who liked the program and, more important, who agreed with its politics. Nonetheless, these cherry-picked listener responses offer some insight into how listeners experienced this radio play. A shared thread in many of these responses is that listeners "took on" the voice of Mian. This actor's voice, explained one listener, "became the voice of the Pakistani heart . . . whatever frustration we wanted to tell Indian animals/beasts, the program would say it beautifully. This is why we would all wait for this feature to air impatiently."[87] Another fan of the program remarked: "Listeners felt that they were hearing the voice of their hearts in a lovely style."[88] On November 27, 1965, the newspaper *Imroz Lahore* noted that "Mian spoke with the flow and accent of regular Pakistani."[89] Mian's voice, however, was far from unmarked.

A radio actor named S. A. Amin played Mian. His fascinating and surprising background provides some insight into the ways Mian's voice was marked. Amin was born in Channapatna, a small town famous for producing wooden toys near Bangalore in South India. Amin left Channapatna for Bombay in the hopes of breaking into the film industry but had little luck. Shortly after the Partition of India, he migrated to Karachi, but most of his family remained in South India.[90] Amin came to radio in a rather roundabout way. He began as an announcer in a crafts exhibition in Karachi, selling his own products and showing his acting ability with impersonations of various radio personalities, including the enormously popular radio character Qazi ji.[91] A radio producer heard Amin's voice in one of these exhibitions and invited him to audition for a staff artist position at Radio Pakistan. During the days of the war, S. A. Amin, like many other Radio Pakistan broadcasters and artists, rose to fame.

On one hand, it is ironic that S. A. Amin, the man behind the so-called voice of Pakistan, had such deep ties to India.[92] On the other, it is deeply revealing of the politics of language in newly formed Pakistan. Urdu, while widely understood in West Pakistan, was the first language of only a minority: the Muhājir community that migrated from India to Pakistan after Partition. S. A. Amin did not speak with the "accent of a regular Pakistani" as one fan claimed. His voice was clearly not that of the Bengalis who made up more than 50 percent of Pakistan's total population, nor was it the voice of speakers of other languages in West Pakistan.

Ultimately, *Nidā-e-Haq* is a story about the power of language and speech. In this play, what Verma calls the "everyday act of verbal exchange" acquires a kind of cult status.[93] The voice becomes so powerful as to be "indistinguishable from force" itself.[94] Many programs end with Mian pointing a gun at Mahashay and saying, "this is the voice of Pakistan." Mahashay trembles in fear: "Ram, Ram, please turn your gun the other way." In *Nidā*, the gun and the voice are one and the same.

Again, radio resonance remains important. Although the listener accounts of *Nidā* emphasize the importance of physically listening to the 1965 war radio plays, they also point to the ways that *Nidā* and other radio plays generated conversation about the war. The racy plot of the radio plays, the characters, and the various voices on the ether were clearly an important topic of discussion during the days of war, just as Nur Jehan's impressive performance was. In this sense, it was not only that Mian "became the voice of the Pakistani heart," as one listener explained, but also that listeners "took on" Mian's voice. In celebrating *Nidā* and Mian's verbal victories, in talking about them with family and friends, they too were promoting and participating in the war's verbal rampage.[95] So while the experience of tuning in to broadcasts took precedence during the 1965 war, radio resonance remained a crucial aspect of the war's sonic experience.

Broken Hearts

In every *Nidā-e-Haq* episode, the Pakistani army is just about to win the war. On the actual battlefield, however, that was far from the truth. Many of the details of the various military encounters remain unclear because Indian and Pakistani armies provided contradictory accounts. Foreign observers, however, noted that the war seemed to be heading toward a stalemate, with no army showing a clear advantage.[96] What was certain was that both countries were wasting not only human lives but also precious resources in a senseless war. India was experiencing a major food crisis that threatened to escalate into an all-out famine, and Pakistan had many other much more pressing issues to address, providing basic facilities for its people not least among them.

The United Nations pressured the Indian and Pakistani leaders to end the fighting. On September 22, Ayub Khan and Shastri agreed on a new cease-fire line.[97] Radio Pakistan's seventeen days of war came to an end that day. Some programs shut down abruptly, whereas others slowly petered out as Radio Pakistan resumed its normal programming. Nur Jehan left the radio station and returned to her home in Lahore, as did many of the singers, musicians, and poets who had joined the war effort. *Nidā-e-Haq* continued to run after the UN agreement, but as a number of listeners commented, these later episodes lacked the "punch" of earlier productions as neither the writers nor the actors seemed committed to the cause any longer.[98]

Although Shastri and Ayub Khan agreed to the ceasefire on September 22, the undeclared war did not formally end until February 1966, when leaders of the Soviet Union offered to help negotiate a final agreement in Tashkent, then part of the Soviet Union.[99] Shastri suffered a fatal heart attack the night after signing the accord. Ayub Khan survived the accord, but, in a way, he too suffered from a broken heart. He had hoped that the war would boost his political career; it had the opposite effect.

In the end, Radio Pakistan's campaign, which Ayub Khan had encouraged if not personally directed, backfired. Pakistani foreign minister, Zulfiqar Ali Bhutto, accused Ayub Khan of copping out of the conflict with India and giving up too quickly. During the United Nations meeting, Bhutto noted that the ceasefire resolution "did not take into account the self-determination of [the] people of Kashmir," and assured the United Nations that the Pakistani public would not accept the agreement.[100] In the months to come, Bhutto and others toiled to ensure that would become true, and they publicly campaigned against Ayub Khan.

Ayub Khan found himself in a difficult position. On one hand, the international community pressured for peace. On the other, many who had been galvanized by the radio broadcasts agreed with Bhutto and demanded that Ayub Khan continue the war. President Johnson of the United States, after a brief meeting with Khan, remarked that the Pakistani president "had gone on adventure and had been licked." Johnson could not help feeling sorry for the embittered Pakistani leader. It is hard "to see such a proud man humble himself," Johnson told his close associates.[101]

It was, however, in Pakistan's eastern wing where the negative effects of the 1965 war and its radio campaign were felt most prominently, if not immediately. East Pakistan had remained unprotected during the war even though there was a very real possibility that India would attack on the eastern border. During the height of the war, one wary U.S. official observed: "The situation in the west can be controlled, but if it expands to the east it cannot be controlled."[102] Radio programs propelled many West Pakistanis to draw the circle of Pakistani nationalism much closer around Punjab and very far from Bengal, where the majority of Pakistan's population resided. To those in East Pakistan, the 1965 radio war—from Nur Jehan's patriotic songs to Billo's innocent cries for her beloved Maulvi and Mian's resonant insults—must have clearly shown that in Pakistan, there was no place for them.[103]

Conclusion

The 1965 war's radio campaign transformed the military skirmish in Punjab into a grand event. Moreover, this radio campaign gave many broadcasters, writers, and artists in Pakistan's western wing the opportunity to showcase their talents and build their careers. As a nation-making project, however, the trials of 1971 and the breakup of the Pakistani nation would soon demonstrate that the campaign ultimately failed. In the end, neither Nur Jehan's sensuous and emotive songs nor Mian's threatening voice (or the radio resonance these songs and plays created) were able to keep the Pakistani nation together. On the contrary, they contributed to the resentment that led to the country's ultimate breakup. Moreover, as I examine in the final chapter, another radio service challenged the ideology of Radio Pakistan's campaign in the decades to come.

CHAPTER 6

THE AIR URDU SERVICE'S LETTERS OF LONGING

On July 13, 1974, the broadcaster Abdul Jabbar read a letter on the airwaves from Mohammed Shafi, who wrote from Karachi to ask if someone could tell him if his former hometown of Bulandshahar in India still had large mango orchards. A few months later, Jabbar read a response to that letter from a listener in Bulandshahar who wrote about the city's orchards and reassured Shafi and other listeners that Bulandshahar's mangos were as tasty then as they had been before Partition.[1] This interchange took place on All India Radio (AIR) Urdu Service's most popular program: *Āvāz De Kahāṅ Hai* (Call to me. Where are you?).

As negotiations in Tashkent for a ceasefire to the 1965 Indo-Pakistan War were well underway, AIR inaugurated an Urdu-language news program for listeners in West Pakistan. The thirty-minute radio service provided daily updates on the diplomatic developments in Tashkent and aimed to counteract Radio Pakistan's successful propaganda during the 1965 war. To attract audiences to the somewhat dry news service, broadcasters began to air a few music programs along with the news bulletins. What began as a brief news service that focused mostly on news and political commentary regarding ceasefire diplomatic negotiations, had expanded to nine hours of daily programming by the end of 1966, with the vast majority of the service focusing on entertainment programs.[2]

The AIR Urdu Service technically formed part of AIR's External Service Division, the branch of AIR dedicated to broadcasting abroad. It received funding to broadcast to West Pakistan as one of India's foreign policy initiatives.[3] Yet the service, which went out of a middle-wave transmitter near the border, was audible throughout western India, as well as in most of the state of Uttar Pradesh and parts of the state of Bihar in North India. Broadcasters took notice of this large local audience during the first months of the service, when they began to receive letters from listeners in India in addition to the regular mail from Pakistan. Rather than ignore this unexpected domestic audience, broadcasters designed programs that consciously catered to their transnational audiences.[4] The AIR Urdu Service was a government-run service, funded and administered by the Indian government with the stated goal of swaying Pakistani public opinion toward the official stances of the Indian nation-state. Yet this service also had a subtle subversive element. By catering programs to audiences on both sides of the divide, broadcasters provided listeners in both India and Pakistan a venue to challenge their respective governments' policies and ideologies and to sustain aural ties across the increasingly impassable border.

Abdul Jabbar was the host of *Āvāz De Kahāṅ Hai*. During the thirty-minute program, Jabbar played Hindi film songs from pre-Partition days and read excerpts from letters sent to him by listeners in India and Pakistan. The program derives its title from one of the singer-actress Nur Jehan's most celebrated film tunes: "Āvāz de kahāṅ hai, duniyā merī javāṅ hai" (Where are you? My world is still young). As detailed in chapter 5, Nur Jehan had played a leading role in Radio Pakistan's campaign during the 1965 war. Her voice personified an independent and warring Pakistan, which bravely stood up to India's aggression. In contrast, in *Āvāz De Kahāṅ Hai*, Nur Jehan's voice became an aural symbol of an unattainable, yet still desirable united India, calling radio listeners on both sides to speak—to offer their voices and their personal stories.

The AIR Urdu Service, which is still in existence albeit in very diminished form, has been broadcasting for more than fifty years. Whereas Radio Pakistan's intensive campaign succeeded in creating a memorable event, following seventeen days of intense broadcasting, the AIR Urdu Service worked slowly, contesting the ideology of the war one broadcast at a time over the course of several decades. In what follows, I focus on what broadcasters describe as the "golden years" of the AIR Urdu Service, the late 1960s and 1970s, when AIR received thousands of letters from both sides of the divide. This is also the time before television's boom, when the widespread availability of radio transistors ensured that radio continued to be a leading medium of communication and entertainment on the subcontinent.[5]

Drawing on in-depth interviews with broadcasters, recordings, and, most important, a rare collection of listeners' letters, this chapter explains how the AIR Urdu Service facilitated cross-border connections at precisely the time when the western Indo-Pakistan border became physically impassible. In the pages that follow, I demonstrate how the practice of writing letters to radio stations enabled listeners on both sides of the divide to maintain dialogue in the decades after the 1965 war. As mentioned earlier, historians of South Asia mark the 1965 Indo-Pakistan War as the time when travel across the western Indo-Pakistan border came to a halt and the border was effectively solidified.[6] I "read" these letters, which were performed on the air by AIR Urdu Service broadcasters, as examples of what Alex Chávez calls "sounds of crossing," that is "sounds that cross the boundaries of both cultural and legal ratio-nalities tethered to nation-states."[7] Through the exchange of letters, listeners across both sides of the Indo-Pakistan divide asserted "their right to exist and know themselves beyond structural violence enacted at the level of the nation-state."[8]

To understand the power of these "sounds of crossing" requires that we first treat these letters as "aural performances." Listeners wrote to radio stations, and broadcasters then selected, edited, and performed these letters on the air. The process therefore required a complex negotiation between listener and broadcaster that blurred the boundaries between the two.[9] In parts 1 and 2, I emphasized the importance of radio resonance and pointed to the many ways in which listeners' voices—discussions, rumors, and gossip—expanded radio's reach and helped cement the medium's influence. In this chapter, I demon-strate how the AIR Urdu Service sought to "give voice" to listeners by quite lit-erally bringing their voices to the airwaves through performances of listeners' letters by radio hosts. In this sense, this chapter shows how radio resonance came to full fruition or reached a point of completion. That process, however, was always a mediated and ultimately limited one. In the final section of this chapter, through a brief comparison to the modern-day photographic blog *Humans of New York*, I grapple with some of the limitations of the AIR Urdu Service. The nostalgia and sentimentalism that AIR Urdu Service broadcast-ers fostered through various programs might have created vital cross-border links but did not result in tangible social action. Moreover, AIR's Urdu Service helped cast Urdu, in postindependence India, into what I call a "language of nostalgia," ensuring that the Urdu in India became associated with bygone pre-Partition days.

The AIR Urdu Service in Context

The AIR Urdu Service's inauguration concurred with other important institu-tional changes to AIR. By the mid-1960s, the Indian government had begun to embrace Hindi film songs and films as part of "Indian culture," moving away from the policies of the 1950s and specifically from B. V. Keskar's diatribe against the film industry. In particular, Indira Gandhi, who became minister of information and broadcasting in 1964 and prime minister of India in 1966, actively supported the film industry. The AIR Urdu Service emerged in this changed scenario of the government's attitude toward the Indian film industry.

The late 1960s and 1970s were decades of rising tension for India and Pakistan. The 1971 war resulted in the breakup of East and West Pakistan and the birth of Bangladesh. Historians agree that the atrocities committed by the Pakistani military constituted nothing short of genocide.[10] The Indian government, then under the leadership of Indira Gandhi, who became prime minister following Lal Bahadur Shastri's unexpected death during the Tashkent negotiations in 1966, intervened in East Pakistan's favor. Tension further escalated between India and Pakistan in the years to follow when India's government tested its first atomic bomb in May 1974. Zulfiqar Bhutto, who led Pakistan after 1971, famously remarked that Pakistan would have its own nuclear bomb, even if it meant that its people would have to resort to "eating grass."[11] It was in this political context of rivalry and resentment that the AIR Urdu Service gained popularity in both India and Pakistan.

The AIR Urdu Service put out a variety of programs, including several Hindi film-song programs, radio dramas, literary programs that discussed new and old works of Urdu literature, and poetry recitation programs (*mušāirā*). The service also put out news programs and commentary that focused on Indo-Pakistan relations. News and political commentary programs provided the justification for the service and the reason why the Indian government continued to fund the service during the decades to follow. Unfortunately, to my knowledge, the vast majority of these news and news commentary programs have not survived. It would be fascinating, for example, to analyze the Urdu Service news broadcasts during the 1971 war.[12] We know, for example, that the Urdu Service broadcasters visited prisoner-of-war camps and recorded the voices of thousands of prisoners who sent greetings to their families.[13] It would be equally interesting to know how the AIR Urdu Service presented India's successful nuclear test in 1974 to Pakistani audiences. On one hand, the unavailability of these more politically oriented programs, which constituted the more explicit form of propaganda, limits the scope of the study. On the other, entertainment programs filled the majority of the AIR's programming time and garnered the largest audience. Therefore, by analyzing the entertainment programs, we are able to focus on what listeners would have considered the most important broadcast numbers.

The AIR Urdu Service and the Politics of Language

The AIR Urdu Service programs went out of transmitters located in Jalandhar, Punjab, and later Rajkot in Gujarat and could be heard throughout most of West Pakistan.[14] AIR broadcasters, however, noted that their programs were popular among two communities in Pakistan: the Muhājir and Punjabis. As discussed in chapter 5, *Muhājir* is the term used in Pakistan to describe refugees (and their descendants) who migrated from India during and after the 1947 Partition of the subcontinent. The Muhājir are the only native-speaking Urdu community in Pakistan. Although Urdu is not a native language in the state of Punjab, Urdu is widely understood, in large part because of the British administration's policies in the region.[15] Incidentally, these are the two communities in the western wing of Pakistan with the strongest ties to India (many Muhājir had relatives in India, and the state of Punjab was divided during 1947, forcing many families to leave their homes). Notably, as argued in the previous chapter, the Muhājir and Punjabis are the two communities that were most active during the 1965 Indo-Pakistan War and likely most influenced by Radio Pakistan's services during the conflict.

Originally, the Indian government planned to erect another medium-wave transmitter in West Bengal, whose transmission could be heard in East Pakistan and would necessarily address audiences in Bengali. Those plans, however, disintegrated as government officials in the years following the 1965 war focused on engaging audiences in West Pakistan.[16] Although available documents do not explain the official rationale for this, government officials were likely most interested in reaching the communities targeted by Radio Pakistan during the "seventeen days of war." Once the service was established, changing or adding languages likely became cumbersome. In interviews, broadcasters noted that there were discussions among personnel about adding programs in Punjabi and Sindhi.[17] These plans, however, never materialized. It is crucial to highlight that the AIR Urdu Service targeted language communities in Pakistan that were the most connected to India and had been most influenced by anti-Indian propaganda during the war. The service was notably less interested in broadcasting to those language communities (e.g., Sindhis and Bengalis) who had greater reason to question the Pakistani state.

Much like Radio Ceylon, AIR Urdu Service broadcasters, who were conscious of their transnational and multireligious audience, stressed the intelligibility of their broadcasts and made a deliberate effort to speak in a manner that would have been accessible to Hindi speakers in India as well as speakers of other linguistically related North Indian and Pakistani languages. When reflecting on the language of the Urdu Service, Mariam Kazmi remarked: "We didn't speak very difficult Urdu. It was easy to understand. The Urdu Service's Urdu was like the common Urdu. In fact, it was not really Urdu. It was Hindustani."[18]

As mentioned earlier, I find it useful to think of Hindustani as a "point of desire" or a "utopian idea." Hindustani represents the aspiration to speak an inclusive language unmarked by religion and accessible to speakers of other Indian and Pakistani languages.[19] It might be tempting to argue that the AIR Urdu Service was actually a Hindustani-language service. Listeners' letters in Devanagari and Nastaliq from both Hindu and Muslim fans provide perhaps the best evidence that the Urdu Service actively embraced the ideology of Hindustani. That said, I believe it would be misleading to take Urdu out of the story of the Urdu Service for two main reasons.

First, Kazmi rightly notes that most broadcasters stressed intelligibility, but a handful of programs did incorporate a higher and more difficult register of Urdu. For example, the literary criticism program, *Āīnā* (Mirror), as well as various poetry recitation programs, necessarily used a register of Urdu that drew heavily on Persian and Arabic vocabulary.[20] In fact, one of the most important differences between Radio Ceylon and the AIR Urdu Service is that, whereas Radio Ceylon almost exclusively broadcast Hindi film-song-related programs, the AIR Urdu Service put out a number of literary programs that drew heavily on Persian and Arabic vocabulary and differed from spoken language.[21]

Additionally, whereas listeners during the 1950s complained that AIR Hindi was unintelligible because it incorporated newly formed words that nobody had ever heard, the more literary-inclined AIR Urdu Service programs did not embrace an artificial version of Urdu. Instead, it incorporated a version of Urdu that drew on a literary tradition with a robust print culture and a diverse multireligious audience.[22]

Second, I believe it would be misleading to claim that the AIR Urdu Service was actually a Hindustani service because for many fans, particularly in India, the higher-register Urdu employed in some of the programs was one of the service's main attractions. In the years following Partition and the successful communalization of Hindi and Urdu, Urdu effectively became the language of the North Indian Muslim minority, whose loyalty to India was constantly questioned. In the decades following Partition, government sponsorship of the language diminished greatly. Few public schools offered Urdu as a medium of education and no state business was conducted in Urdu.[23] This meant that those with a formal education in Urdu had little access to government resources. More important for our purposes, broadcasting in Urdu was limited to a few hours a day in local stations with large Muslim populations, such as the North Indian cities of Bhopal and Lucknow. The AIR Urdu Service, technically aimed at "foreign audiences" in Pakistan, offered one of the few opportunities for audiences in India to enjoy literature, poetry, and radio drama in a higher register of Urdu.

In India, not only Muslims but also older Hindu and Sikh listeners, who had had an Urdu education in colonial India, were among the service's most enthusiastic and loyal listeners. Several AIR broadcasters remembered, for example, the elaborate and passionate letters of an elderly Hindu Punjabi man from Amritsar, who like many of his generation felt most comfortable writing in the Nastaliq script. Unfortunately, his many letters to the station have not survived, but his passion for the service is notable to the point that several broadcasters remembered him (without my prompting). The irony of having to tune in to a "foreign service" to listen to Urdu broadcasting was certainly not lost on Indian listeners. Amita Malik, for example, while praising the Urdu Service program in her *Times of India* column commented this was "a strange way for nationals of a country where the language originated and where it is still loved to get what they want."[24]

AIR Urdu Service broadcasters, most of whom had had a formal education in Urdu at either the primary or university level were conscious of the declining position of Urdu in their native country. They saw their work as part of a larger effort to counter that decline.[25] For these reasons, I believe the AIR Urdu Service, despite its transnational focus and broadcasters' commitment to reaching audiences across the linguistic and political divide, cannot be analyzed separately from Urdu or from Urdu's deteriorating condition in India. The AIR Urdu Service existed somewhere in the space between Hindustani and Urdu, as broadcasters sought a diverse audience and sought to speak a version of Urdu that would be intelligible to non-Urdu speakers and non-Muslims. At the same time, these broadcasters, all of whom were citizens and residents of India, also sought to speak and preserve a more marked version of literary Urdu that they rightly felt was under threat in independent India.

Broadcasters, Border Crossers

The vast majority of AIR Urdu broadcasters, but not all, were Indian Muslims. For example, one of the Urdu Service's most famous voices, K. K. Nayyer, whose initials stand for Kewal Krishan, was born in Rawalpindi to a Hindu family and, like many Hindu Punjabi families, he migrated to Delhi in his early teens after Partition. By the time of the Urdu Service's inauguration, Nayyer was working for AIR and had acquired some fame within the organization for his fondness for Urdu poetry. The director of the Urdu Service recruited Nayyer, and he went on to become one of the service's most renowned voices.

Something that most Urdu Service broadcasters had in common, regardless of religion, was having loved ones, whether family or friends, in Pakistan. Nayyer, for example, had left close friends behind in Rawalpindi. Mujeeb Siddiqui, one of the AIR Urdu Service's founding broadcasters, had an older sister who migrated to Karachi, as well as other relatives in West Pakistan. In interviews, Urdu Service broadcasters shared a sense of feeling a strong connection to their relatives in Pakistan through their work with the Urdu Service, but at the same time feeling physically disconnected from them. Siddiqui, for example, explains, "I had a lot of relatives and they would all hear my voice . . . but I never went to Pakistan. I travelled a lot. I have a daughter who was an airhostess in American Airlines. I didn't go to Pakistan." Similarly, Mariam Kazmi, a leading voice in the AIR Urdu Service, explains: "I have never been to Pakistan. It is ironic since I worked for the AIR Urdu Service for 45 years."[26] She laments, "when my aunt died in Pakistan, I could not attend the funeral services."[27]

Hindi Film Songs as the Beating Heart

Hindi film songs provided an important point of connection with audiences in Pakistan. Nayyer explained that during the service's inaugural years, he and others at the Urdu Service quickly noticed Pakistanis' "weakness" for Hindi film songs and launched a number of programs hoping to capitalize on this weakness. Radio Ceylon's transmitter began to deteriorate in the early 1970s, making it difficult for many, particularly in Pakistan, to tune in and hear it clearly. This deterioration pushed listeners in the region toward the newly inaugurated AIR Urdu Service.[28] In interviews, broadcasters referred to Hindi film songs as the lifeline of the service that ensured listeners would remain tuned in to the programs. Among Hindi film songs, *farmāīš* (song-request) programs were particularly important.

The AIR Urdu Service had three daily song-request programs: *Tāmīle Iršād* (Fulfilling), *Āp Kī Farmāīš* (Your requests), and *Āp Kī Pasand* (Your favorites). As Vebhutti Duggal perceptively argues, *farmāīš* programs constituted a powerful and significant practice that reveals a great deal about the radio listening experience. Embedded in the act of requesting songs on the radio was the desire for "recognition by listeners."[29] Consider, for example, the following song request, written on a piece of scrap paper and addressed to *Tāmīle Iršād*'s host Farrukh Jaffar (figure 6.1): "*Assalāmu alaikum* my heart has been broken. I don't know why, but I still continue to love your voice. As soon as the song-request program starts, I stop everything I am doing and for sixty minutes I make time for your voice. I have sent several song requests, but I don't know why you have not answered them."[30] The letter then breaks into poetry:

Tum jāno tum ko ğair se jo rasm o rāh ho
Mujh ko bhī pūchte raho to kyā gunāh ho

If you wish to be involved with someone, it is your decision
But also ask about me, what sin is there in that?[31]

The listener expresses his love for the broadcaster and then, through this couplet, requests that the broadcaster acknowledge his presence. Requests such as this echoed the rich Urdu poetic tradition, in which love is expressed through analogies of torture and pain. A leading theme in Urdu poetry is the

6.1 Song-request letter addressed to Farrukh Jaffar. The letter was written on what appears to be a scrap piece of paper.

Source: Courtesy of Farrukh Jaffar.

suffering of the lover "*āšiq*" at the mercy of the beloved "*māšūq*." The lover, like the listener, is hungry for recognition. The writer ends the letter by listing his requested song "Pardesīoṅ se na ankhīāṅ milānā, pardesīoṅ ko hai ek din jānā" (Ignore strangers, strangers will leave one day) from the 1965 film *Jab Jab Phūl Khile* (When flowers bloomed). The song, which also deals with the topic of recognition, politely and poetically warns Jaffar that if she continues to ignore his song requests, he too might have no choice but to part ways. More than a warning, however, the song is a desperate cry for recognition as well as an implicit acknowledgment of the lover/listener's ultimately dependent position.

Interestingly, this *farmāīš*, although written in the singular, lists four names—Iqbal, Zameer, Naseem, and Shameem—and requests that the broadcaster read aloud all four names. In this way, this letter also nicely shows how radio listening continued to be a collective practice during this later period and demonstrates the central role that family and friendship bonds played not only in listening practices but also in the practice of writing to the radio station.

Expanding on Duggal's work on *farmāīš*, I argue that beyond recognition, request programs sought to mitigate the distance between listener and broadcaster—to make listeners into broadcasters. Consider the following letter, also from Farrukh Jaffar's collection, written by Dinesh Balasara from Rajkot (figure 6.2): "When your program plays, I greatly enjoy listening to it. But you don't mention my request and my name in the program. This causes me great pain, and I become silent/speechless [*aur ham xāmoš reh jāte haiṅ*]. I want to ask you why you torture me in this way? I am, like others, a listener of the Urdu Service. Why then do you not play my songs and mention my name? I am hopeful that you will consider my request by overlooking my complaint."[32]

Most noteworthy is perhaps the phrase "*aur ham xāmoš reh jāte haiṅ*," which translates into "I become silent" or better yet "I am rendered speechless." The phrase expresses the listener's dire disappointment, but it also conveys the sense that, by not playing his song and acknowledging his name, Jaffar has effectively silenced him. She has denied him a voice. Beyond participation and recognition, song-request programs represented an opportunity for the listener to earn a voice—to become, if only for a moment, a broadcaster. The listener ends the letter with a plea for the opportunity to speak, to join the airwaves: "I am hopeful that after you receive this letter, you will mention my name in the program and play song requests in it and other programs."[33]

Another important point that should not go unnoticed is that this letter was written in Devanagari, but it incorporated Urdu/Hindustani vocabulary and echoed Urdu's poetical tradition. In this way, the letter nicely shows how AIR's Urdu successfully crossed the linguistic divide. In my many conversations with broadcasters, they have noted that letters in Devanagari were as common as letters in Nastaliq and that fluency in both scripts was a necessary, if often unspoken, skill required of all AIR Urdu Service employees.

केवडावाडी- से
दिनेश बालासरा

DT. 2.8.82

प्यारी मेहरबान दीदी,

फर्रुख जाफर बहन,

आदाब-व-अर्ज़ ।

प्यारी बहन,

आप नामालो- इर्शाद प्रोग्राम में आती हैं तो हमें प्रोग्राम सुनने में बहुत ही मज़ा आता है । लेकिन आप हमारी फरमाईशें व नाम इस प्रोग्राम में शामिल नहीं करतें इससे हमें बहुत ही दुःख होता है । इससे हमारा दिल दुःख जाता है और हम नामालिश रह जाते हैं ।

हम आपसे पूछना चाहते हैं कि आप जैसा जुल्म हम पर क्यों करते हैं ? दूसरों की तरह उर्दू सर्विस के नामाईन हैं । फिर भी आप हमारे नाम व नग्में शामिल क्यों नहीं करते ?

हम उम्मीद रखते हैं कि आप हमारी ये शिकायत को नजर अन्दाज नहीं करते हुए जवाब ज़रूर ज़रूर करेंगी ।

6.2A AND 6.2B Letter written by Dinesh Balasara to Farrukh Jaffar for the program *Tamīle Iršād*. The author is from Kevdawadi, Rajkot, in Gujarat, India. This is an example of the kind of poetic language that listeners used to complain when a broadcaster would not play their song requests and mention their names on the radio. The author, indirectly, accuses the broadcaster Farrukh Jaffar of silencing his voice. Note also that the author writes in the Devanagari script, but one that resembles the Gujarati variant of Devanagari, likely the author's native language.

Source: Courtesy of Farrukh Jaffar.

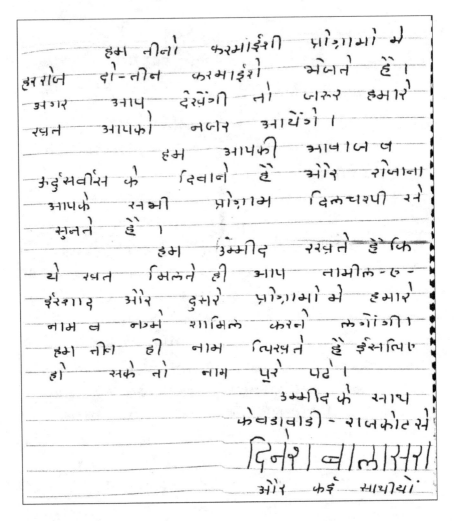

6.2B (*Continued*)

Hindi Film-Song Programs on the AIR Urdu Service

Like Radio Ceylon programs discussed in chapter 4, the AIR Urdu Service
film-song programs also contributed to the decoupling of songs by actively
encouraging listeners to think of songs as entities independent of the films in
which they had first appeared. For example, one of the most iconic programs
was called *Gīton Bharī Kahānī* (Stories filled with songs). As the name suggests, the program consisted of a play sketch—that is, a kind of improvised
radio play that incorporated five to six Hindi film songs. The play's story lines

revolved around film songs but did not bear any direct relation to the films in which the selected songs had originally appeared. Mujeeb Sidiqqui was one of the primary writers for this program and describes himself as a coveted fiction writer. He notes that writing for this program allowed him to exercise his passion for fiction writing. Other broadcasters, including S. M. Shafeeq and Farrukh Jaffar, also wrote drama sketches for the program. One of Farukh Jaffar's scripts provides important clues into the format of the program and reveals how the program created new contexts for listeners to experience film songs. Consider the following story called *Tišnagī* (Thirst), which tells the story of an alcoholic poet.

Told in five scenes, the story opens with the song "Lagī yeh kaisī anbujh āg mitvā" (Dear, how did this inexorable fire start?), following the narrator's description of a dark and lonely night. The song, which originally appeared in the film *Devdās* (1955), sets the mood for the entire story, which explains the origins of the man's internal struggle. The poet asks the narrator for a glass of brandy. When she refuses, he responds, "I am very thirsty. If I don't drink, I will die." As the poet and the narrator converse, we learn that the poet fell in love with a woman who he thought loved him back. Later, he realized that it was not him, but rather his poetry, that she loved. Three more scenes take us to the poet's past, where we meet his lover, a young woman named Salma, who unwillingly admits to loving his poetry more than the poet. We learn that out of anger and desperation, the poet steals Salma's necklace and goes to prison. In prison, Salma attempts to meet him and seek reconciliation, but he refuses. The ending scene features the narrator and the dying poet, who is still unable to forget his love. As the play ends, we hear the song "Kārvāṅ guzar gayā, ǧubār dekhte rahe" (The caravan passed, kept watching the dust).[34]

For some drama sketches, the songs were crucial to the story line. For others, like *Tišnagī*, the songs were meant to set the mood of the story, but they did not necessarily contribute to the story line greatly. In some instances, the songs did little more than provide respite from the subplot. This is not unlike the ways in which they function in the cinematic context. I am most interested, however, in how the program created new movielike contexts for songs and actively encouraged the decoupling of songs from the films.

Yet much like Radio Ceylon's programs, if *Gīton Bharī Kahānī* helped decouple songs from films, other AIR Urdu Service programs actively linked songs to the original films, enabling what Anna Morcom describes as "the double lives" of Hindi film songs—that is, film songs' peculiar ability to be at once linked to films and at the same time exist outside of the filmic context. Perhaps the program that most effectively associated songs with the films in which they originally appeared was *Pardae Sīmiṅ Se* (From the silver screen). The program, which was actually outsourced for production from the AIR Urdu Service, featured edited and shortened versions of an entire movie's soundtrack, including both songs and dialogue (most films were about three hours long, but *Pardae Sīmīṅ Se* was an hour-long program).[35] The program, which featured both old and new films, contributed to the aural circulation of films in India and Pakistan. This was particularly important in Pakistan, where Indian films often were not available in cinemas and where the VCR and pirated cassettes did not arrive until the late 1970s. Notably, far from supplemental, the aural and radiophonic experience of films was often the primary source of filmic experience in the subcontinent. The AIR Urdu Service was an important medium through which Indians and Pakistanis could experience films.

Moreover, AIR Urdu Service programs that might not have been exclusively about film songs also dealt with film-related topics. For example, the program *Rūbarū* (Face-to-face) featured interviews with various personalities, including writers, painters, scientists, and film personalities. Mujeeb Sidiqqui, for example, remembers interviewing Lata Mangeshkar for the service. Siddiqui told Mangeshkar that Pakistani listeners of the program had noted that if India were willing to hand over Lata, as she was normally called, Pakistan would happily give up Kashmir in exchange. To this, Siddiqui claims, Lata responded half in jest: "I have no objection." I have found no evidence of such an interview in AIR's archives, but Siddiqui's comments nicely show how the AIR Urdu Service promoted film culture and specifically an "aural *filmi* culture" as a shared heritage between India and Pakistan, even as it emphasized a kind of rivalry. Kazmi, who also did many of the film-related interviews, notes that interviews with film stars from the 1930s and 1940s were by far some of the most popular programs. In particular, she notes, listeners were thrilled to hear from actors from pre-Partition days. Kazmi, however, also interviewed film personalities from Pakistan, and she fondly remembers interviewing actors Mohammed Ali and Zeba in the AIR studios. "Whenever I learned that any Pakistani film personality was in India, I made sure to bring them to my studio."[36]

"Bore Bore Meṅ Letters Āte" (Letters Arrived in Sacks!)

If film songs were the lifeline of the AIR Urdu Service, whose beats and rhythms powered the service, listener letters were the service's *jigar* (liver), which in Hindi-Urdu poetry and literature represents the part of the body that processes emotion. As explained in the discussion of Radio Ceylon, letters were often the marker of a particular program's popularity. It was, after all, in response to the massive correspondence that Radio Ceylon received in its inaugurating years that the station in Ceylon decided to expand its programming in Hindi. Ameen Sayani, in interviews about *Binaca Geetmala*, always brings up the overwhelming amount of mail correspondence he received as evidence of the program's importance and legacy.[37]

The practice of letter writing to stations was a crucial part of the radio listening experience throughout the world and one that holds special significance in South Asia.[38] Broadcasters encouraged letter writing as a form of listener participation, hoping to get listeners more involved in programs. Yet for the AIR Urdu Service's listeners, letters played another vital role: they enabled listeners across the Indo-Pakistan divide to remain in conversation with each other. For AIR Urdu Service's audiences, the letters were a place of physical contact across the western Indo-Pakistan border, which by that time, for most, had become all but impassable. After visiting the AIR Urdu Service studios in India, Zahida Khan, a Pakistani actress and writer, wrote an editorial in the *Daily Imroz*, in which she related her experience. She wrote that the service's offices were packed with listeners' letters and stressed: "I have seen [them] with my own eyes."[39] Her statement nicely shows the extent to which the materiality of the bundles of letters served as proof of the physical connection between listeners on both sides of the divide.

A large percentage of the letters to the Urdu Service came through a diplomatic avenue. Listeners mailed them to the Indian High Commission in Pakistan using local addresses. While some listeners did mail their letters directly to the Urdu Service in Delhi, the High Commission avenue enabled listeners from Pakistan to pay a much more affordable local postage price.

The AIR Urdu Service had three thirty-minute weekly programs exclusively dedicated to reading and commenting on listeners' letters: *Āp Kā Xat Milā* (We received your letter), *Xat Ke Lie Šukrīā* (Thank you for your letter), and *Āp Ke Xat, Āp Ke Gīt* (Your letter, your song). The first two programs had the following format: two broadcasters, normally a woman and man, read anywhere from five to ten letters and offered short comments or responses to listeners. Mariam Kazmi and Mujeeb Siddiqui, a husband-and-wife team, hosted *Āp Kā Xat Milā* and S. M. Shafeeq and Azra Qureshi hosted *Xat Ke Lie Šukrīā*. The third program *Āp Ke Xat, Āp Ke Gīt*, was a letter-reading program that also included Hindi film songs, but unlike other song-request programs, broadcasters spent most of the time reading and responding to letters and played fewer songs.

To this day, broadcasters remember the names of some listeners and even details from some of the letters; unfortunately, however, the vast majority of this correspondence has not survived. As is the case with a lot of radio-related material in the subcontinent, the abundance of letters seems to have obscured their importance and discouraged their preservation. The AIR Urdu Service personnel regularly discarded letters. Listener response programs could not be rebroadcast, and as a result, these programs usually went on live and were not preserved. The only available letters are the ones that broadcasters, sometimes deliberately, other times by mere accident, retained in their homes and personal files. I rely on the collections of two broadcasters who kindly shared their letters with me: Farrukh Jaffar and Abdul Jabbar.

Profuse praise was part and parcel of this genre of writing. Listeners used elaborate and poetic language to praise their favorite programs and broadcasters. It was not unusual for listeners to express devotion and love for individual broadcasters, for a particular program, or for the entire Urdu Service. For example, Iqbal Jafar praises his favorite broadcaster: "These days, I have really found your program interesting. Whenever I listen to your program, I feel like I am in a daze."[40] In a similar fashion, a woman writing from Lahore compares the beauty of her favorite program, *Āvāz De Kahāṅ Hai*, to the beauty of the prophet Joseph. She explains: "It is well known that God sent one fourteenth of prophet Joseph's beauty to this earth, but I actually think that 12 percent of this fourteenth piece is present in the program *Āvāz De Kahāṅ Hai*."[41] More critical listeners wrote suggestions for improvements for various programs and on some occasions asked for certain programs to be expanded or suggested that they change the time and day of a program to a more convenient time. Kazmi, for example, remembers the detailed letters of two listeners, Deeba Raza and Najma Noushi, who offered useful suggestions for improving programs, many of which, Kazmi notes, broadcasters were able to incorporate.[42]

Listeners often shared details from their personal lives. For example, Iqbal Jafar from Calcutta, mentioned earlier, writes that "he had just started college and that he was not trapped in marriage yet."[43] Listeners sent broadcasters invitations for weddings or important life events. A woman named Harita from Gujarat, for example, shared with Abdul Jabbar the good news that she had now become a university lecturer.[44] Other listeners wrote about personal experiences and trips. Kazmi, for example, remembers reading a letter from a Sikh woman from India, who described her trip to Lahore and the warm welcome she received in neighboring Pakistan.[45] Through the exchange of letters, the AIR Urdu Service promoted what Laura Kunreuther calls "public intimacy"— that is, the notion that "by voicing desire in public, strangers begin to relate to one another as intimates." In this sense, letters allowed not only broadcasters to know listeners intimately but also enabled listeners to know intimate details about one another.[46]

The process of selecting and weeding out inappropriate letters was crucial. As we might expect, broadcasters gave preference to letters that spoke positively about the programs and to letters that explicitly referenced cross-border relations.[47]

Letters of Longing for *Āvāz De Kahāṅ Hai*

Perhaps no program better exemplifies how AIR Urdu Service used listeners' letters and Hindi film songs to promote cross-border connections than *Āvāz De Kahāṅ Hai*. The program, which was inaugurated in the early 1970s, several years after the service's inauguration, combined themes of several listeners' letter-response programs and song-request programs in interesting ways.[48] Moreover, thanks in great part to the commitment and dedication of the program's host, Abdul Jabbar, *Āvāz De Kahāṅ Hai* left a more robust aural and paper trail than other AIR Urdu Service programs.

When asked about the program's origins, Jabbar shared the following story: After the 1965 Indo-Pakistan War, Radio Pakistan curbed its broadcasts of Hindi film songs because of their association with the Bombay film industry. One disappointed radio listener wrote an elaborate editorial to a Pakistani newspaper, in which he argued that Radio Pakistan stations should at the very least broadcast pre-Partition Hindi film songs. After all, India and Pakistan, the editorialist explained, were not separate countries. That editorial, which Jabbar read while browsing through the AIR Urdu Service's copies of Pakistani newspapers, inspired him to design a radio program that would exclusively feature pre-Partition Hindi film songs.[49]

Abdul Jabbar named the program after the Hindi film song "Āvāz de kahāṅ hai, duniyā merī javāṅ hai" from the super-hit film *Anmol Ghaṛī* (Precious moment) released in 1946 (figure 6.3). The title of this song, and consequently the title of the program, evade precise translation. It means something along the lines of "Where are you? Answer me. The world is young" or "Call to me, where are you? I am still youthful." The song featured the voices of the celebrated actor-singers Nur Jehan and Surendra.[50] The program lasted thirty minutes

6.3A AND 6.3B Stills of (a) Nur Jehan and (b) Surendra singing "Āvāz de kahāṅ hai" in *Anmol Ghaṛī*.

Source: *Anmol Ghaṛī* (1946).

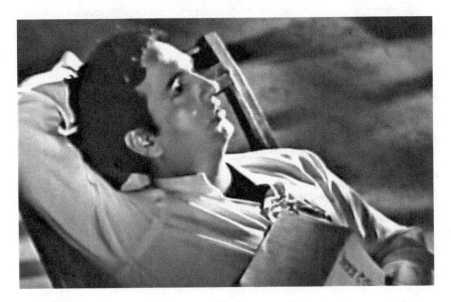

6.3B (*Continued*)

and, during its early years, it aired on Friday evenings. As the program began to attract a robust following, the AIR Urdu Service team decided to rebroadcast it on Sunday evenings and, during a brief period, on Monday evenings as well.[51]

Originally, Jabbar had envisioned *Āvāz De Kahāṅ Hai* as a rather straightforward film-song-request program that would exclusively feature pre-Partition songs. Jabbar went to great lengths to fulfill his audience's requests for old and often forgotten songs. He purchased records in shops, bazaars, and from scrap dealers. In an interview, Jabbar explains that his efforts proved true the well-known Urdu saying: "You can even find God, if you just search."[52] Jabbar recalls that, on one occasion, he found an entire rack full of old records in an old warehouse. Most records were caked with mud and heavily scratched, but he was able, with the help of colleagues, to recover some.[53]

On the air, Jabbar shared sentimental stories about how far he would go to locate records and how much this meant to his listeners (figure 6.4). A seventy-four-year-old listener sent a letter asking him to please play a song from the music directors Husn Lal and Bhagat Ram's debut film *Cānd* (1944) (Moon). The listener warned Jabbar that he was ill and could not wait too long to hear the song. After several months of searching, Jabbar found a damaged record of the song and with the help of a sound engineer friend, Jabbar was able to broadcast a few stanzas of the seventy-four-year-old's favorite song.[54] Even as the program evolved, its vintage music remained one of its key attractions. One listener, referencing the program's title, explains that it was the program's vintage

6.4 Cartoon image of Abdul Jabbar with his collection of old records.

Source: Pioneer (Delhi), March (or May) 9, 1997.

music that attracted him and others to the program: "Really, these songs, *unkī āvāz* [their sounds], pull in listeners."[55]

As the program evolved, listeners wrote not only to make song requests but also to share elaborate descriptions of the memories associated with those songs. For example, in one of the few early recordings that we have of the program, Abdul Jabbar read a letter by Mohammed Iqbal from Agra. Mohammed Iqbal asks that Jabbar play the *qawwali* entitled "Sakhī rī ḍolī meṅ hojā savār" (My dear female friend, it is time to board the palanquin) by Azim Prem Ragi. The *qawwali* is an ode to a bride preparing to leave her parents' home. Mohammed

Iqbal explains in his letter that this particular *qawwali* was very popular when he was in school. It was so well known that he and his classmates would often compose mock versions of the song. Iqbal remarks that he remembers singing "Patelī cūlhe pe hoja savār" (Pot, it is time to board the stove) with his friends.[56]

In a similar fashion, Sitara Jabi Qazi's letter from Karachi also relates songs to childhood memories. Qazi asks that Jabbar play two songs. The first song, "Tū cal cal re naujavān, dūr terā gāoṅ aur thake pāoṅ" (Walk walk, young one, your village is far and your feet are tired), was from the film *Bandhan* (1940). Qazi explains to Jabbar and to listeners that she saw this film in the city of Calcutta, where she lived for a brief period as a child: "The song still echoes in my ears, and I remember the beautiful city of Calcutta, I remember school days and the simplicity of women, the education and music there, I can never forget them."[57] Her second song request—"Ik bār phir kaho zarā ki merī sārī kaināt terī ek nigāh par nisār hai" (Kindly tell me one more time, my entire universe is dedicated to only your one gaze)—is a non-film song performed by Shamshad Begum. The song, Qazi writes, always reminds her of her time in the Indian city of Jalandhar in Punjab. Qazi explains: "I heard this song for the first time when my father was transferred from Bengal to there [Jalandhar]. We were invited to a Sikh gentleman's place for dinner. Their large home was surrounded by gardens. There were vegetables, lentils, pickles, and other things. I heard this *ğazal* there."[58]

Programs that related Hindi film songs to life events were neither new nor exclusive to the AIR Urdu Service (see chapter 4). *Āvāz De Kahāṅ Hai* was unique because of its particular focus on pre-Partition memories and its commitment to encouraging dialogue across the border. The program became an aural forum in which people separated by state borders could publicly reflect on a shared past using film songs as the source of inspiration. Through the exchange of letters, *Āvāz De Kahāṅ Hai* listeners were able to reflect on the meaning of place outside nationalist parameters. Kartar Singh, who migrated from what became Pakistan, wrote to Jabbar to ask about his favorite cinema house in Lahore. A woman from Lahore responded that the Palace Cinema still plays films and that it continues to be a lively place. The same listener from Lahore also responded to another Indian listener's query about Basant celebrations in Lahore. (Basant is a Punjabi festival that is held on the fifth day of the lunar month of Magha, in late January or February, and marks the start of spring.) In her letters, the listener from Pakistan explained that although Basant is not an official holiday in Lahore, people continue to celebrate it with pomp. The Basant kite festival, she noted, is very popular and on that day the sky fills with colorful kites.[59]

To understand the significance of these letters that were aurally performed on the radio, we might briefly consider the practice of *saludados* (literally, "greeted") in cross-border Mexican music performances. *Saludados* are improvised greetings sung during musical performances. They are requested by the audience members and made to relatives or friends who are geographically apart. Alex Chávez, for example, describes a *saludado* performance requested by a man in a ranch in the state of San Luis Postosi, Mexico, for his relatives in Tennessee. *Saludados*, writes Chávez, "are generative compositions that attend to the lives of people who negotiate border politics on a daily level."[60] Yet while the *saludados* will never be heard by those who are being greeted (the family in Tennessee will never hear the specific *saludado*, performed in San Luis), these greetings constitute a "vehicle for voicing solidarities otherwise severed."[61] The AIR Urdu Service letters served a similar intent; the letters can be read as "acts of self-valorization" that enabled a flow and exchange of "sound, language, and expression" across borders.[62]

Listeners from Pakistan and India often asked Jabbar to help them locate friends and relatives on the other side of the divide. One man from Delhi, for example, asked Jabbar to help him find three of his childhood friends: Mohammad, Charaghdeen, and Rehmat, who he believed had migrated to Pakistan shortly after 1947. The listener told Jabbar, in a detailed letter, of the games the four friends would play together and described his affection for his childhood friends. Although Jabbar was unable to find the listener's friends, the man's descriptions of his friends resonated with many listeners, who in turn wrote about friends and family with whom they had lost touch.

Discussion of place was by no way limited to *Āvāz De Kahāṅ Hai*. Place was a leading theme in many other AIR Urdu Service programs. Sarfaraz Ahmad Siddiqui, for example, hosted the long-running program called *Dillī, Jo Šeher Tha* (Delhi, the city it was), which featured hidden and unknown places in Delhi. The program, Khan explains, was particularly popular among the Muhājir in Pakistan who migrated from Delhi or who might have family connections to the city. As the title suggests, nostalgia for a bygone pre-Partition Delhi was the leading theme of the program.

K. K. Nayyer also made a series of radio documentaries about smaller Indian cities, such as Ludhiana and Kanpur. In this program, Nayyer described the factories and neighborhoods of these cities, providing the opportunity for Pakistani listeners unable to physically visit to experience the place through AIR recordings. The program, he notes, was specifically designed for Muhājir, who still had living memories of these cities but, given Indian and Pakistani state politics, had little possibility of ever visiting again.[63] The AIR Urdu Service seems to have effectively tapped into the shifting expression of place and belonging. As Chávez notes, referring to the experience of Mexican immigrants in the United States, "people carry locations with them, here and there, in this way a town in Mexico can be imaginatively involved at performance in Texas, and vice-versa."[64] What was special and noteworthy about *Āvāz De Kahāṅ Hai*—and more likely part of the reason for the program's popularity and longevity—is that, through the exchange of letters, it allowed listeners to take on the role of broadcasters and to reflect for themselves on the meaning of place.

Something else that set *Āvāz De Kahāṅ Hai* apart from other programs is that it deliberately targeted an older generation of people who had experienced Partition and its immediate aftermath as young adults and who would have been at least fifty years old during the program's peak years. When probed about the matter in interviews, Jabbar responds almost defensively that the program was also popular among a younger generation of listeners who were curious about their families' past and who wished to hear stories about India. He is not entirely wrong. One listener, for example, writes in a letter: "*Āvāz De Kahāṅ Hai* is the type of program that the entire house listens to. In our house, from the elderly to the children, all of them like the program. This program is building a bridge between the young and old generations."[65] This listener's self-conscious explanation, as well as Jabbar's somewhat defensive insistence that young people *also* tuned in, betrays an awareness that the program largely catered to an older generation that associated the pre-Partition era with its youth.

Perhaps in part because of its niche focus on an elder generation, *Āvāz De Kahāṅ Hai* developed a loyal band of listeners and letter writers across both sides of the divide. For example, the Urdu-language newspaper *Ajīt* from Punjab reported that it held a "*Āvāz De Kahāṅ Hai* ke sāmaīn kī mehfil" (a gathering of listeners of *Āvāz De Kahāṅ Hai*) in its office building in Jalandhar, in Indian Punjab.[66] A similar event took place in Lahore in the neighborhood of Samanabad. The newspaper reported that devoted listeners from Lahore, as well as Lalpur, Sialkot, gathered on the Muslim holiday of Eid and shared cake with the words "AIR Urdu Service" written on it.[67] Also, a group of devoted listeners in Lahore formed an *Āvāz De Kahāṅ Hai* listeners' association and sent Jabbar a recording of one of their meetings.

The recording is as revealing as it is unique. This group of listeners likely hoped that Jabbar would play a portion of the tape on the air, which because of the recording's amateur quality he was not able to do. Recognition is a leading theme in listeners' conversations. An older man called Pehelvan notes that Jabbar often takes a long time to respond to his letters but that the wait is worthwhile. In Pehelvan's voice, we hear a sense of satisfaction at the knowledge that his dedication to the program is being regularly recognized. A woman named Shagufta explains that she does not write regularly because she has no memories of pre-Partition days and does not feel that she can contribute much to the program. Besides, she notes, it is listening to the "lives [and] to the memories of others" that she really enjoys.

This recording provides us with the rare opportunity to hear from devoted listeners who did not habitually participate in the program but who did listen regularly and were intimately involved in the program from afar. Similarly, a man named Faiyaz notes that he had been diligently listening to the program for five years before he wrote his first letter to Jabbar. Faiyaz admits that he enjoyed hearing his letter on the radio, but that what he really likes is listening to the stories of others. "I really liked the letters of Ram Pal. I greatly look forward to them. He has been writing less." Interestingly, even when listeners like Faiyaz and Shagufta express more interest in listening to other stories than in sharing their own, their recorded voices reveal a palpable sense of excitement in participating as well as a certain degree of comfort in taking on the role of broadcasters. What this rare recording nicely demonstrates is that by making listeners' letters the focus of the program, Jabbar effectively blurred the space between the listeners and the broadcasters. Taking the notion of radio resonance to a whole new level, Jabbar effectively transformed listeners, if only for a brief moment, into broadcasters, offering them "a voice."

As noted earlier, effusive praise and expression of love and desire was a crucial aspect of the radio listeners' letters. *Āvāz De Kahāṅ Hai* listeners often competed with each other for the most creative ways to pay tribute to their favorite program. Rizvana Seher, for example, compares the beauty of the program to the "height of mountains" (*pahāṛoṅ kī bulandīoṅ*), the "depth of oceans" (*samandar kī gehrāīoṅ*), the "singing/modulating of waterfalls" (*ābšāroṅ ke tarannum*), and the "perfume of flowers" (*phūloṅ kī mehek*).[68] Another listener from Lahore praises the program in even more effusive terms: "*Āvāz De Kahāṅ Hai* is [a] constellation of stars, which has been shining in the minds of people in Pakistan and India for some time, [it is a program] for whose beauty you have worked so hard to bring out, and it causes the *anchal* [or 'sari's edge'] to ripple on the horizon of all India, becoming a rainbow."[69] In the same poetic manner, listeners exchanged praise for Jabbar and for his voice. Shagufta Nasreen Hashmi writing from Pakistan tells Jabbar: "When I listen to your voice, it is as if I hear bells and a kind of spell spreads. I wish that the program *Āvāz De Kahāṅ Hai* would never end and forever will beat in the hearts of its listeners. Amen."[70] Listeners addressed Jabbar as *pyāre bhāī* (beloved brother, Jabbar), and when, for any reason, Jabbar would not be able to host the program, they immediately would comment on his absence: "We all badly felt your absence. Thanks to God, you have returned and, like a new moon, are shining."[71]

As discussed earlier, Jabbar was not the only broadcaster to receive this kind of gushing and demonstrative fan mail. Yet Jabbar was unusual in his commitment to personally reading through the letters he received and in carefully selecting and editing the letters he read on the radio. While he succeeded in creating the feeling that listeners were in control of the program, that their letters and voices were most important, his role as mediator and performer was actually a crucial aspect of the program. It is in assessing Jabbar's important role that Kunreuther's analysis of the popular FM Nepali radio program *Mero Kathā, Mero Gīt* (My letter, my song), which aired in the 2000s, proves most helpful. Although from a different time and context, *Mero Kathā, Mero Gīt* bears many similarities to *Āvāz De Kahāṅ Hai*. The more recent Nepali program featured letters from listeners, but these focused on unrequited love and the pain associated with it. Drawing on Mikhail Bhaktin, Kunreuther turns to the idea of "double voicing" to understand the role of the broadcaster as an active mediator. Double voicing is making use of "someone else's discourse for [one's] own purposes by inserting a new semantic intention into a discourse which already has, and which retains an intention of its own." Kunreuther's observations about *Mero Kathā, Mero Gīt* are also true for *Āvāz De Kahāṅ Hai*: "The program's popularity rests on the absent writers," but these writers' "words gain authority, circulation, presence, and the status of 'real' or 'true' through the host's voice."[72] In *Āvāz De Kahāṅ Hai*, the voices of listeners who wrote letters constitute a vital aspect of the program, but it is Jabbar's double voicing that brings a "distinct tone and smoothness" to the program and that lends it a certain kind of authority. In other words, listeners who wrote letters became broadcasters through Jabbar's double-voicing performance. This double voicing, however, depended on an older radio tradition of privileging listeners' voices that had been crucial to the medium's development. During World War II, listeners' voices—discussion, rumors, and gossip—expanded radio's reach at time when radio receivers were not easily available. Three decades later, *Āvāz De Kahāṅ Hai*'s double voicing brought radio resonance to a point of near completion as Jabbar strove to turn listeners into broadcasters. That process, too, however, was mediated and ultimately limited.

The Politics of Sentimentalism and Nostalgia

As we might expect, however, *Āvāz De Kahāṅ Hai* also had its fair share of critics. Some newspaper accounts even noted that the prime minister of Pakistan, Zulfikar Ali Bhutto, actively tried to stop this program's production because he felt it posed a threat to Pakistan's national security.[73] I have not found evidence that Bhutto or any other Pakistani politician publicly denounced this program or any other Urdu service. Yet rumors about Pakistani politicians' opposition to the program seem to have done little to diminish the program's popularity. On the contrary, as is often the case, these rumors appear to have only bolstered the program's relevance and to have given, at least some people, more reason to tune in.

It was debates about the veracity of the letters that Jabbar read on the air that ultimately appear to have had a more a negative effect on the program and on the AIR Urdu Service as a whole. Newspapers across both sides of the border accused Jabbar of reading fake letters on the airwaves. Some claimed that he made up the letters altogether, whereas others put the blame on listeners who, they claimed, told fictitious stories.[74] Jabbar's collection of letters, although far from complete, confirms that the program did receive mail from both Pakistan and India, even during periods of intense hostility between the two nations.

In regard to the second accusation, it is impossible now, as it was then, to check the credibility of letters that Jabbar selected for his program. Was Sitara

Jabi Qazi's story about listening to Shamshad Begum's song at a Sikh man's home in Jalandhar while having a sumptuous vegetarian meal genuine? Did Mohammed Iqbal really hear "Sakhī rī ḍolī meṅ hojā savār" as a child? It is noteworthy that Jabbar comments in the recording of the program that he had already played the song not long ago but that he decided to fulfill Iqbal's request nonetheless. Is it possible that after hearing this song, Iqbal made up his own memory of the song in a desperate attempt to hear his letter on the radio? Or, more generously, is it possible that hearing the song on the radio shaped his memory of the past? Ultimately, however, debating which experiences were likely to be true and which were not would be a futile exercise. A more useful exercise might be to reflect on the fact that the practice of writing to the AIR Urdu Service was mediated and that that mediation inevitably affected the content and topic of the letters as well as reactions to these letters. In her analysis of the Nepali program *Mero Kathā, Mero Gīt*, Kunreuther stresses the importance of the listeners' training. The program's host, she explains, actively "trains his listeners to produce a certain genre. . . . He is training them to see and hear their lives in ways that resonate with new realities."[75] What matters then is not so much whether or not the letters are true but the particular kind of narrative that the program encourages listeners to share.

It is this active fashioning that Khalid Mahmood from Lahore is likely criticizing when he explains in a newspaper editorial: "I read in history books that during the time of Partition in India, Muslims suffered many atrocities." Why weren't these issues described in the program? "The past is not all pink," Mahmood concludes.[76] Mahmood is correct that Jabbar's program did not encourage listeners to address those so-called thorns of the past. His analysis sets the stage for what, in my opinion, is a much stronger criticism of the program, one that resonates with our present-day media world.

It is here that a brief comparison with the popular photographic blog *Humans of New York* (HONY), which features portraits of people in New York City alongside short, often sentimental quotes, could be especially useful.[77] Although from a different time and genre, thinking about the blog HONY, and in particular paying attention to the sharp criticism the blog has received, can help us make sense of *Āvāz De Kahāṅ Hai*'s limitations.

HONY, on its most popular platform, Facebook, boasts more than 16 million followers. One of the most famous of these HONY portraits presents an African American boy named Vidal, who we learn is most inspired by his principal, Ms. Lopez. The quote next to Vidal in a hoody, with the city blurred in the background reads: "When we get in trouble, she doesn't suspend us. She calls us to her office and explains to us how society is built down around us. And she tells us that each time somebody fails out of school, a new jail gets built."

Interestingly, the stories and personal portraits that Jabbar presented on the air, adorned with music from a bygone era, had a great deal in common with

the HONY pictures of ordinary New Yorkers, decorated with their short, sentimental quotes. Both ultimately invite immediate emotional reactions and offer
perhaps an unreal sense that we know something personal and deeply revealing about the subject featured. It is also telling that both forums share similar
development stories. On several occasions, Jabbar explained that the radio program began as a song-request program, but that eventually the letters, which
described pre-Partition memories, took precedence, as radio listeners were
eager to learn about each other's lives. The songs, while still important, took on
a secondary role. Similarly, Brandon Stanton, the founder of the HONY blog,
notes that HONY began as a photo album of strangers from New York. At the
beginning, the album included short descriptions of the people featured, but
as people became more and more interested in these explanations, he began to
include longer quotations about the subjects he featured. Eventually, the quotes
and explanations, like the letters of *Āvāz De Kahāṅ Hai*, became the blog's biggest attraction, drawing millions of followers.

The fiercest critics of HONY have noted that the problem with the blog
is not only that it lacks meaningful conversation about the racial and social
inequality issues that plague New York City, but that the blog actually inhibits
such a dialogue.[78] Melissa Smyth explains: "The problem with sentimentality
[of HONY] is not the infusion of emotion into a political issue. On the contrary, it is the funneling of emotion into mute forms, preventing the marriage
of thought and feeling that produces the most concentrated social action."[79]
Similarly, Vinson Cunningham explains the message of HONY in the following
way: "Vague, flattening humanism, too quick to forget the barriers erected—
even here, and now, in New York—against real equality."[80] We can make similar
critiques of *Āvāz De Kahāṅ Hai*. The program provided an important avenue
for contact across the western Indo-Pakistan border, but it did so through the
avenue of nostalgia and sentimentalism, and in so doing, it severely limited
the stakes of the conversation. A close reading of a moving letter featured in the
program reveals these shortcomings, while simultaneously reminding us of the
program's important subversive elements.

Khalida Begam's Letter and the Longing for a United India

On June 12, 1978, Jabbar broadcast the following letter written by Khalida
Begam from Lakhimpur, a small city in the United Provinces:

> *Greetings Jabbar Bhai.—*
>
> *Again, you have been absent from the* Āvāz De Kahāṅ Hai *program. Well,
> it is OK don't worry about it. I really love this program and listen to it reg-
> ularly. I heard yesterday's Monday, May 15th program. Listening to Malik*

Sahab's wife's story made me cry; the stories that people have shared, the difficulties people have endured. Through Āvāz De Kahāṅ Hai, we hear thousands of stories of people torn apart. Through this program, so many people are able to send their greetings and their stories. When I hear that people before Partition would secretly listen to film songs, I wish I had been among them, but at the time I could not watch films. But I did hear them via the loudspeaker during weddings in the neighborhood and would get an idea: Darde Jigar, Anmol Gharī, Ratan, Pukār, Zīnat—we would really enjoy those film songs. As time passed by, without my noticing, everybody left to Pakistan, and we were left behind. My father and uncle loved India. They were buried here. My brother also left to Pakistan. We were separated from relatives. The memories stayed. If you can play that song from the film, Jugnū . . . I really love it. I remember watching that film with my brother. It a was long time ago, but I can still remember the atmosphere/ feelings [samā] of that time. Nur Jehan sang that song. "Sāze dile purdard nā cheṛ āj kī rāt" [Don't play the music of pained heart, tonight]. I've written many letters to the program, but my letters have not been responded to. I love the Urdu service.[81]

Khalida Begam's letter connects many of the elements discussed earlier (figure 6.5). She opens her note to Jabbar by commenting on his absence to the program. While she falls short of scolding Jabbar for missing the program, she makes it clear that she was displeased by his absence. Immediately after, Khalida Begam comments on her fellow listeners' letters and on the ways in which the program connects people long separated by the making of borders and nation-states. "Listening to Malik Sahab's wife's story made me cry. The stories people have shared, the difficulties they have endured. Through *Āvāz De Kahāṅ Hai*, we hear thousands of stories of people torn apart." In this way, she presents herself as an active member of a radio listeners' community.

Khalida Begam's comments on music and films are equally revealing. She begins by explaining that she was unable to watch films or hear songs in her youth. (Later in her letter, she remarks that she saw the film *Jugnū* with her brother, contradicting her earlier statement.) While her account is somewhat inconsistent, it is worth mentioning that it was rather common for religiously inclined families, both Muslim and Hindu, to discourage children and young adults from watching films or listening to film songs. Her letter offers further evidence of the importance of aural experience of films and the ways in which film songs enabled people to experience films. Even though she could not see the films *Darde Jigar, Anmol Gharī, Ratan, Pukār,* and *Zīnat* in the cinema, she is familiar with these movies because she heard them on the loudspeaker. Khalida Begam asks Jabbar to play the song "Āj kī rāt sāze dile purdard" (The music of pained heart, tonight). Listening to that song, she notes, would help her relive her experience at the theater with her brother, who too had left

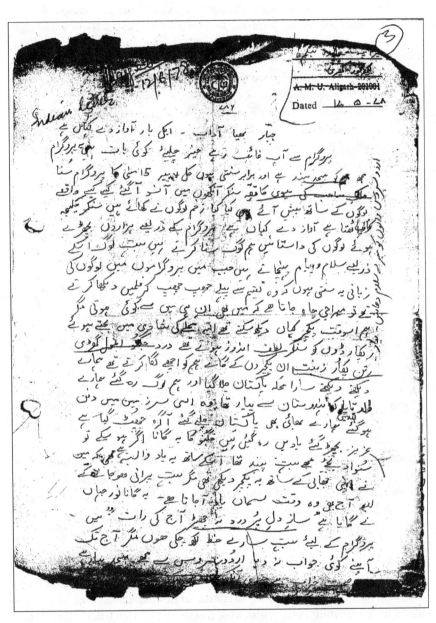

6.5 Letter to Abdul Jabbar by Khalida Begam from Lakhimpur in North India dated May 17, 1978. This letter was read by Jabbar on *Āvāz De Kahāṅ Hai* on June 12, 1978.

Source: Courtesy of Abdul Jabbar.

for Pakistan. Here, Khalida Begam, like other listeners, also connects film songs to her life memories.

Jabbar likely selected this letter and chose to feature it in his program because of Khalida Begam's comments about her experience of Partition. The vast majority of her family, she notes, migrated to Pakistan, but her father and uncle stayed behind. The Urdu/Hindi phrase "dekhte, dekhte sārā mohallā Pakistan chala gaya" is most important here. "Dekhte, dekhte" literally means "watching, watching," but the phrase with its repetition evokes something closer to "right before our eyes, but without us really noticing, the entire neighborhood left to Pakistan." Khalida Begam voices "sentiments and experiences" that many of the program's listeners, and people throughout India for that matter, "could relate to in the flesh."[82] Her letter echoes the primary theme of *Garam Havā* (1974) (Scorching winds), an iconic film about the experience of Partition from the perspective of a Muslim family who stayed in India. The film recounts the struggles of an Indian Muslim businessman, whose family and friends one by one leave to Pakistan during the decade following the Partition. In clear and simple terms, Khalida Begam describes a feeling of abandonment, slow desertion, and ultimately decay, which was experienced by many Muslims who stayed in India after Partition. Khalida Begam's letter, like *Garam Havā*, is subversive, even if subtly so, in that by unapologetically voicing Indian Muslims' suffering and pain in independent India, it contests the government's stance that Muslims ought to be grateful.

Khalida Begam's letter is primarily about loss, the loss of her brother and friends who migrated, but also about the loss of her own youth. If Khalida Begam was twenty when she saw *Jugnū* with her brother, she would have been sixty at the time she wrote to Jabbar. Her letter mourns the loss of her youth, as much as it bemoans the loss of her relatives and friends. In fact, the idea of lost youth was an essential part of the program, ingrained in the program's very own signature tune. The program's title song "Āvāz de kahāṅ hai, duniyā merī javāṅ hai" (Where are you? My world is still young) alludes to that lost youth. If the young Nur Jehan singing in *Anmol Gharī* speaks of her youth and the excitement and opportunity that it presents, the now older Khalida Begam writing to Jabbar speaks of the loss of that youth and the bittersweet feeling that its memory now evokes.

In a similar vein, Mohammed Iqbal's previously mentioned letter to Jabbar where he relates his memories of the song "Sakhī rī ḍolī meṅ hojā savār" (My dear female friend, it is time to board the palanquin) also is about the loss of youth. In his letter, Iqbal explains: "That *qawwali* became popular sixty years ago. That was a simple life. Times have changed."[83] The song also can be read as an ode to lost youth. On the surface, the song is about a young woman, whom the singer tells must prepare to leave her family behind and enter a new and strange world. A deeper reading of the song, however, suggests that the young bride is the listener, who must now, in old age, prepare himself for the new and strange world that follows one's demise. The child, who heard the song and made a funny version of the song with friends, is now an old man. His world is no longer young and he must, like the bride, prepare himself for a trip into the unknown.

Khalida Begam closes her letter by commenting on the practice of writing to the program: "I've written many letters to the program, but my letters have not been responded to." She ends by expressing her deep desire for recognition on the airwaves. Her final line, "I love the Urdu service," is as much a call for reciprocity as it is an expression of affection. She implores Jabbar that he officially recognize her membership in this community by reading her letter and playing her song request—by giving her a voice. On June 12, 1978, Jabbar fulfilled that wish, and again today, thanks to Jabbar's archiving of listeners' letters, we can imagine her voice once more.

Āvāz De Kahāṅ Hai was a deeply nostalgic program that catered to an older generation and invited a discussion about the past. As the earlier quoted critic from Pakistan noted, *Āvāz De Kahāṅ Hai* did not invite an honest and critical reflection of the crimes of the past; instead, it presented pre-Partition India as a "golden era." More problematically, however, by focusing the discussion on sentimentalism for the past, the program inhibited conversation about the future. Although not all of the AIR Urdu Service programs were as explicitly nostalgic or sentimental as *Āvāz De Kahāṅ Hai*, nostalgia was a leading theme in many of its programs, and this had important consequences, particularly in the service's approach to language.

Nostalgia for Urdu

The AIR Urdu Service contested the Pakistani state's official stance that Urdu was a "Muslim" language and belonged in Pakistan by consciously cultivating an Indian (and non-Muslim) audience. At the same time, by speaking exclusively in Urdu to Pakistani audiences (and not broadcasting in other regional languages), the service inadvertently supported the Pakistani state's stance that Urdu was the *only* deserving national language. It was in India, however, where the AIR Urdu Service's particular vision of Urdu was most problematic, if not immediately apparent. Programs like *Āvāz De Kahāṅ Hai* associated Urdu, and to a certain degree Hindustani, with a pre-Partition past. In so doing, the service helped cast Urdu in independent India into what we may call the "language of nostalgia."

Urdu's association with nostalgia has a long history that precedes the Partition of India. In the late nineteenth century, Urdu writers, such as Abdul Halim Sharar, mourned the loss of the Mughal courts and expressed nostalgia during the British colonial period for Muslim-ruled India.[84] In fact, Urdu's association with nostalgia came at the same time that the British government began to grant the language official status and impose it upon other regions. The title of the service's most important program, *Dillī Jo Šeher Thā* (Delhi, the city it was), is a line from a poem by Mir Taqi Mir that describes longing for the capital of the Mughal Empire. The evocative poem idealizes the capital, imagining it as a golden era of expertise. Rather than analyze the reasons for the city's decline or contemplate ways its inhabitants might revive its glory, however, the poem dwells on the memory of the past. The AIR Urdu Service drew on this earlier wave of nostalgia in Urdu literature as it cemented a new form of nostalgia for the Urdu of pre-Partition India on the airwaves.

In his analysis of Faiz Ahmad Faiz's poetry, Aamir Mufti argues that the notion of exile is a defining theme in Faiz's oeuvre—not just exile of the self, but exile of the language. For Faiz, Mufti explains, "modern Urdu writing can only be a writing of exile, a writing that seeks to constantly to displace the relationship of language and self to place."[85] We can extend this notion of exile, Mufti argues, to understand Urdu's larger displacement in South Asia. For the AIR Urdu Service, and for its listeners, particularly those in India, this displacement—the exile—was first and foremost a temporal one. If for Faiz, Urdu had to originate from a place of exile, Urdu, for the Urdu Service's listeners and broadcasters, had to originate from (and express) a sense of nostalgia for bygone past.

In her analysis of the English-language novel *In Custody*, Amina Yaqin points to the ways in which Urdu's association with nostalgia can be harmful. Anita Desai's *In Custody* tells the story of a Hindi literature professor's love for Urdu and his relationship to a once renowned, now mostly forgotten Urdu poet. The novel unambiguously links Urdu to the memory of pre-Partition India. "The central characters . . . are caught in nostalgic remembering of Urdu. . . . Their cultural memory is rooted in premodern past that rejects the values of an evolving present."[86] Yaqin argues that the explicit association of Urdu with a bygone past effectively makes Urdu into a tradition that ought to be "remembered rather than continued."[87] We could propose a similar critique of AIR Urdu Service's programs: they too sought to "remember" rather than to "continue" Urdu.

Conclusion

Rather than end by dismissing the service's limitations, I ask whether we may be demanding too much of a radio service that, after all, aired on a government-run network funded and administered by the Indian government. There were very real limits to what Abdul Jabbar and other AIR Urdu Service broadcasters could say on the air. More important, by developing and nurturing a transnational audience, the AIR Urdu Service broadcasters and its listeners were already sidelining the service's intended purpose.[88] Perhaps nothing shows this more clearly than the amateur recording made by fans of *Āvāz De Kahāṅ Hai* in Lahore, where we can hear the faded voice of an old man named Faiyaz. As noted earlier, somewhat embarrassed, Faiyaz admits that he doesn't write regularly to the program, but that he listens dutifully. He notes that he misses listening to the letters of a fellow listener based in India named Ram Pal.

The phrase "*Āvāz De Kahāṅ Hai*" could be translated in a myriad of ways. It literally means "Give me your voice. Where are you?" But it can also mean "Call to me. Wherever you are?" or even more metaphorically, "Where is your voice?" The program's title and signature tune invited listeners to reflect on the power of radio and on the ways the medium connected with audiences, reminding listeners of the effectiveness of radio resonance. If earlier radio productions had encouraged listeners to "talk," thus expanding the medium's reach, in this program Jabbar, through his performance of listeners' letters on the air, quite literally "gave voice" to his listeners. The program's signature song featuring none other than Nur Jehan's singing also encouraged listeners to reflect on where these voices came from and called attention to radio's ability to cross national borders and to make attainable, if only for a fleeting radio moment, the now impossible dream of a united India. Faiyaz's longing for the voice of Ram Pal—his call out across the border—was a powerful plea, however mediated and limited, in the face of a solidifying border dividing two warring nations.

CONCLUSION

Call to Me. Where Are You?

By the time the program *Āvāz De Kahāṅ Hai* (Call to me. Where are you?) had reached its peak popularity in the late 1970s and early 1980s, radio was already losing its audience to television and to the ubiquity of the cassette.[1] In addition to nostalgia for a united India and for Urdu, the program also summoned nostalgia for radio—or at least for the supremacy the medium had once enjoyed. I found that nostalgia not in Abdul Jabbar's voice, but in listeners' letters, which included descriptions of the joys of listening to the radio. Shaheed Qamar from Karachi explained in 1976: "I locked the door, and made sure I told everyone to keep quiet during the program."[2] Other listeners writing in the early 1980s expressed a preference for listening in the dark, where the absence of visual distractions made the aural experience more enjoyable.[3] This kind of conscious attention to the act of tuning in and hearing voices in the ether is something that earlier radio fans did not include in their letters, and it seems to indicate a keen awareness of an activity later listeners felt was quickly fading out.

My study of Hindi-Urdu broadcasting concludes with the end of radio's reign as the leading electronic medium of daily entertainment and news and with television's hurried coronation. I end here not because radio suddenly disappeared. Radio continued to fuel people's imaginations long after in South Asia, as it did elsewhere. Rather, I end with television's rapid expansion in the subcontinent because I believe that the story of how radio was now forced to share the limelight takes a different turn and is one for others to tell.[4]

Radio for the Millions has traced the history of Hindi-Urdu broadcasting by excavating specific extended moments that illustrate larger social and political changes: World War II, the tumultuous first decade of independence, and the 1965 Indo-Pakistan War and its aftermath. During each of these moments, colonial and national governments attempted to use radio to foster allegiances and fashion national identities, but, as I have demonstrated in each chapter, such attempts were met with mixed success. Sometimes listeners rejected government radio projects immediately in favor of nonstate radio stations; at other times, these projects won immediate success, only to politically backfire soon after.

This, however, is not a straightforward story of resistance to state powers.[5] Rather, it is the story of engagement with state forces, of listeners and broadcasters figuring out ways (sometimes rather unconsciously) to use, fashion, and twist the medium for their own purposes. These alternative radio projects were also not always emancipatory. Axis radio stations promoted a fascist-inflected, misogynistic, and militaristic form of Indian nationalism during World War II. Radio Ceylon enabled important links across the Indian and Pakistani divide and promoted a shared culture and the idea of the subcontinent as a homeland for all faiths. But Radio Ceylon was a moneymaking enterprise that disseminated a commercial form of music that, as several music scholars have shown, stifled other less profitable musical expressions. Last, the All India Radio (AIR) Urdu Service's focus on nostalgia for a united India and for Urdu's lost past in India also could be limiting and ultimately did not lead to social change. At the same time, there can be no doubt that these radio stations challenged "official" cultural, political, and linguistic agendas and enabled listeners and broadcasters to build long-lasting connections across state-sponsored borders.

One might rightfully ask: what difference did it all make? In the end, radio waves could not demolish physical borders, nor did they make it any easier for people to apply for visas or travel across the divide. My answer here is that in failing to listen in to these broadcasting venues that played such a crucial role in people's lives, we run the risk of ceding to the colonial and state governments more power than they actually exercised. This perhaps becomes most evident when addressing issues of language. State documents, and even rich traditions of literature in print, offer plenty of evidence that Partition effectively "killed" Hindustani. Radio sources, in contrast, demonstrate that Hindustani not merely survived but thrived on the airwaves at the very time state governments (and even some writers) denied it existed and had declared it "dead." In taking radio seriously, I am inviting us to acknowledge that radio was a genuine *experience*. I am arguing that sonic experiences—the connections they built, the communities they created—are as valid as any other ones. As Alex Chávez beautifully puts it, "in the midst of anxieties, threats, and failures" these "sounds of crossings take place out of necessity."[6] The idea of a united India, or

Hindustan, as a religiously inclusive regional identity survived not as a political entity, but as a soundscape, and it did so out of necessity.

A guiding conviction of this book has been that the study of media forms, and in particular sound media, is fundamental to the study of history—that South Asian radio history *is* South Asian history. Attention to sound sources forces us to rethink the standard periodization of the region's historiography in important ways, recasting World War II and the 1965 war as watershed events. It also casts serious doubt on a widely accepted narrative that distances the anti-colonial leader, Subhas Chandra Bose, from the fascist governments that sponsored him, showing how his voice—and the talk that surrounded it—circulated in a larger context of Axis radio propaganda to India. Even more important, however, this book makes it clear that Pakistan and India's shared history did not end at Partition. Finally, a study of radio brings attention to South Asian cinema's aurality. Radio provided many opportunities for audiences to hear films, and this sonic encounter was in many cases the *main* way—and in some cases the *only* way—that people experienced them.

If arguing for the centrality of media and sound history has been this book's primary guiding conviction, a secondary one has been a commitment to decolonizing sound studies through an in-depth analysis and excavation of radio-related material in South Asia. Arguing for the importance of radio's resonance calls on scholars of sound and sound reproduction technologies to recognize how listening and talking can be linked intrinsically and to challenge the binary division between "the aural" and "the oral."

Naturally, radio resonance's role in South Asia changed over time. During World War II, "talk" (rumor and gossip) about broadcasts was often more important than the actual broadcast material. Yet by the 1965 war, radio's content as heard by listeners, namely songs and radio plays about the war, took precedence, even as radio resonance helped create the "radio war." By the mid-1970s and early 1980s, radio resonance had reached the airwaves. AIR Urdu Service broadcasters, like Abdul Jabbar, read listeners' letters on the air. In this way, radio resonance and the ways in which oral and aural traditions are intertwined had come full circle.

Notes on Further Research

It seems appropriate to briefly note some possible research I hope this book will inspire. In chronicling radio's role in South Asia, I have found it illuminating to analyze government policies, radio content, and listeners' responses to rethink political histories of the region's transition from British colony to nation-states and to postcolonial state building. I leave the important task of understanding radio as technology in the South Asian context to other scholars, particularly those trained in science and technology studies. Some readers might wonder why I did not cover the role of radio during the 1971 war and foreground the global Cold War in South Asia as I did World War II. Radio, after all, was also an important mode of defiance in East Pakistan (Bangladesh) during the uprising. My answer is that a thorough study of the 1971 war and consequently of the Cold War in South Asia requires an in-depth analysis of Bengali radio sources. What I have attempted in this book is a study of Hindi-Urdu broadcasting during its peak years. I am hopeful, however, that this work has demonstrated the importance of radio to political developments in the region and will inspire further research on radio in other languages and other epochs. I also hope this book will inspire further research on Hindi cinema's aurality and on radio's important liaison to cinema. For example, radio's important role in advertising films and Vividh Bharti and Radio Ceylon's complicated relationship, as both rival and complementary radio stations, deserve further study.

Moving closer to the contemporary moment, FM's earlier boom and radio's most recent rebirth in the form of podcasts are hugely important subjects. In fact, as I complete this book, we are witnessing the growing popularity of the current Hindu-nationalist prime minister's radio program, *Man Kī Bāt* (What my soul/heart says), which airs on AIR but circulates in the form of a podcast, often through social media. The program is a personal rendition of the prime minister's views on the current events, and for many it offers a way to build intimate bonds to the nation's leader and to his Hindu nationalist agenda.[7]

At the time of this book's publication, South Asia as a region is experiencing the rise of communal ideologies and majoritarian governments, and social media has undeniably aided this rise. Opposition certainly has been expressed on social media, but I am sure that to many readers of this book, like me, it has felt muted by much louder calls in support of communalism, majoritarianism, and even authoritarianism. I wish I could confidently say these new media forms will eventually break free from state ideologies, as effectively as radio once did. But the contexts, like the technologies, are vastly different, and it is simply too early to know. The history I tell in this book can offer some hope, but no guarantees, for the future. We can draw, however, at least two clear lessons from this history. First, we should be careful not to ascribe more power to states than they actually hold. Fissures are often not immediately visible (or audible!). After all, some of the most powerful challenges to state projects *on the radio* came at the precise time when imperial and independent governments had tightened their hold over the medium. Second, and most important, a perspective from South Asia is essential to understanding media's relationship to politics on a global scale. More than ever, the region might offer key insight to making sense of our current complex media worlds and the challenges, as well as the moral questions, that they present.

Research as Personal

Finally, if I might be allowed a self-reflexive moment, I would like to comment on my personal relationship to this project.[8] I began studying Hindi and Urdu more than a decade and a half ago. As much as I enjoyed learning languages, it did not come particularly easy to me. I had no problem with aural language (understanding speech and speaking), but in the early years, I struggled with reading and writing. The difficulties I faced in Hindi and Urdu-language classes reminded me of my earlier struggles with learning to read, and especially to write, in Spanish in elementary schools in Mexico and later in English in middle school in the United States. Many years later, I realized that my troubles with written language likely stem from a form of dyslexia and dysgraphia, which often goes undiagnosed because learners can use their aural skills to compensate for other cognitive difficulties. My decision to focus on aural material and to develop a research project that revolves around sound might seem innovative and even somewhat radical for someone trained in a history department and in South Asian studies, fields in which textual studies dominate. The truth is that I chose to do a project on sound not because I wanted to critique highly textual fields or to bring a new perspective, but rather because listening was (and is) so pleasurable for me. It was the sound of voices and my love for what they can convey that kept me going in language classes. In this sense, *Radio for the Millions* is an exploration of that captivation I felt toward sound and language early on, even as the book seeks to demystify and de-fetishize sound and listening cultures, recognizing their place within larger networks of social relations, technologies, and human senses.

There is another way—perhaps less obvious—in which this book is personal. I grew up on the U.S.–Mexico border, in the sister cities of Laredo, Texas, and Nuevo Laredo, Tamaulipas. Growing up, I was witness to the violence of the border and also to the varied ways in which ordinary people go "on living and creating, pushing and pulling at the real and metaphorical edges of nation-state."[9] I think it was this experience that made me particularly attuned to the "sounds of crossing" of South Asia.

My research has taken me thousands of miles away from what I call home and has introduced me to new languages, cultures, and ways of being. Although I certainly did not know it when I first embarked on this journey, my scholarly work has always had a somewhat autobiographical component. A border—similar in some ways and different in others to the one that "crossed" my family and me—also crosses the pages of this book and the lives of the many people I was fortunate to meet along the way. I say this to recognize how personal experiences shape scholarship, but more important, to underscore that any kind of decolonization of scholarship requires that we not make Europe or North America the implicit or default point of comparison, departure, or arrival.[10] My presence in South Asia–related academia in the United States as a minoritized scholar, but one who studies cultures, places, and languages different from her own, often felt to others (and frankly to me as well, at times) bizarre, at best, and completely incongruent, at worst. The expectation in the humanities and social sciences, if often unacknowledged, is that, whereas white scholars can study cultures different from their own, minoritized scholars should study their own cultures and take on representative roles within academia. Not taking on that role presented its own set of complicated challenges. I hope this book has demonstrated that there is value, and indeed potential, in this perspective—just as I hope that this book convinced you of the significance and centrality of the sonic worlds people featured in this text created and inhabited. While searching for sources, conducting oral interviews, listening to recordings, and writing this book, I understood my duty, as a historian of radio in South Asia, to turn an ear to the past and ask in the spirit of the time: "*āvāz de kahāṅ hai?*"

ACKNOWLEDGMENTS

I must begin by thanking the radio broadcasters, listeners, and their families who shared their stories and personal collections. I am especially thankful to Yawar Mehdi in Pakistan; Mariam Kazmi, Farrukh Jaffar, and Ameen Sayani and his son Rajil in India; and Jyoti Parmar in Sri Lanka, who not only generously gave of their time, but also went out of their way to connect me with others. I conducted the bulk of this research in India and Pakistan with fellowships from the American Institutes of Indian and Pakistan Studies. The University of Texas at Austin's South Asia Institute and the Program in British Studies also provided financial support for research trips. The American Institute of Sri Lanka made research in Sri Lanka possible by helping me find a place to stay and enabling me to gain access to various archives. A postdoctorate at the Institute for Historical Studies at the University of Texas at Austin (UT Austin) in fall 2015 as well as a dissertation completion fellowship (2014–2015) and an early career fellowship (2019–2020) from the American Council of Learned Societies made it possible to set aside time for writing during crucial stages of this book's development. I have presented sections of this research at numerous conferences, and I am very thankful for the feedback I received from copresenters and audiences. An earlier version of chapter 3 was published in *Public Culture* in January 2019 and a few paragraphs from chapter 1 were published in *Scroll* in 2016. I appreciate the opportunity to revise and reprint this work.

This project began at UT Austin, where I completed a master's degree in the Department of Asian Languages and Cultures and a doctorate in the

Department of History. There, I benefited greatly from the mentorship of outstanding professors, who have now become friends and colleagues. Gail Minault took me under her wing when I first joined the master's program in 2007 and guided me throughout my graduate career and beyond. Indrani Chatterjee joined the project in 2013 and has been a source of support since then. She has been an insightful and perceptive reader and an encouraging mentor. Kamran Ali also guided me through both my master's and doctoral programs. I am especially grateful for his guidance with research in Pakistan. Judith Coffin and I share a passion for radio scholarship. Her careful feedback on many drafts of my dissertation helped me improve my writing. Shanti Kumar challenged me to better engage South Asian media scholarship. Syed Akbar Hyder encouraged me to think critically about language and literature. I am also grateful to him for voicing his faith in the project; it carried me through the challenging moments.

I wish to thank colleagues in the Department of History at California State University San Bernardino (CSUSB) and the university's awesome Women of Color in Academia (WOCA) group, especially Yvette Saavedra, Liliana Conlisk-Gallegos, Nancy Acevedo, Edna Martinez, and Angie Verissimo. Pursuing my research agenda while at CSUSB with a 3/3/3 (and later 4/4) teaching load would not have been possible without the love and support (and example!) of these friends. I have found a new home at Columbia University's Middle Eastern, South Asian, and African Studies (MESAAS) Department, and I owe a great deal to my colleagues here. In particular, Gil Hochberg, Debashree Mukherjee, Sudita Kaviraj, Laura Fair, Mana Kia, and Manan Ahmed have gone out of their way to make me feel welcomed and have helped me bring this project to completion. Fernando Sanchez, Danny Cervantes, and Jacqueline Anton from CSUSB and Fatima Ahmad and Animesh Joshi from Columbia helped edit and prepare the manuscript at various stages. Sohini Chakrabarty consulted Bangla-language newspapers. I am thankful to Waseem Ahmad for helping with transliteration, but also for being a generous and patient Urdu *ustad* for so many years. Dinyar Patel, Suzanne Schulz, Emilia Bachrach, Sonia Gaind-Krishnan, Gwen Kirk, Salma Siddique, Hoda Bandeh-Ahmadi, J. Daniel Elam, and Ravikant and Peter Knapczyk have read chapter drafts, helped me map out ideas, and/or have been a source of so much support at various stages of the process.

Rumya Putcha, we did it. We published our books! Thank you for assuring me we would persevere. Andrew Amstutz and Asiya Alam have patiently read and re-read each of the chapters of this book more times than I would like to admit. They were with me through every step of the process, and I could not have completed this work without their unwavering support and friendship. Umbreen Bhatt, Gauri Patwardhan, and Agha Talib's beautiful family were amazing hosts in Pakistan. Ajmal Kamal from City Press in Karachi has provided crucial advice and helped trace books and sources during several stages of this project. Saima Iram from Government College in Lahore has been a very helpful interlocutor and a dear friend. Arjumand Ara and Suboor Usmani were hosts in Kolkata and Delhi as well as important interlocutors. Kama Maclean provided helpful advice during a challenging stage, and it made all the difference. Bianca Premo, whom I met during my postdoc at the IHS at UT Austin is the mentor and friend every woman academic needs. I will always be in awe of her wise and on-point guidance and thankful for our friendship. Alaka Basu has been a mentor since I was an undergraduate, and I greatly appreciate her support. Philip Leventhal has been a perceptive reader and an incredibly accommodating and supportive editor as has been Monique Briones. I cannot thank the reviewers of this book enough. Their suggestions, comments, and ideas improved this book tremendously.

Ceara Byrne, Alma Padilla, Crystal Arredondo, and Shahdiba Hasan, I am sorry if I bored you by talking about my work so much. Thank you for listening anyway. A big thanks to Alicia Reyes-Barrientez, a childhood friend, and now also a fellow academic, for believing in me. To family in the United States, Mexico, and India, especially my parents, siblings, sisters-in-law, cousins, nieces, and nephews, thank you. My late father-in-law, Naiyer Masud, always supported this project, and his lifetime of scholarship has been for me, as for many others, such an inspiration. I hope others also will find my father's love for language and poetry in the pages of this book. His insistence on discipline came in handy, particularly at the times when finishing seemed impossible. To the Byrne family, thank you for the many years of love and for giving me a home in Austin.

I met Timsal Masud the summer before I began my doctorate. He has been my partner ever since and has been by my side throughout the ups and downs of this project. Our children, Amalia and Darío, also joined us on this trip. Thank you for your patience and love.

I dedicate Radio for the Millions to the three most important women in my life—my grandmother, Maria Rosa de Leon; my mother, Isabel Alonso de Florida; and my mother-in-law, Sabeeha (Bibi) Khatoon—whose love and support, but above all, sheer enthusiasm for my research and career, made this book possible. The three of them likely would have become scholars and writers had they had the opportunity to do so. All three did everything they could to ensure I had it. Making them proud has been my greatest accomplishment.

NOTES

Introduction: Tuning in to a Radio History

1. Anil Bhargava, *Binaca Geetmala Kā Surīlā Safar* (Jaipur: Vangmāyā Prakāšan, 2007), 27–48. As further described in chapter 4, in this study, I use the term "Radio Ceylon" to refer specifically to Radio Ceylon's Commercial Hindi Service. Binaca is the name of the sponsoring brand, and *Geetmala* is a composite word meaning "garland of songs."

2. For a longer description of *Baiju Bāvrā* and the film's relationship to AIR's social uplift, see Shikha Jhingan, "Re-embodying the 'Classical': The Bombay Film Song in the 1950s," *BioScope: South Asian Screen Studies* 2, no. 2 (2011): 157–79.

3. See chapter 3 and Isabel Huacuja Alonso, "Radio, Citizenship, and the 'Sound Standards' of a Newly Independent India," *Public Culture* 31, no. 1 (2019): 117–44.

4. See Shikha Jhingan, "Re-embodying the 'Classical.'"

5. In the Bombay film industry, film-music composers are normally called music directors. While Naushad disagreed with the government's ban on film songs, he did believe that film-music directors should draw more on native musical traditions and avoid incorporating "western" musical elements. For more details on Naushad's stance and views on this ban, see chapters 3 and 4.

6. S. Dayal, "Well, Keskar Babu?" *Film India*, July 1, 1953, 70, National Film Archive India.

7. The Pakistani press reported on his visit. See chapter 4 for details of press coverage.

8. See Vazira Fazila-Yacoobali Zamindar, *The Long Partition and the Making of Modern South Asia: Refugees, Boundaries, Histories*, Cultures of History (New York: Columbia University Press, 2007).

9. My approach is greatly inspired by the work of Brian Larkin on Nigeria, whose study of media infrastructure focused on "moments" when technologies were introduced. Here, I focus on moments of contention instead. See Brian Larkin, *Signal and Noise: Media, Infrastructure, and Urban Culture in Nigeria* (Durham, NC: Duke University Press, 2008).

10. See Zamindar, *The Long Partition*.

11. I am also inspired by the works on Spanish-language radio in the United States. In particular, Dolores Ines Casillas, *Sounds of Belonging: U.S. Spanish-Language Radio and Public Advocacy* (New York: New York University Press, 2014).

12. See Christopher King, *One Language, Two Scripts: The Hindi Movement in the Nineteenth Century of North India* (Bombay: Oxford University Press, 1994); Vasudha Dalmia, *The Nationalization of Hindu Traditions: Bhāratendū Hariścandra and Nineteenth-Century Banaras* (Delhi: Oxford University Press, 1997); Francesca Orsini, *The Hindi Public Sphere, 1920–1940: Language and Literature in the Age of Nationalism* (New Delhi: Oxford University Press, 2002); and Walter Hakala, *Negotiating Languages: Urdu, Hindi, and the Definition of Modern South Asia* (New York: Columbia University Press, 2016). For work on Urdu's promotion in late colonial India and in indepedent India and Pakistan, see Andrew Amstutz, "Finding a Home for Urdu: Islam and Science in Modern India" (PhD diss., Cornell University, 2017). For works on Urdu as a cosmopolitan language, see Jennifer Dubrow, *Cosmopolitan Dreams: The Making of Modern Urdu Literary Culture in Colonial South Asia* (Honolulu: University of Hawai'i Press, 2018); Peter Knapczyk, "Crafting the Cosmopolitan Elegy in North India: Poets, Patrons, and the Urdu Marsiyah, 1707–1857" (PhD diss., University of Texas at Austin, 2014); and Peter Knapczyk, *Shi'i Devotional Poetry and the Rise of Urdu Literary Culture* (in progress).

13. Alok Rai, "The Persistence of Hindustani," *The Annual of Urdu Studies* 20 (2005): 142.

14. UN data, "A World of Information," http://data.un.org/Search.aspx?q=languages.

15. Following Mandarin. See UN data, "A World of Information."

16. Rebecca P. Scales, *Radio and the Politics of Sound in Interwar France, 1921–1939* (Cambridge: Cambridge University Press, 2018).

17. An excellent example of a work that develops new theoretical tools to "read" broadcasts is Neil Verma, *Theater of the Mind: Imagination, Aesthetics, and American Radio Drama* (Chicago: University of Chicago Press, 2012).

18. The literature that links radio to nationalism is too vast to cite here. Some leading works include Ziad Fahmy, *Ordinary Egyptians: Creating the Modern Nation Through Popular Culture* (Stanford, CA: Stanford University Press, 2011); Joy Elizabeth Hayes, *Radio Nation: Communication, Popular Culture, and Nationalism in Mexico, 1920–1950* (Tucson: University of Arizona Press, 2000); Derek Jonathan Penslar, "Transmitting Jewish Culture: Radio in Israel," *Jewish Social Studies* 10, no. 1 (2003): 1–29; Meltem Ashiska, *Occidentalism in Turkey: Questions of Modernity and National Identity in Turkish Radio Broadcasting* (London: I.B. Tauris, 2010); Kerim Yasar, *Electrified Voices: How the Telephone, Phonograph, and Radio Shaped Modern Japan, 1868–1945* (New York: Columbia University Press, 2018). Two excellent works that explore how radio fosters collective identities include Michele Hilmes, *Radio Voices: American Broadcasting, 1922–1952* (Minneapolis: University of Minnesota Press, 1997); and Susan J. Douglas, *Listening In: Radio and the American Imagination* (Minneapolis: University of Minnesota Press, 2004). Also see Scales, *Radio and the Politics of Sound in Interwar France*. Similarly, there is a rich literature on how radio supported imperial projects. For an example, see Simon J. Porter, *Broadcasting Empire: The BBC and the British World, 1922–1970* (Oxford: Oxford University Press, 2012). Porter shows how BBC helped unite audiences at home with the British settler diaspora.

19. Examples of more theoretical works about radio's listening publics that don't make a nationalist argument but implicitly use the nation as a point of departure or arrival

include Jason Loviglio, *Radio's Intimate Public: Network Broadcasting and Mass-Mediated Democracy* (Minneapolis: University of Minnesota Press, 2005); Kate Lacey, *Listening Publics: The Politics and Experience of Listening in the Media Age* (Cambridge: Polity, 2013); and Verma, *Theater of the Mind*.

20. See also Michele Hilmes, *Network Nations: A Transnational History of British and American Broadcasting* (New York: Routledge, 2012); Derek Valliant, *Across the Waves: How the United States and France Shaped the International Age of Radio* (Champaign: University of Illinois Press, 2017). See also Alejandra M. Bronfman, *Isles of Noise: Sonic Media in the Caribbean* (Chapel Hill: University of North Carolina Press, 2016). Bronfman, focusing on the Caribbean as a region, demonstrates that broadcasting technology originally introduced by various imperial powers was critical to political mobilization against imperial powers in the region. Focusing on radio's influence on literature and studying the BBC's Eastern Service, Daniel Ryan Morse demonstrates how an imperial radio network contributed to the emergence of the global Anglophone novel while still furthering the British Empire's agenda during World War II. Daniel Ryan Morse, *Radio Empire: The BBC's Eastern Service and the Emergence of the Global Anglophone Novel* (New York: Columbia University Press, 2020). Another example of works that take into account transnational perspective is Christine Ehrick, *Radio and the Gendered Soundscape: Women and Broadcasting in Argentina and Uruguay, 1930–1950* (New York: Cambridge University Press, 2015). Her book, however, focusing less on transnational aspects of broadcasting and more on gender dynamics, is particularly helpful for me for addressing issues of gender. For an analysis of this, see the discussion on Nur Jehan in chapter 5.

21. Casillas, *Sounds of Belonging*; and Catherine Squires "Black Talk Radio: Defining Community Needs and Identity," *Harvard International Journal of Press/Politics* 5, no. 2 (2000): 73–95. See also Sonia Robles, *Mexican Waves: Radio Broadcasting Along Mexico's Northern Border, 1930–1950* (Tucson: University of Arizona Press, 2019).

22. Manan Ahmed Asif, *The Loss of Hindustan: The Invention of India* (Cambridge, MA: Harvard University Press, 2020), back cover and 129.

23. Emily Ann Thompson, *The Soundscape of Modernity: Architectural Acoustics and the Culture of Listening in America, 1900–1933* (Cambridge, MA: MIT Press, 2004), 1; citing R. Murray Schafer, *The Soundscape: Our Sonic Environment and the Tuning of the World* (Rochester, VT: Destiny Books, 1994), definition on 274–75.

24. Alex E. Chávez, *Sounds of Crossing: Music, Migration, and the Aural Poetics of Huapango Arribeño* (Durham, NC: Duke University Press, 2017), 33, 235.

25. Chávez, *Sounds of Crossing*, 29, 7.

26. Number of receiver sets in India, statistics gathered by All India Radio, July 2, 1943, AIR and FEB Broadcasting organization, L/I/1/935, India Office, British Library, London (IO hereafter). The report notes that in January 1943, there were 162,000 licensed receiver sets in British India and 17,000 sets in Indian princely states. As I further discuss in chapters 1 and 2, receivers were likely very undercounted in this period for a variety of reasons, including radio listeners' unwillingness to register sets. Nonetheless, receiver ownership rates in India were much lower than in most regions of the world. See chapter 1 for more details.

27. Broadcasting of anti-British propaganda in the Middle East, Persian Gulf, NWF, and Central Asia: BBC broadcasts in Arabic, L/PS/12/4132, IO.

28. Broadcasting of anti-British propaganda in the Middle East, Persian Gulf, NWF, and Central Asia: BBC broadcasts in Arabic, L/PS/12/4132, IO. In explaining how I have

encountered ideas in the archives, I draw inspiration on Durba Mitra's discussion of archives. See Durba Mitra, *Indian Sex Life: Sexuality and the Colonial Origins of Modern Social Thought* (Princeton, NJ: Princeton University Press, 2020), 4.

29. Michael P. Steinberg, "Review: Reason and Resonance: A History of Modern Aurality," *American Historical Review* 116, no. 5 (2011): 1441–42. Veit Erlmann, *Reason and Resonance: A History of Modern Aurality* (Cambridge, MA: MIT Press, 2010). Veit argues that the acoustic and physiological phenomenon of resonance was linked to western ideas of rationality in the early modern period. See also Veit Erlmann, "Resonance," in *Keywords in Sound*, ed. David Novak and Matt Sakakeeny (Durham, NC: Duke University Press, 2015), chapter 15, Kindle. Kate Lacey, also focusing on western traditions, briefly employs the term, but in a much more specific way: to understand the ways certain sounds *resonated* with listeners in ways that they did not necessarily result in speech. Kate Lacey, *Listening Publics: The Politics and Experience of Listening in the Media Age* (Cambridge: Polity, 2013), chapter 8, loc. 3907 of 5736, Kindle.

30. Carolyn Birdsall, *Nazi Soundscapes: Sound, Technology and Urban Space in Germany, 1933–1945* (Amsterdam: Amsterdam University Press, 2012), 34. Birdsall explains: "The loud cheers of massive crowds at the official events not only comprised the affirmations of individual speaking-hearing feedback loops, but also the intensification of the sounds recorded by the microphone, projected through the loud speaker system, and fed back again into the microphone" (34).

31. Bruce Lenthall, *Radio's America: The Great Depression and the Rise of Modern Mass Culture* (Chicago: University of Chicago Press, 2008), chapter 3, Kindle. FDR delivered this speech the day after Japan's bombing of Pearl Harbor, hoping both to convince Congress and the public to support his declaration of war.

32. Sayani also noted that he once made a radio documentary for the BBC titled *Music for the Millions*. Despite many attempts I have been, however, unable to trace this program.

33. Jonathan Sterne, *The Audible Past: Cultural Origins of Sound Reproduction* (Durham, NC: Duke University Press, 2003), 33.

34. Sterne, *The Audible Past*, 33.

35. Sterne, *The Audible Past*, 33.

36. Lacey, *Listening Publics*, 25.

37. Drawing on sources from nineteenth-century Columbia, Ana Maria Ochoa highlights the important links between oral and aural traditions and argues that the disciplining of both was crucial to the making of ideas of personhood and nationhood before the dominance of sound-reproduction technologies. This study shows that links between the oral and aural continued in the twentieth century. Ana Maria Ochoa Gautier, *Aurality: Listening and Knowledge in Nineteenth-Century Columbia* (Durham, NC: Duke University Press, 2014), 140.

38. Lisa Gitelman, *Scripts, Grooves, and Writing Machines: Representing Technologies in the Edison Era* (Stanford, CA: Stanford University Press, 1999). Casillas, for example, perceptively points out that Spanish-language radio in the United States "carrie[s] elements of an oral tradition long familiar to Mexican and Chicano communities." Casillas, *Sounds of Belonging*, 5.

39. Gavin Steingo and Jim Sykes, eds., *Remapping Sound Studies* (Durham, NC: Duke University Press, 2019), 92.

40. Derek Valliant, "Occupied Listeners: The Legacies of Interwar Radio for France During World War II," in *Sound in the Era of Mechanical Reproduction*, ed. David Suisman and Susan Strasser (Philadelphia: University of Pennsylvania Press, 2010), 141–58.

41. In focusing on radio, I align myself with recent historiographical interventions focusing on multisensory archives. For example, Kama Maclean's analysis of visual media in interwar India reveals a much wider and richer history of revolutionaries' violent opposition to colonial rule than historians had previously acknowledged. Similarly, a study of radio, and attention to aural cultures, challenges our understanding of South Asian history in important ways, and centers a story clearly present in popular imagination but largerly absent from scholarly works. See Kama Maclean, *A Revolutionary History of Interwar India: Violence, Image, Voice and Text* (London: Hurst, 2015), 4.

42. In fact, until recently, historians had considered the postcolonial period the territory of political science, sociology, and anthropology. Some groundbreaking history works that study postcolonial India include Zamindar, *The Long Partition*; Benjamin Siegel, *Hungry Nation: Food, Famine and the Making of Modern India* (Cambridge: Cambridge University Press, 2018); Ramchandra Guha, *India After Gandhi: The History of the World's Largest Democracy* (New York: HarperCollins, 2008); Emily Rook-Koepsel, *Democracy and Unity in India: Understanding the All India Phenomenon, 1940–1960*, Routledge Studies in South Asian History (London: Routledge, 2019); Rohit De, *A People's Constitution: The Everyday Life of Law in the Indian Republic* (Princeton, NJ: Princeton University Press, 2018).

43. I am certainly not alone in making this claim. Srirupa Roy makes a similar point in Srirupa Roy, *Beyond Belief: India and the Politics of Postcolonial Nationalism, Politics, History, and Culture* (Durham, NC: Duke University Press, 2007). Mrinalini Sinha made a similar point during a talk. See Mrinalini Sinha, "The Abolition of Indenture: Between Empire and Nation" (Colloquium, SOAS University, London, UK, May 28, 2013). Moreover, just as Priya Jaikumar has shown that imperially themed British films and anticolonial-themed Indian films (and their regulation) filmed "at the end of Empire" do not represent opposing categories but are instead "linked expressions" that emerged during "radical political transform[ing]" moments, I too point to important links between colonial and independent Indian and Pakistani radio projects. See Priya Jaikumar, *Cinema at the End of Empire* (Durham, NC: Duke University Press, 2005), 4.

44. Biswarup Sen, "A New Kind of Radio: FM Broadcasting in India," *Media, Culture, and Society* 36, no. 8 (August 26, 2014): 1084.

45. Indivar Kamtekar, "The Shiver of 1942," *Studies in History* 18, no. 1 (February 1, 2002): 81.

46. In particular, see the following works: Christopher Bayly and Timothy Harper, *Forgotten Armies: The Fall of British Asia, 1941–1945* (London: Allen Lane, 2004); Christopher Bayly and Timothy Harper, *Forgotten Wars: Freedom and Revolution in Southeast Asia* (Cambridge, MA: Harvard University Press, 2007); Indivar Kamtekar, "A Different War Dance: State and Class in India 1939–1945," *Past and Present Society*, no. 176 (August 2002): 187–221; Yasmin Khan, *The Raj at War: A People's History of India's Second World War* (New York: Random House, 2015); Indivar Kamtekar, "The Shiver of 1942," *Studies in History* 18, no. 1 (February 1, 2002): 81–102; Madhushree Mukerjee, *Churchill's Secret War: The British Empire and the Ravaging of India During World War II* (New York: Basic Books, 2010); Raghu Karnad, *Farthest Field: An Indian Story of the Second World War* (London: William Collins, 2015); Srinath Raghavan, *India's War: World War II and the Making of Modern South Asia* (New York: Basic Books, 2016). See essays in a forthcoming special issue of *Modern Asian Studies*, "Between Theaters and Beyond Battles: Rethinking World War II in South Asia," ed. Isabel Huacuja Alonso and Andrew Amstutz. For a more detailed engagement with these works, see chapters 1 and 2.

47. I am specifically in conversation with works on revolutionaries, namely, Maclean, *A Revolutionary History of Interwar India*; and Durba Ghosh, *Gentlemanly Terrorists: Political Violence and the Colonial State in India, 1919–1947* (Cambridge: Cambridge University Press, 2017).

48. A homeland that, as Philip Oldenburg puts it, had not been "sufficiently imagined." Philip Oldenburg, "'A Place Insufficiently Imagined': Language, Belief, and the Pakistan Crisis of 1971," *Journal of Asian Studies* 44, no. 4 (1985): 711–33. On this topic, see also Srinath Raghavan, *1971: A Global History of the Creation of Bangladesh* (Cambridge, MA: Harvard University Press, 2013).

49. I also align myself with film historians, such as Priya Jaikumar, who argues for placing the history of media at the very center of the region's historiography. Jaikumar, *Cinema at the End of Empire*.

50. See, for example, the following postcolonial studies: Roy, *Beyond Belief*; Alyssa Ayres, *Speaking Like a State: Language and Nationalism in Pakistan* (Cambridge: Cambridge University Press, 2009); De, *A People's Constitution*; Siegel, *Hungry Nation*; Guha, *India After Gandhi*; Mubbashir Rizvi, *The Ethics of Staying: Social Movements and Land Rights Politics in Pakistan*, South Asia in Motion (Stanford, CA: Stanford University Press, 2019). Another important recently published book on postcolonial India is Nikhil Menon's *Planning Democracy: Modern India's Quest for Development* (London: Cambridge University Press, 2022). Since it was published after this book's completion, I could not engage with it as much as I would have liked.

51. I am inspired by Zamindar's ethnographic and historical research across the Indo-Pakistan border. Zamindar, *The Long Partition*.

52. South Asia has produced an incredibly rich body of literature on nationalism. In fact, much of the theorization of the region's twentieth-century history written in the past decades has been, in one way or another, about the hardening of identities along religious and national lines. See, for example, Partha Chatterjee, *The Nation and Its Discontents* (Princeton, NJ: Princeton University Press, 1993) and Homi Bhabha, *The Location of Culture* (London: Routledge, 1994). Others have cast doubt on the "native origins" of this imagining and have argued that the idea of the Indian nation as a geographical space bears important links to imperial economic projects and to the rise of capitalist systems in the region and beyond. Scholars also have paid attention to the role of language, art, literature, and print and visual media, in the making and hardening of religious and regional identities prior and after independence. Some examples include Sumathi Ramaswany, *The Goddess and the Nation: Mapping Mother India* (Durham, NC: Duke University Press, 2010); Anna Schultz, *Singing a Hindu Nation: Marathi Devotional Performance and Nationalism* (New York: Oxford University Press, 2012). In fact, some of the most compelling work on media in the subcontinent has effectively linked the rise of the television in the late 1980s in India to political ascent of the Hindu right. See Arvind Rajagopal, *Politics After Television: Hindu Nationalism and the Reshaping of the Public in India* (Cambridge: Cambridge University Press, 2001); Purnima Mankekar, *Screening Culture, Viewing Politics: An Ethnography of Television* (Durham, NC: Duke University Press, 1999). In this book, I propose that careful attention to the domain of sound—and in particular to what was happening on the radio airwaves—reveals that at least until the 1970s, there were significant challenges to these nationalistic projects.

53. Chávez, *Sounds of Crossing*, 33.

54. Chávez, *Sounds of Crossing*, 330. (Emphasis for "sounds of crossing" added. In the original "take place" was italicized. I have removed that emphasis.)

55. J. Daniel Elam, *World Literature for the Wretched of the Earth: Anticolonial Aesthetics, Postcolonial Politics* (New York: Fordham University Press, 2020), Introduction, Kindle.

56. Salman Rushdie, "The Art of Fiction No. 186 Interview with Jack Livings," *Paris Review* 174 (2005): 107–43, cited in Madhumita Lahiri, "An Idiom for India: Hindustani and the Limits of the Language Concept," *Interventions: International Journal of Postcolonial Studies* 18, no. 1 (2016): 60–85.

57. Alok Rai, "The Persistance of Hindustani."

58. Comments on the report accompanying a dispatch from the secretary to the government of India, February 28, 1934, Broadcasting in India, correspondence regarding, L/I/1/445, IO.

59. Jason Beaster-Jones, *Bollywood Sounds: The Cosmopolitan Mediation of Hindi Film Song* (New York: Oxford University Press, 2015), xv.

60. David Lelyveld's pioneering articles, published in the 1990s, demonstrate the various ways that radio in independent India remained loyal to the British centralized system of broadcasting. David Lelyveld, "Colonial Knowledge and the Fate of Hindustani," *Comparative Studies in Society and History* 35, no. 4 (1993): 665–82; David Lelyveld, "Transmitters and Culture: The Colonial Roots of Indian Broadcasting," *South Asian Research* 10, no. 1 (1990): 41–52; David Lelyveld, "Upon the Subdominant: Administering Music on All India Radio," *Social Text* no. 93 (Summer 1994): 111–27. A few recently published works on radio in colonial India have complemented Lelyveld's articles in later years. Joselyn Zivin's research, for instance, examines the lives and work of British broadcasters in India and demonstrates that their vision of the British Empire diverged from that of typical British civil servants. Joselyn Zivin, " 'Bent': A Colonial Subversive and Indian Broadcasting," *Past and Present* 162, no. 1 (1999): 195–220; Joselyn Zivin, "The Imagined Reign of the Iron Lecturer: Village Broadcasting in Colonial India," *Modern Asian Studies* 32, no. 3 (1998): 717–38. Stephen Hughes work on radio in Tamil Nadu is an important addition. See Stephen P. Hughes, "The 'Music Boom' in Tamil South India: Gramophone, Radio and the Making of Mass Culture," *Historical Journal of Film, Radio and Television* 22, no. 4 (2002): 445–73. Garrett Field's work on Sinhala song and poetry also analyzes the crucial role of radio in Sri Lanka. Garrett Field, *Modernizing Composition: Sinhala Song, Poetry and Politics in Twentieth-Century Sri Lanka* (Oakland: University of California Press, 2016). For a work that deals more generally with sound, although not radio specifically, see Laura Brueck, Jacob Smith, and Neil Verma, eds., *Indian Sound Cultures, Indian Sound Citizenships* (Ann Arbor: University of Michigan Press, 2020). This book, while providing an interesting collection of essays on varied topics, clearly makes the Indian nation its point of departure and arrival.

61. Vebhuti Duggal's work on song-request programs also has investigated radio and film's important relationship. See Vebhuti Duggal, "Imagining Sound Through the Pharmaish: Radios and Request-Postcards in North India, c. 1955–75," *BioScope: South Asian Screen Studies* 9, no. 1 (2018): 1–23. See also Duggal, "The Community of Listeners: Writing a History of Hindi Film Music Aural Culture" (PhD diss., Jawaharlal Nehru University, 2015). This fascinating dissertation is a study of the Hindi film song and the various modes of listening it engendered. Ravikant's work on language and Indian media has also investigated these issues. Ravikant, long interested in the ways cinema "pulls in people through other mediums," correctly points out that in this "radio has played a leading role" (71). Ravikant, *Media Kī Bhāṣā Līlā* (New Delhi: Lokchetnā Prakāśan, 2016). In particular, see chapter 5, "Cinema, Bhāṣā, Radio." Moreover, Ravikant's work on the radio set's physical presence in cinema offers new ways to think about radio

and cinema's relationship. See Ravikant, "Śrav-Driṣṭav: Cinema Meṅ Radio," *Pratimān: Samay, Samāj, Sanskriti* 2 (December 2013): 581–600; Narendra Sharma, "Cine-Sangeet Indra Ka Ghora Hai Aur Akashvani Uska Samman Karti Hai!/Film Music Is Lord Indra's Horse and Akashvani Respects It!," Ravikant, trans., *BioScope: South Asian Screen Studies* 3, no. 2 (July 2012): 165–73. A few recent articles concerned with the present-day radio industry have begun to chart radio's past. See, for example, Frederick Noronha, "Who's Afraid of Radio in India?" *Economic and Political Weekly* 35, no. 38 (2000): 385–87; Robin Jeffery, "The Mahatma Didn't Like the Movies and Why It Matters: Indian Broadcasting Policy, 1920s–1990s," *Global Media and Communication* 2, no. 2 (2006): 204–24; Sen, "A New Kind of Radio."

62. Debashree Mukherjee argues that early Indian talkies did not suddenly create a mediated sound, but rather entered an already "densely mediated space of sound technologies," in which the telephone, gramophone, and radio already thrived. See Debashree Mukherjee, *Bombay Hustle: Making Movies in a Colonial City* (New York: Columbia University Press, 2020), 144, 145. Pavitra Sundar, "Of Radio, Remix, and Rang De Basanti: Reimagining History Through Film Sound," *Jump Cut*, no. 56 (Fall 2014), https://www.ejumpcut.org/archive/jc56.2014-2015/RangDeBasanti/index.html, accessed April 15, 2022. Pavitra Sundar also invites us to reverse the primacy of the aural over the visual. See "Usha Uthup and Her Husky, Heavy Voice," in *Indian Sound Cultures, Indian Sound Citizenship*, ed. Brueck, Smith, and Verma, 115–51; "Romance, Piety, and Fun: The Transformation of the Qawwali and Islamicate Culture in Hindi Cinema," in "The Evolution of Song and Dance in Hindi Cinema," special issue, *South Asian Popular Culture* 15, nos. 2–3 (December 2017): 139–53. Similarly, Nilanjana Bhattacharjya's work also argues for the primacy of sound in South Asian cinema. See, for example, Nilanjana Bhattacharjya, "How Sound Helps Tell a Story: Sound, Music, and Narrative in Vishal Bhardwaj's *Omkara*," in *Writing About Screen Media*, ed. Lisa Patti (New York: Routledge University Press, 2019), 149–53.

63. Certainly, some cinema studies scholars have argued that Hindi film songs and their reception should be studied as *the* leading element of Hindi cinema, not as an auxiliary to visual experience. See, for example, Neepa Majumdar, "The Embodied Voice: Song Sequences and Stardom in Popular Hindi Cinema," in *Soundtrack Available: Essays on Film and Popular Music*, ed. Pamela Robertson Wojcik and Arthur Knight (Durham, NC: Duke University Press, 2001), 161–85; Corey Creekmur, "Picturizing American Cinema: Hindi Film Songs and the Last Days of Genre," in *Soundtrack Available: Essays on Film and Popular Music*, ed. Pamela Robertson Wojcik and Arthur Knight (Durham, NC: Duke University Press, 2001), 375–407. Similarly, Debashree Mukherjee's recent work has shown the centrality of sound to early Indian talkies and has argued for the primacy of the aural over the visual. Mukherjee, *Bombay Hustle* (in particular, see chapter 3, "Voice/Awaaz"). See also Pavitra Sundar's works in note 62 in this introduction. Although radio appears in these studies as an important conduit, we are yet to study in more detail the medium's role in shaping the industry. For a longer discussion of these works, see chapter 4.

64. Most prominent is Sugata Bose, *His Majesty's Opponent: Subhas Chandra Bose and India's Struggle Against Empire* (Cambridge, MA: Harvard University Press, 2011), but for more detailed description of Bose's biographies, see chapter 2.

65. Amber H. Abbas, "Disruption and Belonging: Aligarh, Its University, and the Changing Meaning of Place Since Partition," *Oral History Review* 44, no. 2 (2017): 301–21.

66. For example, it was through my interviews with Radio Pakistan's pioneering broadcasters that I came to understand the 1965 Indo-Pakistan War as a pivotal moment in radio

history and that I first learned about the existence of a mostly untouched extensive sound and paper archive about Radio Pakistan's 1965 war campaign in Islamabad.

67. Realizing the importance of these rare sources, I also began to contact the relatives of deceased broadcasters and inquire whether they might be able to share material. Jyoti Parmar, the daughter of Radio Ceylon's Dalbir Singh Parmar, for example, kept a folder of her father's radio-related documents, which included a detailed diary written by a radio listener, which I analyze in chapter 4.

68. Ranajit Guha, *Selected Subaltern Studies*, vol. 1 (New York: Oxford University Press, 1998).

69. Verma, *Theater of the Mind*.

70. Sterne, *The Audible Past*, Introduction, 18–19. For a theoretical analysis of the limitations of archives and the "recovery" of the past, see Gil Z. Hochberg, *Becoming Palestine: Toward an Archival Imagination of the Future* (Durham, NC: Duke University Press, 2021).

71. Santanu Das, *India, Empire, and First World War Culture: Writings, Images, and Songs* (Cambridge: Cambridge University Press, 2018), 14.

72. Raymond Williams, *Marxism and Literature* (London: Oxford University Press, 1977), 132, cited in Santanu Das, *India, Empire, and First World War Culture*, 25.

73. Das, *India, Empire, and First World War Culture*, 25.

74. Verma, *Theater of the Mind*, 8.

1. News on the AIR

1. According to Daniel Todman, by September 1939, the 1935 constitution, "which among other things allowed Indians to hold offices at the regional level," had not legally "come fully into effect" because the "requisite number of princes had not signed up the plan for an Indian federation." This meant that Britain's declaration technically had already "committed India to hostilities" before the viceroy's controversial declaration. Daniel Todman, *Britain's War into Battle, 1937–1941* (New York: Oxford University Press, 2016), 231.

2. Notes by a Bengali observer, Appendix III, Broadcasting in India, Correspondence Regarding, L/I/1/445 India Office, British Library, London, United Kingdom (IO). This document is undated but based on its content, it likely was written in 1939. It is not clear who this Bengali observer was or how this note reached British hands. It appears to be anecdotal and refers to listening practices collected by the British administration and written by so-called native informants. The typed note is added as an appendix to a long file on radio broadcasting.

3. See Sanjoy Bhattacharya, "Wartime Policies of State Censorship and the Civilian Population of Eastern India, 1939–35," *South Asia Research* 17, no. 2 (Autumn 1997): 140–63; and Devika Sethi, *War Over Words: Censorship in India, 1930–1960* (New Delhi: Cambridge University Press, 2019).

4. Broadcasting of anti-British propaganda in the Middle East, Persian Gulf, NWF and Central Asia, etc., BBC broadcasts in Arabic, L/PS/12/4132, IO.

5. Carolyn Birdsall, *Nazi Soundscapes: Sound, Technology and Urban Space in Germany, 1933–1945* (Amsterdam: Amsterdam University Press: 2012), 11–14.

6. Birdsall, *Nazi Soundscapes*, 12.

7. Works that exclusively analyze World War II's influence on South Asia include Christopher Bayly and Timothy Harper, *Forgotten Armies: The Fall of British Asia, 1941–1945* (London: Allen Lane, 2004); Christopher Bayly and Timothy Harper, *Forgotten Wars:*

Freedom and Revolution in Southeast Asia (Cambridge, MA: Harvard University Press, 2007); Indivar Kamtekar, "A Different War Dance: State and Class in India 1939–1945," *Past and Present Society*, no. 176 (August 2002): 187–221; Indivar Kamtekar, "The Shiver of 1942," *Studies in History* 18, no. 1 (February 1, 2002): 81–102; Jagdish N. Sinha, *Science, War, and Imperialism: India in the Second World War* (Leiden: Brill, 2008); Yasmin Khan, "Sex in an Imperial War Zone: Transnational Encounters in Second World War India," *History Workshop Journal* 73, no. 1 (February 28, 2012): 240–58; Yasmin Khan, *India at War: The Subcontinent and the Second World War* (Oxford: Oxford University Press, 2015); Srinath Raghavan, *India's War: World War II and the Making of Modern South Asia* (New York: Basic Books, 2016); Janam Mukherjee, *Hungry Bengal: War, Famine, and the End of Empire* (New York: Oxford University Press, 2015); William Mazzarella, "A Torn Performative Dispensation: The Affective Politics of British Second World War Propaganda in India and the Problem of Legitimation in an Age of Mass Publics," *South Asian History and Culture* 1, no. 1 (2010): 1–24. See also "Proposal for Rethinking WWII in South Asia," prepared by Isabel Huacuja Alonso and Andrew Amstutz. This has been submitted for a special issue of *Modern Asian Studies*, tentatively titled "Between Theaters and Beyond Battles: Rethinking World War II in South Asia."

8. Broadcasting of anti-British propaganda in the Middle East, Persian Gulf, NWF, and Central Asia, etc., BBC broadcasts in Arabic, L/PS/12/4132, IO.

9. See, for example, Ranajit Guha, *Elementary Aspects of Peasant Insurgency in Colonial India* (Delhi: Oxford University Press, 1983).

10. Number of receiver sets in India, statistics gathered by All India Radio, July 2, 1943, AIR and FEB Broadcasting organization, L/I/1/935, IO. The report notes that in January 1943 there were 162,000 licensed receiver sets in British India and 17,000 in Indian princely states. Receivers were likely undercounted for a variety of reasons, including radio listeners' unwillingness to register sets.

11. Luise White, *Speaking with Vampires: Rumor and History in East and Central Africa* (Berkeley: University of California Press, 2000), 84.

12. Christopher Bayly, *Empire and Information: Intelligence Gathering and Social Communication in India, 1780–1870* (Cambridge: Cambridge University Press, 1996), 40.

13. John Reith's interest in broadcasting in India is well known. Reith wrote letters to the government of India expressing interest in broadcasting in the late 1920s and early 1930s. Reith lobbied for the establishment of a public service model similar to the BBC in India. See Charles Stuart, *The Reith Diaries* (London: Collins, 1975); Joselyn Zivin, "'Bent': A Colonial Subversive and Indian Broadcasting," *Past and Present* 162, no. 1 (1999): 203; and Alasdair Pinkerton, "Radio and the Raj: Broadcasting in British India (1920–1940)," *Journal of the Royal Asiatic Society* 18, no. 2 (April 1, 2008): 170.

14. Lionel Fielden, the first controller of broadcasting in India, wrote in his memoirs that before taking the post, he believed that the spoken word could "perform miracles" for a "vast and illiterate country." Lionel Fielden, *The Natural Bent* (London: Andre Deutsch, 1960), 158.

15. U.S.-based Congress leaders took advantage of radio in the United States. J. J. Singh of the India League of America did make use of radio in the United States during World War II. See Dinyar Patel, "One Man Lobby? Propaganda, Nationalism in the Diaspora, and the India League of America During the Second World War," *Journal of Imperial and Commonwealth History* 49, no. 6 (2021): 1110–40.

16. Joselyn Zivin, "The Imagined Reign of the Iron Lecturer: Village Broadcasting in Colonial India," *Modern Asian Studies* 32, no. 3 (1998): 717–38.

17. Radio broadcasting and its future development in India, note by director of wireless, 5 August 1927, 87-R, 1928, Foreign and Political Reforms, National Archives of India, New Delhi, India (NAI).

18. See Syed Zulfiqar Ali Bukhari, *Sarguzašt* (Lahore: Ghalib, 1995), 38. Zulfiqar Bukhari was Patras Bukhari's brother and also a renowned broadcaster in colonial India and later independent Pakistan. For consistency purposes, I use Bukhari in this book for both brothers, but Patras Bukhari sometimes is spelled Patras Bokhari.

19. In 1927, there were 850 license holders in Calcutta and 210 in Bombay. Given the limited numbers of radio owners in India, the colonial government agreed to charge a 10 percent import tax on radio receivers and to transfer the proceeds to the newly formed broadcasting company. All radios had to be imported from Europe because there were no radio manufacturers in India. For information on the number of receivers in 1927, see Wireless Importation Indian Broadcasting Company Bombay Agreement, 1074 CUS 1927, Custom Duties, Central Board of Revenue, NAI; Letter to Earl and Birkenhead, April 28, 1922, 84(5) 1922, Reforms, Mysore Residency, Radio Broadcasting in India, NAI.

20. Letter dated January 12, 1929, Broadcasting in India, L/PO/3/1, IO.

21. Indian vendors later became involved in anticolonial radio stations and thus continued to play an important role in shaping the medium. In 1942, one radio vendor was tried for supporting the Bombay-based Congress Radio, which was on the air during Quit India. Isabel Huacuja Alonso, "'Voice of Freedom' at the End of Empire: Radio SEAC, Underground Congress Radio, and the (Anti) Colonial Sublime" (in progress).

22. Development of broadcasting in India from 1927 to 1933, Broadcasting in India, L/PJ/7/754, IO.

23. Pinkerton, "Radio and the Raj," 176.

24. Telegraph from Viceroy to Eric Dunstan, April 8, 1928, Broadcasting in India, L/PO/3/1, IO.

25. The Empire Broadcasting Service-Proposals of the BBC—Questions of finance and use of languages, Reports as to interest shown in India to the service, L/PJ/6/1996, IO.

26. "Historic Moments from the 1930s," BBC World Services, https://www.bbc.co.uk/worldservice/specials/1122_75_years/page2.shtml, accessed on January 2, 2013.

27. For scholarship on the BBC Empire Service, see Andrew Hill, "The BBC Empire Service: The Voice, the Discourse of the Master and Ventriloquism," in "South Asian Diaspora and the BBC World Service: Contacts, Conflicts and Contestations," special issue, *South Asian Diaspora* 2, no. 1 (2010): 25–38; John M. MacKenzie, "In Touch with the Infinite: The BBC and the Empire, 1923–53," in *Imperialism and Popular Culture*, ed. John M. MacKenzie (Manchester: Manchester University Press, 1986), 165–91.

28. Correspondence regarding Empire Services-1933, Broadcasting in India, Correspondence Regarding, L/I/1/445, IO.

29. Government of India, *Report on the Progress of Broadcasting in India (up to the 31st March 1939)* (Delhi: Manager of Publications, 1939), 1–2.

30. Bukhari, *Sarguzašt*, 38–40.

31. Fielden, *The Natural Bent*, 159; Partha Sarathi Gupta, *Radio and the Raj: 1921–47* (Calcutta: Centre for Studies in Social Sciences, K. P. Bagchi, 1995), 24; H. R. Luthra, *Indian Broadcasting* (New Delhi: Ministry of Information and Broadcasting, 1986), 493–505 (see the timeline of significant events).

32. For more information on early radio clubs in India, see Government of India, *Report on the Progress of Broadcasting*. Lionel Fielden was likely the primary author of this document. The copy I used for this chapter is from the National Documentation Center,

Islamabad, Pakistan. One newspaper account notes that on July 1927, the Bombay Presidency Radio Club broadcast from 5:00 p.m. to 6:00 p.m. and from 7:05 to 7:45 p.m. "Schedules of the Bombay Presidency Radio Club," *Times of India*, July 4, 1927. See also Stephen P. Hughes, "The 'Music Boom' in Tamil South India: Gramophone, Radio and the Making of Mass Culture," *Historical Journal of Film, Radio and Television* 22, no. 4 (2002): 445–73.

33. See chapters 3–4 for discussion on radio and music.

34. As Zivin has noted in her study, these projects were closer in ideology to Reith, as their aim was to uplift the Indian rural poor through educational programs. See Zivin, "The Imagined Reign of the Iron Lecturer," 717–38.

35. See Zivin, "The Imagined Reign of the Iron Lecturer," 717–38. The contrast between retired officers that championed village broadcasting projects and the viceroy demonstrates how the British administration was not monolithic.

36. BBC WAC EI/896/2, quoted and cited in Pinkerton, "Radio and the Raj," 183.

37. Stuart, *The Reith Diaries*, 270; Pinkerton, "Radio and the Raj," 183.

38. Letter from Ian Stephens, Home Department, to Hugh MacGregor India Officer, New Delhi, September 17, 1934, EI/896/2, BBC Written Archives, London, cited in Pinkerton, "Radio and the Raj," 183; Zivin, "'Bent,'" 199. Fielden became the first controller of broadcasting on August 30, 1935. See Luthra, *Indian Broadcasting*, 494.

39. Fielden describes his sexual orientation and his openness about it during his time in India in his autobiography. He also makes note of his dislike for his British colleagues in India. He describes "English officials and their wives" as "the most ignorant, insensitive, arrogant, and stupid conglomeration that the world has ever produced." Fielden, *The Natural Bent*, 179.

40. Fielden, *The Natural Bent*, 179.

41. Fielden, *The Natural Bent*, 181. Fielden also discussed radio with Gandhi who told him that in choosing to disclose his support for the anticolonial movement Fielden would succeed in gaining the distrust of both imperialists and nationalists (*The Natural Bent*, 196). Zulfiqar Bukhari also writes about Fielden's support of the independence movement and friendship with leading Congress members. See Bukhari, *Sarguzašt*. Unfortunately, I cannot do justice to Fielden's fascinating politics and personality in this limited study. For a detailed analysis of Fielden's relationship to anticolonial leaders and his appropriateness for this particular role, see Zivin, "'Bent.'"

42. Luthra, *Indian Broadcasting*, 494–95. See timeline for the name change's dating. For a description of Fielden's version of the name-change story, for which he takes full credit, see Fielden, *The Natural Bent*, 191–93.

43. For example, in June 1938, AIR purchased the Madras Corporation's radio station (Fielden, *The Natural Bent*, 8). He also incorporated a YMCA radio club in Lahore, and a radio station in Madras managed by the local government, which had begun as a radio club. He also incorporated two rural broadcasting schemes into AIR's network, one outside of Delhi and the other in the North-West Frontier Province. See Fielden, *The Natural Bent*, 71.

44. For more detail on these stations, see Luthra, *Indian Broadcasting*.

45. Fielden notes in his autobiography: "I went to India to place myself at the head of a cultural organization in a country whose history I scarcely knew, no one of whose two hundred languages I had mastered, whose customs I had not bothered to study." Fielden, *The Natural Bent*, 154.

46. Fielden's relationship with the elder of the brothers, A. S. Bukhari, appears to have been precarious: the two disagreed on several matters. See Fielden, *The Natural Bent*, 195.

47. Reoti Saran Chandra, interview by author, March 2, 2012. See Ashk, Oral Interview, 208a and 218b, Centre of South Asian Studies, Cambridge—Oral History Collection (CCAS, OHC). For a description of the Lahore station, see Abu al Hasan Naghmi, *Yeh Lahore Hai* (Sang-e-Mīl, 2003). For a description of the Lahore station in late 1930 and the musicians, see Ian Talbot and Tahir Kamran, "Darvarzas and Mohallas," in *Colonial Lahore: A History of the City and Beyond* (Oxford: Oxford University Press, 2017), 41–65.

48. Bukhari, *Sarguzašt*. Bukhari includes descriptions of how AIR recruited *tawaifs* for its music programs.

49. In Britain, by contrast, the BBC provided opportunities for political debate on the radio.

50. In an anonymous article published in the *Times*, Fielden wrote that the colonial government was acting out of duty rather than pleasure and remarked that it developed broadcasting just to ensure nationalist leaders would not take to the airwaves (Zivin, "'Bent,'" 198).

51. These programs are cited in Zivin, "'Bent,'" 215.

52. Notes by a Bengali observer, Appendix III, Broadcasting in India, Correspondence Regarding, L/I/1/445, IO.

53. Letter to Mr. Joyce, December 20, 1939, BBC Indian language services to India, L/I/1/784, IO. Indivar Kamtekar argues that the Japanese caught the Indian government looking the wrong way. During the first half of the war, the administration expected that was there to be an Axis invasion, it would take place through Afghanistan. Kamtekar, "The Shiver of 1942," 6.

54. Policy of His Majesty's Government on the question of jamming—1940, Home, Political, 52/15/40-Poll, NAI.

55. Birdsall, *Nazi Soundscapes*, abstract.

56. Birdsall, *Nazi Soundscapes*, 28.

57. Peter Fritzsche, *Life and Death in the Third Reich* (Cambridge, MA: Belknap, 2009).

58. Haj Amin al-Husseini, a Palestinian leader exiled in Berlin, was one of the service's main voices. This service promoted anti-British sentiments, but also helped formulate a new form of "radical anti-Semitism" in the Middle East, which had important long-term consequences for the region. Jeffrey Herf, "Hate Radio: The Long, Toxic Afterlife of Nazi Propaganda in the Arab World," *Chronicle Review*, November 22, 2009, https://www.chronicle.com/article/Hate-Radio-Nazi-Propaganda-in/49199.

59. Alexander Werth and Walter Harbich, *Netaji in Germany: An Eye-Witness Account of Indian Freedom Struggle in Europe During World War II* (Calcutta: Netaji Research Bureau, 1970), 23.

60. Political situation in India since the outbreak of war-confidential appreciation of the political situation in India, December 18, 1939, L/I/1/777, IO.

61. There was a long history of Indian student activism in Germany. For more on Indian students in Germany and in particular what later became Humboldt University, see Benjamin Zachariah, "Indian Political Activities in Germany, 1914–1945," in *Encounters Between Germany and India: Kindred Spirits in the 19th and 20th Centuries*, Routledge Studies in the Modern History of Asia, ed. Joanne Miyang Cho, Eric Kurlander, and Douglas T. McGetchin (New York: Routledge, 2013), 141–54.

62. Benjamin Zachariah, "Indian Political Activities in Germany"; Daniel Brückenhaus, *Policing Transnational Protest: Liberal Imperialism and the Surveillance of Anticolonialists in Europe, 1905-1945* (Oxford: Oxford University Press, 2017); Fredrik Petersson, "Hub of the Anti-Imperialist Movement: The League Against Imperialism and Berlin, 1927–1933," *Interventions* 16, no. 1 (2014): 49–71; Kris Manjapra, *Age of Entanglement: German and Indian Intellectuals Across Empire* (Cambridge, MA: Harvard University

Press, 2014). See also Eric Kurlander, Joanne Miyang Cho, and Douglas T. McGetchin, eds., *Transcultural Encounters Between Germany and India: Kindred Spirits in the 19th and 20th Centuries* (New York: Routledge, 2013).

63. For information on government censorship of print media during World War II, see Devika Sethi, *War Over Words*. Emily Rook-Koepsel, "Unity, Democracy, and the All India Phenomenon, 1940–1946" (PhD diss., University of Minnesota, 2010); Emily Rook-Koepsel, "Dissenting Against the Defense of India Rules: Emergency Regulations and the Space of Extreme Government Action," *South Asia: Journal of South Asian Studies* 41, no. 18 (August 2, 2018): 642–57; Sanjoy Bhattacharya, *Propaganda and Information in Eastern India 1939–45: A Necessary Weapon of War* (New York: Routledge, 2009). For a study on the English-language All India Press, see Milton Israel, *Communication and Power: Propaganda and the Press in the Indian National Struggle, 1920–1947* (Cambridge: Cambridge University Press, 1994). I agree with Sanjoy Bhattacharya that Milton ultimately underplays the role of censorship of the press during World War II. See Sanjoy Bhattacharya, "Reviewed Work: Communications and Power: Propaganda and the Press in the Indian Nationalist Struggle, 1920–1947 by Milton Israel," *Modern Asian Studies* 31, no. 1 (February 1997): 221–23.

64. The government also censored newspapers through the management of paper quotas. The war brought about a severe paper shortage, and newspapers could "earn" paper quotas through good behavior. For example, one local officer recommended that the *Sansar's*, a Hindi-language publication in Benares, paper quota should be increased because the newspaper, despite being obviously pro-Congress "had given sufficient publicity to the war" from an Allied perspective. See Bhattacharya, "Wartime Policies of State Censorship," 167.

65. Oral interviews with journalists offer further evidence of this. J. N. Sahni, Oral Interview, 203b, CCAS, OHC.

66. Italian News in Hindustani, Date: April 16, 1941, Time: 8:45 p.m., Station: (?). The question mark is in the original document which suggests that the radio monitors were unaware of the radio broadcasts' origins.

67. Moreover, as further described in chapter 2, a few Indian-based anticolonial, nationalist radio stations, managed by anticolonial activists, also appeared in 1942, after Gandhi's call to Quit India. Although these relied on low-power transmitters and had a reception radius of a few miles, they also challenged the colonial government's account of war events. See Isabel Huacuja Alonso, "'Voice of Freedom' at the End of Empire."

68. Alok Rai, "The Persistance of Hindustani," *India International Centre Quarterly* 29, nos. 3/4 (2003): 78.

69. As noted in the introduction, neither Hindi, Urdu, nor Hindustani were accessible throughout most of South India. For a discussion on tensions between Tamil and Hindi, see Sumathi Ramaswmy, *Passions of the Tongue: Language Devotion in Tamil India, 1891–1970* (Berkeley: University of California Press, 1997).

70. Broadcasting of anti-British propaganda in the Middle East, Persian Gulf, NWF and Central Asia, etc.: BBC broadcasts in Arabic, L/PS/12/4132, IO (emphasis added).

71. Fielden also mentions that Axis broadcasts included music. I have been unable to confirm this in transcripts of early Axis radio broadcasts that note music. Fielden, *The Natural Bent*, 214. As noted in chapter 2, Azad Hind Radio did broadcast music.

72. German Topical Talk in Hindustani, Date: January 13, 1942, Time: 8:15 p.m., Station: Berlin, 2(9)/1942, Akashwani, Information and Broadcasting, NAI.

73. German Topical Talk in Hindustani, Date: January 13, 1942.

74. German Talk in Hindustani, Date: January 12, 1942, Time: 8:15 p.m., Station: Berlin, 2(9)/1942, Akashvani, Information and Broadcasting, NAI.

75. Broadcasts from Germany, Date: November 12–18, 1941, Station: Germany, 54/1941, Akashvani, Information and Broadcasting, NAI.

76. Azad Muslim League Radio News in Hindustani, Date: October 28, 1942, Time: 8:00 p.m., Station Saigon (?); News in Hindustani, Date: October 17, 1942, Time: 9:00 p.m., Station: Berlin; German News in Hindustani, Date: October 26, 1942, Time: 9:00 p.m., Station: Berlin, Akashvani, Information and Broadcasting, NAI (question mark in the original).

77. Government of India Department of Information and Broadcasting Counter-Propaganda Directorate Analysis of Foreign Broadcasts Directed to India and the Near East No. 48—New Series September 30–October 6, 1942, 54/1941, Akashvani, Information and Broadcasting, NAI.

78. German Talk in Hindustani by A. Rauf Malik, Date: January 17, 1942, Time: 8:20 p.m., Station: Berlin., 2(9)/1942, Akashvani, Information and Broadcasting, NAI.

79. German Topical Talk in Hindustani, Date: January 27, 1942, Time: 8:15 p.m., Station: Berlin. INA2(9)/1942, Akashvani, Information and Broadcasting, NAI. German Talk in Hindustani, Date: January 5, 1942, Time: 8:15 p.m., Station: Berlin, INA2(9)/1942, Akashvani, Information and Broadcasting, NAI.

80. German Topical Talk in Hindustani, Date: January 27, 1942 (emphasis added).

81. German Talk in Hindustani, Date: July 4 1942, Time: 8:20 p.m., Station: Berlin. 100/1942, Akashvani, Information and Broadcasting, NAI. Radio Himalaya also used this naming and shaming technique, particularly against Indian princes who had encouraged their subjects to join the army.

82. No. 49—New Series, October 7–13, 1942, 217/1942, Akashvani, Information and Broadcasting, NAI.

83. No. 49—New Series, NAI. In his study of World War II, Santanu Das shows that the idea of the mercenary soldier fighting for the British out of economic necessity is as imprecise as the idea of the pro-Empire Indian soldier committed to protecting the British Empire. See Santanu Das, *India, Empire, and First World War Culture: Writings, Images, and Songs* (Cambridge: Cambridge University Press, 2018), 83.

84. Himalaya Radio News in Hindustani, Date: April 1, 1941, Time: 7.55 P.M Station: (?) 8/1941 M.I. 8c, Akashvani, Information and Broadcasting, NAI (question mark in the original).

85. German Talk in Hindustani, Date: January 20, 1942, Time: 8:20 p.m., Station: Berlin, 2(9)/1942, Akashvani, Information and Broadcasting, NAI. As I further explore in chapter 2, Azad Hind Radio's various stations and, in particular Subhas Chandra Bose himself, also took on the issue of race. Bose stressed pan-Asian racial solidarity, noting that Japan's victories disproved ideas about European and "white-skinned" people's racial superiority.

86. German News in Hindustani, Date: October 2, 1942, Time: 9:00 p.m., Station: Berlin. 8/1941 M.I. 8c, Akashvani, Information and Broadcasting, NAI.

87. German Talk in Hindustani, Date: January 6, 1942, Time: 8:15 p.m., Station: Berlin. 2(9)/1942, Akashvani, Information and Broadcasting, NAI.

88. German Talk in Hindustani, Date: January 6, 1942.

89. German Talk in Hindustan, Date: January 6, 1942, Time: 8:15 p.m., Station: Berlin, 8/1941 2(9)1942, Akashvani, Information and Broadcasting, NAI. See also September 1, 1944–September 30, 1944; Berlin News in Hindustani Akashvani, Information and Broadcasting, NAI. September 13, 1944, 41/1944 Akashvani, Information and Broadcasting, NAI. One broadcaster claimed: "All disorder and disturbances which occurred in Germany were not due to Hitler. Only the Jews and the so-called democrats were responsible for them." German Talk in Hindustani, Date: January 6, 1942, Time: 8:15 p.m., Station: Berlin Akashvani, Information and Broadcasting, NAI.

90. September 1, 1944–September 30, 1944; Berlin News in Hindustani. September 13, 1944, 41/1944, Akashvani, Information and Broadcasting, NAI.

91. German Talk in Hindustani, Date: January 6, 1942, Time: 8:15 p.m., Station: Berlin, 2(9)/1942, Akashvani, Information and Broadcasting, NAI.

92. German Talk in Hindustani, Date: January 6, 1942.

93. September 1, 1944–September 30, 1944; Berlin News in Hindustani. September 13, 1944, 41/1944, Akashvani, Information and Broadcasting, NAI.

94. German News in Hindustani, Date: September 19, 1942, Time: 9:00 p.m., Station: Berlin. 215/1942, Akashvani, Information and Broadcasting, NAI.

95. Radio Himalaya also employed patriarchal and misogynistic language. Referencing an Indian army officer who had spoken to the BBC, urging his countrymen to support the Allied cause, one announcer explained: "For the last several years, Major Akbar Khan is to be found in the dark streets of London, where he enjoys himself by cracking jokes with women of the streets. Sometimes, a naughty girl smacks his face, but this son of a usurer enjoys it." The message seems to be that this officer was spineless. If a woman, a lowly woman, can so easily exert power over this officer, then the British clearly had no problem bossing him around. Moreover, the comments about the usury sought to associate this so-called British sympathizer with the "Jewish enemy." Himalaya Radio News in Hindustani, Date: April 1, 1941, Time: 7:55 p.m., Station: (?), 8/1941 M.I. 8c, Akashvani, Information and Broadcasting, NAI (question mark in the original).

96. Confidential Appreciation of the political situation in India, December 18, 1939, Political situation in India since the outbreak of war, L/I/1/777, IO.

97. Measures to check ill effects of German Hindustani Broadcasts, 1940, Home, Political, 60/2/40, Poll, NAI. Broadcasting of anti-British propaganda in the Middle East, Persian Gulf, NWF and Central Asia, etc.: BBC broadcasts in Arabic, L/PS/12/4132, IO.

98. Report on the development of broadcasting in India, August 1940, Home, Political, 52/8 1938, NAI.

99. Broadcasting of anti-British propaganda in the Middle East, Persian Gulf, NWF and Central Asia, etc.: BBC broadcasts in Arabic, L/PS/12/4132, IO (emphasis added).

100. Krishna Bose, Oral Interview, Bengali Intellectuals Oral History Project (BIOHP).

101. Report on broadcasting in India, December 16, 1940, Home, Political, 52/8 1938, NAI.

102. Report on the development of broadcasting in India, August 1940, Home, Political, 52/8 1938, NAI. Enforcement of these laws would have varied from locality to locality, but we know that local officials in Bengal arrested people for listening to Axis radio at "full blast." See Bhattacharya, "Wartime Policies of State Censorship."

103. German News in Hindustani, Date: October 24, 1942, Time: 9:00 p.m., Station: Berlin, 215/1942, Akashvani, Information and Broadcasting, NAI.

104. Summary of Foreign Broadcasts in Asiatic Languages Himalaya News in Hindustani, Date: April 16, 1941, Time: 7:55 p.m., Station: (?), 8/1941 M.I. 8 9c, Akashvani, Information and Broadcasting, NAI (question mark in the original).

105. Azad Hind (Tokyo) in English and Indian Languages, Date: September 24, 1944, Time: 6:45 p.m., Station: Tokyo. 34/1944, Akashvani, Information and Broadcasting, NAI.

106. No. 176, Weekly Series, March 14–20, 1945, Government of India Department of Information Monitoring Office; Analysis of Foreign broadcasts, Akashvani, Information and Broadcasting, NAI.

107. Measures to check ill-effects of German Hindustani Broadcasts, 1940, Home, Political, 60/2/40, Poll, NAI.

108. Number of receiver sets in India, statistics gathered by All India Radio, July 2, 1943, AIR and FEB Broadcasting organization, L/I/1/935, IO. The report notes that in January

1943 there were 162,000 licensed receiver sets in British India and 17,000 sets in Indian princely states.

109. AIR Anti-Piracy campaign, a review of the results achieved, Broadcasting in India, Correspondence Regarding, L/I/1/445, IO. As the Urdu writer Saadat Hasan Manto shows in the radio play *Āo Reḍīo Sunen* (Come listen to radio), many Indian radio receivers were unregistered and did not pay required fees. See Saadat Hasan Manto, "Āo Reḍīo Sunen," in *Dastāvez Manṭo*, ed. Balraj Menra and Sharad Dutt (New Delhi: Rajkamal Prakashan, 1993), 59–66.

110. Even rumors that the British administration did not recognize as "directly traceable to radio" likely also were connected to radio broadcasts. For example, during the second half of the war, the administration noted that "a rumor was afloat that 'Japan is reluctant to invade India and that she will try to negotiate some sort of settlement with India as soon as she achieves independence'" (Srinath Raghavan, *India's War*, 259–62).

111. See, for example, Guha, *Elementary Aspects of Peasant Insurgency*.

112. Bayly, *Empire and Information*, 40. Likewise, Farina Mir demonstrates how Punjabi oral traditions did not compete, but rather buttressed Punjabi texts. See Farina Mir, *The Social Space of Language: Vernacular Culture in British Colonial Punjab* (Berkeley: University of California Press, 2010).

113. Scholars of South Asia have long emphasized the resilience and dynamism of oral networks in the region. See Ranajit Guha, *Elementary Aspects of Peasant Insurgency in Colonial India* (Delhi: Oxford University Press, 1983); Bayly, *Empire and Information*, 204.

114. Guha, *Elementary Aspects*, 251.

115. Guha, *Elementary Aspects*, 256

116. Guha, *Elementary Aspects*, 257.

117. Anjan Ghosh, "The Role of Rumour in History Writing," *History Compass* 6, no. 5 (September 2008): 1235–43.

118. Birdsall, *Nazi Soundscapes*, 12. As noted in the introduction, considering the power of radio resonance allows us to shift the focus away from the act of listening when studying radio and to reflect on the ways in which talking and listening can be intrinsically related. This has important implications for our understanding of radio outside South Asia. Scholars of radio and French history have noted that few in occupied France actually heard Charles de Gaulle's famous L'Appel du 18 juin (Appeal of June 18) speech, which he delivered from the Broadcasting House in London. Thinking about de Gaulle's speech's resonance enables us to account for its wider impact and significance, despite its limited reception. Similarly, Emperor Hirohito's speech after Japan's defeat constitutes another example from the war era. Interestingly, as Kerim Yasar explains, in the Japanese emperor's famous radio speech, the emperor spoke in courtly Japanese that most Japanese listeners would not have been able to understand. Here, too, there is plenty of room to consider how discussion about the Emperor's broadcast is more important than who or how many physically heard (and understood) the emperor. See Derek Valliant, "Occupied Listeners: The Legacies of Interwar Radio for France During World War II," in *Sound in the Era of Mechanical Reproduction*, ed. David Suisman and Susan Strasser (Philadelphia: University of Pennsylvania Press, 2010), 141–58. Kerim Yasar, *Electrified Voices: How the Telephone, Phonograph, and Radio Shaped Modern Japan, 1868–1945* (New York: Columbia University Press, 2018).

119. Policy of His Majesty's Government on the question of jamming, 1940, Home, Political, 52/15/40, Poll, NAI.

120. Supplement to the *Indian Listener* calling radio owners to allow servants to listen to the radio. The advertisement is undated. Based on the context and placement in the archive, it likely was published in late 1941, AIR Library.

121. Mazzarella addresses the peculiarity of the "insurmountable" challenge the British faced in India in trying to garner support for World War II, calling this difficulty a "a torn performative dispensation, a political crisis in which the twin projects of the incitement of mass affect and the articulation of a discourse of sovereignty can no longer be successfully reconciled." Mazzarella continues, "A torn performative dispensation: the affective politics of British Second World War propaganda in India [is a] problem of legitimation in an age of mass publics" (Mazzarella, "A Torn Performative Dispensation," 1).
122. In addition to developing AIR, the British government also founded and funded the BBC Eastern Service, a shortwave service to India, which, like AIR's newly inaugurated news programs, meant to counteract German broadcasts. The Eastern Service began in 1940 as a ten-minute news update in Hindustani, but it grew during the war to include broadcasting in seven languages. As Daniel Morse argues, the Eastern Service did not gain much popularity in India, in part because its transmitters were nowhere near as strong the German transmitters, but also because the service and in particular the English service, had a rather learned and didactic tone, which appealed to limited audience. As Morse explains, "The English-language programs of the BBC's Eastern Service were of a serious intellectual bent, aimed not at the Indian masses nor British officials, but at university students and the native elite" (14). Morse argues, rather convincingly, that the service's most important effect was on literature, and in particular, on in its contributions to the development of the global Anglophobe novel. For an in-depth study of the English programming of the Eastern Service, see Daniel Ryan Morse, *Radio Empire: The BBC's Eastern Service and the Emergence of the Global Anglophone Novel* (New York: Columbia University Press, 2020). For more on the BBC and the Eastern Service, also see Sharika Thiranagama, "Partitioning the BBC: From Colonial to Postcolonial Broadcaster," *South Asian Diaspora* 2, no. 1 (2010): 39–55.
123. For a brief summary of Fielden's work with the Eastern Service after his return to India, see Morse, *Radio Empire*. Z. A. Bhukari also worked with Eastern Service alongside Fielden, while his brother Ahmed Shah Bhukari stayed in India. See Bukhari, *Sarguzašt*.
124. It is notable that many who worked at AIR did not necessarily agree with the Indian government's policies. Many, like Fielden and Patras Bukhari, held anticolonial views. According to one account, Patras Bukhari helped hide the famous underground anticolonial activist Aruna Asaf Ali. K. Khanna, a lawyer and congressman. J. K. Khanna Oral interview, 207c, Cambridge University Centre of South Asian Studies.
125. Change of the designation of the Controller of Broadcasting to that of the Director General-All India Radio, Home, Public, 264/43 1943, NAI. According to this report, AIR employees' salaries were raised, and AIR also became a permanent service.
126. Report on broadcasting in India, December 16, 1940, Home, Political, 52/8 1938, NAI.
127. Broadcasting of anti-British propaganda in the Middle East, Persian Gulf, NWF and Central Asia, etc.: BBC broadcasts in Arabic, L/PS/12/4132, IO; *Statesman's* article clipping, October 1, 1939, Broadcasting in India, Correspondence Regarding, L/I/1/445, IO.
128. Telegraph from Government of India Home Department to Secretary State of India, November 8, 1940, Reuters Service 1938–1942, L/I/1/663, IO.
129. Report on broadcasting in India, May 27, 1940, Home, Political, 52/8 1938, NAI.
130. For example, participant of the Indian Navy mutiny, B. C. Dutt, notes in a February 1946 oral interview, that after the munity was reported on AIR, navy mutineers knew the event had become common knowledge. Before the war began, AIR had been hesitant to report such matters. By the war's end, it had become routine. B. C. Dutt, Oral Interview, 237b, Audio Archive, CCAS OHC.

131. Delhi rural broadcasting scheme for year ending in September 1941, Government of India report on the development of broadcasting, L/I/1/967, IO.

132. A [?] copy of an express letter, from Baluchistan Quetta to Foreign Office in New Delhi, October 20, 1939, BBC Indian language services to India, L/I/1/784, IO (question mark in the original).

133. A [?] copy of an express letter, IO.

134. Report on the working of the Delhi Rural Broadcasting scheme for the period of October 1941 to March 1944, Government of India reports on the development of broadcasting, L/I/1/967, IO. In reality, the presence of radio, even when taking into account the power of oral communication networks, would have been limited in rural areas. Radio had a stronger presence in urban centers, where people would have been in closer proximity to radios and were more likely to engage in discussions about broadcasts.

135. Report on the working of the Delhi Rural Broadcasting scheme for the period of October 1941 to March 1944.

136. Report on broadcasting in India, December 16, 1940, Home, Political, 52/8 1938, NAI. In addition to Indian public figures, AIR also brought in British administrators to its studios to speak on war-related matters. For example, the viceroy of India, the marquess of Linlithgow, gave a speech on May 26, 1940, titled, "Unity, Courage, and Faith." His message was translated to Hindustani and broadcast from all AIR stations.

137. Memorandum by the Department of Information and Broadcasting, Questions affecting the Department of Information and Broadcasting, 1945, L/I/1/1132, IO.

138. Dropdi Nandan, "The All India Radio: Its Administration and Programmes," *Modern Review* 70, no. 2 (August 1941): 153, cited in Rook-Koepsel, "Unity, Democracy, and the All India Phenomenon, 1940–1946," 66.

139. He was known as Patras Bukhari. His best-known work is *Patras Ke Mazāmīn*, which is a collection of essays published in 1927.

140. He was also a poetry connoisseur and performed *marsiya*, a type of elegy. Radio Pakistan archives have collections of his *marsiya* performances. Bukhari writes about the accusations that AIR was too pro-Urdu in Bukhari, *Sarguzašt*, 162.

141. Both Zulfiqar Bukhari and Fielden note this accusation in their biographies. See Fielden, *The Natural Bent*, 195; and Bukhari, *Sarguzašt*, 81.

142. In 1944, Bukhari actually drafted an entire plan for independent India, arguing for a decentralized system of All India Radio. See "Basic Plan for the Development of Broadcasting in India (1944)," in Home-Public, 179/1946, NAI.

143. Rook-Koepsel, "Unity, Democracy, and the All India Phenomenon, 1940–1946," 64.

144. David Lelyveld, "Colonial Knowledge and the Fate of Hindustani," *Comparative Studies in Society and History* 35, no. 4 (1993): 680. The exact date when work on lexicon began is unclear, but it happened while S. A. Bukhari was in charge of the Delhi station in the 1940s.

145. Bukhari also invited Ashk, a renowned Hindi writer, to help him recruit Hindi writers. Chandra, interview by author. Ashk, Oral Interview, 208a and 218b, CCAS, OHC.

146. Report on the development of Broadcasting 1944, Government of India reports on the development of broadcasting, L/I/1/967, IO.

147. For an excellent study of the Anjuman, see Andrew Amstutz, "Finding a Home for Urdu: Islam and Science in Modern India" (PhD diss., Cornell University, 2017); Andrew Amstutz, "A Partitioned Library: Changing Collecting Priorities and Imagined Futures in Divided Urdu Library, 1947–9," *South Asia* 43, no. 3 (2020): 505–21.

148. Luthra, *Indian Broadcasting*, 257. For a more detailed account of the Hindi-Urdu controversy in AIR, see Lelyveld, "Colonial Knowledge and the Fate of Hindustani."

As Lelyveld has pointed out, all the evidence seems to show that Bukhari's vision aligned with Congress's search for Hindustani in the 1930s. Lelyveld, "Colonial Knowledge and the Fate of Hindustani." Ahmed Bukhari left AIR and migrated to Pakistan in 1947. He joined the Government College of Lahore, where he had taught prior to his work with All India Radio.

149. As Rook-Koepsel notes, "for proponents of Hindi, Hindustani was associated with the kind of accommodations that Muslims were asking for politically." Rook-Koepsel, "Unity, Democracy, and the All India Phenomenon, 1940–1946," 67.

150. For an in-depth discussion of language policies in AIR, see Kamaluddin Siddiqui, *Urdu Radio Television Meṅ Tarsīl o Iblāğ Kī Zabān* (New Delhi: Qaumī Konsil Barāe Faroğe Urdu Zabān, 1998). For a longer description of Urdu's contentious place in independent Pakistan, see part III.

151. Rotem Geva, "The Scramble for Houses: Violence, a Factionalized State, and Informal Economy in Post-Partition Delhi," *Modern Asian Studies* 51, no. 3 (2017): 778–82.

152. David Lelyveld, "Upon the Subdominant: Administering Music on All India Radio," *Social Text*, no. 93 (Summer 1994): 111–27.

153. This description is from a short essay by Moiz Fatima about life in colonial India. Asiya Alam shared this record with me, for which I am thankful. For more of Moiz Fatima and women's Urdu writing in colonial India, see Asiya Alam, *Women, Islam, and Familial Intimacy in Colonial South Asia* (Leiden: Brill, 2021).

154. S. A. Robertson, Oral Interview, 20d, CCAS, OHC.

155. Janam Mukherjee, *Hungry Bengal: War, Famine, and the End of Empire* (New York: Oxford University Press, 2015), 20.

156. Broadcasting of anti-British propaganda in the Middle East, Persian Gulf, NWF and Central Asia. BBC broadcasts in Arabic, L/PS/12/4132, IO.

157. Broadcasting in India, Correspondence regarding, Appendix III, Notes by a Bengali Observer, L/I/1/445, IO.

2. Netaji's "Quisling Radio"

1. "Axis Propaganda Barrage Badgers Britain on India," *Newsweek*, November 21, 1943, cited in Ranjan Borra, "The Image of Subhas Chandra Bose in American Journals During World War II," *Oracle* 1, no. 1 (1979): 20. Netaji Research Bureau, Kolkata, India (NRB).

2. "Axis Propaganda Barrage Badgers Britain on India"; Borra, "The Image of Subhas Chandra Bose," 20.

3. Note that the Indian National Congress (INC) did not function as a unified bloc. There were important divisions in the party, and Bose had been central to those divisions as the leader of the Forward Bloc, a left-leaning faction within the Indian National Congress founded in 1939.

4. Bose formed part of a larger group of anticolonial activists from throughout the world that sought the help of the Nazi government between 1941 and 1945. For an analysis of the Nazi government's complicated relationship to this group, see David Motadel, "The Global Authoritarian Moment and the Revolt Against Empire," *American Historical Review* 124, no. 3 (2019): 843–77. In addition to Bose, the group included "prominent Arabs, including the Iraqi nationalist Rashid 'Ali al-Kaylani, the Syrian rebel leader Fawzi al-Qawauqji, and Amin al-Husayni, the notorious Mufti of Jerusalem; Irish radicals, such as Sean Russell; and nationalist revolutionaries from Central Asia and the Caucus—Turkestanis, Azerbaijanis, Chechens, and others" (843). As Motadel notes:

"The relationship between Berlin's anticolonial revolutionaries and the regime was full of tension. Whereas Germans sought to use the exiles to destabilize their adversaries' territories, the exiles sought practical assistance for their liberation struggles and official recognition of their legitimacy and their countries' sovereignty" (848).

5. Lauren Derby, "Imperial Secrets: Vampires and Nationhood in Puerto Rico," *Past and Present* 199, no. 3 (January 1, 2008): 292.

6. This is rapidly changing, however; for works on World War II and India, see chapter 1.

7. Lok Sabha Starred Qu.Dy.No. 8502 for 20-8-69 by Shri Samar Guha regarding broadcast by Netaji Subhas Chandra Bose on Radio Moscow after signing of Tashkent Pact File No. c/125/11/69/JP, "Netaji Subhas Chandra Bose Papers," National Archives of India, New Delhi, India (NAI). See also 1/12014/13/2000-IS.D-III, Vol. II, Order/Directions passed by Justice Mukherjee Commission of Inquiry-compliance thereof by MHA etc., Ministry of Home Affair (MHA), NAI.

8. In recent years, the Bharatiya Janata Party (BJP), and particularly Prime Minister Narendra Modi, has embraced the memory of Subhas Chandra Bose as a symbol of strong and valiant India, even though Bose had been a member of the Indian National Congress, the predecessor to the BJP's most prominent political opponent. For another example of the phrase being used in contemporary India, see "Air India Orders Crew to Say '*Jai Hind*' After Every Flight Announcement," *Scroll.In*, March 4, 2019, https://scroll.in /latest/915401/air-india-orders-crew-to-say-jai-hind-after-every-flight-announcement.

9. For more detailed accounts of the two armies, see Leonard Gordon, *Brothers Against the Raj: A Biography of Indian Nationalists Sarat and Subhas Chandra Bose* (New York: Columbia University Press, 1990); Sugata Bose, *His Majesty's Opponent: Subhas Chandra Bose and India's Struggle Against Empire* (Cambridge, MA: Harvard University Press, 2011).

10. As explained later in this chapter, there were other lesser-known anticolonial activists who did manage to bring their message to the airwaves for a short time. See section on Congress Radio.

11. The most important scholarly biographies include Gordon, *Brothers Against the Raj*; Bose, *His Majesty's Opponent*; Sisir Kumar Bose, Alexander Werth, and S. A. Ayer, eds., *A Beacon Across Asia: A Biography of Subhas Chandra Bose* (Calcutta: Orient Longman, 1973); Rudrangshu Mukherjee, *Nehru and Bose: Parallel Lives* (New Delhi: Penguin, 2014); Romain Hayes, *Subhas Chandra Bose in Nazi Germany 1941–43* (New York: Columbia University Press, 2011). Mukherjee's *Nehru and Bose* and Hayes's *Subhas Chandra Bose in Nazi Germany* provide a more critical view of Bose's alliance with fascism and Nazism, but neither read his campaign in the context of Axis broadcasts to India. Other popular biographies of Bose include Nemai Sadhan Bose, *Deshnayak Subhas Chandra* (in Bengali) (Calcutta: Ananda, 1997); Nilanjana Sengupta, *A Gentleman's Word: The Legacy of Subhas Chandra Bose in Southeast Asia* (Singapore: Institute of Southeast Asian Studies, 2012). For an important critical review of Sugata Bose's *His Majesty's Opponent*, see Benjamin Zachariah, "Review of *His Majesty's Opponent: Subhas Chandra Bose and India's Struggle Against Empire*, by Sugata Bose," *American Historical Review* 117, no. 2 (2012): 509–10. For a biographical essay with an extensive list of works in English and German related to Bose, see "Biographical Essay" in Hayes, *Subhas Chandra Bose in Nazi Germany*.

12. John Durham Peters, *Speaking Into the Air: A History of the Idea of Communication* (Chicago: University of Chicago Press, 1999), 210.

13. Bruce Lenthall, *Radio's America: The Great Depression and the Rise of Modern Mass Culture* (Chicago: University of Chicago Press, 2008), chapter 3, Kindle.

14. Bose, *His Majesty's Opponent*, 192.

15. Mukherjee, *Nehru and Bose*, 222.

16. Mukherjee, *Nehru and Bose*, 99, 102. During this trip Bose appears to have hardened his commitment to socialism. He also seems to have developed an interest in fascism. During this exile abroad, Bose met Mussolini and tried, unsuccessfully, to meet Hitler.

17. Bose, *His Majesty's Opponent*, 111–21. In this Bose was not alone; other Indian communists had supported Nazism. See, for example, Benjamin Zachariah, "Indian Political Activities in Germany, 1914–1945," in *Encounters Between Germany and India: Kindred Spirits in the 19th and 20th Centuries*, Routledge Studies in the Modern History of Asia, ed. Joanne Miyang Cho, Eric Kurlander, and Douglas T. McGetchin (New York: Routledge, 2013).

18. Bose, *His Majesty's Opponent*, 111–21.

19. Bose, *His Majesty's Opponent*, 198. Hayes argues that there was an important difference between earlier trips to Germany and this last one. "His arrival in Berlin was not akin to one of his 1930s visits to Germany but rather a deliberate attempt to engage the Nazi regime during its most aggressive, expansionist, and brutal phase." Hayes, *Subhas Chandra Bose in Nazi Germany*, 25.

20. Hayes makes an interesting argument that forming an exile government in Germany might have hurt Bose's case. See Hayes, *Subhas Chandra Bose in Nazi Germany*, 149.

21. Yasmin Khan, *India at War: The Subcontinent and the Second World War* (Oxford: Oxford University Press, 2015), 77.

22. See Amit K. Gupta, "Defying Death: Nationalist Revolutionism in India, 1897–1938," *Social Scientist* 25, nos. 9/10 (1997): 3–27. The British government made every effort to keep the Indian Legion from public knowledge, just as it strove in later years to contain news of the Indian National Army. For example, Yasmin Khan writes that when a London-based newspaper published a picture of a Sikh soldier sporting a German uniform, Leo Amery, the secretary of state for India immediately scolded the newspaper. Khan, *India at War*, 77–78.

23. See Alexander Werth and Walter Harbich, *Netaji in Germany: An Eye-Witness Account of Indian Freedom Struggle in Europe During World War II* (Calcutta: Netaji Research Bureau, 1970). See also Bose, *His Majesty's Opponent*. Interestingly, however, it was the soldiers of the Indian Legion that first began calling Bose "*Netaji*." The word *neta* means politician or leader in several Indian languages and the suffix *ji* is a term of respect, but also one of endearment, similar to the honorific prefix *don/doña* in Spanish. We cannot and should not, however, altogether disregard the epithet's resemblance to Hitler's own Führer, or Mussolini's Il Duce, with which the Indian Legion soldiers certainly would have been familiar.

24. See Bose, *His Majesty's Opponent*; Gordon, *Brothers Against the Raj*; Milan Hauner, *India in Axis Strategy: Germany, Japan, and Indian Nationalists in the Second World War*, vol. 7 (Stuttgart, Germany: Klett-Cotta, 1981).

25. In the spring of 1941, as he began to chart the work he could do in Germany, Bose first connected with Indians residing in Berlin. N. G. Swami from Madras was in Berlin and so were M. R. Vyas and N. G. Ganpuley. Abid Hasan and Habibur Rehman, both students in Berlin, also joined Bose's team. In addition, Bose managed to convince others in Vichy France to move to Berlin, including A. C. N. Nambiar, a correspondent for several Indian newspapers, and Girija Mukherjee, a journalist and teacher. B. K. Banerji, who had been active in communist organizations and had a doctorate from Souborne, also came from Vichy France. For more details, see Zachariah, "Indian Political Activities in Germany," and Hayes, *Subhas Chandra Bose in Nazi Germany*.

26. See Eric Kurlander, "The Orientalist Roots of National Socialism? Nazism, Occultism, and South Asian Spirituality, 1919–1945," in *Transcultural Encounters Between Germany*

and India, ed. Joanne Cho, Eric Kurlander, and Douglas T. McGetchin (London: Routledge, 2013), 141–54.

27. Bose, *His Majesty's Opponent*, 225.

28. Subhas Chandra Bose et al., *Netaji Collected Works*, vol. II, *The Indian Struggle, 1920–1942*, ed. Sisir Kumar Bose and Sugata Bose (Calcutta: Netaji Research Bureau, 1980), 77. In 1921, Bose congratulated M. K. Gandhi for promoting national pride and for successfully reintroducing Hindustani into the Indian National Congress as the official language.

29. "Extracts from Presidential Address of Subhas Chandra Bose at the Fifty-First Session of the Congress at Haripura, February 19, 1938," reprinted in *Subhas Chandra Bose and the Indian National Movement*, ed. Harihara Dasa (Delhi: Sterling, 1983).

30. Werth and Harbich, *Netaji in Germany*, 28.

31. See, for example, Vikram Sampath, *"My Name Is Gauhar Jaan!": The Life and Times of a Musician* (New Delhi: Rupa, 2010).

32. By November 1941, the British government became aware of Bose's location. This, according to Hayes, was a big blow to Bose, who wished to be the one that announced his location, but only after Hitler had offered an official declaration of support. Hayes, *Subhas Chandra Bose in Nazi Germany*, 68.

33. Mukund R. Vyas, *Passage Through a Turbulent Era: Historical Reminiscences of the Fateful Years, 1937–47* (Bombay: Indo-Foreign, 1982), 34.

34. Vyas, *Passage Through a Turbulent Era*, 34.

35. Vyas, *Passage Through a Turbulent Era*, 34.

36. Hayes, *Subhas Chandra Bose in Nazi Germany*, 61. Interestingly, also according to Hayes, Goebbels, the propaganda minister, however, did follow Bose's broadcasts very carefully and seems to have been deeply satisfied with them. "Bose's appeal has made a deep impression on world public opinion" / "In London there is boundless wrath about the appeal of Bose." Entry March 2, 1942, Goebbels, Joseph. *The Goebbels Diaries*, ed. Louis Paul Lochner (London: Hamilton, 1948), cited in Hayes, *Subhas Chandra Bose in Nazi Germany*, 90.

37. As described in more detail later in the chapter, K. A. Abbas makes note of this confusion about radio stations in an oral interview. K. A. Abbas, Oral Interview, 123b, University of Cambridge, Centre of South Asian Studies, Oral History Collection, Cambridge, United Kingdom (CCAS, OHC).

38. See Akashvani, Monitoring Reports, NAI. For a more detailed analysis of shortwave and audibility, see chapter 1.

39. "1942: Singapore Forced to Surrender," BBC—History: On This Day (n.d.), http://news.bbc.co.uk/onthisday/hi/dates/stories/february/15/newsid_3529000/3529447.stm, accessed on June 23, 2018.

40. Subhas Chandra Bose, "The Fall of Singapore: First Broadcast, February 19, 1941," in *Azad Hind: Writings and Speeches, 1941–1943*, ed. Sisir Kumar Bose and Sugata Bose (London: Anthem, 2002), 63–64.

41. Khan, *India at War*, 113.

42. Bose, "The Fall of Singapore," 63–64.

43. Khan, *India at War*, 113.

44. Subhas Chandra Bose, "India Has No Enemy Outside Her Own Frontiers," in *Azad Hind: Writings and Speeches, 1941–1943*, ed. Sisir Kumar Bose and Sugata Bose (London: Anthem, 2002), 73.

45. Subhas Chandra Bose, *Testament of Subhas Bose, Being a Complete and Authentic Record of Netaji's Broadcast Speeches, Press Statements, Etc., 1942–1945* (Delhi: Rajkamal, 1946), 6.

46. Bose, *Testament of Subhas Bose*, 2.

47. Subhas Chandra Bose, "Join India's Epic Struggle Broadcast, 31 August 1942," in *Azad Hind: Writings and Speeches, 1941–1943*, ed. Sisir Kumar Bose and Sugata Bose (London: Anthem, 2002), 133.

48. Bose, "Join India's Epic Struggle Broadcast," 133.

49. Confidential appreciation of the political situation in India, May 26, 1943, Political situation in India since the outbreak of war, L/I/1/777, India Office, British Library, London, United Kingdom (IO).

50. For a detailed summary of Nehru's opposition to Bose's alliance with Germany and Japan, see Mukherjee, *Nehru and Bose.*

51. Gandhi did, however, eventually take to the airwaves, particularly after independence when he led several prayer meetings, which were broadcast on AIR. See Joseph Leylved, *Great Soul: Mahatma Gandhi and His Struggle with India* (New York: Knopf, 2011). See also "The Mahatma Did Not Like Films," *Media and Communications* 2, no. 2 (2006): 204–24. For Gandhi's relationship to U.S. and British media, see Chandrika Kaul, *Communications, Media and the Imperial Experience: Britain and India in the Twentieth Century* (London: Palgrave Macmillan, 2014).

52. Abul Kalam Azad, *India Wins Freedom* (Hyderabad: Orient Longman, 1988), 40, cited in Bose, *His Majesty's Opponent*, 217.

53. For example, during the Cripps Mission, Bose tried to influence Indian leaders' decision from thousands of miles away. Sir Stafford Cripps, a Labor Party British politician, came to India late in March 1942 to negotiate an agreement with nationalist leaders. Cripps promised to give India dominion status after the war in exchange for Indian leaders' support for the British war effort. On the radio, Bose urged politicians to reject Cripps's offer. For a detailed account of Bose's response to Cripps, see Hayes, *Subhas Chandra Bose in Nazi Germany.*

54. See Sen Gupta, Oral Interview, 211b, CCAS, OHC.

55. Number of receiver sets in India, statistics gathered by All India Radio, July 2, 1943, AIR and FEB Broadcasting organization, L/I/1/935, IO.

56. As noted earlier, the lack of electricity in rural areas made radio's presence there more difficult.

57. For a more detailed analysis of how the government of India tried to stop people from listening to Axis radio and when and how it prosecuted those who did tune in, see chapter 1.

58. Krishna Bose, Oral Interview, Bengali Intellectuals Oral History Project, Tufts University, Boston (BIOHP).

59. Moreover, the British government tightened censorship of print media during World War II, reviving the Defense of India Rules. The result was that radio became one of the few places people could access alternative accounts of the war. See chapter 1.

60. One of the most important economic works on the famine is Amartya Sen, "Starvation and Exchange Entitlements: A General Approach and Its Application to the Great Bengal Famine," *Cambridge Journal of Economics* 1, no. 1 (March 1977): 35–59. For a more recent historical analysis, see Benjamin Siegel, *Hungry Nation: Food, Famine and the Making of Modern India* (Cambridge: Cambridge University Press, 2018). See also Janam Mukherjee, *Hungry Bengal: War, Famine, and the End of Empire* (New York: Oxford University Press, 2015); and on the famine in Travancore, see Aditya Balasubramanian, "A Forgotten Famine '43? Tranvancore's Muffled 'Cry of Distress,'" *Modern Asian Studies* (forthcoming).

61. For information on the significant and effective efforts by the government to censor news of the famine in Indian newspapers, see Devika Sethi, *War Over Words, Censorship*

in India, 1930–1960 (New Delhi: Cambridge University Press, 2019). The broadcasting schedules of the *Indian Listener* and *Awaz* make it clear that AIR avoided famine related topics. Daniel Ryan Morse notes that the BBC Eastern Service also did not broadcast on the famine. See Daniel Ryan Morse, *Radio Empire: The BBC's Eastern Service and the Emergence of the Global Anglophone Novel* (New York: Columbia University Press, 2020), 16, 129. Morse writes about the writer and broadcaster Mulk Raj Anand's frustration with the service's refusal to broadcast on the famine. In response, Mulk Raj Anand wrote a play about the famine. See also Babli Sinha, "The BBC Eastern Empire Service and the Crisis of Cosmopolitanism," *Historical Journal of Film, Radio and Television* 39, no. 2 (2019): 309–21.

62. Subhas Chandra Bose, "The Bengal Famine: Press Statement 20 August 1943," in *Chalo Delhi: Writings and Speeches, 1942–1945*, ed. Sisir Kumar Bose and Sugata Bose (Calcutta: Netaji Research Bureau, 2007), 79.

63. File 114/43-Poll (I) September 1, 1943, IO, cited in Bose, *His Majesty's Opponent*, 250.

64. Patricia Meyer Spacks, *Gossip* (New York: Knopf, 1985), 57.

65. Subhas Chandra Bose, "Differentiate Between Internal and External Policy: Broadcast, June 17, 1942," in *Azad Hind: Writings and Speeches, 1941–1943*, ed. Sisir Kumar Bose and Sugata Bose (London: Anthem, 2002), 111.

66. Kama Maclean, *A Revolutionary History of Interwar India: Violence, Image, Voice and Text* (London: Hurst, 2015), 78.

67. "Axis Submarine Berlin and Bose," *Times of India*, April 9, 1942. The *Times of India* claims that the original report of his death had emanated from Axis sources first, which the BBC later rebroadcast.

68. Subhas Chandra Bose, "My Death Is Perhaps an Instance of Wishful Thinking," in *Azad Hind: Writings and Speeches, 1941–1943*, ed. Sisir Kumar Bose and Sugata Bose (London: Anthem, 2002), 76.

69. Bose, *His Majesty's Opponent*, 216.

70. Khan, *India at War*.

71. See Sanjoy Bhattacharya, "Wartime Policies of State Censorship and the Civilian Population of Eastern India, 1939–35," *South Asia Research* 17, no. 2 (Autumn 1997): 140–63; and Sethi, *War Over Words*.

72. Sethi, *War Over Words*, 162.

73. For this study, with the help of Sohini Chakrabarty, I consulted three Bengali publications: *Desh Patrika* (National Library of India in Kolkata) and *Jugantar* and *Amrita Bazar Patrika* (after 1942, *Amrita Bazaar* was published in English) at the Center for Studies in Social Sciences in Calcutta. Bose's radio addresses appear to be mostly absent from these publications. It is noteworthy that in September 1939, *Jugantar* covered Bose's political work in great detail but did not cover his speeches from 1942 onward. This leads me to believe that these newspapers were subjected to censorship like many other publications.

74. "Find of Subhas Bose Posters; Arrested Men Discharged," *Times of India*, May 28, 1942.

75. Subhas Chandra Bose, "The Quit India Movement: Broadcast, 17 August 1942," in *Azad Hind: Writings and Speeches, 1941–1943*, ed. Sisir Kumar Bose and Sugata Bose (London: Anthem, 2002), 128.

76. Bose, "Our National Honour: Broadcast from Tokyo on 21 June 1943," in *Chalo Delhi*, 20.

77. Bose, "Our National Honour: Broadcast from Tokyo on 21 June 1943," in *Chalo Delhi*, 20.

78. Frantz Fanon, "The Voice of Algeria," in *A Dying Colonialism* (London: Writers and Readers, 1980).

79. Bose, "Comment on First Wavell Offer: Statement Broadcast by the 'Provisional Government of Azad Hind Broadcasting Station,' Saigon, on 18 June 1945," in *Chalo Delhi*, 333.

See also reports of broadcasts from Japanese and Japanese-controlled radio stations regarding Mr. Subhas Chandra Bose's arrival in Tokyo from Germany and the text of Mr. Bose's speech from Tokyo radio on June 21, 1943, Home Political, 1/6/1943 poll, NAI.

80. Bose, *His Majesty's Opponent*, 185.

81. Vyas, *Passage Through a Turbulent Era*, 312.

82. The personal staff, household and private affairs of S. C. Bose, Appendix A to CSDIC (I) 2, Sec. report no. 996, Documents from the National Archives of India, ordered by Sugata Bose, NRB.

83. Maclean, *A Revolutionary History of Interwar India*, 75, 222; J. Daniel Elam, "The Martyr, the Moviegoer: Bhagat Singh at the Cinema," *BioScope: South Asian Screen Studies* 8, no. 2 (2017): 181–203.

84. Maclean, *A Revolutionary History of Interwar India*, 222. S. A. Ayer, who worked with Bose in Southeast Asia and was in charge of the INA's publicity, also points to the importance of radio resonance in an interview: "We knew that it was not everybody who could openly listen to the broadcasts from, say our station in Singapore. But as I said earlier, I had confirmation after I reached India, from various quarters and various parts of the country, that people inside India did listen to our broadcasts and by *word of mouth*. The fact was made known to many people to many others that Netaji Subhas Chandra Bose had formed an INA and was leading it across in the India-Burma border and was determined to drive the British out of India." S. A. Ayer, Oral Interview, 172a and 172b, CCSA OHC (emphasis added).

85. On Quit India, see Srinath Raghavan, *India's War: World War II and the Making of Modern South Asia* (New York: Basic Books, 2016); Gyanendra Pandey, *The Indian Nation in 1942* (New Delhi: Centre for Studies in Social Sciences, 1988); *Calcutta: The Stormy Decades*, Tanika Sarkar and Sekhar Bandyopadhyay, ed. (New York: Routledge, 2018).

86. Raghavan, *India's War*, 263. Raghavan sees the Quit India movement as a turning moment and the beginning of the Raj's collapse. Moreover, it is important to note that if Quit India was an important moment for Bose and his radio voice, it was also an important moment for the medium of radio. During Quit India, the government not only clamped down on pro-Axis publications, but also more carefully monitored any publications critical of the administration's policies and actively tried to stop the flow of information and news between provinces to prevent information about the rebellion from traveling. For example, the postal office prohibited the transmission of "sensational telegrams" in East Bengal and post office administrators began to monitor and censor mail correspondence as well. Sethi, *War Over Words*, 123. See Sanjoy Bhatacharya, *Propaganda and Information in Eastern India 1939–45: A Necessary Weapon of War* (New York: Routledge, 2009). As the British increased censorship, listeners turned to radio even more eagerly.

87. Hayes, *Subhas Chandra Bose in Nazi Germany*, 113.

88. Subhas Chandra Bose, "Independence Day: Speech, January 26, 1943," in *Azad Hind: Writings and Speeches, 1941–1943*, ed. Sisir Kumar Bose and Sugata Bose (London: Anthem, 2002), 180–81.

89. Bose, "Independence Day: Speech," 180–81.

90. Bose, "Independence Day: Speech," 180.

91. Subhas Chandra Bose, "The Quit India Movement: Broadcast, August 17, 1942," in *Azad Hind: Writings and Speeches, 1941–1943*, ed. Sisir Kumar Bose and Sugata Bose (London: Anthem, 2002), 129.

92. Bose, "The Quit India Movement: Broadcast," 130.

93. "Broadcast in English from Berlin, August 19, 1942," Time 8:15 p.m., Wavelength 19.56 cm, Documents from the National Archives of India related to Bose, NRB.

94. Subhas Chandra Bose, "The Fall of Singapore: First Broadcast, 19 February 1941," in *Azad Hind: Writings and Speeches, 1941–1943*, ed. Sisir Kumar Bose and Sugata Bose (London: Anthem, 2002), 63–64.

95. Subhas Chandra Bose, "Join India's Epic Struggle: Broadcast 31 August 1942," in *Azad Hind: Writings and Speeches, 1941–1943*, ed. Sisir Kumar Bose and Sugata Bose (London: Anthem, 2002), 139.

96. Subhas Chandra Bose, "The Pledge of the INA: Address to the Indian Legion in Europe and Broadcast: Broadcast June 17, 1942," in *Azad Hind: Writings and Speeches, 1941–1943*, ed. Sisir Kumar Bose and Sugata Bose (London: Anthem, 2002), 106–118.

97. Subhas Chandra Bose, "The Bluff and Bluster Corporation of British Imperialists: Speech, Late January/Early February 1943," in *Azad Hind: Writings and Speeches, 1941–1943*, ed. Sisir Kumar Bose and Sugata Bose (London: Anthem, 2002) (emphasis added).

98. Bose, "India Has No Enemy Outside Her Own Frontiers," 74.

99. Bose, "The Quit India Movement: Broadcast," 130–31.

100. German Talk in Hindustani by Habibur Rahman, Date: 3.1.1942, Time: 8:20 p.m., Station: Berlin. 2(9), 1942, Akashvani, Information and Broadcasting, NAI.

101. Himalaya News in Hindustani, Date: April 12, 1941, Time: 7:55 p.m. Station: (?), 8/1941 M.I. 8c, Akashvani, Information and Broadcasting, NAI (question mark in the original).

102. With the exception of the Radio Himalaya from Italy, which had supported the Muslim League, German and Japanese radio broadcasts were unfailingly anticommunal. Announcers would go as far as presenting Japan and Germany as examples of the ideal kind of national unity that Indians should strive to emulate. One Tokyo-based broadcaster claimed that "in Japan, for instance, there are 500 religious sects but Japan can always depend upon her own national unity in the time of any national crisis." Azad Hind (Tokyo) in English and Indian Languages, Date: September 22, 44 [corrected to September 21, 1944], Time: 1845 hrs, Station: Tokyo, 34/1944, Akashvani, Information and Broadcasting, NAI.

103. Azad Hind (Tokyo) in English and Indian Languages, NAI.

104. German News in Hindustani, Date: November 2, 1942, Time: 9:00 p.m., Station: Berlin, 8/1941 M.I. 8c, Akashvani, Information and Broadcasting, NAI.

105. Bose, "Gandhiji's Part in India's Fight: Broadcast from Bangkok Delivered on 2 October 1943," in *Chalo Delhi*, 102–4.

106. Bose, "Gandhiji's Part in India's Fight: Broadcast from Bangkok Delivered on 2 October 1943," in *Chalo Delhi*, 104. Bose, too, did not hesitate to overstate Gandhi's support for Bose's military campaign. For example, broadcasting from Rangoon on May 18, 1944, as his armies prepared to fight in northeastern India, Bose said: "Mahatmaji will be glad when the National Army enters Calcutta and he will send me a congratulatory telegram." Although less critical of Bose than Nehru, Gandhi did not explicitly endorse Bose's military campaign.

107. Abbas, CCAS, OHC. Pandey has also alluded to this: "Quit India might be fairly summed up as a popular nationalist upsurge that occurred in the name of Gandhi but went substantially beyond the confines that Gandhi may have envisaged for the movement." The movement used Gandhi's name but "ultimately Gandhi had little command." Pandey, *The Indian Nation in 1942*, 5–6.

108. Abbas, CCAS, OHC. I align myself with recent studies on the nationalist movement that have emphasized that Congress did not have a monopoly on the movement, in particular Maclean's and Ghosh's works on anticolonial violence. Maclean, *A Revolutionary History of Interwar India*; Durba Gosh, *Gentlemanly Terrorists: Political Violence and the Colonial State in India, 1919–1947* (Cambridge: Cambridge University Press, 2017).

109. Radio Waziristan's leading voice was a man from Hyderabad named M. N. Sultan, who, at least according to memoirs, was well regarded for his command of Urdu.

110. Azad Muslim League News in Hindustani, Date: February 24, 1943, Time: 2000 hrs, 5/1943, Akashvani, Information and Broadcasting, NAI.

111. Azad Muslim League Radio News in Hindustani, October 28 (no year), Time: 8:00 p.m., Station: Saigon (?), 217/1942, Akashvani, Information and Broadcasting, NAI (question mark in the original).

112. Azad Muslim League News in Hindustani, October 21, 1942, Station: Saigon (?), 219/1942, Akashvani, Information and Broadcasting, NAI (question mark in the original).

113. Oct 1942 Indian National Congress Radio, 217/1942, Akashvani, Information and Broadcasting, NAI.

114. Oct 1942 Indian National Congress Radio, NAI.

115. See Syamalendu Sengupta and Gautam Chatterjee, *Secret Congress Broadcasts and Storming Railway Tracks During the Quit India Movement*, South Asia Books (New Delhi: Navrang, 1988). One interesting anecdote is that in an oral interview, Usha Mehta, one of the organizers of Congress Radio, a small-scale radio station based in Bombay that was explicitly not pro-Axis, repeatedly refers to All India Radio (AIR) as "Anti-India Radio," a term Bose used in radio broadcasts. Mehta's use of that name provides further evidence of Bose's important aural presence. Usha Mehta, Oral Interview, 107, CCAS, OHC. For a more detailed study of the Bombay-based underground Congress Radio, which was on the air for about two months, see Usha Thakkar, *Congress Radio: Usha Mehta and the Underground Radio Station 1942* (Delhi: Penguin Viking, 2022). For a study of this underground station in the context of World War II, see Isabel Huacuja Alonso, "'Voice of Freedom' at the End of Empire: Radio SEAC, Underground Congress Radio, and the (Anti) Colonial Sublime" (in progress).

116. Abbas, CCAS, OHC.

117. Clive Branson, *British Soldier in India: Letters of Clive Branson* (London: Communist Party, 1944), 24.

118. No. 40-New Series, August 5–11, 1942, 217/1942, Akashvani, Information and Broadcasting, NAI.

119. German News in Hindustani, Date: October 18, 1942, Time: 9:00 p.m., Station: Berlin, 215/1942, Akashvani, Information and Broadcasting, NAI.

120. German News in Hindustani, NAI (emphasis added).

121. Provisional Government of Azad Hind (Saigon), in Hindustani, Date: April 28, 1945, Time: 2015–2030 hrs, Station: Saigon, 17/1945, Akashvani, Information and Broadcasting, NAI.

122. Bose, "Broadcast from Tokyo on June 21, 1943," in *Chalo Delhi*, 20–21.

123. C. K. Narayanswami, Oral Interview, 120d, CCAS, OHC.

124. Bose, "Statement at Press Conference Held in Tokyo on 19 June 1943," in *Chalo Delhi*, 18–19.

125. Bose, "Statement at Press Conference Held in Tokyo on 19 June 1943," in *Chalo Delhi*, 18–19.

126. Bose, *His Majesty's Opponent*. For an in-depth description of the INA, see Sugata Bose, "Roads to Delhi," in *His Majesty's Opponent* (Cambridge, MA: Harvard University Press, 2011), 231–304. For more details on the INA, also see Christopher Bayly and Timothy Harper, *Forgotten Armies: The Fall of British Asia, 1941–1945* (London: Allen Lane, 2004).

127. Khan, *India at War*, 188. "In many ways, Indian soldiers often felt more inner conflict about joining the INA than the local populace, who solidly backed Bose." Khan, *India at War*, 119.

128. "Occupied South-East Asia was a strange twilight world for Indians caught between two imperial masters, and a world in which political allies could be fickle and the borderline between the Indian Army, the INA and civilian life was sometimes surprisingly porous. Sepoys went undercover as waiters, porters and merchants." Khan, *India at War*, 118.

129. Bose also used the radio to spread his message in Southeast Asia and to recruit supporters in Singapore and other cities. My focus in this chapter, however, is on the ways in which he used the radio to take his message to India.

130. Lakshmi Sahgal, "Broadcast by Capt. Mrs. Lakshmi," *Young India* 1, no. 42 (1943), NRB.

131. The INA orchestra reassembled in Delhi after Partition and recorded some of their most popular songs. Gramophone records of these songs are available at the NRB.

132. New Songs Rally, No 10A/APS/46, Documents from the National Archives, NRB.

133. Sisir Kumar Bose, Subhas Chandra Bose, and Atulendu Sen, *The Voice of Netaji: Netaji Research Bureau Presents Selected Speeches and Radio Broadcasts of Netaji Subhas Chandra Bose 1938–1944* (Calcutta: Saregama, 1985), CD, NRB.

134. *The Voice of Netaji*, CD, NRB.

135. Bose, "Indian National Army in Action: Addresses to the INA and statements broadcast during the months of January to March 1944," in *Chalo Delhi*, 177.

136. Lenthall, *Radio's America*, chapter 3, Kindle.

137. Lenthall, *Radio's America*, chapter 3, Kindle. Of course, there are crucial differences. Bose allied with the Axis; Franklin Delano Roosevelt with the Allies. FDR was president of the United States, soon to be the dominant economic and political force in the world. Bose was a fugitive Indian anticolonial leader. Simply to reach the Indian public via radio, Bose had to escape house arrest, travel across the world, and ally with Nazi Germany. In contrast, since his first day as president, FDR enjoyed almost unlimited access to the airwaves.

138. Alex E. Chávez, *Sounds of Crossing: Music, Migration, and the Aural Poetics of Huapango Arribeño* (Durham, NC: Duke University Press, 2017), chapter 2, loc. 1806 out of 10316, Kindle.

139. Peters, *Speaking Into the Air*, 210.

140. Peters, *Speaking Into the Air*, 215.

141. Even if Bose had actively tried to take on a speaking style similar to FDR's, shortwave reception in India was simply not good enough for his listeners to react in the same way as listeners in the United States. Whereas listeners in the United States could hear FDR's voice on the medium wave clearly, listeners in India had to deal with a great deal of static.

142. Bose, "Changing Tactics of Enemy Propaganda: Broadcast on 12 July 1944," in *Chalo Delhi*, 256.

143. Ayer, CCAS, OHC.

144. I am thankful to one of the anonymous reviewers for pointing this out.

145. Confidential appreciation of the political situation in India, May 26, 1943, Political situation in India since the outbreak of war, L/I/1/777, IO.

146. Appendix B, Anti JIFC propaganda, War Series, L/I/I/1084, IO. In an oral interview, S. A. Ayer, the minister of propaganda and publicity, uses the word "intimacy" to describe Bose. "Netaji Subhas Chandra Bose, by this background of *intimate* contact with the masses and with his knowledge of the mind of the masses inside India, was convinced beyond the shadow of a doubt that when the full story of the INA was known to the people inside India, after the war was over, there would be a tremendous upheaval throughout the country (and) the people would feel tremendously proud that an Indian went outside India and organized a national army of liberation." Ayer, CCAS, OHC.

147. Bose, "The Situation in Europe: Broadcast on 8 July 1944," in *Chalo Delhi*, 223–31.

148. Bose, "The German Defeat: Statement on the Situation in Europe from an Undisclosed Base Outside Burma on 22 May 1945, and Broadcast by the Provisional Government of Azad Hind Radio, Singapore on 25 May 1945," in *Chalo Delhi*, 328.

149. Bose, "The Situation in Europe: Broadcast on 8 July 1944," in *Chalo Delhi*, 236.

150. Bose, "The Situation in Europe: Broadcast on 8 July 1944," in *Chalo Delhi*, 239.

151. Bose, "The Situation in Europe: Broadcast on 8 July 1944," in *Chalo Delhi*, 239.

152. Bose, "No Compromise on Independence: Broadcast from Singapore on 19 June 1945," in *Chalo Delhi*, 345.

153. 12014/13/2000-IS.D-III (MHA), NAI.

154. "Subhas Bose Still Alive," *Times of India*, January 3, 1946.

155. W. McK Wright, New Delhi, to Major Courtenay Young, Intelligence Division, Singapore, February 19, 1946, no. C-5, Intelligence Bureau, Home Department, New Delhi, File 273, INA. This file is originally from the NAI, but the copy I accessed was housed in the NRB. It is also cited in Bose, *His Majesty's Opponent*, 6.

156. Krishna Bose, interview by Kris Manjapra, 2009, BIOHP.

157. Further research is needed to understand and contextualize the important connection between Bose's voice and the proliferation of his image after the war and the proliferation of printed copies of his speeches in various languages. So far, I have been able to compile a list of more than one hundred books, in various languages, with Bose's speeches published during and after 1945, which suggests that there was a publishing boom of Bose's speeches after the end of the war.

158. On March 30, 1946, Gandhi took back his words. He wrote in the *Harijan*, "I appeal to everyone to forget what I have said and . . . to reconcile themselves to the fact that Netaji has left us." Cited in Bose, *His Majesty's Opponent*, 310.

159. For evidence of this, see "Netaji Subhas Chandra Bose Papers," NAI.

160. Lok Sabha Starred Qu.Dy.No. 8502 for 20-8-69, NAI; see also 1/12014/13/2000-IS.D-III (MHA), NAI. See also "Moscow Ne Mān Liā Subhas Chandra Yahāṅ Haiṅ," in *Vishwa Neta*, in "Netaji Subhas Chandra Bose Papers," NAI.

161. Bose, *His Majesty's Opponent*, 319.

162. Focusing on colonial Africa, Luise White explains that fantastic stories about vampires sucking Africans' blood actually tell a great deal about the many qualms Africans have with imperial technologies and medicine. See Luise White, *Speaking with Vampires: Rumor and History in East and Central Africa* (Berkeley: University of California Press, 2000). In the context of Puerto Rico, Lauren Derby argues that the *chupacabras* rumors of the 1990s "were a reflection of how the imperial U.S. state is seen in the political imagination of Puerto Ricans." Derby, "Imperial Secrets: Vampires and Nationhood in Puerto Rico," 293.

163. Wright, New Delhi, to Major Courtenay Young, INA.

3. The "Sound Standards" of a New India

1. B. V. Keskar, "Development Plans for All India Radio," *Indian Listener*, October 26, 1952, 59.

2. Keskar, "Development Plans for All India Radio," 8.

3. I have been unable to locate an official statement banning film songs. Newspaper and magazine accounts, broadcaster memoirs, and, most important, AIR broadcasting schedules, however, do reveal that for all intents and purposes AIR stopped broadcasting film songs in 1952.

4. Alison E. Arnold, "Hindi *Filmigit*: On the History of Commercial Indian Popular Music" (PhD diss., University of Illinois at Urbana-Champaign, 1991); Anna Morcom, *Hindi Film Songs and the Cinema*, SOAS Musicology Series (Hampshire: Ashgate, 2007); Anna Morcom, "Film Songs and the Cultural Synergies of Bollywood in and Beyond South Asia," in *Beyond the Boundaries of Bollywood: The Many Forms of Hindi Cinema*, ed. Rachel Dwyer and Jerry Pinto (Delhi: Oxford University Press, 2011), 156–87; Aswin Punathambekar, "'We're Online, Not on the Streets': Indian Cinema, New Media, and Participatory Culture," in *Global Bollywood*, ed. Anandam P. Kavoori and Aswin Punathambekar (New York: New York University Press, 2008), 282–97; Ravikant, "Śrav-Driṣṭav: Cinema Meṅ Radio," *Pratimān: Samay, Samāj, Sanskriti* 2 (December 2013): 581–600; Ravikant, *Media Kī Bhāṣā Līlā* (New Delhi: Lokchetnā Prakāśan, 2016).

5. "2007 Interview with Ameen Sayani," interview by Kamla Bhatt. March 27, 2007, http://kamlashow.com/podcast/2007/03/25/in-conversation-with-ameen-sayani-part-i/; see also Aswin Punathambekar, "Ameen Sayani and Radio Ceylon: Notes Towards a History of Broadcasting and Bombay Cinema," *BioScope* 1, no. 2 (2010): 189–97.

6. "2007 Interview with Ameen Sayani"; Punathambekar, "Ameen Sayani and Radio Ceylon."

7. Ravikant, *Media Kī Bhāṣā Līlā*, XIX. See also Ravikant, "Words in Motion: A Social History of Language in 'Hindi' Cinema (c. 1931 till present)" (PhD diss., 2015), 305. Cited in Vebhuti Duggal, "Imagining Sound Through the Pharmaish: Radios and Request-Postcards in North India, c. 1955–75," *BioScope: South Asian Screen Studies* 9, no. 1 (2018): 1–23.

8. As noted in the introduction, following the work of Murray Schafer and Emily Thompson, I define the term "soundscape" as an "auditory landscape." Much "like a landscape, a soundscape is simultaneously a physical environment and a way of perceiving that environment." Emily Ann Thompson, *The Soundscape of Modernity: Architectural Acoustics and the Culture of Listening in America, 1900–1933* (Cambridge, MA: MIT Press, 2004), 1; citing R. Murray Schafer, *The Soundscape: Our Sonic Environment and the Tuning of the World* (Rochester, VT: Destiny Books, 1994), definition on 274–75. See also R. Murray Schafer, *The Soundscape: Our Sonic Environment and the Tuning of the World* (Toronto: McClelland and Stewart, 1977).

9. Rajendra Prasad, "President's Speech," *Indian Listener*, November 16, 1958, 10.

10. I have not found a statement by Nehru in which he explicitly endorses Keskar's work at AIR. Nehru, however, appointed Keskar to the ministry and continued to support him throughout his decade-long term. See Jawaharlal Nehru, *Selected Works of Jawaharlal Nehru*, 64 vols. (New Delhi: Jawaharlal Nehru Memorial Fund, 1984). Ravikant, however, does point to an interesting anecdote that suggests Nehru's disagreement with AIR's policies. He notes that AIR, specifically Keskar, wished to censor the film *Ganga Jamuna* (1961), but Nehru ultimately approved it. Ravikant, *Media Kī Bhāṣā Līlā*, 83.

11. David Lelyveld, "Upon the Subdominant: Administering Music on All India Radio," *Social Text*, no. 93 (Summer 1994): 117.

12. Benjamin Siegel, "Self-Help Which Ennobles a Nation: Development, Citizenship and the Obligations of Eating in India's Austerity Years," *Modern Asian Studies* 50, no. 3 (2016): 975–1018.

13. K. H. Miller, *Segregating Sound: Inventing Folk and Pop Music in the Age of Jim Crow* (Durham, NC: Duke University Press, 2010).

14. Srirupa Roy, *Beyond Belief: India and the Politics of Postcolonial Nationalism, Politics, History, and Culture* (Durham, NC: Duke University Press, 2007), 44; Siegel, "Self-Help Which Ennobles a Nation."

15. Other recent works that do deal with ideas of sound and citizenship include Erich Nunn, *Sounding the Color Line* (Athens: Univeristy of Georgia Press, 2015); Brian Ward, *Radio*

and the Struggle for Civil Rights in the South (Gainesville: University Press of Florida, 2004); Rebecca P. Scales, Radio and the Politics of Sound in Interwar France, 1921–1939 (Cambridge: Cambridge University Press, 2018), chapter 2. On citizenship and sound in South Asia, but focusing on a later period, see Aswin Punathambekar and Sriram Mohan, "A Sound Bridge: Listening for the Political in a Digital Age," International Journal of Communication 11 (2017); 4610–29. See also a revised version of this essay: "Sound Clouds: Listening and Citizenship in Indian Public Culture," in Indian Sound Cultures, Indian Sound Citizenships, ed. Laura Brueck, Jacob Smith, and Neil Verma (Ann Arbor: University of Michigan Press, 2020), 19–43. Lakshmi Subramanian in Singing Gandhi's India turns to Gandhi's relationship to music. While citizenship is not her main interest, she explains that Gandhi's "overriding concern was to create conditions for the constitution of the perfect moral subject, the satyagrahi, and thereby facilitate his/her pursuit of swaraj or self-rule." For Gandhi, music, Subramanian argues, formed part of that project. His approach, however, differed depending on the context. In the ashram, he linked music to prayer and made it mandatory, but "when music leaked into the public domain . . . Gandhi moderated his enthusiasm and linked the issue to the larger question of appropriate traditions for faith practice." Lakshmi Subramanian, Singing Gandhi's India: Music and Sonic Nationalism (New Delhi: Roli, 2020), Epilogue, Kindle.

16. Ana Maria Ochoa Gautier, Aurality: Listening and Knowledge in Nineteenth-Century Colombia (Durham, NC: Duke University Press, 2014), 127.

17. Scales, Radio and the Politics of Sound in Interwar France, 20.

18. Roy, Beyond Belief, 136.

19. Alison E. Arnold, The Garland Encyclopedia of World Music, Vol. 5, South Asia: The Indian Subcontinent (New York: Routledge, 2013).

20. Katherine Butler Schofield, "Reviving the Golden Age Again: 'Classicization,' Hindustani Music, and the Mughals," Ethnomusicology 54, no. 3 (2010): 63.

21. Amanda J. Weidman, Singing the Classical, Voicing the Modern: Postcolonial Politics of Music in South India (Durham, NC: Duke University Press, 2006), 9.

22. Janaki Bakhle, Two Men and Music: Nationalism in the Making of an Indian Classical Tradition (New York: Oxford University Press, 2005), 4, 8.

23. Schofield, "Reviving the Golden Age Again," 490.

24. Schofield, "Reviving the Golden Age Again," 490.

25. B. V. Keskar, "Ustad Fayyaz Khan," in Indian Music (Bombay: Popular Prakashan, 1955), 88.

26. B. V. Keskar, "Problems and Prospects," in Indian Music (Bombay: Popular Prakashan, 1967), 2.

27. Keskar, "Problems and Prospects," 2.

28. Keskar, "Problems and Prospects," 3.

29. Keskar, "Problems and Prospects," 28.

30. B. V. Keskar, "An Article on Music" (undated), B. V. Keskar Papers, Jawaharlal Nehru Memorial Museum and Library, New Delhi, India (NMML).

31. Keskar, "Problems and Prospects," 12.

32. Schofield, "Reviving the Golden Age Again."

33. B. V. Keskar, "Music and Arts in Modern Indian Society," in Indian Music (Bombay: Popular Prakashan, 1962), 59.

34. Keskar, "Ustad Fayyaz Khan," 88.

35. Keskar, "Problems and Prospects," 5–7.

36. Keskar, "Problems and Prospects," 13.

37. Keskar, "Problems and Prospects," 14.

38. Keskar, "An Article on Music," NMML.
39. As noted, recent scholarship has pointed to the many ways in which British colonialism influenced Indian musical traditions.
40. Keskar, "An Article on Music," NMML.
41. Keskar, "Problems and Prospects," 6; see also Lelyveld, "Upon the Subdominant."
42. Keskar, "Problems and Prospects," 9.
43. Keskar, "Problems and Prospects," 9.
44. Fahmy's work reveals a similar search for respectability through sound in Egypt, where a growing middle class used sounds to distinguish itself from the Egyptian "masses." See Ziad Fahmy, *Street Sounds: Listening to Everyday Life in Modern Egypt* (Stanford, CA: Stanford University Press, 2020).
45. Fahmy, *Street Sounds*, 12.
46. Fahmy, *Street Sounds*, 12.
47. Jonathan Sterne, *The Audible Past: Cultural Origins of Sound Reproduction* (Durham, NC: Duke University Press, 2003); see also Judith G. Coffin, "From Interiority to Intimacy: Psychoanalysis and Radio in Twentieth-Century France," *Cultural Critique* 91, no. 1 (2015): 114–49.
48. Coffin, "From Interiority to Intimacy," 3.
49. Sterne, *The Audible Past*.
50. See Kapila Vatsyayan, *Bhāratā: Nāṭyaśāstrā* (New Delhi: Sāhityā Academy, 2006).
51. Katherine Butler Schofield, "Did Aurangzeb Ban Music? Questions for the Historiography of His Reign," *Modern Asian Studies* 41, no. 1 (2007): 109.
52. Francesca Orsini and Katherine Butler Schofield, eds., *Tellings and Texts: Music, Literature and Performance in North India* (Cambridge: Open Book, 2015); Bonnie C. Wade, *Imagining Sound: An Ethnomusicological Study of Music, Art, and Culture in Mughal India* (Chicago: University of Chicago Press, 1999). See also Katherine Butler Schofield, "Emotions in Indian Music History: Anxiety in Late Mughal Hindustan," *South Asian History and Culture* 12, nos. 2–3 (2021): 182–205.
53. Sterne, *The Audible Past*, 14–18.
54. Prasad, "President's Speech," 10.
55. Prasad, "President's Speech," 10.
56. Keskar, "Problems and Prospects," 28.
57. Keskar, "Problems and Prospects," 12.
58. Gautier, *Aurality*, 20.
59. Gautier, *Aurality*, 20.
60. For example, Narciso Gonzales Lineros, senator of the republic, wrote "it is known that music is the most powerful element in sociability; and the egotistical passions fomented by the incomplete civilization of which nineteenth century boasts will give way to the sweet, generous, compassionate affects awoken in the heart by the cultivation of the divine art." Cited in Gautier, *Aurality*, 20.
61. Keskar, "Problems and Prospects," 2–5.
62. See Bakhle, *Two Men and Music*; Schofield, "Reviving the Golden Age Again"; Weidman, *Singing the Classical, Voicing the Modern.*
63. Bakhle, *Two Men and Music*, 14.
64. B. V. Keskar, "Keskar's Speech," *Indian Listener*, November 16, 1958, 10.
65. Keskar, "Keskar's Speech."
66. David Lelyveld, "Transmitters and Culture: The Colonial Roots of Indian Broadcasting," *South Asian Research* 10, no. 1 (1990): 41–52. Garrett Field's research suggests that a similar process might have taken place in Sri Lanka in the 1950s through the

national network of Radio Ceylon (broadcasting in Sinhala to a national audience). Although focusing on poetry and song composition, rather than radio per se, Field notes the ways in which radio composers promoted certain types of nationalization and created new forms of "classical" compositions specifically for the radio. Garrett Field, *Modernizing Composition: Sinhala Song, Poetry and Politics in Twentieth-Century Sri Lanka* (Oakland: University of California Press, 2016), chapter 4.

67. The British government, however, did seriously consider a decentralized system, at least for a short period. As Joselyn Zivin remarks in the 1920s, Indian administrators promoted a village broadcasting system: "Indian listeners would congregate in the village square or headman's courtyard to hear official 'uplift' programming in the local vernacular blaring from a community receiver." By 1937, AIR had subsumed most village broadcasting systems, effectively dismantling the possibility of a decentralized broadcasting system. Joselyn Zivin, "The Imagined Reign of the Iron Lecturer: Village Broadcasting in Colonial India," *Modern Asian Studies* 32, no. 3 (1998): 717–38. Moreover, for more information on pre-independence radio and the "colonial roots" of AIR, see Lelyveld, "Transmitters and Culture."

68. Lelyveld, "Upon the Subdominant."

69. B. V. Keskar, "Inauguration Speech," *Indian Listener*, October 16, 1952, 5; Siegel, "Self-Help Which Ennobles a Nation."

70. "Listening Post: Aurangabad Radio Station," *The Statesman*, October 24, 1953, NMML.

71. Nehru was, of course, not alone in promoting this kind of government centralization. Nehru's attitude aligned with other socialism, including that of the postwar Labour Party in Britain. See, for example, Laura Beer, *Your Britain: Media and the Making of the Labour Party* (Cambridge, MA: Harvard University Press, 2010).

72. B. V. Keskar, "Standards in Music," in *Indian Music* (Bombay: Popular Prakashan, n.d.), 31.

73. Daniel M. Neuman, *The Life of Music in North India: The Organization of an Artistic Tradition* (Chicago: University of Chicago Press, 1990), 78.

74. Ravi Shankar, *Raga Mala: The Autobiography of Ravi Shankar*, ed. George Harrison and Oliver Craske (New York: Welcome Rain, 1999), 118.

75. "A Musician's Notebook, An Indian Orchestra," Newspaper clipping, March 8, 1953, Bonnie C. Wade Collection, Miscellaneous folder No. 9, Archive and Research Center for Ethnomusicology, New Delhi, India (ARCE). According to this article, the orchestra had no brass instruments and used only Indian percussion instruments. Before Vādya Vrinda's inauguration, a number of individuals had experimented with orchestration of Indian instruments. At the turn of the nineteenth century, Maula Bakhsh, a celebrated court musician from the princely state of Baroda in western India formed a small Indian instrumental ensemble. British-born musicologist, John Fouldes, who worked for AIR during the last decades of British rule, founded a small ensemble of Indian instruments. For a discussion of Fouldes, see Lelyveld, "Upon the Subdominant," 114.

76. Actual scores of Ravi Shankar's compositions for the National Orchestra are available in Ravi Shankar, *Shankar ka Orchestra*, ed. Lakshmi Garg Narayan (Hathras, UP: Prabhulal Garg Sangīt Kāryālae, n.d.). Interestingly, western-style conducting was a feature that film-music composers had adopted a few years earlier. Alison Arnold explains that when music directors began to use western music styles, they also began to conduct their orchestras in "western fashion even though their *tabla* player or other Indian drummer was playing traditional rhythmical patterns." It might not be a big leap of faith to suggest that Keskar's insistence on conducting was, at least partially, influenced by the film industry. Arnold, "Hindi *Filmigit*," 139.

77. "A Musician's Notebook, An Indian Orchestra," ARCE.

78. Shankar, *Raga Mala*, 118.

79. See program schedules printed in *Indian Listener*, 1952–1962. Copies available at the All India Radio, Library, New Delhi, India (AIR Library).

80. Mohan Nadkarni, "The Last Titan," *Illustrated Weekly*, July 15, 1984, 159. Shikha Jhingan, "Re-embodying the 'Classical': The Bombay Film Song in the 1950s," *BioScope: South Asian Screen Studies* 2, no. 2 (2011): 157–79.

81. Max Katz, "Institutional Communalism in North Indian Classical Music," *Ethnomusicology* 56, no. 2 (2012): 91.

82. "A.I.R. Policy Vigorously Defended by Dr. Keskar," *Times of India*, April 9, 1954.

83. Naresh Kumar, "From Centerstage to the Margins: Hindustani Classical Music in Radio, Television, and the Music Industry," *Sangeet Natak* 44, no. 3 (n.d.): 22; Nadkarni, "The Last Titan," 40.

84. B. V. Keskar, "Letter to Jawaharlal Nehru from B. V. Keskar dated September 21," B. V. Keskar Papers, 1962, NMML. Interestingly, this is one of the few letters in which Keskar's defensive tone hints at some friction between Nehru and Keskar over broadcasting policies. Nehru's letters to Keskar during the height of AIR controversy over Hindi film songs suggest that Nehru was rather unconcerned in the AIR's reforms. During the height of the controversy over AIR's alleged film-song ban, Nehru corresponded with Keskar about other unrelated matters and maintained a friendly tone. For example, on September 1, 1953, Nehru wrote to Keskar to complain about the Goan journalist Frank Moraes's pro-Portuguese stance. In March 1956, Nehru wrote enthusiastically that the Mountbattens and Churchill greatly enjoyed the two documentaries on the Republic Day Parade. See Nehru, *Selected Works*.

85. Rotem Geva, "The Scramble for Houses: Violence, a Factionalized State, and Informal Economy in Post-Partition Delhi," *Modern Asian Studies* 51, no. 3 (2017): 778–82.

86. Lelyveld, "Upon the Subdominant."

87. H. R. Luthra, *Indian Broadcasting* (New Delhi: Ministry of Information and Broadcasting, 1986), 270–72; Kamaluddin Siddiqui, *Urdu Radio Television Meṅ Tarsīl o Iblāğ Kī Zabān* (New Delhi: Qaumī Konsil Barāe Faroğe Urdu Zabān, 1998).

88. See also Syed Zulfiqar Ali Bukhari, *Sarguzašt* (Lahore: Ghalib, 1995). Zulfiqar Bukhari was Patras Bukhari's brother and also a renowned broadcaster in colonial India and later independent Pakistan.

89. Luthra, *Indian Broadcasting*, 255–77.

90. "Listening Post: AIR's Opportunity in Language Development," *The Statesman*, January 10, 1954, NMML.

91. This is a famous joke still repeated in contemporary India.

92. Keskar, "Letter to Jawaharlal Nehru from B. V. Keskar," NMML.

93. Keskar, "Ustad Fayyaz Khan," 88.

94. Keskar, "Problems and Prospects," 26–28.

95. Ministry of Information and Broadcasting, *Annual Report* (New Delhi: Ministry of Information and Broadcasting, 1954). Receiver licenses were a poor indicator of the size of radio audiences in India for a variety of reasons.

96. Siegel, "Self-Help Which Ennobles a Nation," 980.

97. Roy, *Beyond Belief*, 44. Similarly, William Mazzarella explains that as early as 1930, British colonial censors in India invoked ideas about the relationship between film spectatorship and citizenship. The notion of "spectator-citizen," Mazzarella notes, remained part of the rhetoric of film censorship in the postcolonial period (81–88 and 146–51). William Mazzarella, *Censorium: Cinema and the Open Edge of Mass Publicity* (Durham, NC: Duke University Press, 2013). Manishita Dass, also focusing on the colonial period,

studies how filmmakers imagined film viewers as members of "cohesive national public." Dass argues that filmmakers imagined the screen as "site for project fantasies of a truly national and more inclusive public sphere" (191). Manishita Dass, *Outside the Lettered City: Cinema, Modernity, and the Public Sphere in Late Colonial India* (Oxford: Oxford University Press, 2016).

98. Roy, *Beyond Belief*.

99. Keskar, "Problems and Prospects," 28.

100. Jason Beaster-Jones, *Bollywood Sounds: The Cosmopolitan Mediation of Hindi Film Song* (New York: Oxford University Press, 2015), loc. 341 of 7018, Kindle. For a concise and accessible summary of Hindi cinema's relationship to Hindi film songs, see Corey Creekmur, "Popular Hindi Cinema and the Film Song," in *Traditions in World Cinema*, ed. Steven Jay Schneider and R. Barton Palmer (New Brunswick, NJ: Rutgers University Press, 2006), 193–202.

101. Kathryn Hansen, *Grounds for Play: Nautanki Theatre of North India* (Berkeley: University of California Press, 1991).

102. Arnold, "Hindi *Filmigit*," 78; also see Alison E. Arnold, "Popular Film Song in India: A Case of Mass Market Musical Eclecticism," *Popular Music* 7, no. 2 (1998): 177–88; Beaster-Jones, *Bollywood Sounds*.

103. Arnold, "Hindi *Filmigit*," 139; also see Beaster-Jones, *Bollywood Sounds*, chapters 2 and 3.

104. Arnold, "Hindi *Filmigit*," 144.

105. Arnold, "Popular Film Song in India," 177; Morcom, *Hindi Film Songs and the Cinema*, 65.

106. Arnold, "Hindi *Filmigit*," 79.

107. Arnold, "Hindi *Filmigit*," 145.

108. Keskar, "Development Plans for All India Radio," 59.

109. Madhumita Lahiri, "An Idiom for India: Hindustani and the Limits of the Language Concept," *Interventions: International Journal of Postcolonial Studies* 18, no. 1 (2016): 60–85.

110. Raza Ali Abidi, *Naǧmāgar* (Lahore: Sang-e-Mīl, 2013).

111. See Neepa Majumdar, *Wanted Cultured Ladies Only: Female Stardom and Cinema in India; 1930s–1950s* (Champaign: University of Illinois Press, 2010).

112. Dass, *Outside the Lettered City*, Introduction, Kindle.

113. S. G. Bapat, "Cheers and Jeers: Two Pills for Dr. Keskar. Sweet," *Movie Times*, 1952, 1, National Film Archive of India, Pune (NFAI).

114. Bapat, "Cheers and Jeers," NFAI.

115. B. V. Keskar, "Inauguration Speech," *Indian Listener*, October 16, 1952, 8.

116. Keskar, "Inauguration Speech."

117. See also "Govt Will Consult Industry. Dr. Keskar's Assurance Awards for Good Films: Idea to be Considered, Dropping Film Names on AIR," *Movie Times*, 1952, 14, NFAI.

118. "IMPPA Gives Notice to AIR to Stop Film Music," *Movie Times*, 1952, 7, NFAI.

119. "Readers Write to the Editor," *Screen*, 1952, 2, NFAI.

120. K. Ahmed, "Cheers and Jeers: Film Music Goes West," *Movie Times*, 1952, 10, NFAI.

121. Ahmed, "Cheers and Jeers," NFAI.

122. "Music Orchestra Should Suit Context, Advises R. C. Boral," *Screen*, 1952, 12, NFAI.

123. "Music Orchestra Should Suit Context," NFAI.

124. See Jhingan, "Re-embodying the 'Classical'"; Nikhil Menon, *Planning Democracy: Modern India's Quest for Development* (London: Cambridge University Press, 2022); Nikhil Menon, "'Help the Plan-Help Yourself': Making Indians Plan-Conscious," in *The Postcolonial Moment in South and Southeast Asia*, ed. Gyan Prakash, Nikhil Menon, and Michael Laffan (London: Bloomsbury, 2018).

125. Ravikant provides excellent examples from the film magazine *Madhuri* and *Shankar's Weekly* of further resistance to the AIR's ban on film songs. Ravikant, *Media Kī Bhāṣā Līlā*, 70–87.

126. These were printed in "And Now Film Music," *Filmfare*, 1952, NFAI.

127. "And Now Film Music," NFAI (emphasis added).

128. H. P. Mahalik, "Music and the Common Man," *Movie Times*, 1952, NFAI (emphasis added).

129. "A.I.R. Policy Vigorously Defended by Dr. Keskar."

130. U. L. Baruah, *This Is All India Radio: A Handbook of Radio Broadcasting* (New Delhi: Ministry of Information and Broadcasting, 1983), 137.

131. "Listening Post: AIR Talk Series Disappointing," *The Stasteman*, October 4, 1953, NMML.

132. "Listening Post: Calcutta Leads in Light Music Broadcasts," *The Statesman*, December 28, 1952, NMML.

133. "Listening Post: Calcutta Leads in Light Music Broadcasts," NMML.

134. "Listening Post: AIR Talk Series Disappointing," NMML.

135. "Listening Post: New Light Music Fails to Satisfy," *The Statesman*, December 12, 1953, NMML.

136. G. C. Awasthy, *Broadcasting in India* (Bombay: Allied, 1965), 53–54.

137. Narendra Sharma, "Cine-Sangeet Indra Ka Ghora Hai Aur Akashvani Uska Samman Karti Hai!/Film Music Is Lord Indra's Horse and Akashvani Respects It!," Ravikant, trans., *BioScope: South Asian Screen Studies* 3, no. 2 (July 2012): 165–73.

138. As Ravikant explains, Vividh Bharti continued to censor film songs and "the puritan, pedagogical impulse," and even in postliberalization India, the Indian government refused to allow FM to broadcast news. See also Ravikant, "Šrav-Driṣṭav: Cinema Meṅ Radio," *Pratimān: Samay, Samāj, Sanskriti* 2 (December 2013): 581–600.

139. These conceptualizations might also be useful for the contemporary period. For example, Anaar Desai-Stephens's work has shown how the relationship to sound and citizenship continue to be important in the postcolonial periods. See Anaar Desai-Stephens, "The Age of Aspiration? Music Classes and the Limits of Gendered Self-Transformation in Mumbai," *MUSICultures* 44, no. 1 (2018): 74–96.

4. Radio Ceylon, King of the Airwaves

1. WO 165/111, National Archives United Kingdom, London, United Kingdom (NA-UK), cited in Eric Hitchcock, *Making Waves: Admiral Mountbatten's Radio SEAC, 1945–1949* (Solihull, England: Helion, 2014), 57.

2. Report on the discussion regarding forces broadcasting for India and South East Asia command, November 11, 1944, L/I/1/937, India Office, British Library, London, United Kingdom (IO).

3. Letter to Secretary of State from Lord Mountbatten, WO 203/5207, NA-UK; Radio SEAC, WO 203/5207, NA-UK; Hitchcock, *Making Waves*, 294. A new station represented no small expenditure for the already financially stretched British government. The station's principal piece of equipment, a state-of-the-art 100kW Marconi transmitter, cost over a quarter million pounds.

4. Radio SEAC, WO 203/5207, NA-UK; see also Hitchcock, *Making Waves*, 72.

5. For an excellent description of Mountbatten and media during his post as viceroy, see Chandrika Kaul, *Communications, Media and the Imperial Experience: Britain and India in the Twentieth Century* (London: Palgrave Macmillan, 2014). In particular, see chapter 5, "Operation Seduction: Mountbatten, the Media and Decolonisation in 1947."

6. See, for example, Sugata Bose and Ayesha Jalal, *Modern South Asia: History, Culture, Political Economy*, 4th ed. (New York: Routledge, 2018).

7. As supreme commander, Mountbatten technically served both U.S. and British forces. U.S. soldiers, however, joked that SEAC actually stood for "Saved England's Asian Colonies" because Mountbatten seemed most intent on recovering the empire's prestige in Asia and in improving the morale of British forces. Philip Ziegler, *Mountbatten: The Official Biography* (London: Phoenix Press, 2001).

8. Ceylon was a crown colony governed more closely from London than India, which had its own administrative body and separate office. Moreover, Ceylon had not witnessed mass opposition to colonial rule. Hence, in Ceylon, Mountbatten could enjoy much greater independence. In a letter, Mountbatten explained: "I want to make sure that my staff can stand on their own two feet." He went on to note: "It will be a good thing to get away from the social and political attitude" of New Delhi. Lady Pamela Hicks Papers, May 19, 1944, cited in Ziegler, *Mountbatten*, 90.

9. Letter to Claude Auchinleck from Lord Mountbatten, February 7, 1945, WO 203/5207, NA-UK; see also L/I/1/440, "Appendix A: Directive Station Commander Radio Unit SEAC," IO. For a longer and more elaborate history of Radio SEAC and Mountbatten's relationship to the station, see Isabel Huacuja Alonso, " 'Voice of Freedom' at the End of Empire: Radio SEAC, Underground Congress Radio, and the (Anti) Colonial Sublime" (in progress).

10. Eric Hichtcock, "Radio SEAC's Transmitters: Eric Hitchcock Brings Us a Tale of 1940s Broadcasting from the Indian Ocean," *Shortwave Magazine*, 2000, 45–52.

11. Letter to Secretary of State from Lord Mountbatten, January 20, 1946, WO 203/5207, NA-UK. When Mountbatten left Ceylon, the transmitter had been operating for only a month. Hitchcock, *Making Waves*, 111.

12. Barbara Kingler, "Pre-cult: Casablanca, Radio Adaptation, and Transmedia in the 1940s," *New Review of Film and Television Studies* 13, no. 1 (2015): 48; Henry Jenkins, *Convergence Culture: Where Old and New Media Collide* (New York: New York University Press, 2006). Kingler notes: "Like any theory that creates a disciplinary paradigm shift, Jenkins's account of transmedia has drawn scrutiny." Matt Hills, for example, has criticized Jenkins for "emphasizing" transmedia's "organization unity over less coordinated, yet culturally significant story enterprises." Siobhan O'Flynn, in turn, has criticized Jenkins for the "difficulty of drawing boundaries between rampant intertexts that define media circulation and consumption." See Matt Hills, "Sherlock's Epistemological Economy and the Value of 'Fan' Knowledge," in *Sherlock and Transmedia Fandom: Essays on the BBC Series*, ed. Louisa Ellen Stein and Kristina Busse (Jefferson, NC: McFarland, 2012), 27–40; Siobhan O'Flynn, "Epilogue," in *A Theory of Adaptation*, ed. Linda Hutcheon, 2nd ed. (London: Routledge, 2013), 179–206.

13. Kingler, "Pre-cult," 48.

14. I align myself with cinema studies scholars who have argued that Hindi film songs and their reception should be studied as *the* leading element of Hindi cinema, not as an auxiliary to visual experience or as "interruptions" to visual films. See Neepa Majumdar, "The Embodied Voice: Song Sequences and Stardom in Popular Hindi Cinema," in *Soundtrack Available: Essays on Film and Popular Music*, ed. Pamela Robertson Wojcik and Arthur Knight (Durham, NC: Duke University Press, 2001), 161–85; Corey Creekmur, "Picturizing American Cinema: Hindi Film Songs and the Last Days of Genre," in *Soundtrack Available*, 375–407; Ravikant, *Media Kī Bhāṣā Līlā* (New Delhi: Lokchetnā Prakāśan, 2016), XVIII. See also Vebhuti Duggal, "Imagining Sound Through the Pharmaish: Radios and Request-Postcards in North India, c. 1955–75," *BioScope: South Asian*

Screen Studies 9, no. 1 (2018): 1–23, and "The Community of Listeners: Writing a History of Hindi Film Music Aural Culture" (PhD diss., Jawaharlal Nehru University, 2015).

15. John Durham Peters, "Broadcasting and Schizophrenia," *Media, Culture, and Society* 32, no. 1 (2010): 127; John Durham Peters, *Speaking Into the Air: A History of the Idea of Communication* (Chicago: University of Chicago Press, 1999), 206–25. Paddy Scannell uses a similar concept. See Paddy Scannell, "For-Anyone-as-Someone Structures," *Media, Culture, and Society* 22, no. 1 (2000): 5–24.

16. Jonathan Sterne, *The Audible Past: Cultural Origins of Sound Reproduction* (Durham, NC: Duke University Press, 2003), 23.

17. Information Services Committee Commercial Broadcasting, Broadcasting—Radio SEAC Ceylon, L/I/1/440, IO. The new government refused to let their former colonial rulers run a military station in their territory. The document states: "The Ceylon government [is] unwilling to allow the station to remain in United Kingdom ownership now that Ceylon is independent."

18. Letters signed by P. C. Shaw, April 9, 1948, T 219/91, NA-UK.

19. Letters signed by P. C. Shaw, NA-UK.

20. Inward Telegram to Commonwealth Relations, April 15, 1948, Broadcasting—Radio SEAC Ceylon, L/I/1/440, IO.

21. Letters signed by P. C. Shaw, NA-UK (emphasis added).

22. Hitchcock, "Radio SEAC's Transmitters," 45–52. In the end, Prime Minister Senanayake made two concessions that helped ease British officials' worries: he promised to give preference to British and commonwealth clients and agreed to let BBC staff use the transmitter to relay news to the remaining British troops in Asia for a few hours a day for two years. Memorandum, HO 256/279, NA-UK.

23. "Clifford Dodd," *Ceylon Radio Times*, September 24–October 7, 1950, British Library Newspapers at Colindale (BL-Colindale). Ivan Corea, "Eighty Years of Broadcasting," *Daily News*, December 27, 2005, http://archives.dailynews.lk/2005/12/27/fea02.htm.

24. For more on the Australian system, see Bridget Griffen-Foley, "The Birth of a Hybrid: The Shaping of the Australian Radio Industry," *Radio Journal: International Studies in Broadcast and Audio Media* 2, no. 3 (December 2004): 153–69.

25. Nandana Karunanayake, *Broadcasting in Sri Lanka: Potential and Performance* (Colombo: Center for Media and Policy Studies, 1990), 103–13. Moreover, Garrett Field's work on Sinhala song and film takes studio productions from Radio Ceylon's national network. See Garrett Field, *Modernizing Composition: Sinhala Song, Poetry and Politics in Twentieth-Century Sri Lanka* (Oakland: University of California Press, 2016).

26. See *Ceylon Radio Times* magazines, 1948–1951, BL-Colindale. Music from the United States made up most of Radio Ceylon's broadcasts, but the station also occasionally aired radio serials. Among them was *Superman* and *Front Page Lady*, likely a radio adaptation of the successful war film *Front Page Woman*, which related the struggles of a female journalist. In addition to news and music, Radio Ceylon relayed news from the BBC and Voice of America alongside a weekly local news program titled *Home News from Ceylon*.

27. For the listing of early Hindi programs, see the collection of *Ceylon Radio Times* magazines for 1951, BL-Colindale. The Sri Lanka National Museum (SLNM) also houses copies of these magazines, but the Colindale collection is more complete. Ameen Sayani noted in an interview that early Hindi broadcasters did little more than play gramophone records of Hindi film songs on the air. Ameen Sayani, interview by author, July 25, 2016.

28. H. P. Mahalik, "Music and the Common Man," *Movie Times*, February 6, 1953, National Film Archive of India, Pune-India (NFAI). In 1962, All India Radio began to make

plans to take over Radio Goa. See Taking Over Radio GOA by AIR, States, Broadcasting Policy, 1962, 8(1) 62-B(P), NAI.

29. Azam Khan, interview by author, January 23 and 24, 2012.

30. S. Dayal, "Well, Keskar Babu?" *Film India*, July 1, 1953, 70, NFAI.

31. Radio Ceylon is now called Sri Lankan Broadcasting Corporation. For a description of the library, see Gopal Sharma, *Āvāz Kī Duniyā Ke Dostoṅ* (Mumbai: Gopal Sharma, 2007), 74. For an emotive description of the library, see Manohar Mahajan, *Yādeiṅ Radio Ceylon Kī* (Jaipur: Vangmāyā Prakāśan, 2010). In his description of the library, Mahajan writes that when he first saw the library, "I almost fainted. I couldn't believe that I was in that library" (64). In this, Mahajan also describes spending many hours listening to the records in the small room made especially for that purpose.

32. A controversy about royalties and Radio Ceylon emerged in 1965. See, for example, "AIR Should Provide Substitute to Radio Ceylon Publicity," *Cinema Advance*, July 1, 1965, 70, NFAI.

33. The politics of language in Sri Lanka, while outside the scope of this study, are interesting here. Ironically, it seems that the government of Sri Lanka supported an inclusive form of Hindustani in North India and Pakistan (through Radio Ceylon's commercial Hindi Service) at the same time that it excluded Tamil-speaking populations in its own country. More research with Sinhala and Tamil sources is needed to properly analyze the relationship between the politics of language in Sri Lanka and the service's embrace of Hindustani. Sources in English and Hindi, however, imply that Dodd and others at Radio Ceylon chose to broadcast in Hindustani because it made commercial sense, rather than for ideological reasons. On Sri Lankan–language politics, see Neil DeVotta, *Blowback: Linguistic Nationalism, Institutional Decay, and Ethnic Conflict in Sri Lanka* (Stanford, CA: Stanford University Press, 2004). On Sri Lankan ethnic politics and the BBC, see Sharika Thiranagama, "Ethnic Entanglements: The BBC Tamil and Sinhala Services Amidst the Civil War in Sri Lanka," *Journalism* 12, no. 2 (2011): 153–69.

34. Vishnu Prakash, CIBA director of communication, interview by author, July 29, 2016. Prakash noted that CIBA was able to sidestep this restriction because it had its European offices pay for Indian product advertisements on Radio Ceylon. Other foreign companies that advertised on Radio Ceylon did the same.

35. Ameen Sayani, interview by Kamla Bhatt, March 27, 2007, http://kamlashow.com/podcast/2007/03/25/in-conversation-with-ameen-sayani-part-i/.

36. The names listed here appear on Radio Ceylon's programming schedules. See *Radio Ceylon Times*, 1952–1965, BL-Colindale and SLNM.

37. Sayani, interview by Kamla Bhatt; Sayani, interview by author. Arun Chaudhuri, *Indian Advertising: 1780 to 1950 A.D.* (New Delhi: Tata McGraw Hill, 2009), 227–35.

38. Sayani, interview by Kamla Bhatt; Sayani, interview by author; Ameen Sayani, "The Strange and Amusing History of Indian Commercial Radio" (Sayani graciously shared a copy of this unpublished article with me). RES staff had deep connections to the film industry. It was not unusual for RES employees to also work in film productions. Listen to Ameen Sayani, *Geetmala Kī Chāoṅ Meṅ*, RPG Enterprises, vols. 1–5, 2009, compact discs. The celebrated actor Sunil Dutt worked for RES before his debut in the film *Railway Platform*, released in 1955. See Namrata Kumar-Dutt and Priya Dutt, *Mr. and Mrs. Dutt: Memories of Our Parents* (New Delhi: Lustre/Roli, 2007), 28.

39. Vijay Kishore Dubey helped build up Radio Ceylon's Hindi studios. After working for RES in Bombay, Dubey moved to Colombo. In Ceylon, Dubey made it a point to recruit broadcasters from India with a passion for films and film music. Gopal Sharma made this point emphatically during an interview. Gopal Sharma, interview by author,

July 27, 2016. Sayani also makes this point in Sayani, *Geetmala Kī Chāoṅ Meṅ*. See also Sharma, *Āvāz Kī Duniyā Ke Dostoṅ*. We should not underestimate the importance of these broadcasters as stars and performers, who, in many cases, were as famous as the singers they promoted. As Ravikant correctly notes, for radio listeners, broadcasters' names were often as important and familiar as Lata Mangeshkar's name. See Ravikant, *Media Kī Bhāṣā Līlā*, XVIII.

40. It was not unusual, however, for Radio Advertising Services broadcasters to join Radio Ceylon's studios in Colombo or vice versa.

41. Anonymous, "Bedari—Another Plagiarised Version," *Pakistan Times*, December 13, 1957, 6, cited in Salma Siddique, "From Gandhi to Jinnah: National Dilemmas in the Stardom of Rattan Kumar," in *Indian Film Stars: New Critical Perspectives*, ed. Michael Lawrence (London: Bloomsbury, 2020), 109–23. I am thankful to Salma Siddique for sharing this important reference with me. See also Salma Siddique, *Evacuee Cinema: Travels of Film Cultures Between Bombay and Lahore (1940–60)* (Cambridge: Cambridge University Press, 2022).

42. "Readers Forum: 'Radio Pakistan and Film Songs,'" *Eastern Film*, August 1962. The listener also notes that more listeners were turning to Indian stations. These Indian stations broadcasting on medium-wave transmitters would have had limited reception and would have been heard only in bordering regions.

43. Vishnu Prakash noted that, to his knowledge, CIBA did not advertise in Pakistan, but I found printed CIBA (and *Geetmala*) advertisements for Pakistani audiences that appear to be from the 1960s circulating on various social media sites. Despite many attempts, I was unable to trace the original source. Vishnu Prakash, interview by author, July 28, 2016.

44. Sharma, interview by author. See also Mahajan, *Yādeiṅ Radio Ceylon Kī*.

45. For example, the June 19–July 2, 1961, edition of *Ceylon Radio Times* notes that Radio Ceylon played Pakistani songs on Friday nights at 8:45. *Ceylon Radio Times*, June 19–July 2, 1961, BL-Colindale.

46. "Hum TV Ke Progrām Meṅ Ameen Sayani Adākār Nadīm Se Bāt Cīt Kar Rahe Haiṅ," *Navā-e-vaqt*, May 8, 2007; "Pāk Bhārat Dostī Mazbūt Rište Meṅ Bandh Jāe: Ameen Sayani," *Express*, May 8, 2007; "Hum TV's Tribute to Ameen Sayani—the Legend," *Regional Tunes*, May 7, 2007; "Ameen Sayani Ek Muddat Tak Muhabbat Kī Mālā Bunte Rahe," *Gateway*, May 9, 2007; "Merī Āwāz Hī Pahcān Hai, Gar Yād Rahe," *Super Star Dust*, June 2007; "Sayani Jaise Sadākār Ke Līye Radio Āj Bhī Muntazir," *QVS Audio Video*, June 2007, Newspaper and Magazine Clippings, Sultan Ahmad Arshad personal papers.

47. "Bollywood" is the term more commonly used now to reference commercial Hindi cinema. Madhumita Lahiri, "An Idiom for India: Hindustani and the Limits of the Language Concept," *Interventions: International Journal of Postcolonial Studies* 18, no. 1 (2016): 2.

48. Lahiri, "An Idiom for India." See also Ravikant, *Media Kī Bhāṣā Līlā*. Ravikant correctly notes that the film industry's use of Hindustani was not without controversy. He points to a telling incident when the film-song lyricist Sahir Ludhianvi was severely criticized in the film magazine *Madhuri* for saying that Hindi films were actually Urdu films (74). Ravikant also notes that some disapproving critics noted that the film industry's use of Hindustani was actually nothing more than an excuse to bring in "Urdu through the back door" and to consequently exclude Hindi (76). Ultimately, however, Ravikant agrees that cinema managed to keep the spirit of Hindustani alive. David Lunn reaches a similar conclusion. See David Lunn, "The Eloquent Language: Hindustani in 1940s Cinema," *BioScope: South Asian Screen Studies* 6, no. 1 (2015): 1–26. Lunn argues that "cinema largely side-stepped the vitriol and bright-line divisions that characterized the literary and publishing worlds."

49. For a discussion of the language issues faced by AIR, see David Lelyveld, "Colonial Knowledge and the Fate of Hindustani," *Comparative Studies in Society and History* 35, no. 4 (1993): 665–82.

50. Ameen Sayani called the language he spoke on the radio "simple Hindustani." Ameen Sayani and Rajil Sayani, email exchange with author, October 19, 2012.

51. *Binaca Geetmala* program copies from Sri Lanka Broadcasting Corporation Library (SLBC-Library). Although undated, these programs appear to be from the 1980s, but Ameen Sayani notes that he did this in earlier programs as well.

52. Ameen Sayani, *Geetmala Kī Chāoṅ Meṅ*.

53. In an interview, Sayani remarked that it took him seven years to feel at ease broadcasting in Hindi and noted that even now, after more than four decades of broadcasting in Hindi, he feels his speech is still far from perfect. Ameen Sayani, interview by author.

54. The vast majority of programs Radio Ceylon aired were Hindi film-song programs that did not require the more difficult vocabulary of literary tradition.

55. Padmini Pereira, interview by author, July 26, 2016.

56. The Ministry of Information and Broadcasting estimated that by 1954 there were 759,643 registered receiver licenses in India. Mininistry of Information and Broadcasting, *Annual Report* (1954), Jawaharlal Nehru Memorial Museum and Library, New Delhi, India (NMML).

57. See Duggal, "Ubiquitous Listening: Technologies, Transmission, and the Circulation of Film Song," chapter 1 in "The Community of Listeners: Writing a History of Hindi Film Music Aural Culture" (PhD diss., Jawaharlal Nehru University, 2015). It appears that a similar cottage industry of transistors developed in Pakistan as well and it too proliferated in the early 1960s. The film magazine, *Eastern Film*, includes ads for what appear to be locally produced transistors (see chapter 5).

58. Duggal includes interviews with radio sellers. One shop owner, for example, notes that during these two decades, buyers would often ask for a "Radio Ceylon" when purchasing receivers because they did not consider the radio station to be "separate from the devise they were purchasing." Duggal, "Ubiquitous Listening," 59.

59. Duggal, "Ubiquitous Listening," 67.

60. In her study of the Hindi film song, Duggal pays attention to these localities in particular. Duggal, "Ubiquitous Listening," 46–47.

61. Duggal, "Ubiquitous Listening," 66.

62. Sayani, interview by author.

63. Sayani, interview by author.

64. Anil Bhargava, *Binaca Geetmala Kā Surīlā Safar* (Jaipur: Vangmāyā Prakāśan, 2007), 30.

65. Aswin Punathambekar, "Ameen Sayani and Radio Ceylon: Notes Towards a History of Broadcasting and Bombay Cinema," *BioScope* 1, no. 2 (2010): 189–97. Sayani interview by author.

66. For a more detailed analysis of *Geetmala's* four-decade run, see Isabel Huacuja Alonso, "Songs by Ballot: *Binaca Geetmala* and the Making of a Hindi Film Song Radio Audience, 1952–1994," *BioScope: South Asian Screen Studies* (forthcoming, 2022).

67. Duggal also makes notes of this. She notes that one of her informants commented, "If we wanted to listen to *Binaca Geetmala* we would go to a restaurant at 7 pm, we would order and keep sitting there." Duggal, "The Community of Listeners," 40.

68. For a more detailed analyses of *Geetmala's* end-of-year program, see Huacuja Alonso, "Songs by Ballot."

69. Duggal, "The Community of Listeners," 48.

70. Aswin Punathambekar, "'We're Online, Not on the Streets': Indian Cinema, New Media, and Participatory Culture," in *Global Bollywood*, ed. Anandam P. Kavoori and Aswin Punathambekar (New York: New York University Press, 2008), 282–99.

71. Sultan Arshad Ahmad, email exchange with author, March 14, 2015. Ahmad worked for HUM TV and played an important role in helping organize Ameen Sayani's visit to Karachi in 2007.

72. Jyoti Parmar kindly shared copies of this diary that a listener gifted to her father when he worked for Radio Ceylon.

73. Bhargava, *Binaca Geetmala Kā Surīlā Safar*.

74. See Huacuja Alonso, "Songs by Ballot."

75. Lisa Gitelman, *Scripts, Grooves, and Writing Machines: Representing Technologies in the Edison Era* (Stanford, CA: Stanford University Press, 1999). For a longer discussion of the relationship between writing and listening and the importance of writing Hindi film songs, see Duggal, "A Community of Listeners," chapter 6.

76. Sayani, interview by Bhatt.

77. For details, see Huacuja Alonso, "Songs by Ballot."

78. See Duggal, "A Community of Listeners," chapter 2.

79. "Undated list of radio clubs, names, and addresses," Ameen and Rajil Sayani personal papers. For a more in-depth analysis of this list and this particular collection with radio club material, see Huacuja Alonso, "Songs by Ballot."

80. Duggal, "A Community of Listeners," chapter 2.

81. Radio Club names are from "Undated list of radio clubs, names and addresses," Ameen and Rajil Sayani personal papers.

82. Unfortunately, we do not have lists of songs that were played at the time, but interviews with broadcasters as well as Radio Ceylon's collection of Pakistani gramophone records suggest that programs sometimes also featured Pakistani film songs in sustenance programs. Songs from the India-based film industry, however, would have made up the majority of broadcasts.

83. Peters, "Broadcasting and Schizophrenia," 127; Peters, *Speaking Into the Air*, 206–25. Paddy Scannell uses a similar concept. See Scannell, "For-Anyone-as-Someone Structures," 5–24.

84. Sterne, *The Audible Past*, 23.

85. Jason Beaster-Jones, *Bollywood Sounds: The Cosmopolitan Mediation of Hindi Film Song* (New York: Oxford University Press, 2015), Kindle. Stephen P. Hughes, "The 'Music Boom' in Tamil South India: Gramophone, Radio and the Making of Mass Culture," *Historical Journal of Film, Radio and Television* 22, no. 4 (2002): 445–73; G. N. Joshi, "A Concise History of the Phonograph Industry in India," *Popular Music* 7, no. 2 (May 1988): 147–56; Michael Kinnear, *The Gramophone Company's First Indian Recordings, 1899–1908* (Mumbai: Popular Prakashan, 1994).

86. The names and times of radio programs are listed in *Radio Ceylon Times* magazines from the 1950s and 1960s. These are housed in BL–Colindale and the Sri Lanka Public Library. In his biography, Gopal Sharma includes detailed descriptions of these programs. I also asked Jyoti Parmar to describe the radio programs listed on the schedules during my visit to the Sri Lanka Broadcasting Corporation. Jyoti Parmar is a Hindi broadcaster for the Sri Lanka Broadcasting Corporation (the successor of Radio Ceylon) and resides in Colombo. She is the daughter of the Radio Ceylon broadcaster Dalbir Singh Parmar, who joined Radio Ceylon in the mid-1960s, and has been involved in broadcasting since her youth.

87. Sharma, *Āvāz Kī Duniyā Ke Dostoṅ*, 91.

88. These song titles are meant to imitate sounds and do not have a specific meaning.

89. J. Firoze, "Stock Words in Songs," *Movie Times*, November 14, 1952, 24, NFAI.

90. "Listening Post: AIR Talk Series Disappointing," *The Statesman*, October 4, 1953, NMML.

91. Anna Morcom, "Film Songs and the Cultural Synergies of Bollywood in and Beyond South Asia," in *Beyond the Boundaries of Bollywood: The Many Forms of Hindi Cinema*, ed. Rachel Dwyer and Jerry Pinto (Delhi: Oxford University Press, 2011), 162.

92. Morcom, "Film Songs and the Cultural Synergies."

93. Jyoti Parmar, interview by author, November 27, 2012.

94. As he notes, "*alag mazā ātā hai*" (xix) (it is a different kind of enjoyment). See Ravikant, *Media Kī Bhāṣā Līlā*, XIX. Salma Siddique has also pointed out in conversations that some fans in Pakistan who would hear songs on Radio Ceylon would express disappointment at seeing the picturization of the song. See also Siddique, *Evacuee Cinema*.

95. For example, in the op-ed section of *Eastern Film*, film lovers often describe Indian films. But the descriptions usually, in one way or another, revolve around songs.

96. "Programs Service," *Ceylon Radio Times*, June 19–July 2, 1961, BL-Colindale. Newspaper clippings, Siraj Syed personal papers.

97. Creekmur, "Picturizing American Cinema," 389.

98. What we need to fully make sense of this commercial relationship is an in-depth study of the process of convergence and transmedia, focusing specifically on understanding the financial transaction between radio and film and how that evolved over time. Unfortunately, such a study is outside the scope of this book.

99. As Creekmur notes, "Aside from the sheer presence of music, the most distinctive characteristic of Hindi film music, and perhaps of Indian sound practice, is the regular and acknowledged use of a relatively small number of playback singers to perform the hundreds of songs produced annually by the film industry." Creekmur, "Picturizing American Cinema," 395.

100. Majumdar, "The Embodied Voice," 165. See also Kiranmayi Indraganti, "Of 'Ghosts' and Singers: Debates Around Singing Practices of 1940s Indian Cinema," *South Asian Popular Culture* 10, no. 3 (October 2012): 296–306. As Amanda Weidman points out, "playback singers are an essential part of the popular film industries of India. Playback singing is thus a realm of vocality that has become intricately encoded with meaning." Amanda J. Weidman, "Neoliberal Logics of Voice: Playback Singing and Public Femaleness in South India," *Cultural, Theory, and Critique* 55, no. 2 (April 2014): 175. See also Amanda J. Weidman, *Brought to Life by the Voice: Playback Singing and Cultural Politics in South India* (Oakland: University of California Press, 2021).

101. Ashok Ranade, "The Extraordinary Importance of the Indian Film Song," *Cinema Vision India* 1, no. 4 (1980): 4–11. Nur Jehan migrated to Pakistan. Majumdar, "The Embodied Voice," 165. Weidman also points to an important gender dynamic among the female playback singers of the 1950s and 1960s: "The female playback voice that emerged in the 1950s and 60s can be interpreted as a solution to the problem of how women (both singers themselves and the female characters in films) could appear in the newly defined public sphere while keeping their modesty intact." Weidman, "Neoliberal Logics of Voice."

102. Ranade, "The Extraordinary Importance of the Indian Film Song," 171.

103. Majumdar, "The Embodied Voice," 164.

104. Majumdar, "The Embodied Voice," 165.

105. Majumdar, "The Embodied Voice," 164.

106. This was one of the most common and popular programs on Radio Ceylon.

107. Majumdar, "The Embodied Voice," 171. For biographical information about Talat Mahmood and descriptions of his music, see Pratap Singh, *Talat Geet Kosh* (Kanpur: 1992), cited in Ravikant, *Media Kī Bhāṣā Līlā*, XXIX–XXX.

108. The first mention in *Radio Ceylon Times* of this program is in 1954 schedules under the English name *Today's Artist*. The program *Āj Ke Kalākār* appears in later schedules as well.

109. Majumdar, "The Embodied Voice," 170.

110. For a more in-depth description of the program, see "Programmes and People Commercial Service," *Radio Ceylon Times*, June 8–June 21, 1959, BL-Colindale. I have heard listeners also refer to this program as *Āj Aur Kal*. See also Sharma, *Āvāz Kī Duniyā Ke Dostoṅ*, 83, 84, 89, 90. Broadcasters developed other variations. *Do Pahlū Do Gīt*, for example, only featured film songs interpreted by two different playback singers. Pereira, interview by author.

111. Sharma, interview by author.

112. Sharma, *Āvāz Kī Duniyā Ke Dostoṅ*, 91.

113. Producers began to purposefully employ commercially successful music directors to increase their chances of producing a popular film. Radio Ceylon's boom in the early 1950s further contributed to this trend by training listeners to identify music directors' compositional style.

114. Pereira, interview by author. A sponsored program produced in Bombay by radio advertising staff called *Burnaol Gītānjalī* was similar to *Sur Sancār* and *Āj Ke Kalākār*. It featured the works of a different music director or playback every week, but because the program was recorded in Bombay, the anchor was sometimes also able to offer the added bonus of including interviews with these musical celebrities.

115. Peters, *Speaking Into the Air*, 206.

116. Even as AIR began to retract Keskar's policies, it never quite shed the paternalistic ethos toward listeners. As Ravikant explains, Vividh Bharti continued to censor songs even after Keskar left AIR, albeit in a less invasive way. See Ravikant, *Media Kī Bhāṣā Līlā*, 88.

5. Radio Pakistan's Seventeen Days of Drama

1. File 41a, Folder: Vol. 3, Indo-Pak War, State Department History, Box: 24 National Security Council Histories/South Asia, 1962–1966, Lyndon B. Johnson Library and Museum, Austin, TX (LBJ).

2. Some experiments in televised broadcasting had begun in Pakistan, but the vast majority of Pakistanis did not have access to television then.

3. "Seventeen days of war" is a phrase that Radio Pakistan uses in official publications to reference the 1965 war programming. See, for example, Radio Pakistan, *Ten Years of Development: Radio Pakistan 1958–68* (Karachi: Serajsons, 1968).

4. I rely on sources from the 1965 Indo-Pakistan War Collection, Central Production Unit, Pakistan Broadcasting Corporation, Islamabad, Pakistan (CPU).

5. Scannell employs the distinction to examine TV and radio coverage of Princess Diana's death in Britain in August 1997. Her death "began as a happening: a car crash, an accidental death, a meaningless tragedy. It ended as a solemn event: her funeral service and burial." Yet "between these two moments . . . there was a complex unfolding process, a process of resolution, a process of transforming a meaningless happening into a meaningful event." Paddy Scannell, "The Death of Diana and the Meaning of Media Events," *Media, Information and Society: Journal of the Institute of Socio-information and Communication Studies* 4 (1999): 27–51.

6. Judith G. Coffin, "From Interiority to Intimacy: Psychoanalysis and Radio in Twentieth-Century France," *Cultural Critique* 91, no. 1 (2015): 114–49.

7. Comment by Sher Mohammad Akhtar, reprinted in Naseer Anwar, *Nidā-e-Haq*, ed. Syed Tafazul Zia (Lahore: Maktabae Jadeed, 1965), 21.

8. Neil Verma, *Theater of the Mind: Imagination, Aesthetics, and American Radio Drama* (Chicago: University of Chicago Press, 2012).

9. Radio Pakistan personnel prided themselves on the fact that AIR radio accused Radio Pakistan of having prepared broadcast material beforehand. Radio Pakistan broadcasters noted that AIR's false accusations actually demonstrated just how effective the Radio Pakistan campaign had been. Amrah Malik, "The Spirit of Creativity," *The Nation*, June 7, 2007; Maqsood Gauhar, "Jaṅg Sitambar Ke Tarānoṅ Kī Recording Mere Liye Faxr Aur Ejāz Kī Bāt Hai," *Family Magazine*, newspaper clippings, Azam Khan personal papers. The title of this article can be translated as "for me, the recording of the September war is a matter of pride and dignity."

10. Moreover, the few available war programs listed in the AIR recording library are not open to scholars. I identified a number of recordings that might have been broadcast during the war at AIR's recordings collection, but was unable to procure permission to listen to them or take copies of the recordings. I, however, was able to listen to a section of AIR's *Radio Jhūṭistān* (Radio nation/place of lies). This program mocked versions of Radio Pakistan's news and poked fun at Radio Pakistan's news propaganda, specifically the famed Pakistani newsreader Shakeel Ahmad.

11. Following a wave of protests in East Pakistan, the constituent assembly granted official status to Bengali in 1954; this reform, however, was not implemented equitably. Moreover, the military government formed by Ayub Khan made several attempts to reestablish Urdu as the sole national language. For a concise history of East Pakistan, see Willem Van Schendel, *A History of Bangladesh* (Cambridge: Cambridge University Press, 2009).

12. The Maharaja initially wanted his state to become an independent country. The viceroy of India, Lord Mountbatten, however, called on Singh to choose either Pakistan or India. File 41a, LBJ. For a concise summary of the First Kashmir War, see Sumit Ganguly, "Avoiding War in Kashmir," *Foreign Affairs* 69, no. 5 (1990): 57–58.

13. Jawaharlal Nehru chose a nonaligned position but leaned closer to the Soviet Union both in thinking and in rapport. Ayub Khan's alliance with the United States was more opportunist than ideological.

14. Indeed, during the Cold War, the United States provided training and military equipment for the Pakistani army. See File 41a, LBJ.

15. File 41a, LBJ. In November 1962, China launched a series of military attacks on the disputed India-China border. The United States provided prompt military aid to the Indian government.

16. File 41b, LBJ.

17. File 41a and 41b, LBJ. One U.S. official explained: "Motivation for Pak irregular warfare initiative would therefore seem to be desire to create overt situation which would either cause GOI to react against Pakistan in what could be portrayed by GOP as aggressive manner, or to create set of circumstances which GOP could use to justify their employment of regular forces to 'protect' Indian Kashmiris." See also Farooq Bajwa, *From Kutch to Tashkent: The Indo-Pakistan War of 1965* (London: Hurst, 2013). It is not clear which sources the author uses to draw conclusions.

18. File 41a, LBJ.

19. Also see Altaf Gauhar, "Four Wars, One Assumption," *The Nation*, September 5, 1999. Altaf Gauhar was a close associate of Ayub Khan. He later admitted to the Pakistani army's complicity in the uprising in Kashmir.

20. Gauhar, "Four Wars, One Assumption"; File 64 and 41m, LBJ. Ayub Khan wrote to the Johnson administration in a telegraph: "The Indian armed forces launched an armed attack in full strength against Pakistan on the West Pakistan border thereby unleashing a war of aggression against this country." See File 41m, LBJ.

21. File 41p, LBJ.

22. Ayub Khan, "Address to the Nation," *Daily Motion*, September 6, 1965, http://www.dailymotion.com/video/x29hkaf_ayub-khan-address-s-to-the-nation-on-start-of-indo-pak-1965-war-6-9-1965-wmv_news. The recording of this broadcast is also available in the Pakistan Broadcasting Corporation archives, CPU.

23. Khan, "Address to the Nation."

24. In 1959, Karachi, Hyderabad, Quetta, Lahore, Rawalpindi, Peshawar, Dacca, Chittagong, and Rajshani had medium-wave transmitters. Additionally, Karachi, Lahore, and Dacca had shortwave transmitters, which means their broadcasts could be heard in a wider area. This information is listed in Radio Pakistan, *Ten Years of Development*.

25. Imdaad Nizaami, "Un Ke Cāroṅ Jānib Maut Kā Raqs Jārī Thā, Aur Voh Zindagī Kā Paiġām Sunā Rahe They," *Roznāmā Anjān*, January 3, 1966, newspaper clippings, Azam Khan personal papers. The title of the article can be translated as follows: "They were surrounded by the dance of death, and they were reciting the message of life."

26. C. M. Naim reaches a similar conclusion regarding the participation of poets during the war. He concludes that the government did not coerce poets to participate. See Chaudhuri Mohammed Naim, "The Consequences of Indo-Pakistani War for Urdu Language and Literature: A Parting of the Ways?" *Journal of Asian Studies* 28, no. 2 (1969): 269–70.

27. Nizaami, "Un Ke Cāroṅ Jānib Maut Kā Raqs Jārī Thā, Aur Voh Zindagī Kā Paiġām Sunā Rahe They."

28. *Safar Hai Šart*, interview by Nur Jehan, CPU. This recording is undated but based on the sound quality and on the location of the recording, I estimate it was broadcast in the early 1990s. The title of this program can be translated roughly as "when/if you travel."

29. The names are listed in the war catalog. See "1965 Indo-Pakistan War Catalog," CPU.

30. Naim, "The Consequences of Indo-Pakistani War," 272. C. M. Naim does not mention Kishwar Naheed in his study of 1965 war poetry, but according to the CPU catalog, she composed the lyrics to two Urdu songs "Mādar-e-vatan" (Homeland) and "Aye Sialkot tumko merā salām" (Oh Sialkot, I salute you). Naim also does not mention the poet John Elia who, according to the catalog, also composed many songs.

31. Naim, "The Consequences of Indo-Pakistani War," 269–83; see also "1965 Indo-Pakistan War Catalog," CPU.

32. Naim, "The Consequences of Indo-Pakistani War," 273.

33. Naim, "The Consequences of Indo-Pakistani War," 273. It appears that Faiz composed the poem "Blackout" during the days of war. The poem, to my knowledge, was not broadcast and was published later in collection. As Aamir Mufti notes in his analysis of this poem, "Blackout" can be read as a subtle but powerful critique of the politics of the war. Aamir Mufti, *Enlightenment in the Colony: The Jewish Question and the Crisis of Postcolonial Culture* (Princeton, NJ: Princeton University Press, 2007), 225–32. See also Iftikhar Dadi, *Modernism and the Art of Muslim South Asia* (Chapel Hill: University of North Carolina Press, 2010). Dadi explains that the artist Shakir Ali's works also criticized the war's politics.

34. "1965 Indo-Pakistan War Catalog," CPU.

35. Azam Khan, interview by the author, January 23 and 24, 2012.

36. "1965 Indo-Pakistan War Catalog," CPU.

37. For example, the pages of *Eastern Film* (available at LBJ), which include many ads for transistors. Transistors' huge boom, which ensured that radio became ubiquitous, took place slightly after the war in the late 1960s and 1970s.

38. Abdus Salam Khurshid notes that, in 1966, there were 933,233 radio licenses for receivers in a population of 120 million; however, these statistics are no longer considered to be valid because transistors did not have to be registered. Abdus Salam Khurshid, "Mass Communication Media in Pakistan" (paper presented at the AMIC Travelling Seminar, Asian Mass Communication Research and Information Centre, Singapore, September 5–29, 1971), https://dr.ntu.edu.sg/bitstream/10356/90890/1/AMIC_1971_09_10.pdf.

39. I was able to purchase a number of these CDs in Lahore.

40. The names of musicians are from Gauhar, "Jaṅg Sitambar Ke Tarānoṅ." Azam Khan confirmed that these musicians accompanied Nur Jehan's singing.

41. "1965 Indo-Pakistan War Catalog," CPU.

42. "1965 Indo-Pakistan War Catalog," CPU.

43. Malik, "The Spirit of Creativity," newspaper clippings, Azam Khan personal papers.

44. Khalid Hassan made note of this book in his essay on Nur Jehan. I have not been able to find a copy. Khalid Hasan, "Awaaz De Kahan Hai: A Portrait of Nur Jehan," in *City of Sin and Splendour: Writings on Lahore*, ed. Bapsi Sidhwa (New Delhi: Penguin, 2005), 206. Salma Siddique discusses Shaukat Hussain Rizvi's migration to Pakistan in "The Cacophony of Partition," in *Evacuee Cinema: Travels of Film Cultures Between Bombay and Lahore (1940–60)* (Cambridge: Cambridge University Press, 2022), chapter 1. See Shaukat Hussain Rizvi, *Nur Jehan Aur Maiṅ* (Lahore: Atish Publication, 1984), cited in *Evacuee Cinema*.

45. Saadat Hasan Manto, *Nur Jehan, Surūr-e-Jāṅ* (Lahore: Maktaba-e-šer-o-adab, 1975), 18, 27, 40–43, 51–62. The title of this book can be translated as "Nur Jehan, the intoxication of life."

46. Nur Jehan's political voice during the 1965 war can also be read as having earlier roots. Nur Jehan belonged to the generation of pioneering early Indian talkie actresses, who lent their voices to the first "talking" films. As Debashree Mukherjee shows, in the early and mid-1930s, "public concerns about actresses' singing voices were confronted" through "filmic speechmaking by fictional female characters" (145). As part of this generation of early talkie actress, Nur Jehan had already been involved in a "public argument against the moral surveillance of female cine-workers." She had quite literally participated in the "acoustic battles" of the 1930s (145). See Debashree Mukherjee, *Bombay Hustle: Making Movies in a Colonial City* (New York: Columbia University Press, 2020).

47. The biographical details are from Hasan, "Awaaz De Kahan Hai," 205–20.

48. Hasan, "Awaaz De Kahan Hai," 219.

49. Alison E. Arnold, "Hindi *Filmigit*: On the History of Commercial Indian Popular Music" (PhD diss., University of Illinois at Urbana-Champaign, 1991), 145.

50. Neepa Majumdar, "The Embodied Voice: Song Sequences and Stardom in Popular Hindi Cinema," in *Soundtrack Available: Essays on Film and Popular Music*, ed. Pamela Robertson Wojcik and Arthur Knight (Durham, NC: Duke University Press, 2001), 174.

51. It is telling, for example, that Nur Jehan chose to sing the song "Aye vatan ke sajīle javānoṅ" in an interview about her career. *Safar Hai Šart*, interview by Nur Jehan, CPU.

52. Hasan, "Awaaz De Kahan Hai," 208–9.

53. John Durham Peters, *Speaking Into the Air: A History of the Idea of Communication* (Chicago: University of Chicago Press, 1999), 221.

54. Hasan, "Awaaz De Kahan Hai," 208–9.

55. Khan, interview by the author.

56. Naveeda Khan, "Review of *Speaking Like a State: Language and Nationalism in Pakistan*, by A. Ayres," *Linguistic Anthropology* 22, no. 1 (2012): 133. For an excellent study of Punjabi in the colonial period, see Farina Mir, *The Social Space of Language: Vernacular Culture in British Colonial Punjab* (Berkeley: University of California Press, 2010). For a study of the Punjabi movement "Punjabiyat" in the postcolonial period and its rise in the 1980s, see Alyssa Ayres, *Speaking Like a State: Language and Nationalism in Pakistan* (Cambridge: Cambridge University Press, 2009), chapters 4 and 5, Kindle. For an excellent study of Punjab in the decades leading to Partition, see Neeti Nair, *Changing Homelands: Hindu Politics and the Partition of India* (Cambridge, MA: Harvard University Press, 2011).

57. Verma, *Theater of the Mind*.

58. Not to be confused with the younger short-story writer and columnist by the same name.

59. In fact, one of the difficulties that the present study faces is that there is little secondary literature on Indian or Pakistani radio drama or any other radio production, for that matter.

60. This summary is based on the printed version of the radio drama. See Ashfaq Ahmad, *Jaṅg-Ba-Jaṅg* (Lahore: Sang-e-Mīl, 2001), 3–302.

61. There is an interesting play on words here. *Talqeen* means reciting or the act of reciting. The main character, Talqeen was always preaching about how to be a better human being while he himself engaged in dishonest and manipulative behavior.

62. *Maulvī jī*, Radio Drama Catalog, CPU. According to the catalog, the play was produced and written by Syed Imtiaz Ali Taj. This catalog, however, has many errors. Because the play does not appear in Syed Imtiaz Ali Taj's complete anthology of radio drama, I suspect that Imtiaz Ali Taj was not the author. Some broadcasters have told me that the writer and actor Naim Tahir (son-in-law of Syed Imtiaz Ali Taj) was the author of this play. I have not been able, however, to confirm that information.

63. Verma, *Theater of the Mind*, see section I.

64. Verma, *Theater of the Mind*, 68.

65. Verma, *Theater of the Mind*, 67.

66. I was not able to locate original recordings of this broadcast, which unfortunately did not make it to the Central Production Unit's 1965 war archive, which contains only songs and poetry. The following analysis is based on a published transcription of the program, which includes some sound directions; a recording of a reenactment of the play by the original actors, which S. A. Ameen's son kindly shared with me; and newspaper accounts of the play. Anwar, *Nidā-e-Haq*.

67. "Arts Player Will Present a Comic Play," *Roznama Maghribi Pakistan*, Lahore. February 27, 1966, newspaper clippings, S. A. Amin personal papers.

68. Adriana Cavavero, *For More Than One Voice: Toward a Philosophy of Vocal Expression*, trans. Paul A. Kottman (Stanford, CA: Stanford University Press, 2005), 6. For more on the voice's relationship to the "bodies" and performance, see Rumya Sree Putcha, *The Dancer's Voice: Performance and Womanhood in Transnational India* (Durham, NC: Duke University Press, 2022).

69. Christine Ehrick, *Radio and the Gendered Soundscape: Women and Broadcasting in Argentina and Uruguay, 1930–1950* (New York: Cambridge University Press, 2015), Introduction, Kindle. Shenila Khoja-Moolji's understanding of masculinity and Muslimness in affective politics in contemporary Pakistan is also useful to understanding this

earlier period and *Nidā* specifically. As Khoja-Moolji perceptively notes "gender and Muslimness become the very means through which sovereignty is performatively iterated in Pakistan." Shenila Khoja-Moolji, *Sovereign Attachments: Masculinity, Muslimness, and Affective Politics in Pakistan* (Oakland: University of California Press, 2022), Introduction, Kindle.

70. *Amos 'n' Andy*, like *Nidā*, is a comedy that derives humor from pushing a litany of stereotypes. Both plays are also similarly focused on speech and dialogue.

71. Comment by Makeen Ahsan Kaleem, reprinted in Anwar, *Nidā-e-Haq*, 20.

72. Gerd Horten, "'Propaganda Must Be Painless': Radio Entertainment and Government Propaganda During World War II," *Prospects* 21 (1996): 385.

73. Verma, *Theater of the Mind*, 131.

74. Anwar, *Nidā-e-Haq*, 78.

75. Anwar, *Nidā-e-Haq*, 121–26.

76. Anwar, *Nidā-e-Haq*, 134.

77. Anwar, *Nidā-e-Haq*, 134.

78. Anwar, *Nidā-e-Haq*, 68.

79. Anwar, *Nidā-e-Haq*, 68.

80. Anwar, *Nidā-e-Haq*, 161–62.

81. The food situation in India, November 16, 1965, Narrative and Guide to Documents, Vol. I, Background Tab 3, Box: 25 National Security Histories, Indian Famine, August 1966–February 1967, LBJ.

82. Anwar, *Nidā-e-Haq*, 157–58.

83. Comment by Rais Ahmad Jafri, reprinted in Anwar, *Nidā-e-Haq*, 15.

84. Comment by Mohammad Ajmal from Government College Lahore, reprinted in Anwar, *Nidā-e-Haq*, 13.

85. Anwar, *Nidā-e-Haq*, 13.

86. Mohammed Ali Jinnah, *Speeches as Governor-General of Pakistan, 1947–1948* (Karachi: Ferozesons, n.d.), cited in Philip Oldenburg, "'A Place Insufficiently Imagined': Language, Belief, and the Pakistan Crisis of 1971," *Journal of Asian Studies* 44, no. 4 (1985): 176.

87. Comment by Ahsan originally printed in *Roznāmā Kohistān, Lahore*, reprinted in Anwar, *Nidā-e-Haq*, 18.

88. Comment by Zahur Alam Shaheed, reprinted in Anwar, *Nidā-e-Haq*, 27.

89. Anwar, *Nidā-e-Haq*, 28.

90. No title, *Āhaṅg*, July 1987; "S. A. Amin Passed Away," *Āhaṅg*, February 1992; "S. A. Amin (1927–1991): The Sketch of His Artistic Life," newspaper clippings, S. A. Ameen personal papers. S. A. Ameen's full name was Syed Ahmad Ameen, but he preferred the abbreviated form.

91. Shaukat Thanvi, *Qāzi Ji* (Lahore: Idāra-e-Faroǧ-e-Urdu, 1948).

92. "Ke Mīyaṅ Jī Jin Kī Garajdār Āvāz Se Mahāšae Kāṅpne Lagte Haiṅ," *Roznāmā Šahar*, December 14, 1964, newspaper clippings, S. A. Amin personal papers.

93. Verma, *Theater of the Mind*, 153.

94. Verma, *Theater of the Mind*, 132.

95. Comment by Ahsan originally printed in *Roznāmā Kohistān, Lahore*, reprinted in Anwar, *Nidā-e-Haq*, 18.

96. File 41a, LBJ.

97. File 51 and 55, LBJ.

98. Listeners in particular complained that when Naseer Anwar stopped writing the script the play lost its charm, in Anwar, *Nidā-e-Haq*, 21. Also see Ahmad Nadim Qasmi's letter, reprinted in Anwar, *Nidā-e-Haq*, 29.

99. File 62, LBJ. The September 22 ceasefire marked the end of Radio Pakistan's "seventeen days of drama," but not the end of the armies' fighting. Five days after the ceasefire, the Indian and Pakistani armies had yet another skirmish. For the entire text of the Tashkent declaration, see File 69, LBJ.

100. Files 58, 62, and 69, LBJ.

101. File 79, LBJ.

102. File 41u, LBJ.

103. For an excellent study of the high politics of the 1971 Bangladesh War in a global perspective, see Srinath Raghavan, *1971: A Global History of the Creation of Bangladesh* (Cambridge, MA: Harvard University Press, 2013). Srinath Raghavan argues that there was "nothing inevitable either about the breakup of united Pakistan or about the emergence of an independent Bangladesh. Rather it was the product of historical current and conjunctures that ranged far beyond South Asia" (9). This cultural study of radio presents a counterpoint to Raghavan's work and notes that the seeds of the issues of 1971 were planted in 1965.

6. The AIR Urdu Service's Letters of Longing

1. "A Touch of Nostalgia: Listening Post," *Statesman*, June 21, 1981, newspaper clippings, Abdul Jabbar personal papers.

2. 10/9/66-BA, "Introduction of Daily Programme to East and West Pakistan," Information and Broadcasting, 1926–1970, October 9, 1966, National Archives of India (NAI).

3. "Introduction of Daily Programme to East and West Pakistan."

4. Author interviews with AIR Urdu Service broadcasters. In particular, Mujeeb Siddiqui, who was among the group of founding broadcasters, stressed this point. Mujeeb Siddiqui, interview by author, July 10, 2016.

5. For works on television, see Shanti Kumar, *Gandhi Meets Primetime: Globalization and Nationalism in Indian Television* (Urbana: University of Illinois Press, 2006); Purnima Mankekar, *Screening Culture, Viewing Politics: An Ethnography of Television, Womanhood, and Nation in Postcolonial India* (Durham, NC: Duke University Press, 1999).

6. Vazira Fazila-Yacoobali Zamindar, *The Long Partition and the Making of Modern South Asia: Refugees, Boundaries, Histories*, Cultures of History (New York: Columbia University Press, 2007).

7. Alex E. Chávez, *Sounds of Crossing: Music, Migration, and the Aural Poetics of Huapango Arribeño* (Durham, NC: Duke University Press, 2017), Introduction, loc. 804 out of 10316, Kindle.

8. Chávez, *Sounds of Crossing*, chapter 1, loc. 1395 out of 10316, Kindle.

9. As I further elaborate in this chapter, here I draw on the work of Vebhuti Duggal and Laura Kunreuther. Vebhuti Duggal, "Imagining Sound Through the Pharmaish: Radios and Request-Postcards in North India, c. 1955–75," *BioScope: South Asian Screen Studies* 9, no. 1 (2018): 1–23; Laura Kunreuther, *Voicing Subjects: Public Intimacy and Mediation in Kathmandu* (Berkeley: University of California Press, 2014).

10. Yasmin Saikia, *Women, War, and the Making of Bangladesh: Remembering 1971* (Durham, NC: Duke University Press, 2011); Srinath Raghavan, *1971: A Global History of the Creation of Bangladesh* (Cambridge, MA: Harvard University Press, 2013).

11. Feroz Khan, *Eating Grass: The Making of the Pakistani Bomb* (Stanford, CA: Stanford University Press, 2012).

12. AIR Pakistan inaugurated a similar campaign during the 1971 war. The campaign was nowhere near as successful. Both broadcasters and listeners had told me that many tuned in to the BBC during the war when they wished to hear accurate news. A study of 1971 war broadcasts would require knowledge of Bengali and, therefore, is outside of the scope of this limited study.

13. K. K. Nayyer, interview by author, March 17 and 18, 2012; Siddiqui, interview by author.

14. 10/9/66-BA, "Introduction of Daily Programme to East and West Pakistan," NAI.

15. For an excellent study of Punjabi in the colonial period, see Farina Mir, *The Social Space of Language: Vernacular Culture in British Colonial Punjab* (Berkeley: University of California Press, 2010). For a study of the Punjabi movement "Punjabiyat" in the postcolonial period and its rise in the 1980s, see Alyssa Ayres, *Speaking Like a State: Language and Nationalism in Pakistan* (Cambridge: Cambridge University Press, 2009), chapters 4 and 5, Kindle.

16. 10/9/66-BA, "Introduction of Daily Programme to East and West Pakistan," NAI.

17. S. M. Shafeeq, interview by author, August 24, 2016; Siddiqui, interview by author. At least one newspaper account notes that listeners in the Indian Punjab wished the AIR Urdu Service would add Punjabi-language programs. See undated article in the *Daily Ajeet*, newspaper clippings, Abdul Jabbar personal papers.

18. Mariam Kazmi, interview by author, July 21 and 28, 2016. Kazmi's exact words were "Urdu service kī Urdu bilkul ām tarah kī Urdu bhī nahīṅ thī, Hindustani thī."

19. Alok Rai, "The Persistence of Hindustani," *India International Centre Quarterly* 29, nos. 3/4 (2003): 78.

20. Some transcripts of this program are available in the Urdu magazine *Āwāz*. I procured the copies of *Āwāz* from the AIR Library and from Jamia University's library.

21. *Gītoṅ Bharī Kahānī* is an example of the AIR Urdu Service Hindi film-song programs.

22. See Jennifer Dubrow, *Cosmopolitan Dreams: The Making of Modern Urdu Literary Culture in Colonial South Asia* (Honolulu: University of Hawai'i Press, 2018). See also Frances Prichett, *Nets of Awareness: Urdu Poetry and Its Critics* (Berkeley: University of California Press, 1994).

23. Ather Farouqui, "Urdu Education in India: Four Representative States," *Economic and Political Weekly* (2 April 1994): 782–85.

24. Amita Malik, "More on Urdu Service," *Times of India*, November 27, 1977.

25. This topic came up repeatedly in interviews with AIR Urdu Service broadcasters.

26. Mariam Kazmi, interview by author, June 21 and 26, 2016.

27. Kazmi, interview with author, June 21 and 26, 2016.

28. Vishnu Prakash who worked for CIBA, a company that sponsored many of Radio Ceylon's programs, confirmed this point. Vishnu Prakash, CIBA director of communication, interview by author, July 29, 2016.

29. Vebhuti Duggal, "Imagining Sound Through the Pharmaish: Radios and Request-Postcards in North India, c. 1955–75," *BioScope: South Asian Screen Studies* 9, no. 1 (2018): 1–23.

30. Author's name unknown, place unknown, Farrukh Jaffar personal papers. In her later years, after she had left a career in broadcasting, Farrukh Jaffar became an actress. She first gained fame after her performance in the acclaimed film *Peepli Live* (2015) and has performed in dozens of films since then and received several awards. She unfortunately passed in 2021.

31. This is a well-known couplet by Ghalib.

32. Letter by Dinesh Balasara to Farrukh Jaffar for *Tāmīle Irśād* from Kevdavadi, Rajkot, in Gujarat, India, August 2, 1982, Farrukh Jaffar personal papers.

33. Letter by Dinesh Balasara, August 2, 1982, Farrukh Jaffar personal papers.

34. Farrukh Jaffar, "Script of *Tišnagī*," for *Gītoṅ Bharī Kahānī* (undated).

35. This was one of the few programs that was outsourced and included little or almost no commentary by AIR Urdu Service broadcasters.

36. Kazmi, interview by author, June 21 and 26, 2016.

37. Ameen Sayani, interview by author, 2014 and 2016.

38. See, for example, Laura Kunreuther, *Voicing Subjects: Public Intimacy and Mediation in Kathmandu* (Berkeley: University of California Press, 2014), chapter 4.

39. Zahida Khan, *Daily Imroz*, October 21, 1978, newspaper clippings, Abdul Jabbar personal papers.

40. Letter by Iqbal Jafar from Calcutta to Farrukh Jaffar, Farrukh Jaffar personal papers. I wish to emphasize that this kind of praise of broadcasters is by no means unique to the Urdu Service or this time period. Casillas's work on Spanish in the United States has documented the kind of devotion that broadcasters have received. Similarly, Laura Kunreuther writes of the deep devotion that FM radio hosts in the early 2000s in Nepal could garner. Dolores Ines Casillas, *Sounds of Belonging: U.S. Spanish-Language Radio and Public Advocacy* (New York: New York University Press, 2014), and Kunreuther, *Voicing Subjects*.

41. Letter by Naila Bee, Lahore to *Āvāz De Kahāṅ Hai*. The Urdu version reads, "*Sunā hai Allāh Tālā ne Hazrat Yūsuf (alehissalām) ke husn o jamāl kā chaudahvāṅ hissā is duniyā meṅ bhejā. Magar hameṅ to yūṅ lagtā hai chaudā meṅ se bārā fīsad is progrām ke hisse meṅ āyā hai.*"

42. Kazmi, interview by author, June 21 and 24, 2016.

43. Letter by Iqbal Jafar from Calcutta to Farrukh Jaffar, Farrukh Jaffar personal papers.

44. Recording of *Āvāz De Kahāṅ Hai* (undated), letters and recordings, Abdul Jabbar personal papers.

45. Recording of *Āvāz De Kahāṅ Hai*.

46. Kunreuther, *Voicing Subjects*, 25.

47. Both male and female broadcasters received overt declarations of love that went well beyond the accepted form of elusive overtures expected of this genre. Similarly, it was not unusual for readers to send harsh criticisms of programs, which would be inappropriate to broadcast on the air. Listeners also sometimes wrote to criticize the Indian government's official explanation of events as presented in news programs.

48. The exact date that this program was inaugurated is unclear. Some newspapers note that the program was inaugurated in 1974, others say 1973.

49. This same story is repeated in various newspaper clippings of the programs shared with me by Abdul Jabbar, newspaper clippings, Abdul Jabbar personal papers. For example, "The Voice That Bridges a Generation," *Pioneer Delhi*, March or May [unclear in the clipping] 9, 1997, and "AIR Steps to Reclaim Old Musical Hits," *Hindu*, July 6, 1998. Azam Khan, who worked for Radio Pakistan, confirmed Jabbar's points about the restriction of film songs in Radio Pakistan during certain time periods. Azam Khan, interview by author, January 23 and 24, 2011; also see chapter 5.

50. The title of this song is difficult to translate. The title of the film can be translated as "precious/priceless moment/watch/time."

51. "The Voice That Bridges a Generation," *Pioneer Delhi*. Based on Khalida Begam's letter, I believe the program might have been broadcast on Mondays during this period (see the section "Khalida Begam's Letter and the Longing for a United India").

52. The Urdu/Hindi version of this phrase is "*Dūṅḍhne se Xudā bhī milegā.*"

53. "AIR Steps to Reclaim Old Musical Hits," *Hindu*, July 6, 1998.

54. "The Voice That Bridges a Generation," *Pioneer Delhi*.
55. Letter to *Āvāz De Kahāṅ Hai* by Sitara Jabi Qazi, February 14, 1981, played on April 5, 1981, letters and recordings, Abdul Jabbar personal papers. The Urdu reads: "*vāqaī yeh naġme unkī āvāz le kar apnī taraf mutavajjeh kar lete haiṅ.*"
56. Recording of *Āvāz De Kahāṅ Hai* (undated), letters and recordings, Abdul Jabbar personal papers.
57. Recording of *Āvāz De Kahāṅ Hai* (undated), letters and recordings, Abdul Jabbar personal papers.
58. Recording of *Āvāz De Kahāṅ Hai* (undated), letters and recordings, Abdul Jabbar personal papers.
59. Letter from Lahore, February 2, 1978, played on the air February 24, 1978, author's name unintelligible, letters and recordings, Abdul Jabbar personal papers.
60. Chávez, *Sounds of Crossing*, chapter 5, loc. 5916 out of 10316, Kindle.
61. Chávez, *Sounds of Crossing*, chapter 5, loc. 5918 out of 10316, Kindle.
62. Chávez, *Sounds of Crossing*, chapter 5, loc. 6066 and 5931 out of 10316, Kindle.
63. Nayyer, interview by author. Among the recordings and interviews that he collected was an interview with Nur Jehan, which I found in the archives. Moreover, Nayyer was one of few AIR Urdu Service broadcasters who was able to travel to Pakistan. (His being Hindu might have been one of the reasons why the Indian government granted him permission for travel to Pakistan.) He brought several hours of recordings from the cities he visited in Pakistan, which he later edited into a popular series about cities and places in Pakistan.
64. Chávez, *Sounds of Crossing*, Introduction, loc. 783 out of 10316, Kindle.
65. Letter by Uzma Ali to *Āvāz De Kahāṅ Hai*, September 1, 1979, Lahore, Pakistan.
66. "'Āvāz De Kahāṅ Hai' Ke Sāmaīn Kī Ajīt Bhavan Meṅ Mehfil Kā Ineqād," *Punjab Daily Ajīt* (undated), newspaper clippings, Abdul Jabbar personal papers.
67. "Pāk-Hind Avām Kī Yakjahtī Kā Nazārā," *Daily Avām* (undated), newspaper clippings, Abdul Jabbar personal papers.
68. Letter to *Āvāz De Kahāṅ Hai* from Rizvana Seher, September 19, 1979 (location unknown), letters and recordings, Abdul Jabbar personal papers.
69. Letter to *Āvāz De Kahāṅ Hai* (name unintelligible), February 2, 1978, played on February 24, 1978, letters and recordings, Abdul Jabbar personal papers.
70. Letter to *Āvāz De Kahāṅ Hai* by Shagufta Nasreen Hashmi, from Mandi Faridke (undated), letters and recordings, Abdul Jabbar personal papers. The Urdu reads "*āp kī āvāz sun kar kānoṅ meṅ ghanṭīāṅ sī bajne lagtī haiṅ. Aur ek sehar sā chā jātā hai. Aur jī cāhtā hai 'Āvāz De Kahāṅ Hai' kabhī aur kabhī xatm na ho, hameśā yuṅhī sāmaīn ke dil kī dharkan banā rahe. Āmīn.*"
71. Letter to *Āvāz De Kahāṅ Hai* (name unintelligible), February 2 and 15, 1978, played on February 24, 1978, letters and recordings, Abdul Jabbar personal papers.
72. Kunreuther, *Voicing Subjects*, chapter 4, Kindle. Mikhail Bakhtin, *Problems of Dostoevsky's Poetics (Theory and History of Literature)*, ed. and trans. Carl Emerson (Minneapolis: University of Minnesota Press, 1984), 218.
73. "If Music Be Food of Love—Play On," *MID-DAY Showbiz*, November 7, 1997, newspaper clippings, Abdul Jabbar personal papers.
74. "If Music Be Food of Love—Play On."
75. Kunreuther, *Voicing Subjects*, chapter 4, Kindle.
76. Khalid Mohammed, "Hindustan Aur Pakistan Ke Buzurg Hazrāt Apne Daure Bacpan Aur Javānī Kī Bāteṅ Aur Yādeṅ Baṛe Faxr Se Bayān Karte Haiṅ," *Axbār Xvātīne Pakistan*, August 1984, newspaper clippings, Abdul Jabbar personal papers.

77. Brandon Stanton, *Humans of New York* (London: St. Martin's Press, 2013); *Humans of New York* (blog), accessed November 3, 2019, https://www.humansofnewyork.com/.

78. Starting in 2015, Stanton began to travel abroad and collect pictures and stories. His first trip was to Pakistan and Iran. He also interviewed refugees fleeing the crisis in Syria.

79. Melissa Smyth, "On Sentimentality: A Critique of Humans of New York," *Warscapes* (online magazine), January 16, 2015, accessed April 15, 2022, http://warscapes.com/opinion /sentimentality-critique-humans-new-york.

80. Vinson Cunningham, "Humans of New York and the Cavalier Consumption of Others," *New Yorker*, November 3, 2015.

81. Letter to Abdul Jabbar by Khalida Begam from Lakhimpur in North India dated May 17, 1978, but read by Jabbar on *Āvāz De Kahāṅ Hai* on June 12, 1978.

82. Kunreuther, *Voicing Subjects*, chapter 4, Kindle.

83. Recording of a single program of *Āvāz De Kahāṅ Hai* (undated), letters and recordings, Abdul Jabbar personal papers.

84. C. Ryan Perkins, "A New Pablik: Abdul Halim Sharar, Volunteerism, and the Anjuman-e Dar-us-Salam in Late Nineteenth-Century India," *Modern Asian Studies* 49, no. 4 (2015): 1049–90. See also Manan Ahmed Asif, *The Loss of Hindustan: The Invention of India* (Cambridge, MA: Harvard University Press, 2020), chapter 6.

85. Aamir Mufti, *Enlightenment in the Colony: The Jewish Question and the Crisis of Post-colonial Culture* (Princeton, NJ: Princeton University Press, 2007), 210, 243. Another reference from Aamir Mufti is found in his analysis of the artist Zarina's work. Zarina used her sister's letters in Urdu to make prints about exile, so letters, longing, and displacement using Urdu is evoked in her work in a parallel visual register. Aamir Mufti, "Zarina's Language Question," *Marg* 68, no. 1 (September 1, 2016): 26–34; see also his essay in Allegra Pesenti, *Zarina: Paper like Skin* (Los Angeles: Hammer Museum, University of California, 2012).

86. Amina Yaqin, "The Communalization and Disintegration of Urdu in Anita Desai's *In Custody*," *Annual of Urdu Studies*, no. 19 (2004): 139.

87. Yaqin, "The Communalization and Disintegration of Urdu."

88. Siddiqui, interview by author (see note 4).

Conclusion: Call to Me. Where Are You?

1. Television made a later entrance in South Asia. Although it was introduced in 1959, it was not until the early 1980s that it boomed. For details, see Shanti Kumar, *Gandhi Meets Primetime: Globalization and Nationalism in Indian Television* (Urbana: University of Illinois Press, 2006); Arvind Rajagopal, *Politics After Television: Hindu Nationalism and the Reshaping of the Public in India* (Cambridge: Cambridge University Press, 2001); Purnima Mankekar, *Screening Culture, Viewing Politics: An Ethnography of Television, Womanhood, and Nation in Postcolonial India* (Durham, NC: Duke University Press, 1999); and Elizabeth Bolton, "Personalizing Politics: Producing Accountability on Pakistan's News Television" (PhD diss., University of Texas at Austin, 2017). See also *BioScope*'s special issue on television in Pakistan. Lotte Hoek, Debashree Mukherjee, Kartik Nair, S. V. Srinivas, Salma Siddique, and Rosie Thomas, eds., "Televisual Pakistan," special issue, *BioScope: South Asian Screen Studies* 10, no. 2 (2010): 105–10. Moreover, the ubiquity of the cassette tape and its recorders in the 1980s allowed almost everyone to make their own mixtapes and circulate them. The cassette revolution also engendered the circulation of localized music and created new types of music

audiences. See Peter Manuel, *Cassette Culture: Popular Music and Technology in North India* (Chicago: University of Chicago Press, 1993).

2. Shaheed Qamar to Abdul Jabbar for *Āvāz De Kahāṅ Hai*, September 1, 1976, letters and recordings, Abdul Jabbar personal papers.

3. Unknown author to Abdul Jabbar for *Āvāz De Kahāṅ Hai*, September 14, 1981 (aired on April 5, 1981), letters and recordings, Abdul Jabbar personal papers.

4. For a study of FM radio in Nepal, see Laura Kunreuther, *Voicing Subjects: Public Intimacy and Mediation in Kathmandu* (Berkeley: University of California Press, 2014). Casillas's book reminds us how the golden age of radio did not end with the rise of television in the United States. See Dolores Ines Casillas, *Sounds of Belonging: U.S. Spanish-Language Radio and Public Advocacy* (New York: New York University Press, 2014).

5. Rohit De makes a similar point regarding people's engagement with the constitution. See Rohit De, *A People's Constitution: The Everyday Life of Law in the Indian Republic* (Princeton, NJ: Princeton University Press, 2018).

6. Alex E. Chávez, *Sounds of Crossing: Music, Migration, and the Aural Poetics of Huapango Arribeño* (Durham, NC: Duke University Press, 2017), Epilogue, loc. 7304 out of 10316, Kindle.

7. For an in-depth study of this program, see Praseeda Gopinath, "Narendra Modi Speaks to the Nation: Masculinity, Radio and Voice," in *Indian Sound Cultures, Indian Sound Citizenships*, ed. Laura Brueck, Jacob Smith, and Neil Verma (Ann Arbor: University of Michigan Press, 2020), 152–73.

8. Reading Rumya Putcha's self-reflective prologue inspired me to include this section. See Rumya Sree Putcha, *The Dancer's Voice: Performance and Womanhood in Transnational India* (Durham, NC: Duke University Press, 2022).

9. Chávez, *Sounds of Crossing*, 2.

10. I want to recognize privileges that made this research possible. To begin with, a foreign passport (Mexican passport and later U.S. passport) made it possible to gain visas and travel to both India and Pakistan, a privilege which many Indian and Pakistani nationals simply do not have.

BIBLIOGRAPHY

Archives and Libraries

All India Radio, Library, New Delhi, India (AIR Library).

Archive and Research Center for Ethnomusicology, New Delhi, India (ARCE).

Bengali Intellectuals Oral History Project, Tufts University, Boston, Massachusetts, United States (BIOHP).

British Library Newspapers, Colindale, London, United Kingdom (BL-Colindale).

Central Production Unit, Radio Pakistan, Islamabad, Pakistan (CPU).

Centre of South Asian Studies, Oral History Collection, University of Cambridge, United Kingdom (CCAS, OHC).

India Office, British Library, London, United Kingdom (IO).

Jawaharlal Nehru Memorial Museum and Library, New Delhi, India (NMML).

Lyndon B. Johnson Library and Museum, Austin, Texas, United States (LBJ).

National Archives of India, New Delhi, India (NAI).

National Archives of Sri Lanka, Colombo, Sri Lanka (NASL).

National Archives United Kingdom, London, United Kingdom (NA-UK).

National Documentation Center, Islamabad, Pakistan (NDC).

National Film Archive of India, Pune, India (NFAI).

Netaji Research Bureau, Kolkata, India (NRB).

Sri Lanka Broadcasting Corporation Library (SLBC Library).

Sri Lanka National Museum (SLNM).

Personal Papers (Shared with the Author)

Ahmad, Sultan Arshad. Newspaper clippings of Ameen Sayani's visit to Pakistan.

Amin, S. A. Newspaper clippings and recordings.

Bhargava, Anil. Newspaper clippings, recordings, letters, and diaries.

Jabbar, Abdul. Newspaper clippings, letters, and recordings.
Jaffar, Farrukh. Newspaper clippings and letters.
Khalid, Toor. Newspaper clippings and recordings.
Khan, Azam. Newspaper clippings.
Khan, Lutfullah. Recordings and letters.
Kulkarni, J. J. Personal diary.
Mehdi, Yawar. Newspaper clippings.
Parmar, Dalbir Singh. Newspaper clippings.
Sayani, Rajil, and Ameen Sayani. Radio club listings and recordings.
Syed, Siraj. Newspaper clippings, recordings, and letters.

Selected Oral Interviews

2010

Abbas, Qasim. 2010.
Ahmad, Nihal. 2010.
Azadi, Mohammed Iqbal. 2010.
Farrukhi, Aslam. 2010.
Jafri, Hashmat Husain. 2010.
Mehdi, Yawar. 2010, 2015, and 2017.
Naseem, Agha. 2010.
Rizvan, Badr. 2010.
Rizvi, Syed Qamar. 2010.
Zaidi, Anees. 2010.

2011

Arif, Iftikhar. 2011.
Bhatti, Nasreen Anjum. 2011.
Khan, Azam. 2011.
Khan, Ustad Abdul Latif. 2011.
Menon, Nisar. 2011.
Naheed, Kishwar. 2011.
Qureshi, Nazar. 2011.
Rehman, Afzal. 2011.
Riaz, Mahmood. 2011.
Tahir, Yasmeen. 2011.
Tirmizi, Sajjad. 2011.
Toor, Khalid. 2011.

2012

Abdi, Syed Tasweerul Hasan. 2012.
Chandra, Reoti Saran. 2012.
Hanafi, Shameem. 2012.
Nayyer, K. K. 2012.
Raj, Yog. 2012.
Raza, Salima. 2012.

Rizvi, Zubair. 2012.
Siddiqui, Kamal Ahmad. 2012.
Siddiqui, Shahid Ali. 2012.

2014–2016

Sayani, Ameen. 2014, 2016.
Sharma, Gopal. 2014, 2016.

2016

Parmar, Jyoti. 2016.
Pereira, Padmini. 2016.
Prakash, Vishnu. 2016.
Shafeeq, S. M. 2016.
Siddiqui, Mujeeb. 2016.
Siddiqui, Sarfaraz Ahmad. 2016.
Syed, Siraj. 2016.

2016–2017

Kazmi, Mariam. 2016, 2017.
Singh, Harmandir (Hamraaz). 2016, 2017.

2017

Bhargava, Anil. 2017.

2017–2018

Jaffar, Farrukh (with Mehru Jaffar). 2017, 2018.

Selected Books, Articles, and Resources

Abbas, Amber H. "Disruption and Belonging: Aligarh, Its University, and the Changing Meaning of Place Since Partition." *Oral History Review* 44, no. 2 (2017): 301–21. https://doi.org/10.1093/ohr/ohx066.
Alam, Asiya. *Women, Islam, and Familial Intimacy in Colonial South Asia*. Leiden: Brill, 2021.
Amstutz, Andrew. "Finding a Home for Urdu: Islam and Science in Modern India." PhD diss., Cornell University, 2017.
——. "A Partitioned Library: Changing Collecting Priorities and Imagined Futures in Divided Urdu Library, 1947–9." *South Asia* 43, no. 3 (2020): 505–21.
Amstutz, Andrew, and Isabel Huacuja Alonso. "Proposal for Rethinking WWII in South Asia." *Modern Asian Studies* (in review).
Anwar, Naseer. *Nidā-e-Haq*. Edited by Syed Tafazul Zia. Lahore: Maktabae Jadeed, 1965.
Arnold, Alison E. *The Garland Encyclopedia of World Music*. Vol. 5, *South Asia: The Indian Subcontinent*. New York: Routledge, 2013.
——. "Hindi *Filmigit*: On the History of Commercial Indian Popular Music." PhD diss., University of Illinois at Urbana-Champaign, 1991.

——. "Popular Film Song in India: A Case of Mass Market Musical Eclecticism." *Popular Music* 7, no. 2 (1998): 177–88.

Ashfaq, Ahmad. *Jaṅg-Ba-Jaṅg*. Lahore: Sang-e-Mīl, 2001.

Ashiska, Meltem. *Occidentalism in Turkey: Questions of Modernity and National Identity in Turkish Radio Broadcasting*. London: I.B. Tauris, 2010.

Asif, Manan Ahmed. *The Loss of Hindustan: The Invention of India*. Cambridge, MA: Harvard University Press, 2020.

Awasthy, G. C. *Broadcasting in India*. Bombay: Allied, 1965.

Ayres, Alyssa. *Speaking Like a State: Language and Nationalism in Pakistan*. Cambridge: Cambridge University Press, 2009.

Bajwa, Farooq. *From Kutch to Tashkent: The Indo-Pakistan War of 1965*. London: Hurst, 2013.

Bakhle, Janaki. *Two Men and Music: Nationalism in the Making of an Indian Classical Tradition*. New York: Oxford University Press, 2005.

Bakhtin, Mikhail. *Problems of Dostoevsky's Poetics (Theory and History of Literature)*. Edited and translated by Carl Emerson. Minneapolis: University of Minnesota Press, 1984.

Balasubramain, Aditya. "A Forgotten Famine '43? Tranvancore's Muffled 'Cry of Distress.'" *Modern Asian Studies* (forthcoming).

Baruah, U. L. *This Is All India Radio: A Handbook of Radio Broadcasting*. New Delhi: Ministry of Information and Broadcasting, 1983.

Bataille, George. *The Accused Share*. Vol. 1, *Consumption*. New York: Zone, 1991.

Bayly, Christopher. *Empire and Information: Intelligence Gathering and Social Communication in India, 1780–1870*. Cambridge: Cambridge University Press, 1996.

Bayly, Christopher, and Timothy Harper. *Forgotten Armies: The Fall of British Asia, 1941–1945*. London: Allen Lane, 2004.

——. *Forgotten Wars: Freedom and Revolution in Southeast Asia*. Cambridge, MA: Harvard University Press, 2007.

Beaster-Jones, Jason. *Bollywood Sounds: The Cosmopolitan Mediation of Hindi Film Song*. New York: Oxford University Press, 2015. Kindle.

Bhabha, Homi. *The Location of Culture*. London: Routledge, 1994.

Bhargava, Anil. *Binaca Geetmala Kā Surīlā Safar*. Jaipur: Vangmāyā Prakāśan, 2007.

Bhattacharjya, Nilanjana. "How Sound Helps Tell a Story: Sound, Music, and Narrative in Vishal Bhardwaj's *Omkara*." In *Writing About Screen Media*, edited by Lisa Patti, 149–53. New York: Routledge University Press, 2019.

Bhattacharya, Sanjoy. *Propaganda and Information in Eastern India 1939–45: A Necessary Weapon of War*. New York: Routledge, 2009.

——. "Reviewed Work: Communications and Power: Propaganda and the Press in the Indian Nationalist Struggle, 1920–1947 by Milton Israel." *Modern Asian Studies* 31, no. 1 (February 1997): 221–23. www.jstor.org/stable/312865.

——. "Wartime Policies of State Censorship and the Civilian Population of Eastern India, 1939–35." *South Asia Research* 17, no. 2 (Autumn 1997): 140–77.

Birdsall, Carolyn. *Nazi Soundscapes: Sound, Technology and Urban Space in Germany 1933–1945*. Amsterdam: Amsterdam University Press, 2012.

Bolton, Elizabeth. "Personalizing Politics: Producing Accountability on Pakistan's News Television." PhD diss., University of Texas at Austin, 2017.

Booth, Gregory D. *Behind the Curtain: Making Music in Mumbai's Film Studios*. Oxford: Oxford University Press, 2008.

Borra, Ranjan. "The Image of Subhas Chandra Bose in American Journals During World War II." *Oracle* 1, no. 1 (1979).

Bose, Nemai Sadhan. *Deshnayak Subhas Chandra (Bengali)*. Calcutta: Ananda, 1997.

Bose, Sisir Kumar, Subhas Chandra Bose, and Atulendu Sen. *The Voice of Netaji: Netaji Research Bureau Presents Selected Speeches and Radio Broadcasts of Netaji Subhas Chandra Bose 1938–1944.* Calcutta: Saregama, 1985.

Bose, Sisir Kumar, and Sugata Bose. *Chalo Delhi: Writings and Speeches, 1942–1945.* Vol. 12. Edited by Sisir Kumar Bose and Sugata Bose. Calcutta: Netaji Research Bureau, 2007.

Bose, Sisir Kumar, Alexander Werth, and S. A. Ayer, eds. *A Beacon Across Asia: A Biography of Subhas Shandra Bose.* Calcutta: Orient Longman, 1973. Compact Disc.

Bose, Subhas Chandra. *Azad Hind: Writings and Speeches, 1941–1943.* Edited by Sisir Kumar Bose and Sugata Bose. London: Anthem, 2002.

——. *Netaji Collected Works.* Vol. II, *The Indian Struggle, 1920–1942.* Edited by Sisir Kumar Bose and Sugata Bose. Calcutta: Netaji Research Bureau, 1980.

——. *Testament of Subhas Bose, Being a Complete and Authentic Record of Netaji's Broadcast Speeches, Press Statements, Etc., 1942–1945.* Delhi: Rajkamal, 1946.

Bose, Sugata. *His Majesty's Opponent: Subhas Chandra Bose and India's Struggle Against Empire.* Cambridge, MA: Harvard University Press, 2011.

Bose, Sugata, and Ayesha Jalal. *Modern South Asia: History, Culture, Political Economy.* 4th ed. New York: Routledge, 2018.

Bronfman, Alejandra M. *Isles of Noise: Sonic Media in the Caribbean.* Chapel Hill: University of North Carolina Press, 2016.

Brückenhaus, Daniel. *Policing Transnational Protest: Liberal Imperialism and the Surveillance of Anticolonialists in Europe, 1905–1945.* Oxford: Oxford University Press, 2017.

Brueck, Laura, Jacob Smith, and Neil Verma, eds. *Indian Sound Cultures, Indian Sound Citizenships.* Ann Arbor: University of Michigan Press, 2020.

Bukhari, Syed Zulfiqar Ali. *Sarguzašt.* Lahore: Ghalib, 1995.

Casillas, Dolores Ines. *Sounds of Belonging: U.S. Spanish-Language Radio and Public Advocacy.* New York: New York University Press, 2014.

Cavavero, Adriana. *For More Than One Voice: Toward a Philosophy of Vocal Expression.* Translated by Paul A. Kottman. Stanford, CA: Stanford University Press, 2005.

Chakrabarty, Dipesh. *Provincializing Europe: Postcolonial Thought and Historical Difference.* Princeton, NJ: Princeton University Press, 2000.

Chatterjee, Partha. *The Nation and Its Discontents.* Princeton, NJ: Princeton University Press, 1993.

Chaudhuri, Arun. *Indian Advertising: 1780 to 1950 A.D.* New Delhi: Tata McGraw Hill, 2009.

Chávez, Alex E. *Sounds of Crossing: Music, Migration, and the Aural Poetics of Huapango Arribeño.* Durham, NC: Duke University Press, 2017. Kindle.

Coffin, Judith G. "From Interiority to Intimacy: Psychoanalysis and Radio in Twentieth-Century France." *Cultural Critique* 91, no. 1 (2015): 114–49.

Creekmur, Corey. "Picturizing American Cinema: Hindi Film Songs and the Last Days of Genre." In *Soundtrack Available: Essays on Film and Popular Music,* edited by Pamela Robertson Wojcik and Arthur Knight, 375–407. Durham, NC: Duke University Press, 2001.

Cunningham, Vinson. "Humans of New York and the Cavalier Consumption of Others." *New Yorker,* November 3, 2015. www.newyorker.com/books/page-turner/humans-of-new-york-and-the-cavalier-consumption-of-others.

Dadi, Iftikhar. *Modernism and the Art of Muslim South Asia.* Chapel Hill: University of North Carolina Press, 2010.

Dalmia, Vasudha. *The Nationalization of Hindu Traditions: Bhartendu Harishchandra and Nineteenth-Century Banaras.* Delhi: Oxford University Press, 1997.

Das, Santanu. *India, Empire, and First World War Culture: Writings, Images, and Songs.* Cambridge: Cambridge University Press, 2018.

Dasa, Harihara, ed. *Subhas Chandra Bose and the Indian National Movement*. Delhi: Sterling, 1983.

Dass, Manishita. *Outside the Lettered City: Cinema, Modernity, and the Public Sphere in Late Colonial India*. Oxford: Oxford University Press, 2016.

De, Rohit. *A People's Constitution: The Everyday Life of Law in the Indian Republic*. Princeton, NJ: Princeton University Press, 2018.

Derby, Lauren. "Imperial Secrets: Vampires and Nationhood in Puerto Rico." *Past and Present* 199, no. 3 (January 1, 2008): 290–312.

Desai-Stephens, Anaar. "The Age of Aspiration? Music Classes and the Limits of Gendered Self-Transformation in Mumbai." *MUSICultures* 44, no. 1 (2018): 74–96. https://journals .lib.unb.ca/index.php/MC/article/view/26079.

DeVotta, Neil. *Blowback: Linguistic Nationalism, Institutional Decay, and Ethnic Conflict in Sri Lanka*. Stanford, CA: Stanford University Press, 2004.

Douglas, Susan J. *Listening In: Radio and the American Imagination*. Minneapolis: University of Minnesota Press, 2004.

Dubrow, Jennifer. *Cosmopolitan Dreams: The Making of Modern Urdu Literary Culture in Colonial South Asia*. Honolulu: University of Hawai'i Press, 2018.

Duggal, Vebhuti. "The Community of Listeners: Writing a History of Hindi Film Music Aural Culture." PhD diss., Jawaharlal Nehru University, 2015.

——. "Imagining Sound Through the Pharmaish: Radios and Request-Postcards in North India, c. 1955–75." *BioScope: South Asian Screen Studies* 9, no. 1 (2018): 1–23. doi.org/10.1177 /0974927618767270.

——. "Seeing Print, Hearing Song: Tracking the Film Song Through Hindi Popular Print Sphere, c. 1955–75." In *Music Modernity and Publicness in India*, edited by Tejaswini Niranjana, 135–57. Delhi: Oxford University Press, 2020.

Ehrick, Christine. *Radio and the Gendered Soundscape: Women and Broadcasting in Argentina and Uruguay, 1930–1950*. New York: Cambridge University Press, 2015.

Elam, J. Daniel. "The Martyr, the Moviegoer: Bhagat Singh at the Cinema." *BioScope: South Asian Screen Studies* 8, no. 2 (2017): 181–203.

——. *World Literature for the Wretched of the Earth: Anticolonial Aesthetics, Postcolonial Politics*. New York: Fordham University Press, 2020. Kindle.

Erlmann, Veit. *Reason and Resonance: A History of Modern Aurality*. Cambridge, MA: MIT Press, 2010.

——. "Resonance." In *Keywords in Sound*, edited by Novak and Sakakeeny, Chapter 15. Durham, NC: Duke University Press, 2015. Kindle.

Fahmy, Ziad. *Ordinary Egyptians: Creating the Modern Nation Through Popular Culture*. Stanford, CA: Stanford University Press, 2011.

——. *Street Sounds: Listening to Everyday Life in Modern Egypt*. Stanford, CA: Stanford University Press, 2020.

Fanon, Frantz. "The Voice of Algeria." In *A Dying Colonialism*, edited by Frantz Fanon, Haakon Chevalier, and Adolfo Gilly, 69–99. London: Writers and Readers, 1980.

Farouqui, Ather. "Urdu Education in India: Four Representative State." *Economic and Political Weekly* (April 2, 1994): 782–85.

Field, Garrett. *Modernizing Composition: Sinhala Song, Poetry and Politics in Twentieth-Century Sri Lanka*. Oakland: University of California Press, 2016.

Fielden, Lionel. *The Natural Bent*. London: Andre Deutsch, 1960.

Fritzsche, Peter. *Life and Death in the Third Reich*. Cambridge, MA: Belknap, 2009. www.hup .harvard.edu/catalog.php?isbn=9780674034655.

Ganguly, Sumit. "Avoiding War in Kashmir." *Foreign Affairs* 69, no. 5 (1990): 57–73.

Gauhar, Altaf. "Four Wars, One Assumption." *The Nation*, September 5, 1999.

Gautier, Ana Maria Ochoa. *Aurality: Listening and Knowledge in Nineteenth-Century Colum-bia*. Durham, NC: Duke University Press, 2014.

Geva, Rotem. "The Scramble for Houses: Violence, a Factionalized State, and Informal Economy in Post-Partition Delhi." *Modern Asian Studies* 51, no. 3 (2017): 769–825.

Ghosh, Anjan. "The Role of Rumour in History Writing." *History Compass* 6, no. 5 (September 2008): 1235–43.

Ghosh, Durba. *Gentlemanly Terrorists: Political Violence and the Colonial State in India, 1919–1947*. Cambridge: Cambridge University Press, 2017.

Gitelman, Lisa. *Scripts, Grooves, and Writing Machines: Representing Technologies in the Edison Era*. Stanford, CA: Stanford University Press, 1999.

Goebbels, Joseph. *The Goebbels Diaries*. Edited by Louis Paul Lochner. London: Hamilton, 1948.

Gopal, Sangita, and Sujata Moorti, eds. *Planet Bollywood: The Transnational Travels of Hindi Song-and-Dance Sequences*. Minneapolis: University of Minnesota Press, 2008.

Gopinath, Praseeda. "Narendra Modi Speaks to the Nation: Masculinity, Radio and Voice." In *Indian Sounds Cultures, Indian Sound Citizenships*, edited by Laura Brueck, Jacob Smith, and Neil Verma, 152–73. Ann Arbor: University of Michigan Press, 2020.

Gordon, Leonard. *Brothers Against the Raj: A Biography of Indian Nationalists Sarat and Subhas Chandra Bose*. New York: Columbia University Press, 1990.

Goswami, Manu. *Producing India: From Colonial Economy to National Space*. Chicago: University of Chicago Press, 2004.

Government of India. *Report on the Progress of Broadcasting in India (up to the 31st March 1939)*. Delhi: Manager of Publications, 1939.

Griffen-Foley, Bridget. "The Birth of a Hybrid: The Shaping of the Australian Radio Industry." *Radio Journal: International Studies in Broadcast and Audio Media* 2, no. 3 (December 2004): 153–69.

Guha, Ramchandra. *India After Gandhi: The History of the World's Largest Democracy*. New York: HarperCollins, 2008.

Guha, Ranajit. *Elementary Aspects of Peasant Insurgency in Colonial India*. Delhi: Oxford University Press, 1983.

——. *Selected Subaltern Studies*. Vol. 1. New York: Oxford University Press, 1998.

Gupta, Amit K. "Defying Death: Nationalist Revolutionism in India, 1897–1938." *Social Scientist* 25, nos. 9/10 (1997): 3–27.

Gupta, Partha Sarathi. *Radio and the Raj: 1921–47*. Calcutta: Centre for Studies in Social Sciences, K. P. Bagchi, 1995.

Hakala, Walter. *Negotiating Languages: Urdu, Hindi, and the Definition of Modern South Asia*. New York: Columbia University Press, 2016.

Hansen, Kathryn. *Grounds for Play: Nautanki Theatre of North India*. Berkeley: University of California Press, 1991.

Hasan, Khalid. "Awaaz De Kahan Hai: A Portrait of Nur Jehan." In *City of Sin and Splendour: Writings on Lahore*, edited by Bapsi Sidhwa, 205–20. New Delhi: Penguin, 2005.

Hauner, Milan. *India in Axis Strategy: Germany, Japan, and Indian Nationalists in the Second World War*. Vol. 7. Stuttgart, Germany: Klett-Cotta, 1981.

Hayes, Joy Elizabeth. *Radio Nation: Communication, Popular Culture, and Nationalism in Mexico, 1920–1950*. Tucson: University of Arizona Press, 2000.

Hayes, Romain. *Subhas Chandra Bose in Nazi Germany 1941–43*. New York: Columbia University Press, 2011.

Herf, Jeffrey. "Hate Radio: The Long, Toxic Afterlife of Nazi Propaganda in the Arab World." *Chronicle Review*, November 22, 2009. www.chronicle.com/article/Hate-Radio-Nazi-Propaganda-in/49199.

Hill, Andrew. "The BBC Empire Service: The Voice, the Discourse of the Master and Ventriloquism." In "South Asian Diaspora and the BBC World Service: Contacts, Conflicts and Contestations." Special issue, *South Asian Diaspora* 2, no. 1 (2010): 25–38. doi.org/10.1080/19438190903541952.

Hills, Matt. "Sherlock's Epistemological Economy and the Value of 'Fan' Knowledge." In *Sherlock and Transmedia Fandom: Essays on the BBC Series*, edited by Louisa Ellen Stein and Kristina Busse, 27–40. Jefferson, NC: McFarland, 2012.

Hilmes, Michele. *Network Nations: A Transnational History of British and American Broadcasting*. New York: Routledge, 2012.

——. *Radio Voices: American Broadcasting, 1922–1952*. Minneapolis: University of Minnesota Press, 1997.

Hitchcock, Eric. *Making Waves: Admiral Mountbatten's Radio SEAC, 1945–1949*. Solihull, England: Helion, 2014.

——. "Radio SEAC's Transmitters: Eric Hitchcock Brings Us a Tale of 1940s Broadcasting from the Indian Ocean." *Shortwave Magazine*, 2000, 45–52.

Hochberg, Gil Z. *Becoming Palestine: Toward an Archival Imagination of the Future*. Durham, NC: Duke University Press, 2021.

Hoek, Lotte, Debashree Mukherjee, Kartik Nair, S. V. Srinivas, Salma Siddique, and Rosie Thomas, eds. "Televisual Pakistan." Special issue, *BioScope: South Asian Screen Studies* 10, no. 2 (2010): 105–10.

Horten, Gerd. "'Propaganda Must Be Painless': Radio Entertainment and Government Propaganda During World War II." *Prospects* 21 (1996): 373–95. doi.org/10.1017/S0361233300006591.

Huacuja Alonso, Isabel. "Songs by Ballot: *Binaca Geetmala* and the Making of a Hindi Film Song Radio Audience, 1952–1994." *BioScope: South Asian Screen Studies* (forthcoming, 2022).

——. "Radio, Citizenship, and the 'Sound Standards' of a Newly Independent India." *Public Culture* 31, no. 1 (2019): 117–44.

——. "'Voice of Freedom' at the End of Empire: Radio SEAC, Underground Congress Radio, and the (Anti) Colonial Sublime." (in progress).

Hughes, Stephen P. "The 'Music Boom' in Tamil South India: Gramophone, Radio and the Making of Mass Culture." *Historical Journal of Film, Radio and Television* 22, no. 4 (2002): 445–73. doi.org/10.1080/0143968022000012129.

Imdad, Sabri, ed. *Subhāṣ bābū kī taqrīreṅ*. Delhi: Ālā, n.d.

Indranti, Kiranmayi. "Of 'Ghosts' and Singers: Debates Around Singing Practices of 1940s Indian Cinema." *South Asian Popular Culture* 10, no. 3 (October 2012): 296–306.

Israel, Milton. *Communication and Power: Propaganda and the Press in the Indian National Struggle, 1920–1947*. Cambridge: Cambridge University Press, 1994.

Jaikumar, Priya. *Cinema at the End of Empire*. Durham, NC: Duke University Press, 2005.

——. *Where Histories Reside: India as Film Space*. Durham, NC: Duke University Press, 2019.

Jeffery, Robin. "The Mahatma Didn't Like the Movies and Why It Matters: Indian Broadcasting Policy, 1920s–1990s." *Global Media and Communication* 2, no. 2 (2006): 204–24.

Jenkins, Henry. *Convergence Culture: Where Old and New Media Collide*. New York: New York University Press, 2006.

Jhingan, Shikha. "Re-embodying the 'Classical': The Bombay Film Song in the 1950s." *BioScope: South Asian Screen Studies* 2, no. 2 (2011): 157–79.

Joshi, G. N. "A Concise History of the Phonograph Industry in India." *Popular Music* 7, no. 2 (May 1988): 147–56.

Kamtekar, Indivar. "A Different War Dance: State and Class in India 1939–1945." *Past and Present Society*, no. 176 (August 2002): 187–221. www.jstor.org/stable/3600730.

——. "The Shiver of 1942." *Studies in History* 18, no. 1 (February 1, 2002): 81–102. doi.org /10.1177/025764300201800104.

Karnad, Raghu. *Farthest Field: An Indian Story of the Second World War*. London: William Collins, 2015.

Karunanayake, Nandana. *Broadcasting in Sri Lanka: Potential and Performance*. Colombo: Center for Media and Policy Studies, 1990.

Katz, Max. "Institutional Communalism in North Indian Classical Music." *Ethnomusicology* 56, no. 2 (2012): 279–98.

Kaul, Chandrika. *Communications, Media and the Imperial Experience: Britain and India in the Twentieth Century*. London: Palgrave Macmillan, 2014.

Kavoori, Anandam P., and Aswin Punathambekar, eds. *Global Bollywood*. New York: New York University Press, 2008.

Keskar, B. V. *Indian Music*. Bombay: Popular Prakashan, 1962.

Khan, Feroz. *Eating Grass: The Making of the Pakistani Bomb*. Stanford, CA: Stanford University Press, 2012.

Khan, Naveeda. *Muslim Becoming: Aspiration and Skepticism in Pakistan*. Durham, NC: Duke University Press, 2012.

——. "Review of *Speaking Like a State: Language and Nationalism in Pakistan*, by A. Ayres." *Linguistic Anthropology* 22, no. 1 (2012): 132–34.

Khan, Pasha. *The Broken Spell: Indian Storytelling and the Romance Genre in Persian and Urdu*. Detroit, MI: Wayne State University Press, 2019.

Khan, Yasmin. *India at War: The Subcontinent and the Second World War*. Oxford: Oxford University Press, 2015.

——. *The Raj at War: A People's History of India's Second World War*. New York: Random House, 2015.

——. "Sex in an Imperial War Zone: Transnational Encounters in Second World War India." *History Workshop Journal* 73, no. 1 (February 28, 2012): 240–58. doi.org/10.1093/hwj/dbr026.

Khoja-Moolji, Shenila. *Sovereign Attachments: Masculinity, Muslimness, and Affective Politics in Pakistan*. Oakland: University of California Press, 2022. Kindle.

King, Christopher. *One Language, Two Scripts: The Hindi Movement in the Nineteenth Century of North India*. Bombay: Oxford University Press, 1994.

Kingler, Barbara. "Pre-cult: Casablanca, Radio Adaptation, and Transmedia in the 1940s." *New Review of Film and Television Studies* 13, no. 1 (2015): 45–62.

Kinnear, Michael. *The Gramophone Company's First Indian Recordings, 1899–1908*. Mumbai: Popular Prakashan, 1994.

Knapczyk, Peter. "Crafting the Cosmopolitan Elegy in North India: Poets, Patrons, and the Urdu Marsiyah, 1707–1857." PhD diss., University of Texas at Austin, 2014.

——. *Shi'i Devotional Poetry and the Rise of Urdu Literary Culture* (forthcoming).

Kumar, Naresh. "From Centerstage to the Margins: Hindustani Classical Music in Radio, Television, and the Music Industry." *Sangeet Natak* 44, no. 3 (n.d.): 15–37.

Kumar, Shanti. *Gandhi Meets Primetime: Globalization and Nationalism in Indian Television*. Urbana: University of Illinois Press, 2006.

Kumar-Dutt, Namrata, and Priya Dutt. *Mr. And Mrs. Dutt: Memories of Our Parents*. New Delhi: Lustre/Roli, 2007.

Kunreuther, Laura. *Voicing Subjects: Public Intimacy and Mediation in Kathmandu*. Berkeley: University of California Press, 2014.

Kurlander, Eric, Joanne Miyang Cho, and Douglas T. McGetchin, eds. *Transcultural Encounters Between Germany and India: Kindred Spirits in the 19th and 20th Centuries*. New York: Routledge, 2013.

Lacey, Kate. *Listening Publics: The Politics and Experience of Listening in the Media Age.* Cambridge: Polity, 2013. Kindle.

Lahiri, Madhumita. "An Idiom for India: Hindustani and the Limits of the Language Concept." *Interventions: International Journal of Postcolonial Studies* 18, no. 1 (2016): 60–85.

Larkin, Brian. *Signal and Noise: Media, Infrastructure, and Urban Culture in Nigeria.* Durham, NC: Duke University Press, 2008.

Lelyveld, David. "Colonial Knowledge and the Fate of Hindustani." *Comparative Studies in Society and History* 35, no. 4 (1993): 665–82.

——. "Transmitters and Culture: The Colonial Roots of Indian Broadcasting." *South Asian Research* 10, no. 1 (1990): 41–52.

——. "Upon the Subdominant: Administering Music on All India Radio." *Social Text*, no. 93 (Summer 1994): 111–27.

Lenthall, Bruce. *Radio's America: The Great Depression and the Rise of Modern Mass Culture.* Chicago: University of Chicago Press, 2008. Kindle.

Leylved, Joseph. *Great Soul: Mahatma Gandhi and His Struggle with India.* New York: Knopf, 2011.

Loviglio, Jason. *Radio's Intimate Public: Network Broadcasting and Mass-Mediated Democracy.* Minneapolis: University of Minnesota Press, 2005.

Lunn, David. "The Eloquent Language: Hindustani in 1940s Cinema." *BioScope: South Asian Screen Studies* 6, no. 1 (2015): 1–26.

Luthra, H. R. *Indian Broadcasting.* New Delhi: Ministry of Information and Broadcasting, 1986.

MacKenzie, John M. "In Touch with the Infinite: The BBC and the Empire, 1923–53." In *Imperialism and Popular Culture*, edited by John M. Mackenzie, 165–91. Manchester: Manchester University Press, 1986.

Maclean, Kama. *A Revolutionary History of Interwar India: Violence, Image, Voice and Text.* London: Hurst, 2015.

Mahajan, Manohar. *Yādeṅ Radio Ceylon Kī.* Jaipur: Vangmāyā Prakāśan, 2010.

Majumdar, Neepa. "The Embodied Voice: Song Sequences and Stardom in Popular Hindi Cinema." In *Soundtrack Available: Essays on Film and Popular Music*, edited by Pamela Robertson Wojcik and Arthur Knight, 161–85. Durham, NC: Duke University Press, 2001.

——. *Wanted Cultured Ladies Only: Female Stardom and Cinema in India; 1930s–1950s.* Champaign: University of Illinois Press, 2010.

Malik, Amrah. "The Spirit of Creativity." *The Nation*, June 7, 2007.

Manjapra, Kris. *Age of Entanglement: German and Indian Intellectuals Across Empire.* Cambridge, MA: Harvard University Press, 2014.

Mankekar, Purnima. *Screening Culture, Viewing Politics: An Ethnography of Television, Womanhood, and Nation in Postcolonial India.* Durham, NC: Duke University Press, 1999.

Manto, Saadat Hasan. "Āo Radio Suneṅ." In *Dastāvez Manṭo*, edited by Balraj Merna and Sharad Dutt, 59–66. New Delhi: Rajkamal Prakāśan, 1993.

——. *Nur Jehan, Surūr-e-Jāṅ.* Lahore: Maktaba-e-šer-o-adab, 1975.

Manuel, Peter. *Cassette Culture: Popular Music and Technology in North India.* Chicago: University of Chicago Press, 1993.

Mazzarella, William. *Censorium: Cinema and the Open Edge of Mass Publicity.* Durham, NC: Duke University Press, 2013.

——. *Shoveling Smoke: Advertising and Globalization in Contemporary India.* Durham, NC: Duke University Press, 2003.

——. "A Torn Performative Dispensation: The Affective Politics of British Second World War Propaganda in India and the Problem of Legitimation in an Age of Mass Publics." *South Asian History and Culture* 1, no. 1 (2010): 1–24.

Menon, Nikhil. "'Help the Plan-Help Yourself': Making Indians Plan-Conscious." In *The Postcolonial Moment in South and Southeast Asia*, edited by Gyan Prakash, Nikhil Menon, and Michael Laffan, 221–42. London: Bloomsbury, 2018.

——. *Planning Democracy: Modern India's Quest for Development*. London: Cambridge University Press, 2022.

Miller, K. H. *Segregating Sound: Inventing Folk and Pop Music in the Age of Jim Crow*. Durham, NC: Duke University Press, 2010.

Ministry of Information and Broadcasting. *Annual Report*. New Delhi: Ministry of Information and Broadcasting, 1954.

Mir, Farina. *The Social Space of Language: Vernacular Culture in British Colonial Punjab*. Berkeley: University of California Press, 2010.

Mitra, Durba. *Indian Sex Life: Sexuality and the Colonial Origins of Modern Social Thought*. Princeton, NJ: Princeton University Press, 2020.

Morcom, Anna. "Film Songs and the Cultural Synergies of Bollywood in and Beyond South Asia." In *Beyond the Boundaries of Bollywood: The Many Forms of Hindi Cinema*, edited by Rachel Dwyer and Jerry Pinto, 156–87. Delhi: Oxford University Press, 2011.

——. *Hindi Film Songs and the Cinema*. SOAS Musicology Series. Hampshire: Ashgate, 2007.

Morse, Daniel Ryan. *Radio Empire: The BBC's Eastern Service and the Emergence of the Global Anglophone Novel*. New York: Columbia University Press, 2020.

Motadel, David. "The Global Authoritarian Moment and the Revolt against Empire." *American Historical Review* 124, no. 3 (2019): 843–77.

Mufti, Aamir. *Enlightenment in the Colony: The Jewish Question and the Crisis of Postcolonial Culture*. Princeton, NJ: Princeton University Press, 2007.

——. "Zarina's Language Question." *Marg* 68, no. 1 (September 1, 2016): 26–34.

Mukerjee, Madhushree. *Churchill's Secret War: The British Empire and the Ravaging of India During World War II*. New York: Basic Books, 2010.

Mukherjee, Debashree. *Bombay Hustle: Making Movies in a Colonial City*. New York: Columbia University Press, 2020.

Mukherjee, Janam. *Hungry Bengal: War, Famine, and the End of Empire*. New York: Oxford University Press, 2015.

Mukherjee, Rudrangshu. *Nehru and Bose: Parallel Lives*. New Delhi: Penguin, 2014.

Naghmi, Abu al Hassan. *Yeh Lahore Hai*. Sang-e-Mīl, 2003.

Naim, Chaudhuri Mohammed. "The Consequences of Indo-Pakistani War for Urdu Language and Literature: A Parting of the Ways?" *Journal of Asian Studies* 28, no. 2 (1969): 269–83.

Nair, Neeti. *Changing Homelands: Hindu Politics and the Partition of India*. Cambridge, MA: Harvard University Press, 2011.

Nandan, Dropdi. "The All India Radio: Its Administration and Programmes." *Modern Review* 70, no. 2 (August 1941): 153.

Nehru, Jawaharlal. *Selected Works of Jawaharlal Nehru*. 64 vols. New Delhi: Jawaharlal Nehru Memorial Fund, 1984.

Neuman, Daniel M. *The Life of Music in North India: The Organization of an Artistic Tradition*. Chicago: University of Chicago Press, 1990.

Noronha, Frederick. "Who's Afraid of Radio in India?" *Economic and Political Weekly* 35, no. 38 (2000): 385–87.

O'Flynn, Siobhan. "Epilogue." In *A Theory of Adaptation*, edited by Linda Hutcheon, 2nd ed., 179–206. London: Routledge, 2013.

Oldenburg, Philip. "'A Place Insufficiently Imagined': Language, Belief, and the Pakistan Crisis of 1971." *Journal of Asian Studies* 44, no. 4 (1985): 711–33.

Orsi, Robert A. *Between Heaven and Earth: The Religious World People Make and the Scholars Who Study Them*. Princeton, NJ: Princeton University Press, 2005.

Orsini, Francesca. *The Hindi Public Sphere, 1920–1940: Language and Literature in the Age of Nationalism*. New Delhi: Oxford University Press, 2002.

Orsini, Francesca, and Katherine Butler Schofield, eds. *Tellings and Texts: Music, Literature and Performance in North India*. Cambridge: Open Book, 2015.

Pandey, Gyanendra. *The Indian Nation in 1942*. New Delhi: Centre for Studies in Social Sciences, 1988.

Patel, Dinyar. "One Man Lobby? Propaganda, Nationalism in the Diaspora, and the India League of America During the Second World War." *Journal of Imperial and Commonwealth History* 49, no. 6 (2021): 1110–40.

Penslar, Derek Jonathan. "Transmitting Jewish Culture: Radio in Israel." *Jewish Social Studies* 10, no. 1 (2003): 1–29.

Perkins, C. Ryan. "A New Pablik: Abdul Halim Sharar, Volunteerism, and the Anjuman-e Dar-us-Salam in Late Nineteenth-Century India." *Modern Asian Studies* 49, no. 4 (2015): 1049–90.

Pesenti, Allegra. *Zarina: Paper like Skin*. Los Angeles: Hammer Museum, University of California, 2012.

Peters, John Durham. "Broadcasting and Schizophrenia." *Media, Culture, and Society* 32, no. 1 (2010): 123–40.

——. *Speaking Into the Air: A History of the Idea of Communication*. Chicago: University of Chicago Press, 1999.

Petersson, Fredrik. "Hub of the Anti-Imperialist Movement: The League Against Imperialism and Berlin, 1927–1933." *Interventions* 16, no. 1 (2014): 49–71.

Pinkerton, Alasdair. "Radio and the Raj: Broadcasting in British India (1920–1940)." *Journal of the Royal Asiatic Society* 18, no. 2 (April 1, 2008): 167–91. doi.org/10.1017/S1356186307008048.

Pinney, Christopher. "Hot Bricolage: Magical Mimesis in Modern India." In *Art and Aesthetics in a Globalizing World*, edited by Raminder Kaur and Parul Dave-Mukherji, 85–98. London: Bloomsbury, 2014.

Porter, Simon J. *Broadcasting Empire: The BBC and the British World, 1922–1970*. Oxford: Oxford University Press, 2012.

Prasad, Rajendra. "President's Speech." *Indian Listener*, November 16, 1958.

Prichett, Frances. *Nets of Awareness: Urdu Poetry and Its Critics*. Berkeley: University of California Press, 1994.

Punathambekar, Aswin. "Ameen Sayani and Radio Ceylon: Notes Towards a History of Broadcasting and Bombay Cinema." *BioScope* 1, no. 2 (2010): 189–97.

——. " 'We're Online, Not on the Streets': Indian Cinema, New Media, and Participatory Culture." In *Global Bollywood*, edited by Anandam P. Kavoori and Aswin Punathambekar, 282–97. New York: New York University Press, 2008.

Punathambekar, Aswin, and Sriram Mohan. "A Sound Bridge: Listening for the Political in a Digital Age." *International Journal of Communication* 11 (2017): 4610–29.

Putcha, Rumya Sree. *The Dancer's Voice: Performance and Womanhood in Transnational India*. Durham, NC: Duke University Press, 2022.

Radio Pakistan. *Ten Years of Development: Radio Pakistan 1958–68*. Karachi: Serajsons, 1968.

Raghavan, Srinath. *1971: A Global History of the Creation of Bangladesh*. Cambridge, MA: Harvard University Press, 2013.

——. *India's War: World War II and the Making of Modern South Asia*. New York: Basic Books, 2016.

Rai, Alok. "The Persistance of Hindustani." *The Annual of Urdu Studies* 20 (2005): 135–42.

Rajagopal, Arvind. *Politics After Television: Hindu Nationalism and the Reshaping of the Public in India*. Cambridge: Cambridge University Press, 2001.

Ramaswamy, Sumathi. *The Goddess and the Nation: Mapping Mother India*. Durham, NC: Duke University Press, 2010.

——. *Passions of the Tongue: Language Devotion in Tamil India, 1891–1970*. Berkeley: University of California Press, 1997.

Ranade, Ashok. "The Extraordinary Importance of the Indian Film Song." *Cinema Vision India* 1, no. 4 (1980): 4–11.

Ravikant. *Media Kī Bhāṣā Līlā*. New Delhi: Lokchetnā Prakāśan, 2016.

——. "Śrav-Driṣṭav: Cinema Meṅ Radio." *Pratimān: Samay, Samāj, Sanskriti* 2 (December 2013): 581–600.

Raza, Ali Abidi. *Naǧmāgar*. Lahore: Sang-e-Mīl, 2013.

Rizvi, Mubbashir. *The Ethics of Staying: Social Movements and Land Rights Politics in Pakistan*. South Asia in Motion. Stanford, CA: Stanford University Press, 2019.

Robles, Sonia. *Mexican Waves: Radio Broadcasting Along Mexico's Northern Border, 1930–1950*. Tucson: University of Arizona Press, 2019.

Rook-Koepsel, Emily. *Democracy and Unity in India: Understanding the All India Phenomenon, 1940–1960*. Routledge Studies in South Asian History. London: Routledge, 2019.

——. "Dissenting Against the Defense of India Rules: Emergency Regulations and the Space of Extreme Government Action." *South Asia: Journal of South Asian Studies* 41, no. 18 (August 2, 2018): 642–57.

——. "Unity, Democracy, and the All India Phenomenon, 1940–1946." PhD diss., University of Minnesota, 2010. http://hdl.handle.net/11299/191456.

Roy, Srirupa. *Beyond Belief: India and the Politics of Postcolonial Nationalism, Politics, History, and Culture*. Durham, NC: Duke University Press, 2007.

Rushdie, Salman. "The Art of Fiction No. 186 Interview with Jack Livings." *Paris Review* 174 (2005): 107–43.

Saikia, Yasmin. *Women, War, and the Making of Bangladesh: Remembering 1971*. Durham, NC: Duke University Press, 2011.

Sampath, Vikram. *"My Name Is Gauhar Jaan!" The Life and Times of a Musician*. New Delhi: Rupa, 2010.

Sarkar, Tanika, and Sekhar Bandyopadhyay. *Calcutta: The Stormy Decades*. New York: Routledge, 2018.

Sayani, Ameen. *Geetmala Kī Chāoṅ Meṅ*, RPG Enterprises, vols. 1–5 (2009). Compact Discs.

Scales, Rebecca P. *Radio and the Politics of Sound in Interwar France, 1921–1939*. Cambridge: Cambridge University Press, 2018.

Scannell, Paddy. "The Death of Diana and the Meaning of Media Events." *Media, Information and Society: Journal of the Institute of Socio-information and Communication Studies* 4 (1999): 27–51.

——. "For-Anyone-as-Someone Structures." *Media, Culture, and Society* 22, no. 1 (2000): 5–24.

Schafer, R. Murray. *The Soundscape: Our Sonic Environment and the Tuning of the World*. Rochester, VT: Destiny Books, 1994.

——. *The Soundscape: Our Sonic Environment and the Tuning of the World*. Toronto: McClelland and Stewart, 1977.

Schofield, Katherine Butler. "Did Aurangzeb Ban Music? Questions for the Historiography of His Reign." *Modern Asian Studies* 41, no. 1 (2007): 77–120.

——. "Emotions in Indian Music History: Anxiety in Late Mughal Hindustan." *South Asian History and Culture* 12, nos. 2–3 (2021): 182–205.

——. "Reviving the Golden Age Again: 'Classicization,' Hindustani Music, and the Mughals." *Ethnomusicology* 54, no. 3 (2010): 464–517.

Schultz, Anna. *Singing a Hindu Nation: Marathi Devotional Performance and Nationalism.* New York: Oxford University Press, 2012.

Sen, Biswarup. "A New Kind of Radio: FM Broadcasting in India." *Media, Culture, and Society* 36, no. 8 (August 26, 2014): 1084–99. doi.org/10.1177/0163443714544998.

Sengupta, Nilanjana. *A Gentleman's Word: The Legacy of Subhas Chandra Bose in Southeast Asia.* Singapore: Institute of Southeast Asian Studies, 2012.

Sengupta, Syamalendu, and Gautum Chatterjee. *Secret Congress Broadcasts and Storming Railway Tracks During the Quit India Movement.* South Asia Books. New Delhi: Navrang, 1988.

Sethi, Devika. *War Over Words: Censorship in India, 1930–1960.* New Delhi: Cambridge University Press, 2019.

Shankar, Ravi. *Raga Mala: The Autobiography of Ravi Shankar.* Edited by George Harrison and Oliver Craske. New York: Welcome Rain, 1999.

——. *Shankar ka Orchestra.* Edited by Lakshmi Garg Narayan. Hathras, UP: Prabhulal Garg Sangīt Kāryālae, n.d.

Sharma, Gopal. *Āvāz Kī Duniyā Ke Dostoṅ.* Mumbai: Gopal Sharma, 2007.

Sharma, Narendra. "Cine-Sangeet Indra Ka Ghora Hai Aur Akashvani Uska Samman Karti Hai!" [Film Music Is Lord Indra's Horse and Akashvani Respects It!]. Ravikant, trans. *BioScope: South Asian Screen Studies* 3, no. 2 (July 2012): 165–73.

Siddique, Salma. "Archive Filmaria: Cinema, Curation, and Contagion." *Comparative Studies of South Asia, Africa and the Middle East* 39, no. 1 (2019): 196–211.

——. *Evacuee Cinema: Travels of Film Cultures Between Bombay and Lahore (1940–60).* Cambridge: Cambridge University Press, 2022.

——. "From Gandhi to Jinnah: National Dilemmas in the Stardom of Rattan Kumar." In *Indian Film Stars: New Critical Perspectives*, edited by Michael Lawrence, 109–23. London: Bloomsbury, 2020.

Siddiqui, Kamaluddin. *Urdu Radio Television Meṅ Tarsīl o Iblāğ Kī Zabān.* New Delhi: Qaumī Konsil Barāe Faroğe Urdu Zabān, 1998.

Siegel, Benjamin. *Hungry Nation: Food, Famine and the Making of Modern India.* Cambridge: Cambridge University Press, 2018.

——. "Self-Help Which Ennobles a Nation: Development, Citizenship and the Obligations of Eating in India's Austerity Years." *Modern Asian Studies* 50, no. 3 (2016): 975–1018.

Singh, Pratap. *Talat Gīt Koš.* Kanpur, 1992.

Sinha, Babli. "The BBC Eastern Empire Service and the Crisis of Cosmopolitanism." *Historical Journal of Film, Radio and Television* 39, no. 2 (2019): 309–21.

Sinha, Jagdish N. *Science, War, and Imperialism: India in the Second World War.* Leiden: Brill, 2008.

Sinha, Mrinalini. "The Abolition of Indenture: Between Empire and Nation." Colloquium, SOAS University, London, UK, May 28, 2013.

Smyth, Melissa. "On Sentimentality: A Critique of Humans of New York." *Warscapes* (online magazine), January 16, 2015, accessed April 15, 2022. http://warscapes.com/opinion/sentimentality-critique-humans-new-york.

Spacks, Patricia Meyer. *Gossip.* New York: Knopf, 1985.

Squires, Catherine. "Black Talk Radio: Defining Community Needs and Identity." *Harvard International Journal of Press/Politics* 5, no. 2 (2000): 73–95.

Stanton, Brandon. *Humans of New York.* London: St. Martin's Press, 2013.

Steinberg, Michael P. "Review: Reason and Resonance: A History of Modern Aurality." *American Historical Review* 116, no. 5 (2011): 1441–42.

Steingo, Gavin, and Jim Sykes, eds. *Remapping Sound Studies.* Durham, NC: Duke University Press, 2019.

Sterne, Jonathan. *The Audible Past: Cultural Origins of Sound Reproduction*. Durham, NC: Duke University Press, 2003.

Stuart, Charles. *The Reith Diaries*. London: Collins, 1975.

Subramanian, Lakshmi. *Singing Gandhi's India: Music and Sonic Nationalism*. New Delhi: Roli, 2020. Kindle.

Sundar, Pavitra. "Gender, Bawdiness, and Bodily Voices: The 'Ethnic' Woman and Bombay Cinema's Audiovisual Contract." In *Locating the Voice in Film: Critical Approaches and Global Practices*, edited by Tom Whittaker and Sarah Wright, 63–82. New York: Oxford University Press, 2016.

——. "Of Radio, Remix, and Rang De Basanti: Reimagining History Through Film Sound." *Jump Cut*, no. 56 (Fall 2014). https://www.ejumpcut.org/archive/jc56.2014-2015/RangDeBasanti /index.html, accessed April 15, 2022.

——. "Romance, Piety, and Fun: The Transformation of the Qawwali and Islamicate Culture in Hindi Cinema." In "The Evolution of Song and Dance in Hindi Cinema." Special issue, *South Asian Popular Culture* 15, nos. 2–3 (December 2017): 139–53.

——. "Usha Uthup and Her Husky, Heavy Voice." In *Indian Sound Cultures, Indian Sound Citizenship*, edited by Laura Brueck, Jacob Smith, and Neil Verma, 115–51. Ann Arbor: University of Michigan Press, 2020.

Talbot, Ian, and Tahir Kamran. "Darvarzas and Mohallas." In *Colonial Lahore: A History of the City and Beyond*. Oxford: Oxford University Press, 2017.

Thakkar, Usha. *Congress Radio: Usha Mehta and the Underground Radio Station 1942*. Delhi: Penguin Viking, 2022.

Thanvi, Shaukat. *Qazi Ji*. Lahore: Idāra-e-Farog̃-e-Urdu, 1948.

Thiranagama, Sharika. "Ethnic Entanglements: The BBC Tamil and Sinhala Services Amidst the Civil War in Sri Lanka." *Journalism* 12, no. 2 (2011): 153–69.

——. "Partitioning the BBC: From Colonial to Postcolonial Broadcaster." *South Asian Diaspora* 2, no. 1 (2010): 39–55.

Thompson, Emily Ann. *The Soundscape of Modernity: Architectural Acoustics and the Culture of Listening in America, 1900–1933*. Cambridge, MA: MIT Press, 2004.

Todman, Daniel. *Britain's War into Battle, 1937–1941*. New York: Oxford University Press, 2016.

Valliant, Derek. *Across the Waves: How the United States and France Shaped the International Age of Radio*. Champaign: University of Illinois Press, 2017.

——. "Occupied Listeners: The Legacies of Interwar Radio for France During World War II." In *Sound in the Era of Mechanical Reproduction*, edited by David Suisman and Susan Strasser, 141–58. Philadelphia: University of Pennsylvania Press, 2010.

Van Schendel, Willem. *A History of Bangladesh*. Cambridge: Cambridge University Press, 2009.

Vatsyayan, Kapila. *Bhāratā: Nāṭyaśāstrā*. New Delhi: Sāhityā Academy, 2006.

Verma, Neil. *Theater of the Mind: Imagination, Aesthetics, and American Radio Drama*. Chicago: University of Chicago Press, 2012.

Vyas, Mukund R. *Passage Through a Turbulent Era: Historical Reminiscences of the Fateful Years, 1937–47*. Bombay: Indo-Foreign, 1982.

Wade, Bonnie C. *Imagining Sound: An Ethnomusicological Study of Music, Art, and Culture in Mughal India*. Chicago: University of Chicago Press, 1999.

Weidman, Amanda J. *Brought to Life by the Voice: Playback Singing and Cultural Politics in South India*. Berkeley: University of California Press, 2021.

——. "Neoliberal Logics of Voice: Playback Singing and Public Femaleness in South India." *Cultural, Theory, and Critique* 55, no. 2 (April 2014): 175–93.

——. *Singing the Classical, Voicing the Modern: Postcolonial Politics of Music in South India*. Durham, NC: Duke University Press, 2006.

Werth, Alexander, and Walter Harbich. *Netaji in Germany: An Eye-Witness Account of Indian Freedom Struggle in Europe During World War II*. Calcutta: Netaji Research Bureau, 1970.

White, Luise. *Speaking with Vampires: Rumor and History in East and Central Africa*. Berkeley: University of California Press, 2000.

Williams, Raymond. *Marxism and Literature*. London: Oxford University Press, 1977.

Yaqin, Amina. "The Communalization and Disintegration of Urdu in Anita Desai's *In Custody*." *Annual of Urdu Studies*, no. 19 (2004): 120–41.

Yasar, Kerim. *Electrified Voices: How the Telephone, Phonograph, and Radio Shaped Modern Japan, 1868–1945*. New York: Columbia University Press, 2018.

Zachariah, Benjamin. "Indian Political Activities in Germany, 1914–1945." In *Encounters Between Germany and India: Kindred Spirits in the 19th and 20th Centuries*. Routledge Studies in the Modern History of Asia, edited by Joanne Miyang Cho, Eric Kurlander, and Douglas T. McGetchin, 141–54. New York: Routledge, 2013.

——. "Review of *His Majesty's Opponent: Subhas Chandra Bose and India's Struggle Against Empire*, by Sugata Bose." *American Historical Review* 117, no. 2 (2012): 509–10.

Zamindar, Vazira Fazila-Yacoobali. *The Long Partition and the Making of Modern South Asia: Refugees, Boundaries, Histories*. Cultures of History. New York: Columbia University Press, 2007.

Ziegler, Philip. *Mountbatten: The Official Biography*. London: Phoenix Press, 2001.

Zivin, Joselyn. "'Bent': A Colonial Subversive and Indian Broadcasting." *Past and Present* 162, no. 1 (1999): 195–220. doi.org/10.1093/past/162.1.195.

——. "The Imagined Reign of the Iron Lecturer: Village Broadcasting in Colonial India." *Modern Asian Studies* 32, no. 3 (1998): 717–38.

INDEX